MAC'S BOYS

MAC'S BOYS

BRANCH McCRACKEN AND THE LEGENDARY 1953 HURRYIN' HOOSIERS

Jason Hiner

INDIANA UNIVERSITY PRESS
BLOOMINGTON AND INDIANAPOLIS

This book is a publication of

Indiana University Press
601 North Morton Street
Bloomington, IN 47404-3797 USA

http://iupress.indiana.edu

Telephone orders 800-842-6796
Fax orders 812-855-7931
Orders by e-mail iuporder@indiana.edu

The paper used in this publication meets the minimum requirements of American National Standard for Information Sciences—Permanence of Paper for Printed Library Materials, ANSI Z39.48-1984.

Manufactured in the United States of America

Library of Congress Cataloging-in-Publication Data
Hiner, Jason, date
   Mac's boys : Branch McCracken and the legendary 1953 Hurryin' Hoosiers / Jason Hiner.
      p. cm.
   Includes bibliographical references and index.
   ISBN 0-253-21814-4 (pbk. : alk. paper)   1. McCracken, Branch, 1908–1970.   2. Indiana University, Bloomington—Basketball—History.   3. Indiana Hoosiers (Basketball team)—History. I. Title.
   GV885.43.I53H56 2006
   796.323'6309772255—dc22
                                                    2006012692

1 2 3 4 5   11 10 09 08 07 06

This is dedicated to the two women who always believed in me.
You know who you are.

History is a guide to navigation in perilous times.
History is who we are and why we are the way we are.

—David McCullough

CONTENTS

Contents

x

Acknowledgments

I was born more than twenty years after the events of this story took place, so I needed the help and the patience of many different people to be able to tell the tale of this great basketball team. First and foremost, I am deeply indebted to the surviving players, the student managers, the family members of the players who are no longer with us, the players from opposing teams, IU students who were on campus at the time, and many others who allowed me to take their time to interview them about their memories of the 1953 Hoosiers and of college basketball during the 1950s. That list includes Bobby Leonard, Burke Scott, Charlie Kraak, Dick White, Paul Poff, Phil Byers, Jim Schooley, Ernie Andres, Goethe Chambers, Sam Esposito, Ron Taylor, Jack Wright, Dick Hendricks, Ron Fifer, Don Defur, James Fitzpatrick, John Heiney, Bob Howard, Marge Farley, Louise McCracken, Bill Schlundt, Gloria Schlundt, Mark Schlundt, B. H. Born, Johnny "Red" Kerr, Chuck Mencel, Pete Newell, Dick Rosenthal, Clyde Lovellette, Dean Smith, Charles Cogan, John "Hap" Dragoo, Jack Gilbert, Dudley Miller, John Robertson, and Martin Weissert.

The work of numerous journalists from the early 1950s also served as critical source material for unearthing many of the details of this story and for confirming the veracity of anecdotes that were five decades old. I'm especially indebted to Herb Michelson and Jack Sellers of the *Indiana Daily Student* and George Bolinger of Bloomington's *Daily Herald-Telephone* for their excellent coverage throughout the 1952–53 season.

I'd also like to thank Brad Cook in the IU archives for gathering an exhaustive collection of photos from the 1952–53 season, and Pete

Rhoda in the IU athletic department for allowing me access to the 1953 manager's book and other records from that era that exist in the athletic department's archives in Assembly Hall.

A sincere thanks also goes to Bob Sloan and Indiana University Press for believing in this project from the beginning and being flexible with me as the vision and scope of this book evolved. All along, I felt like the highest priority of Indiana University Press was producing the best book possible, and their flexibility allowed me to fully tell the story the way it deserved to be told.

And, most of all, I want to thank my wife Heather and my son Noah for their tireless patience and encouragement throughout this project. They sacrificed as many nights and weekends as I did during the course of writing this book, and so part of the victory in bringing it to completion also belongs to them.

PART ONE

EXPANSION AND CRISIS

1

The tall children of basketball have been consumed by the
slot machine racket of sports. . . . They have forfeited honor
at an age when the dream of life should be beautiful. We
should weep when we come upon a boy who has been
fleeced of principles before he is a man.
　　　　　—JIMMY CANNON, *New York Post,* 1951

In the early 1950s, basketball had three epicenters—New York City,
Kansas, and Indiana. New York City earned its place because of Madison Square Garden, which hosted the prestigious National Invitation
Tournament along with an annual slate of prominent college basketball
games pitting New York City colleges against each other and against
other national basketball powers. Those games often featured Clair
Bee's Long Island University (LIU) team, Nat Holman's City College
of New York (CCNY) squad, the local Catholic powerhouse St. John's,
or New York University (NYU). Meanwhile, 1,200 miles west of the
Big Apple, Kansas gained its prominence because Kansas University
had been the longtime host of the game's inventor, Dr. James Naismith, and had also been the longtime coaching post for the man
Naismith called "the father of basketball coaching"—Dr. Forrest C.
"Phog" Allen. Naismith died in 1938, but the moniker he gave Allen
was nothing less than prophetic, as Allen's two most prominent coaching pupils were Adolph Rupp and Dean Smith, who both held the
record for the winningest coach in the history of college basketball.

The third basketball capital, Indiana, was simply known as the "basketball state" because of its key role in the early development of the game and because its citizens contracted a contagious form of hysteria every year between December and March when they lived and died with the fortunes of their local high school basketball teams.

As the tumultuous 1940s turned into the prosperous 1950s, basketball was flourishing in all three places. In New York City, basketball games were packing Madison Square Garden with capacity crowds on a regular basis. Four New York City teams—NYU, Manhattan, St. John's, and CCNY—made it into the 1949 NIT. The next year, in 1950, Nat Holman's sophomore-dominated CCNY squad pulled off the first—and last—"Grand Slam" in college basketball history by winning both the NIT and NCAA tournaments in the same season. And the championship games of both tournaments were played in the Big Apple at Madison Square Garden.

At Kansas, Phog Allen fulfilled his highest aspiration and kept the promise he made to his 1948 recruiting class when he led the Jayhawks to the 1952 NCAA championship and then to a spirited run to the finals of the Olympic trials. As a result, Allen and seven of his Kansas players got to represent the United States in the 1952 Olympic Games in Helsinki, Finland. That year, Team USA swept their way to a gold medal, including two wins over the Soviet Union, and Kansas's Clyde Lovellette was the team's leading scorer.

In the Hoosier state, Indiana's high school basketball tournament was setting new attendance records and was drawing the eye of NCAA officials, who were looking to expand and revamp the NCAA Tournament. In 1946, one of college basketball's most intense and successful basketball coaches, Branch McCracken, returned to Indiana University after a voluntary stint in the U.S. Navy during World War II, and he quickly re-established the Hoosiers as one of the perennial leaders in the Big Ten and one of the top-ranked college teams in the nation.

Other areas were also making upstart bids to join the basketball elite. Although obscured by the shadow of New York City, Philadelphia had already established a notable basketball tradition of its own with a cluster of prominent teams and a crown jewel in The Palestra, one of the coziest venues in the country to watch a college basketball game. Henry Iba had built a basketball juggernaut at Oklahoma A&M (later Oklahoma State). The Aggies became the first team to win back-to-back NCAA titles in 1945 and 1946 and introduced college basketball to its first great seven-footer in Bob Kurland. At the same time, Adolph Rupp, a former Kansas player, had turned the University of Kentucky Wildcats into a perennial national contender, winning national championships in 1948, 1949, and 1951. That included a victory over Iba's Aggies in the national championship game in 1949, as well as one of the first great championship game upsets in NCAA Tournament history in 1951, when Kentucky upended a high-powered Kansas State team that was widely considered at the time to be the greatest basketball team to ever grace the college court.

College basketball, which had drawn respectable crowds on campuses for decades, was riding the tidal wave of interest in spectator sports that was spreading across America after World War II. There were now many more students on college campuses, and a rapidly expanding economy had given Americans more disposable income to spend and more leisure time to spend it.

This rising tide certainly was not overlooked by the NCAA. By the mid-1940s, after years of debate and speculation over which was the premier postseason venue, the NCAA Tournament officially overtook the NIT as the tournament that crowned the national champion. The moment when the NCAA Tournament gained symbolic top-dog status came in 1945, when the NCAA winner, Oklahoma A&M, played the NIT winner, DePaul, in Madison Square Garden to decide the "Champion of Champions," with the proceeds benefiting the Red Cross in this wartime confrontation. That game also featured a high-profile matchup between two indomitable centers—Oklahoma A&M's Bob Kurland and DePaul's George Mikan. Kurland and his NCAA champion Aggies prevailed 52-44.

Throughout the 1940s, both the NIT and NCAA were limited to a field of only eight teams each. In 1949, the NIT expanded to twelve teams. The NCAA went even further, expanding to sixteen teams in 1951, twenty-two teams in 1953, and twenty-four teams in 1954. Beginning with the 1953 tournament, the NCAA also stipu-

5

lated that to be eligible for an NCAA bid, a team could play in only one postseason tournament, which meant that some top teams that had previously competed in both the NIT and the NCAA tournaments now had to choose. Most of them elected to go to the NCAA Tournament when faced with that choice, and as a result the NIT was slowly relegated to second-class status. However, the expansion and development of the NCAA Tournament wasn't the only blow struck against the NIT in the early 1950s. In fact, the greatest blow came from much closer to home.

As a result of all the World War II veterans who got college degrees through the G.I. Bill, in the postwar era there were more upwardly mobile college alumni in the United States than ever before. By the early 1950s, most of these veterans had finished their degrees and moved on to chase the American dream. Many of them took a passionate interest in the sports programs of their respective alma maters, and some of them began making generous donations to their college athletic departments. As a result, a new factor was soon introduced into college athletics—the full-ride athletic scholarship.

Prior to World War II, when a college basketball coach coveted a high school player and wanted to recruit him, the coach would typically promise to find the player a job around campus that would pay enough money to cover the bulk of the player's college costs. These jobs weren't glamorous and were usually fairly rudimentary—such as working as a janitor in the athletic facilities, working in the kitchen in a dorm or fraternity house, or working as a secretary for someone in the athletic department—but these jobs paid the bills and allowed the athlete to get a free—or at least a very low-cost—education.

However, in the wake of World War II, as new affluence spread across America and alumni contributions swelled athletic department budgets, colleges could now offer full athletic scholarships to top athletes—mostly in football and basketball. At Indiana University, for example, a basketball player could now have all tuition, fees, and books paid for, along with room and board in a dorm and a small stipend. If a player chose to live in a fraternity house rather than the dorm, then the player had to get a job at that fraternity (usually in the kitchen) to cover the costs.

With more money being donated into athletics and larger and larger crowds filling the arenas for collegiate athletic events, there was also a rising uneasiness among a significant faction of college faculty members and administrators who believed that college athletics was getting too much attention and was becoming too money-oriented. This group wanted to see college athletics kept in their proper place and wanted to make sure student-athletes were students first and athletes second. If these educators were concerned by what they saw developing in the late 1940s, then they were appalled by the news they heard on February 18, 1951.

Along with the growing national interest in spectator sports and the rising population of students on college campuses, there was another, more nefarious factor fueling the rising interest in college basketball—the point spread. During the 1940s, the point spread truly began to flourish, and it was most frequently used with college basketball games. All the additional money in America meant there were a lot more bookies running around promising to help people turn their five dollars into ten dollars in the blink of an eye.

Prior to the point spread, betting on basketball games was based on odds, just like horse racing. For example, a powerful team like Kentucky might be a 5-2 favorite to beat Tennessee. The point spread made college basketball games much more interesting to bet on. If the point spread had St. John's favored by ten against Temple, then St. John's had to win by at least eleven for someone who bet on St. John's to win the bet. Conversely, if Temple lost by nine points or less (or, heaven forbid, won the game) then someone who wagered on Temple would win the bet. Since teams could score quickly and in bunches in basketball, for those who wagered, the point spread made the games intriguing to the end, even when the matter of which team actually won the game was already decided. As a result, for many of the leading bookies in New York City in the late 1940s around 80 percent of the money they handled was wagered on college basketball games.[1]

The dark side of the point spread was the phenomenon of "point shaving." A group of influential players on a good team could, once the victory was close to being wrapped up, keep the winning margin under the point spread. They would be hired to do this by a big-time gambler who would place a large wager against the team whose players he had struck a deal with. When the gambler won a large sum, he would shuffle some of the money (usually around $1,000 per game) to each of the players involved.

While most college basketball coaches were caught up in the rising success and interest in the game in the mid- to late 1940s and didn't believe gamblers and game-fixers could affect their teams, or any of the top squads in the college game for that matter, there were a few coaches who were deeply troubled by the rumors they heard and by the well-sourced reports they received from their network of contacts. The most vocal of these was Kansas's Phog Allen. In September 1944, Allen called for college athletics to name a commissioner like the one major league baseball had in Kenesaw Mountain Landis. "Judge Landis is fighting betting on professional baseball in his vigorous manner," stated Allen, "but the colleges are doing nothing about it, and as sure as you live the thing is going to crack wide open sometime when they lay bare a scandal that will rock the college world. It has already happened in Madison Square Garden, but the newspapers have kept it quiet."[2]

Of course, Allen had a reputation for loving the sound of his own voice and he enjoyed pontificating about the state of the game to anyone who would listen—the press most of all. Hence, much of the basketball world simply shook their heads, curled their lips into wry smiles, and waived off Allen's statement like they would the sound of an annoying insect that wouldn't stop buzzing. Still, Allen's words spawned a public feud between him and Ned Irish, the Madison Square Garden promoter. Irish summed up the feelings of many of the people in college basketball when he dismissed Allen's claims by saying, "He's been doing this sort of thing for years now, and the mystery to me is that people take him seriously in light of his previous false prophecies."[3]

Irish insisted that Madison Square Garden took illegal gambling on college sports very seriously and that anyone arrested for gambling was unequivocally banned from the facility. "It is extremely unlikely that any gambling can emanate from the building here," said Irish.[4]

Most of the basketball world believed Irish—or at least sincerely wanted to believe him—and they turned against Allen. Emil Liston, who had formerly been coached by Allen and was the executive director of the National Association of Intercollegiate Basketball at the time, castigated Phog's "deplorable lack of faith in the American youth and meager confidence in the integrity of coaches."[5]

NCAA leaders also criticized Allen for bringing down negative publicity on college sports. Throughout the fall of 1944, sports columnists and commentators from across the country chimed in about the controversy, and there were some who applauded Allen for taking a stand against money and corruption. In the *Denver Post,* Jack Carberry wrote, "Phog Allen has thrown down the gauntlet. Let the colleges of our land pick it up."[6]

Other columnists took a more pragmatic approach to the situation. In *Stars & Stripes,* Andy Rooney wrote, "The fact is, if [Irish] stamped out gambling he would stamp out a great deal of Garden basketball. Not all of those 17,000 people were at the Garden the other night because either St. Francis or Muhlenberg were dear to their hearts. They were there for the same reasons they go to watch the horse races—and that ain't to watch the nags run. The hardest comment to answer about such gambling is 'So what?' But it is true that gambling makes for a bad smell and dishonesty."[7]

In January 1945, four months after Phog made his controversial comments, two gamblers and five Brooklyn College basketball players were arrested for planning to fix the team's game against Akron in the Boston Garden. When the news broke, Allen stated, "Now, who's the bumpkin?"[8] Most of college basketball simply waived him off again and chalked up the Brooklyn College scandal as an isolated incident. Seven years later, there were a lot of people in college basketball who wished they would have listened to Phog Allen's outrageous pronouncement in 1944.

It's the oldest excuse in the world for doing something morally questionable. It's as simple as it is predictable. It's as easy as it is simple.

"Everybody's doing it." That's what the gamblers told college basketball players when asking them to shave a few points off their winning scores and keep their teams from covering the spread. If they did it, they'd earn some extra money. "Everybody's doing it," the gamblers said. "You'd be stupid not to," they added. "It's not hurting anybody. And it pays $1,000 per game. If you don't do it, somebody else will and they'll get the money. Everybody's doing it."

In retrospect, Phog Allen was simply one of the first to recognize the vultures circling college basketball. Gamblers had started taking an uncommon interest in college campuses during the 1940s, placing operatives around campuses to get the latest rumors on which players were hurt, which ones were in a shooting slump, and which teams were having chemistry problems. The gamblers tried to do everything they could to get an advantage before placing their bets, but eventually that wasn't enough. Many of the high-stakes gamblers in big cities were also doing everything they could to get close to the players themselves. Once they got close enough, it wasn't long before the gamblers started offering players big money to influence the outcomes of games. It was the kind of money that most adults in America had never seen before—let alone twenty-year-old kids.

When boys—even ones with common sense and street smarts— are faced with the type of temptation that would buckle the resolve of more than a few disciplined men, the results are often tragic. For college basketball and its boys, the dark tragedies of the 1940s and early 1950s were hatched behind the scenes in dark corners, in back alleys, in the lavish New York City apartments of shady characters, and in a series of summer resorts in the Catskill Mountains west of the Big Apple.

Beginning in the 1930s, the summer resorts in the Catskills started hiring college basketball players as waiters, busboys, and bellhops. Then, after dinner, the players would play pickup games to entertain the hotel guests. The games weren't well organized. There were rarely any formalized leagues or regular teams, and the games were often played on outdoor courts. But the competition was excellent. By the 1940s, there were usually around five hundred college basketball players who spent their summers in the Catskills, including many of the best players in the country, players like George Mikan from DePau Alex Groza from Kentucky, and Bob Cousy from Holy Cross.[9]

The Catskill resorts were also where some players first learned ho to shave points. It started innocently at first. At one of the resorts, a hat would be passed around the stands and audience members could put in a dollar and pick the score of the winning team. The players would split the pot with the winners, which usually earned them an extra ten to fifteen bucks per game. Sometimes the players would try to hit the number held by a specific audience member, if there was something extra in it for them. For example, "If the chef had number 154, we'd make sure that was all the points we'd score. Then we'd eat like kings for a week," said one former CCNY player.[10]

The Catskills were also where many college basketball players from across the nation were first introduced to high-stakes gamblers from New York City. And the Catskills were where a Long Island University player named Eddie Gard first met a Sicilian entrepreneur and con man named Salvatore Sollazzo. Together, the two of them engineered the most ambitious and well-coordinated point-shaving scheme ever discovered by authorities. Their ultimate ambition was to have a fix on every game played in Madison Square Garden plus the NIT and NCAA championship games—and they nearly succeeded.[11]

Usually gamblers would orchestrate a fix for an individual game here or there in order to make a quick buck. Some gamblers had their favorite teams to work with and some teams, most notably Long Island University, worked with several different gamblers. Eddie Gard was intimately familiar with this loosely organized system of "dumping" games at the lucrative behest of big-stakes gamblers and mafia agents. When Gard joined the LIU varsity during the 1947–48 season, he almost immediately joined a cadre of players that was in cahoots with gamblers to dump an occasional game to earn some extra money, already an established tradition at LIU. While other New York City schools were occasionally haunted by rumors of fixes throughout the 1940s, there was an almost constant stream of rumors swirling about LIU—and many of them were true. The fixing even transcended LIU's Hall of Fame coach Clair Bee. It started in force at LIU during the early 1940s when Bee roamed the sidelines, but when Bee was in the merchant marines during World War II, the fixing continued while interim coach Red Wolfe was there. Wolfe once threatened to turn in any player he caught trying to dump a game. The players kept shaving points anyway, and either Wolfe simply couldn't catch them doing it or didn't have the resolve to go through with his threat.[12]

Gard eventually became the leader of the LIU coterie of players who were offering their services to gamblers, and he took the operation to a new level. He didn't want to simply be constantly brokering services, always looking for someone to sell a fix to. He thought it would be better to have one guy they could regularly do business with, and he also thought the fix could be extended to other New York City teams if he found a high roller with enough ambition and cash. That's where Salvatore Sollazzo came in.

It was through Gard that Sollazzo gained the services of a kid who was arguably the most talented player in the nation—Sherman White. In the middle of the 1949–50 season, when Gard was a senior and White was a junior, the LIU Blackbirds lost a 55-52 contest to North Carolina State in Madison Square Garden because of several late miscues by Gard, who was in Sollazzo's pocket for the game. In the locker room, White confronted Gard and two other players (one was Dolf Bigos, who was also in on the fix) and asked about their poor play. They shrugged it off, but Gard went back to Sollazzo and told him that White would have to be cut in for any future fixes because "[h]e's getting too good. . . . He can turn a game around all by himself."[13] Gard brought White to Sollazzo's upscale apartment where Sollazzo's gorgeous wife Jeanne, an ex-model in a sultry dress, served them a lavish dinner. Gard and Sollazzo explained point shaving to Sherman and told him "everybody's doing it." White nervously agreed to go along. LIU finished the season 19-5 and was ranked in the top ten almost all season, and never lower than fourteenth. Only one of the team's losses was honest, a 60-53 loss to seventh-ranked Duquesne on February 16, 1950, when LIU was ranked sixth. The other four losses were all in games that the Blackbirds were trying to shave points, including a first-round defeat to Syracuse in the NIT.

The next season, Gard had graduated, but LIU continued to excel as White became a senior and a consensus All-American, averaging

27.7 points per game. Gard maintained close ties with his former LIU teammates and continued to orchestrate fixes. The Blackbirds started the next season 16-0 and rose to No. 2 in the AP poll. In the middle of that great run, Coach Clair Bee got an anonymous tip that three of his players were shaving points. After Bee confronted White and the two others, Sherman White told Gard that it was over and there would be no more dumping or point shaving. However, LIU eventually went into a late-season tailspin, caused partly by a poor western road trip and partly by the ominous storm clouds of scandal that engulfed college basketball during January and February of 1951 and gave several of LIU's best players a terrible ache in the pits of their stomachs. Sherman White's stomach ached worst of all.

Eddie Gard didn't stop with his own LIU team. He and Sollazzo propositioned other teams, both in New York City as well as visiting teams from around the country that came to Madison Square Garden to play on what was then college basketball's greatest stage. Gard and Sollazzo were successful in lining up several other fixes, but they were also rebuffed by several teams. For example, when Oklahoma came to town in December 1950, Sollazzo invited some of the Sooners to his apartment both before and after their game. He solicited their services, but none of them showed any interest in shaving points for him. As it turned out, Sollazzo's other major client ended up being New York City's other big college team during that era, City College of New York (CCNY).

At first glance, CCNY would have seemed one of the least likely teams to be involved in point shaving. "City," as it was simply called by New Yorkers, had a reputation as an academic school. While nearly every other major college basketball team was offering full scholarships by the early 1950s, CCNY still was not. Its players earned their way with jobs—usually easy jobs, but jobs nonetheless. While other schools were starting to eagerly recruit out-of-state talent for their basketball programs, City relied almost exclusively on hometown kids from the Big Apple. And while other schools—most notably its New York neighbor LIU—were stretching the boundaries of propriety by setting up athletes with easy courses and providing them with a variety of fringe benefits, City still had a reputation as a school that was hard to get into and where its athletes had to do the same tough schoolwork as the other students. Their greatest fringe benefit was supposed to be having a degree with the prestigious CCNY stamp on it. As a result, some of New York City's top basketball talent had started to shy away from City during the 1940s.

CCNY coach Nat Holman was a basketball institution in New York City, known simply as "Mr. Basketball" in the Big Apple. However, by the mid-1940s, Holman knew he needed top players to continue to be successful, so he put added pressure on his assistant coach Bobby Sand, who did virtually all the recruiting. Sand delivered with CCNY's 1948 recruiting class, which was surprisingly loaded. It was later learned that in order to land that class, a number of sins had been committed, including altering transcripts, offering a free ride to a player's sibling, offering a job to a player's father, and the use of a mysterious "student loan" fund. Nevertheless, Nat got what he needed (though he had unknowingly sold the soul of CCNY for it). If those players looked exciting on paper, then they looked even better once they arrived on campus and started playing on the freshman team. Ed Roman, Ed Warner, Al Roth, and Floyd Layne were the core members of a freshman squad that went 11-3. Warner and Layne were African American, so the team had a multicultural appeal at a time when black athletes were just beginning to break the color barrier in college basketball (during that season, 1948–49, Bill Garrett joined the Indiana University varsity and became the first black basketball recruit to play in the Big Ten).

In the 1949–50 season, CCNY's stellar recruiting class moved up to the varsity. They had a successful but up-and-down season as the young guys learned the ropes. They were unranked going into post-season play, but they caught fire in March. In the NIT, CCNY upset San Francisco in the first round, emasculated third-ranked Kentucky 89-50 in the quarterfinals, easily beat Duquesne in the semis, and then shocked top-ranked Bradley 69-61 in the championship game. Then they moved on to the NCAA Tournament. CCNY barely slipped past second-ranked Ohio State 56-55 in the first round and then beat North Carolina State 78-73 to advance to the title game and a rematch with top-ranked Bradley in Madison Square Garden. In the rematch, CCNY pulled ahead early and led by ten halfway through the second half. Bradley made a rip-roaring comeback in the final minutes, but came up short and CCNY won 69-68. Previously, four other NIT champions had tried to recreate their magic in the NCAA, and all had failed.

Because of their NIT-NCAA sweep, CCNY was crowned as the greatest undisputed champion in college basketball history. They were the darling of American sportswriters and made the front pages of newspapers across the country. Since their four best players were sophomores, they looked like a dynasty in the making and were the immediate favorite to repeat as national champions in 1951 and 1952. Then they could go out in a blaze of glory by winning the 1952 Olympic trials and representing the United States with a gold medal win in the 1952 Olympics in Helsinki. Their destiny looked perfectly scripted, but only eleven months later that destiny disintegrated in scandal.

City's destiny was eventually lost because the young CCNY sophomores, in addition to learning college basketball from their upperclassmen teammates, also learned how to dump games. During City's championship 1949–50 season, senior sixth man Norm Mager brokered fixes between a contingent of CCNY's top players—including fellow senior Irv Dambrot and sophomores Ed Roman and Al Roth—and a prominent fixer named Eli Kaye, who worked for the mafia. Mager was a 6' 5", 160-pound sharpshooter who hated the abrasive style of Nat Holman, who was old school even back then. Holman rarely gave any of his players credit for doing something right, but he would chap their ass for the smallest mistake. "Sometimes I get violent," Nat admitted.[14] However, Nat's philosophy on the matter was simple: "Easygoing guys who don't demand the best from their players don't win many games."[15] And although he didn't show it outwardly, Holman did care for his players. After the scandals broke, he never publicly ridiculed or denounced any of them. He only expressed sorrow for their bad choices.

Still, not all of his players adjusted well to Nat's coaching tactics, and Norm Mager was the malcontent on that 1950 CCNY team.

"Norm was Nat's scapegoat that year and he hated Nat with a passion. . . . Norm would have dumped for nothing," said one former CCNY player.[16] However, Mager and his young teammates didn't shave points for free; they did it for big money and the fixes were in effect for a variety of games throughout their double-championship season.

Heading into the next season, Magers and Dambrot moved on, but the point shaving didn't stop. CCNY simply fell into the clutches of a new fixer—Salvatore Sollazzo. Despite his success in fixing LIU games, Sollazzo's gambling had landed him in a financial hole and he was looking for even more fixes to help dig himself out. Sollazzo's front man Eddie Gard started working on CCNY's Ed Warner by telling him that several of his teammates had been fixing games the previous season. Warner was shocked. Then Gard told him about how much money the university was making on basketball games while Warner and the other players weren't getting a dime. Warner agreed to shave points, and eventually his three classmates, Roth, Roman, and a reluctant Floyd Layne, all joined in the fix.

The defending national champs got off to a rough start in 1950–51. They were 5-3 by the time January rolled around, losing a couple of games in which they were trying to shave points. Meanwhile, across town, LIU and Sherman White were the talk of the college basketball world. In early January, Sollazzo failed to pay the CCNY Beavers all the money he owed them after a fix against Boston College. They decided to play it straight the rest of the season and quit doing business with Sollazzo and Gard.

It was around that same time that Clair Bee got his inside tip that some of his LIU players were shaving points and approached Sherman White, who told Sollazzo and Gard that there would be no more fixes with LIU. Unfortunately, both CCNY and LIU soon learned that it was too late for redemption.

In the early 1950s, Sherman White was perhaps the greatest all-around talent the college game had ever seen. He was 6' 8", lithe, and strong. He could shoot, rebound, and dribble. He played facing the basket and with his back to the basket. And he was an unselfish team-mate who opened up opportunities for other players around him. Today, he remains one of the greatest talents to have ever graced a collegiate floor in any era. However, his name has largely been forgotten, like a long-lost relative who was once the pride of the family but whose name now only brings grimaces of pain and disappointment. When we think of the great stars of the early 1950s, we now think of guys like Clyde Lovellette, Bob Houbregs, and Bobby Leonard. Sherman White was probably a better player than all three of them, but history has dealt him the unkindest blow of all—to be forgotten. He is no longer remembered as a great player, only as a cheater. Sherman White was not a bad kid. He was not a selfish kid. He was not even a stereotypical street kid. He was just an average American kid from a good family, like most of the guys involved in the point-shaving scandals. That's what made the scandals so shocking.

At the beginning of January 1951, newspaperman Max Kase tipped off New York district attorney Frank Hogan that he needed to keep an eye on Eddie Gard. Hogan was already investigating several college basketball fixes, but when his investigators started watching Eddie Gard, they hit the jackpot. On January 17, 1951, Hogan's previous top case, against Manhattan College, went public and three gamblers and two players from the 1949–50 Manhattan team were booked. The news made headlines the next day and sent shock waves through college basketball in New York. Nat Holman called a special meeting and told his CCNY players to steer clear of gamblers. Meanwhile, LIU, 16-0 and one of the top-ranked teams in country, was getting ready to leave on a western road trip at the time, but with a cloud of uncertainty hanging over their star players, LIU lost four out of five games on the road trip and started on a downward spiral.

On Saturday, February 17, 1951, a different kind of destiny finally caught up with CCNY, as a chain of events was triggered that eventually consumed them, Sollazzo and Gard, LIU, and, surprisingly, a handful of other teams beyond the confines of the Empire State. On February 17, the CCNY Beavers were on a train on their way back to the city after shredding the zone defense of the Temple Owls for a 95-71 win in Philadelphia. On the train with them were two detectives who approached Coach Holman and told him that three of

17

his players—Ed Roman, Al Roth, and Ed Warner—were suspected of dealing with gamblers and would need to come to the police station to answer some questions when the train reached New York. A shocked Holman told the boys to go willingly and tell the truth. The three players were handcuffed and taken away. That same night, the D.A.'s office also rounded up Eddie Gard and Salvatore Sollazzo. Roman, Roth, Warner, and Gard all confessed to their crimes, and the dominoes began to fall.

In exchange for his tip about Gard, Hogan gave Max Kase the story about the CCNY players and the news broke in the *New York Journal-American* newspaper, sending shock waves of grief and disbelief across the five boroughs of New York City. Three days after the first CCNY players were nailed, Sherman White was named the college player of the year by the *Sporting News*. At the time, he was only seventy-seven points away from setting the all-time collegiate career scoring record. But he never got a chance at it. The D.A.'s office soon nabbed him, and with a heavy heart he confessed to dumping.

After arresting the stars of the CCNY team that had been crowned the greatest in college basketball history less than a year earlier, then bringing down the guy who was arguably the college game's best player, the New York D.A.'s office used their confessions to round up the rest of the CCNY and LIU players who were involved in fixing games. CCNY played out its 1951 schedule with a patchwork roster, while LIU, which was 20-4 at the time and poised for an NIT and NCAA run, saw its championship season implode. Around the country, many basketball fans simply shook their heads and called the scandals a tragic but isolated New York City phenomenon.

Phog Allen stated, "Out here in the Midwest these scandalous conditions, of course, do not exist. But in the East, the boys, particularly those who participate in the resort leagues during the summer months, are thrown into an environment which cannot help but breed the evil which more and more is coming to light."[17]

Meanwhile, Kentucky's Adolph Rupp boasted, "Gamblers couldn't get to my boys with a ten-foot pole."[18]

That spring, seven-footer Bill Spivey and clutch man Cliff Hagan sparked Kentucky to an upset over high-powered Kansas State in the

NCAA title game. It was Rupp's third national championship in four years.

However, if the Midwest at first looked squeaky clean and the point-shaving scandals appeared to be limited to New York City, that illusion was blown away in July 1951 when Frank Hogan revealed point-shaving allegations against players at Toledo University (in Toledo, Ohio) and Bradley University (in Peoria, Illinois). Both teams had connections with a group of New York City gamblers that included Eli Kaye, the mafia-connected fixer who had done business with CCNY players before they fell into the clutches of Salvatore Sollazzo and Eddie Gard. Then, in October, Hogan jolted the college basketball world again when he apprehended former Kentucky Wildcats Ralph Beard, Alex Groza, and Dale Barnstable. Beard and Groza were two of college basketball's golden boys. They had led the Wildcats to NCAA titles in 1948 and 1949 and had been key members on the U.S. Olympic team that won gold at the 1948 games in London. After leaving Kentucky, they became founding members of a hot new NBA franchise, the Indianapolis Olympians, which offered the Kentucky stars an ownership stake for signing on to play in the Circle City. By their second season in the league in 1950–51, both Beard and Groza were NBA all-stars and appeared destined for landmark pro careers. That future quickly evaporated when they were arrested by Hogan for shaving points in a 1949 NIT game in Madison Square Garden for the gambling syndicate spearheaded by Eli Kaye. Under interrogation, Beard, Groza, and Barnstable all confessed to their crimes, which included other fixes as well.

However, the New York D.A. wasn't finished with Kentucky. On February 20, 1952, Hogan arrested Jim Line, an assistant coach on Kentucky's 1951 championship team, and Walter Hirsch, a senior on the 1951 championship team, and Line and Hirsch implicated Wildcat All-American Bill Spivey. There was never enough evidence to convict the three of them, but suspicions continued to surround Spivey, who was convicted of a lesser charge of perjury for untrue statements he made to a grand jury. It was later learned that Line, Hirsch, and Spivey had conspired with gamblers during the 1950–51 season. Spivey originally decided to sit out the 1951–52 season (his senior year) until he could clear his name, but after UK did its own internal investigation, it officially suspended the All-American seven-footer and ended his prominent collegiate career. The NBA then refused to allow him into its league. The investigation of Kentucky's basketball program by the D.A.'s office and the NCAA also turned up other unsavory allegations, including academic fraud, illegal recruiting, illegal subsidies to players, and disregard for the physical welfare of the student-athletes. Kentucky officials, however, said that Rupp was blameless and they refused to sanction him.

When the dust finally cleared in 1952, the last four NCAA championship teams—Kentucky in 1948 and 1949, CCNY in 1950, and Kentucky again in 1951—were all implicated in the point-shaving scandals. The pristine reputation of college basketball and its amateur athletes, supposedly unsullied by commercialism, was in public shambles.

People tried to find reasons. Most of them blamed the money that was pouring into college sports. It was becoming a big business and the joy of amateur competition was being sold out. Some people blamed the athletic scholarship and the new sense of entitlement that went with it. Essentially, they said that kids had it too easy and didn't have to work hard enough for what they got. In a letter to the editor, one New York citizen said the problem started before kids reached college age. "Sturdy teenagers scorn snow shoveling and lawn mowing," the letter writer stated. "They would rather pester front doors like well-clad beggars asking for money to buy uniforms and athletic paraphernalia. Soft-hearted adults provide a wealth of public recreational facilities, and the kids grow up thinking everything coming their way—including bribes—should be accepted as their due."[19]

Whatever the reasons, the scandals struck a heavy blow. Irving Marsh of the *New York Herald Tribune* predicted, "Basketball is through as a big-time sport."[20] At that dark and uncertain hour, college basketball desperately needed new heroes, but not just any heroes. It needed honest heroes with a pristine image. It needed scandal-free heroes. It needed heroes who represented the values of a patriotic America that had just endured the Great Depression and World War II and was gearing up for the Cold War. It needed the type of boys that Americans would like to have seen their daughters bring home. And, of course, they also needed to be able to shoot the lights out, crash the boards, and win ball games with guts and honor. College basketball found those heroes in the American heartland. It found them in Indiana.

BOBBY

2

[Bobby Leonard] was cocky. Bobby knew he was a good basketball player and he wasn't afraid to tell you that. Of course, he didn't have to tell you. He'd show you.

—GOETHE CHAMBERS

Even in childhood, Bobby Leonard was decisive and determined when he knew what he wanted. The difference between Bobby and most other kids his age was that he understood early on what it took to get what he wanted—and Bobby always seemed to want it just a little bit more than everybody else.

Leonard was part of a generation of kids that were born just as America was sliding into the Great Depression in the early 1930s. When he was growing up, poverty and privation were as much a part of his family as his two sisters. Up through Bobby's elementary school years, the family lived on Elm Street near the railroad tracks on the north side of Terre Haute in a tough, working-class Catholic neighborhood. The Leonards weren't Catholic—in fact, they weren't very religious at all. But Bobby's father Ray was working-class to the core. He was a steamfitter, and during the Depression he had a tough time finding work, just like everybody else. The house on Elm Street didn't have indoor plumbing, so the family had to use an old outhouse in the backyard.

In those lean times, Bobby found his refuge in sports, even though the rest of his family didn't have much of a history or interest in any type of athletics. Leonard played every sport he could find and grew to love competition as a way to distinguish himself. Since Bobby was small for his age, he also developed a toughness and self-reliance that came from defending himself against bigger kids in his dog-eat-dog neighborhood. "I was independent. I was always by myself," said Bobby. "You come from around the railroad tracks in Terre Haute and you didn't have the clothes and some of the other things the other kids had. And that was probably good because I developed a fascination for a ball going through a basket and I spent all my time working on that. Other guys didn't want to spend that much time."

When Bobby was in elementary school he desperately wanted a basketball of his own so he could practice by himself whenever he wanted. "One year at Christmas we got Bob a bicycle," said Hattie Leonard, Bobby's mother. "We thought he would like it. But he and some friends took it apart and sold the parts. He was disappointed that he didn't get a basketball."[1]

Since he didn't have a basketball of his own, Bobby had to make friends with others who did have one. Fortunately, although Bobby was independent, he was also gregarious and good-natured, and so he was a natural at making friends with different kinds of people. When he was ten, he befriended some young marines who lived up the alley from him. Those guys had gone to Terre Haute Gerstmeyer Technical High School, but nearly all of them—even some who hadn't finished high school yet—joined the marines after the Japanese bombed Pearl Harbor, and they ended up serving in many of the major battles in the Pacific during World War II. After the war, many of them returned to Terre Haute and finished high school or went to trade school. Several of them got together and welded a sturdy basketball goal that they hung under a big tree in Ma Sullivan's backyard, then strung a light out there so they could play ball at night. What they didn't realize was that they had given Bobby Leonard his first full-time basketball court.

Bobby was always hanging around wanting to play ball. The ex-marines took a liking to the kid and taught him how to spit-shine shoes. They would leave their shoes for him on Ma Sullivan's back porch on Fridays so that Bobby could shine them up before the boys went out on the town on Friday nights. Then on Sunday afternoons they would all go out and play pickup games on their homemade basketball rim, and they would let Bobby—barely a teenager—play with them. "Here I was a little kid playing against grown guys and they beat the hell out of me," said Bobby. "They liked me but they weren't going to give me an inch."

After they got done playing, the guys would sit on the porch and drink coffee and tell stories. "They'd sit up there and tell stories about the invasions, and they'd tell stories about the Japs," Bobby said. "They'd tell about Japs coming out of caves with white flags [pretending to surrender]. They said they forgot the white flags and just mowed 'em down. They said they weren't taking no prisoners at all. It was brutal over there. My eyes were big as silver dollars listening to the stories they told."

After World War II, there was a lot more work to go around and Ray Leonard moved his family to a better house on 13½ Street. It didn't take long for Bobby to find a new hangout where he could shoot baskets and join pickup games with older guys. Right around the corner from Leonard's new house was the 13th Street firehouse. Bobby made friends with the firemen and ended up getting more than basketball out of the deal. "Those firemen they cooked their own meals in the firehouse," said Bobby, "so I used to go over there and they would let me eat with them and they had a basketball goal out in the back and I used to go out there and shoot all the time."

By the time he entered McLean Junior High School, Bobby was already a basketball wizard in the making. "He wasn't too big but he had a lot of natural ability when he first came to McLean," said Phil Cartwright, the McLean coach. "I think Bob was more interested in basketball to the exclusion of everything else than any kid that I have ever known. He was the best player on the team both years that I had him."[2]

Bobby got his first taste of organized basketball at McLean, but when he moved up to Gerstmeyer Technical High School in 1946, he got the full course in basketball fundamentals from legendary coach

Howard Sharpe, who was already recognized as one of the top coaches in the Hoosier state and who would go on to become the winningest coach in the history of Indiana high school basketball. Sharpe was a pupil of the legendary Glenn Curtis, who had coached John Wooden at Martinsville, and during Bobby Leonard's first two years at Gerstmeyer, Wooden was in Terre Haute coaching the Indiana State Sycamores. Since Sharpe and Wooden shared the same mentor, they were natural colleagues, and both of them were pioneers of teaching the one-handed jump shot. Bobby Leonard would become one of the first prep disciples of the jump shot.

At that time, basketball was still dominated by the two-handed set shot (and occasionally a one-handed set shot). With the two-handed set shot, a player would typically cock the ball near his chest and then push it straight forward—with a fairly low release. With the jump shot, the player would cock the ball over his head and then elevate into the air and throw the ball toward the basketball with one hand—and a high release. The jump shot was much more difficult to defend and allowed players to release shots under pressure, shots that might have been blocked or stolen had they been two-handed set shots. The jump shot revolutionized the game, and Bobby Leonard became one of the first Indiana high school players to truly perfect it.

At the start of his sophomore year at Gerstmeyer, Leonard stood just 5' 4", and he failed to make the varsity basketball squad. Nevertheless, Coach Sharpe kept a close eye on Leonard, knowing he had the potential to be a terrific player. Sharpe also made a prediction that few others—including Bobby himself—would have made. Sharpe said he believed Leonard would grow to over six feet tall because he had a long humerus (the bone that runs from the shoulder to the elbow). "I predicted that he'd grow to be 6' 3" or 6' 4" and he made me a prophet," said Sharpe.[3] Leonard was 5' 10" by the end of his sophomore year and 6' 3½" by the time he was a junior.

Bobby not only made the varsity as a junior, he quickly became the heart of the team. Gerstmeyer opened the 1948–49 season with a game in Evansville against Bosse High School, which had won back-to-back state titles in 1944 and 1945. It wound up being Bobby's coming-out party. He scored twenty-one and Gerstmeyer upset tradition-rich Bosse 41-37. Bobby continued his high-scoring pace throughout the season and became one of the top players in the state. Sharpe commented, "He was simply a great high school player. He had radar-like shooting range from 21–25 feet. We played him at forward but I set up our offense to screen for him so he could shoot his one-handers from the top of the circle. He was deadly."[4]

By the time Bobby was a senior, he earned a reputation as a kid who would "rather die than lose a basketball game." During one road trip to northwest Indiana where Gerstmeyer played two tough teams— East Chicago Roosevelt and Whiting—Leonard rang up a total of sixty-seven points in two games, which was a huge number in that era. At the end of the season, he led Gerstmeyer to its first sectional title in five years and only the third in school history. In the finals of the Martinsville regional, Gerstmeyer lost to Ellettsville on a buzzer-beater that brought Leonard's high school career to a dramatic end. However, it was obvious that Bobby's basketball career was far from over.

Since the 1930s, Indiana had been known across America as "the basketball state" because of its famous high school basketball tournament and the passion its citizens had for the game. When college basketball began moving toward tournament play with the NIT and NCAA tournaments, universities began coveting Indiana high school coaches, who had abundant experience coaching in postseason tournaments. During the 1930s and 1940s, nine coaches of Indiana high school state championship teams landed head coaching jobs at major universities, and once they got to their colleges, many of them recruited Indiana high school players to join them. The most prominent Indiana high school coach to make the jump was Everett Case, who took over the reins at North Carolina State in 1946 after leading Frankfort to four state titles (1925, 1929, 1936, and 1939). Case, known as the "Old Grey Fox," compiled a record of 376-133 (.739) in eighteen seasons with the Wolfpack and became one of the founding fathers of the Atlantic Coast Conference. Case's successful teams at NC State were built largely with Hoosier recruits.

At first, it was a matter of pride throughout the Hoosier state that its coaches were so widely sought after and that they were able to build successful programs with Indiana boys on their rosters. From the perspective of the Indiana fan, it was like they were spreading the truth and converting the infidels to the world's best brand of basketball. And Indiana boys filling out rosters at colleges outside of the Hoosier state was definitely noticed by others as well. For example, the University of Southern California had seven Indiana players on its roster in 1938, and when the Trojans played at the University of California they were taunted by the home band with a rendition of "Back Home Again in Indiana." A few years later in a game between Vanderbilt and Mississippi, there were twelve players from Indiana on the two rosters, all from high schools within a fifty-square-mile area in the southern part of the Hoosier state.[5]

However, by the mid-1940s it wasn't just coaches originally from Indiana who were coming into the state and trying to pluck away the top basketball talent. Other coaches from around the country noticed that many of these guys were winning with Hoosier kids on their rosters, so they decided to recruit in Indiana as well. The situation finally came to a head in 1948. Two things happened that year that brought about the inevitable backlash of Indiana basketball fans getting fed up with watching their best high school players leave the state. The first was that Adolph Rupp's Kentucky Wildcats won the NCAA title. Afterwards, the impetuous Rupp bragged, "Indiana has not only lost its leadership as the top basketball state, but the South has replaced the Midwest as the home of basketball."[6] Many Indiana fans scoffed at that, especially since that spring the Indiana high school all-stars trounced the Kentucky high school all-stars 70-47 in their annual border war game (up until 1954 the two teams played only one game each year rather than the "home and home" series that developed later). The 1948 win was Indiana's sixth victory over Kentucky in the seven-year history of the series. Nevertheless, Rupp's words did strike a nerve. Rupp had already started coming into Indiana to try to woo the top Hoosier players down to Lexington, and while Kentucky was winning the NCAA championship in 1948, Indiana University—

which had been one of the favorites to win the Big Ten—was suffering through an injury-plagued 8-12 season and ended up tied for last place in the Big Ten.

The other big thing that happened in 1948 was that the Hoosier state's top recruit, 6' 9" center Clyde Lovellette from Terre Haute, made a last-minute decision to attend Kansas University. The national championship runs of Oklahoma A&M with Bob Kurland and Kentucky with Bill Spivey had convinced Indiana University coach Branch McCracken and many other college basketball coaches that winning on a national level now required a dominant big man. Lovellette was the big man that McCracken wanted to build around, and Lovellette had definitely appeared headed to IU. He had attended multiple Indiana games in Bloomington during his senior year, and late in the summer after he graduated he went down to the IU campus to meet with Coach McCracken and make it official that he was coming to Indiana, even selecting the courses he was going to take that fall. But he told McCracken that he needed to go back home to Terre Haute and get his clothes before school started, and McCracken said that was fine but to only take a few days. Kansas coach Phog Allen was still convinced that Lovellette was interested in his school. So he approached Lovellette about visiting Kansas before making his final decision. Lovellette initially refused, but Allen was undeniably persistent and he eventually persuaded Lovellette to make a short visit to Lawrence, even driving to Indiana and picking up Lovellette to drive him to Lawrence. Ten days after Lovellette left Bloomington to get his clothes from Terre Haute, a news story hit the wire that the big center from Terre Haute had enrolled at Kansas. When it was announced, Allen explained that Lovellette had asthma and the air in Kansas was better for him. Lovellette went along with that story, but later said that he simply liked the fact that Kansas was a much smaller campus than IU and that he hit it off with his Jayhawk teammates.

Whatever the reason for Lovellette's change of heart, it stunned and outraged McCracken. For the IU coach, it was the final straw in watching Indiana's top basketball talent getting plundered by out-of-state schools. McCracken threw down the gauntlet. He publicly declared that every year he was going to pinpoint the top five prospects in the state of Indiana and offer those boys the honor of playing for Indiana University. The rest of the country could have its pick of the leftovers.

To reinforce his plan, McCracken set up a series of clinics for Indiana high school basketball coaches in which he shared his philosophy and his system so that players could begin their schooling in Indiana University's fast break style and fundamentals before they ever arrived on the IU campus. McCracken also built a network of contacts with coaches and athletic directors (many of them IU alumni) who could help him pinpoint the best talent in the state, and he appealed to them that it was something akin to their civic duty to help steer players toward IU. Pretty soon, the best basketball players in the state started hearing subtle messages such as "You're too good to play anywhere but Indiana."[7]

By the 1949–50 season, McCracken's plan was in full swing, and the timing was perfect because there was an outstanding crop of seniors in Indiana high schools that year. One of the hot prospects was, of course, a brash young sharpshooter from Terre Haute Gerstmeyer named Bobby Leonard. After a stellar senior year, Leonard was heavily recruited by several major programs. Everett Case of NC State made a strong bid for Leonard. Coach Peck Hickman of Louisville offered him a scholarship. Kentucky's Adolph Rupp flew Leonard down to Lexington—Bobby's first ride on an airplane—and had him scrimmage against one of the Wildcat reserves. When Bobby soundly beat the kid in a game of one-on-one, Rupp immediately offered him a scholarship. However, in his heart Bobby already knew where he wanted to go. At the end of Leonard's senior year, McCracken had come to Gerstmeyer for a visit after he targeted Leonard as one of the top prospects in the state. Leonard was impressed by McCracken's imposing 6' 5" stature and the way he carried himself. "He had a great personality. He had a magnetism about him that drew people to him," Leonard said. "He could walk in anywhere, and people would say with awe, 'That's Branch McCracken of IU!'[8]

"I used to lay in bed at night listening to IU play on the radio, so I knew about McCracken and all the guys from Indiana. Deep down,

I knew that I wanted to go to IU." Shortly after he got his scholarship offer from McCracken, Bobby let the Indiana coach know that he was committed to playing for the Hoosiers.

But as good as Bobby Leonard was in high school, he was not McCracken's top target in the state that year. In fact, of the four Indiana high school ballplayers who got IU scholarships in the graduating class of 1950, Leonard was probably no higher than fourth on the list at the time. McCracken focused a lot of his attention on New Castle High School, which was one of the state's basketball powerhouses and featured a 5' 10" forward whom McCracken had been recruiting since his sophomore year—Jack Wright. During the fall of his senior year, Wright had been invited to Bloomington for an IU football game, and before the game he was treated to brunch at McCracken's house, where Mac and his wife Mary Jo charmed the youngster with home cooking and friendly midwestern hospitality.

If Bobby Leonard wasn't known as the best outside shooter in Indiana at that time, it was because Jack Wright had already locked up the honor. Wright had been nailing long-range bombs at a remarkably consistent pace for three years at New Castle. He was a swish artist with his two-handed set shot, and he also possessed a deadly running hook that he could fire with either hand. As a senior, Wright led the Hoosier state's prestigious North Central Conference in scoring and finished his career as the all-time leading scorer in conference history. He was heavily recruited by North Carolina State's Everett Case, and Wright made a trip down to Raleigh, North Carolina, to visit the campus. Wright gave NC State serious consideration, but in the end he couldn't resist the lure of McCracken and Indiana. It just felt natural to follow in the footsteps of New Castle's great stars of the past, such as Vern Huffman and Marv Huffman, and play for the Hoosiers. "I'd always been an IU fan and most everybody that played for New Castle went to IU," said Wright. "I guess I was destined for IU."

With Wright and Leonard, McCracken had two potent outside scorers, and he added another excellent scorer when he locked up Marion's Pat Klein, the 1950 Indiana Mr. Basketball and winner of the prestigious Trester Award for Mental Attitude at the Indiana state finals. Those were three outstanding players and three pretty big names—and Mac still had one big fish left to catch in Indiana—but like other coaches, McCracken was no longer limiting himself to recruiting basketball players in his home state. In fact, with the class of 1950, McCracken landed four out-of-state players—the most he had ever landed in a single recruiting class until then. And he nabbed all four of them from the state of Illinois.

With the loss of Clyde Lovellette in 1948, McCracken was still desperately looking for a big man. In 1950, he plucked two promising centers out of Illinois high schools. One of them was 6' 5" Charlie Kraak from Collinsville, Illinois, just across the river from St. Louis. Kraak was a classic late bloomer. He sat on the bench during his sophomore and junior years in high school, then grew six inches in the summer following his junior year. That got him an opportunity at the starting spot at center and he ran with it, earning all-state honors and carrying his team to the Illinois state finals as a senior. That brought him a flood of attention from college basketball coaches, and he was heavily recruited by Kansas, St. Louis, Illinois, Indiana, and several other Big Ten schools. "The people of Illinois, of course, wanted me to go to the University of Illinois," said Charlie. "[Illinois coach Harry Combes] came down to visit me and that was probably the place that most people thought I'd go." However, Charlie, who was an only child, had never been out of Collinsville, so the thought of going away to college appealed to him. When he visited Bloomington, Indiana, with his parents at the end of his senior year to see the campus and meet with McCracken, he knew he had found the right fit. "They really treated me well and I loved the campus," Kraak said. "So I deserted the state of Illinois and ended up in Bloomington."

At 6' 5", Kraak was best suited to play forward in college. It was the other high school center from Illinois whom McCracken hoped to turn into a college center. His name was Lou Scott and he played for Chicago Vocational High School on the south side of the Windy City in the famous Chicago Public League. Scott was 6' 10" in his bare feet and possessed long arms and broad shoulders on top of a thin frame. He certainly was not a superstar in high school—he didn't play basketball at all until his senior season—but he was aggressive, somewhat coordinated, and eager to learn. If McCracken couldn't find a topflight big man, then by God, he was going to make one. And that's exactly what he set out to do with Lou Scott.

McCracken also picked up two guards in Chicago from the 1950 graduating class, one of them Lou Scott's teammate Ron Taylor. After an outstanding senior year, Taylor was leaning heavily toward playing for the North Carolina Tar Heels until McCracken swooped in at the eleventh hour, offered Taylor a tryout in Bloomington, and then convinced him to come and play for the Hoosiers.

The other Chicago guard was a 5' 9" mighty mouse named Sammy Esposito, who played for Fanger High School in the Chicago Public League. Esposito was an all-city performer in football, basketball, and baseball during his senior year at Fanger and was recruited to play college ball in all three sports. He used his lightning-quick speed and agility to become a standout quarterback in football and a sweet-hitting shortstop in baseball. On the basketball court, he could run and shoot all night. In one memorable game as a senior, he scored an unbelievable eighty-one points to set Chicago's single-game scoring record for a high school player. Esposito was so good in baseball that he had a few teams interested in signing him directly to a minor league contract. However, his older brother had gone to college and he decided he should do the same. He had plenty of suitors, but he wanted to play both basketball and baseball in college, and he didn't want to go too far from home. There was a loyal IU alumnus in the area and he made contact with Sammy. "He came to my games and talked about Indiana all the time," said Esposito. That led to Sammy getting an invitation to come to the Bloomington campus over the holiday break during his senior year. He took the train from Chicago to Bloomington and then took a cab to the IU Fieldhouse and asked for Coach McCracken. Mac was on the floor conducting a practice session with the varsity, so he had Esposito suit up and scrimmage with the team. It didn't take long for Mac to see that he was looking at an outstanding athlete. Afterwards, McCracken immediately offered Sammy a scholarship and said he would love to have him at Indiana. The assistant basketball coach, Ernie Andres, was IU's head baseball coach, so Esposito could also play for the Hoosier baseball team. "I was going to go to a school in Illinois," said Esposito. "But I changed my mind at the last minute and ended up at IU."

That spring of 1950 at the Indiana-Kentucky all-star game in Indianapolis, Bobby Leonard sat with Branch McCracken and Mary Jo McCracken. Surprisingly, Leonard was only an alternate on the Indiana all-star team. Only ten players were selected at that time and it was heavily weighted toward the teams that made the state finals and supplemented by one player from each of the state's main regions. Of course, IU recruit Pat Klein wore the honorary number 1 jersey that was reserved for Mr. Basketball. While Leonard was certainly disappointed that he didn't make the all-star team, he was thrilled to get the chance to watch the game with his future coach. "He and Mac never stopped talking basketball during the entire contest," said Mary Jo McCracken. "Bobby had already announced that he was going to attend Indiana, and he and Mac really went over that all-star game. When the game ended, Bobby looked at Mac and said, 'Coach, I'm going to be the best basketball player that ever played for you. All you have to do is tell me what to do, and I'll do it.'"9

One of the guys McCracken and Leonard watched on the Indiana team that day was Dick Farley from Winslow High School, a tiny rural school in southwestern Indiana. Leonard did not know it at the time, but he would help McCracken put the finishing touches on recruiting Farley to play for IU, and Farley would eventually become Leonard's closest friend at Indiana.

To his family, Dick Farley was always known as "Richard." He didn't really pick up the name "Dick" until he was a young man in high school and college. His parents were both widowers who married each other later in life and had children from previous marriages. Richard was the youngest of their seven children and the only child they had together, and as a result, he was doted on by his older siblings. Richard's father, who was in his late fifties when Richard was born, was a coal miner, and the family was very, very poor, but they were a close-knit group and were happy enough that being poor was just part of life. When Richard was born, the family's house was already bursting at the seams and there was barely room for another body. Once he was old enough to sleep by himself, the family put a feather bed out on their back porch and that became Richard's bedroom until one of the older siblings moved out. Up through his high school years, the house still had dirt floors in several rooms and didn't have an indoor toilet or a shower.

As Farley grew to be one of the tallest kids his age, people naturally asked him if he was going to play basketball. He gave it a try, loved it, and was hooked. He used to regularly take a basketball to school with him. As he walked to school over dirt and gravel roads, he would dribble the ball all the way from his driveway to the schoolhouse. He became a standout on his grade school and junior high school basketball teams, then became a town celebrity when he reached Winslow High School and led the underdog Eskimos to an improbable run in the 1950 state tournament, winning sectional and regional championships and making it all the way to the semistate finals. Farley's Winslow squad became known statewide as the "giant killers" because they knocked off several powerhouse schools during their magnificent run in the Indiana high school tournament.

Farley's inspired play in the state tournament turned a lot of heads and made him a hot commodity among college basketball coaches. Kentucky's Adolph Rupp made a strong bid for his services, and so did coaches from several other major basketball powers. However, at 6' 3" and 180 pounds, Farley played center for Winslow, and there were some who questioned whether he could make the transition to forward in college. Most of those who posed that question did so because they had never actually seen Farley play. He could nearly do it all on the basketball court—pass, dribble, rebound, shoot one-handers from the outside, drive to the hoop, and play flypaper defense. And although he was quiet and forbearing off the court, he was aggressive and desperately competitive on the court.

For Indiana coach Branch McCracken, Farley reminded him a lot of a player from the late 1920s—himself. McCracken was a 6' 4" center who led minuscule Monrovia High School on a giant-killing spree during his final two years on the varsity. As a result, McCracken had high hopes for Farley and made a strong appeal for Farley to come and play for his home state Indiana Hoosiers. By the middle of the summer after his senior year, Farley was leaning heavily toward IU. McCracken closed the deal by making one final trip down to Winslow that summer—but he didn't make the trip alone.

After watching the Indiana-Kentucky all-star game and hitting it off with McCracken, Bobby Leonard wanted to get his college basketball career started as soon as possible. He didn't have a summer job, so McCracken lined up summer work for Leonard at a Bloomington stone quarry, and Leonard was able to spend his evenings at the old Men's Gym on the IU campus, where there were nightly scrimmages with current IU players as well as former players who were back on campus for the summer to finish up their coursework.

"Once I decided to go to IU, I immediately went down to Bloomington because I needed a summer job and Branch got me the hardest job he could find, working on one of those stone-cutting machines. That was enough to make you realize you needed a college education," said Bobby. "So I'm lifting stone all day long. Once [McCracken] came out to the stone quarry. I'm out there dying and he says, 'Boy, this is gonna make you tough, this is gonna make you stronger, and you're gonna be brown as a bear.' And I said, 'yeah, if it doesn't kill me.' . . . When I got off work then I'd go up there in the nighttime and play pickup games, so I was in great shape."

One day, McCracken came and picked up Leonard and said, "I want you to ride down with me to see Dick Farley." So Leonard joined his silver-haired mentor for a scenic ninety-mile drive through the lush green hills of southern Indiana between Bloomington and Winslow. As they came down the dirt road that pulled up to the Farley house, Leonard noticed that Dick's number 7 Indiana all-star jersey was hanging on the clothesline. From the front porch of Farley's house, they could see a neighbor's barn, some fields, and the gently sloping hills of thick southern Indiana forest.

Dick was very soft-spoken, but he and Bobby spent a little time talking and Leonard told Farley, "We're putting together a good team." Of course, McCracken talked to Farley directly and reconfirmed that he thought it would be great for Farley to play for IU. Adolph Rupp and other coaches were after Farley pretty hard at that point and Farley hadn't committed anywhere, so McCracken didn't want to see him slip away to another school. "[Dick] was very impressed and his family was very impressed with Branch McCracken," remembered Marge Farley, Dick's wife (whom he met at IU). After McCracken's summer visit, Farley made it official that he was also committed to playing for Indiana.

Farley's commitment gave McCracken an eight-man recruiting class: Bobby Leonard, Jack Wright, Pat Klein, and Dick Farley from Indiana, and Lou Scott, Charlie Kraak, Sam Esposito, and Ron Taylor from Illinois. It was Indiana's best recruiting class since the 1937 graduates formed a nine-man class recruited by Everett Dean and then coached by McCracken to the 1940 NCAA championship.

The seed of nearly every national championship team is a great recruiting class. When McCracken wrapped up his 1950 class, it was clear that the recruiting plan he had set in motion a few years earlier was now bearing fruit. Mac was quietly jubilant over the prospects of his 1950 recruits and even let it slip to a few friends that he might be able to win it all with this group. However, he didn't stop there. The next year he went out and landed another sensational recruiting class— one that included the blue-chip big man he'd been searching for since he lost Clyde Lovellette.

THE OX

3

[Don] Schlundt was one of the first of the really good big men. There were some big ball players around, but they were mediocre. They played mainly due to their size. But Don was an excellent basketball player.

—Bob Collins, *Indianapolis Star*

Don Schlundt couldn't get enough of sports. He loved to play ball and he played all year round from a young age growing up in South Bend, Indiana. Don had an easy smile and was laid-back by nature, but he loved to compete and he loved to win. Baseball was actually his first love, but he also picked up football early on, and he was a good player in both sports. Then, when he was eleven, he started playing basketball, but that game didn't come to him as easily. "I wasn't much good," said Don. "Probably the only reason I got to play in my neighborhood was that I owned the ball."[1]

One of the things that kept Don from being an effective basketball player was that he didn't exactly have the slender frame of a gazelle. "He was kind of pudgy as a youngster. He looked well-fed," said Bill Schlundt, Don's older brother. Still, Don developed a special love for basketball. He liked the fact that he could go out and practice by himself, and he developed a great rhythm for putting up shot after shot, hour after hour. Eventually he started making a bunch of them.

With his brother Bill, who was two and a half years older, Don

37

also had a rival he could play basketball with nearly every day. Bill was tall and a good player in his own right, and the two of them spent a lot of time playing against each other. "We had a basketball court on dirt out beside our house," said Bill. "During the wintertime when you'd get those nice moonlit nights, we'd go out there and shovel the snow off and play basketball by moonlight."

By the time Don was a fourteen-year-old freshman at Washington-Clay High School, a small township school on the outskirts of South Bend, he had become a very tough basketball player. However, he was still haunted by his girth. As a freshman, he was 5' 9" and 170 pounds. "His freshman year he was told by one of the assistant coaches that he wouldn't make a basketball player because he was too short and heavy," said Bill. Nevertheless, Don persisted and made the freshman team as a reserve guard.

Then something unexpected happened that transformed Don's basketball career and his future. He grew seven inches between the spring of his freshman year and the fall of his sophomore year, sprouting from 5' 9" to 6' 4" in a few short months. "I guess mother got the biggest surprise," said Don. "She bought four pairs of slacks for me at a fire sale in April, figuring I'd be able to wear the pants all winter—but when she pulled them out of the closet in September, I couldn't get into them."[2]

Washington-Clay basketball coach Herschel Eaton quickly realized that he now had a 6' 4" sophomore who possessed the skills and versatility of a guard. He immediately converted Schlundt to center and began working to develop him into a pivot man. That included a lot of work outside of the normal high school practice routine. "Schlundt was mighty awkward at first, but he had two great assets—height and patience," said Eaton. "He'd skip rope for half an hour to improve his footwork; then he'd practice his hook shot for hours. He'd stay around the gym until the janitor turned out the lights. He practiced in and out of season. After school closed in June, he worked on an outdoor court. There was hardly a day in Don's last three years in high school that he didn't shoot a basketball for at least an hour."[3]

Don became Washington-Clay's starting center as a sophomore and had an excellent season. He brought a lot of attention to small-time Washington-Clay, which had a cramped little home gym that only seated about eighty spectators. The gym had six rows of bleachers along each sideline and the out-of-bounds line ran right against the bleachers. The basket on one end was in front of a stage and the basket on the other end was flush against a wall. After Don's breakout sophomore season, a lot of people in the area figured he would change schools and end up at South Bend Central. Don's brother Bill had transferred to Central a few years earlier because there were a lot more academic options at Central and Bill had his sights set on going to college. Bill, who was 6' 5", also played on the basketball team at Central and was good enough to go on to play for the University of Dayton as a freshman.

"A lot of people just assumed that [South Bend Central] was where [Don] was going to go to school," said Bill. "Don just didn't want to go there. He wanted to stay out at Washington-Clay. It was close to home. We only lived two blocks from the high school." The other factor that kept Schlundt at Washington-Clay was Coach Eaton, with whom Schlundt developed a close relationship—in fact, Schlundt remained close to Eaton until the coach passed away, long after Don's basketball career was over.

During his junior and senior years, Don grew to 6' 9" and added a lot of extra polish to his skills. He drew so much attention from local basketball fans and college recruiters that Washington-Clay could no longer play its home games in the school's minuscule gym. Instead, they moved the majority of their home contests to nearby John Adams High School, which had a gym that could seat more than two thousand. Washington-Clay's familiarity with the Adams High School court became an advantage during Schlundt's senior year when the local sectional of the state tournament was held at Adams and Schlundt led Washington-Clay to only the second sectional title in school history.

There were also two off-the-court developments during his junior and senior years that would ultimately have an important effect on Don's basketball career. The first was that he developed a large calcium deposit on the side of his left thigh during his junior year, which had to be removed surgically after the school year ended. The surgery left him with a long scar up his left thigh and tenderness in the thigh that lasted throughout his basketball career. When the pain was at its worst, Don would place a football thigh guard over the tender area and hold it in place with athletic tape. "It bothered him if somebody would hit it," said Bill Schlundt, "and that's what some of the opposing ballplayers would do. One time in a high school game, the [players on the] other team kept hitting him on the leg when they would go by him. He actually lost his cool once during that ball game. He took off after one of the ballplayers. The play was going one way and him and this ballplayer were going the other way. Even in college, they would hit him on that leg all the time."

The other major off-the-court development for Don during that time was that he met Gloria Blyton and fell in love. Gloria was the same age as Don but she was a student at South Bend Central. She had a cousin who went to Washington-Clay and one time she went to a basketball game with her cousin and afterward they went to a church-sponsored youth dance, where she met Don. The two of them became very close and by the end of their senior year the relationship had gotten serious. "By then, we had both pretty much decided that we were going to get married," said Gloria.

By that time, Don's life had also gotten extremely chaotic, as he and his family entertained an endless stream of college basketball coaches and tried to sort through a flood of offers—including some that included additional "incentives." Several coaches offered cash to Don's father to try to persuade Don to go to their school, but Don's father, who was a longtime employee at the Studebaker factory and earned a solid living, was not influenced by the offers of money. Almost all the coaches offered to pay for the family to come to games to watch Don play. Adolph Rupp sent one of his representatives to South Bend to visit with Don and invited the whole family and Gloria down to the University of Kentucky for a visit. So Gloria, Don, and his parents flew to Lexington and got the red carpet treatment. They had dinner with Rupp the first night, and Rupp personally took them around campus for a tour the next day and introduced Don to Kentucky All-American Bill Spivey, the center Rupp was recruiting

Schlundt to succeed. "Adolph Rupp was at his height around that time and that made an impression on you," said Don.[4] Thus, Kentucky was the early favorite in the Don Schlundt sweepstakes.

Hometown Notre Dame pursued Schlundt as aggressively as anyone. "Notre Dame thought they had him all locked up," said Bill. During the fall of Don's senior year, Notre Dame gave him a job at the football stadium selling programs, an easy job that didn't take much for a kid to earn good money at. Selling programs at football games was at the time one of the most sought-after jobs for college basketball players to earn extra money. Down at Kansas, Clyde Lovellette was selling football programs for twenty-five cents each (keeping a nickel for each one sold) and was making $40 to $50 per game.[5] That Notre Dame offered a job selling football programs to a high school kid showed just how much they wanted Schlundt.

Gloria was surprised by the intensity of the recruiting efforts and the various bonus offers that were being thrown around. Some of them even spilled over to her. "It was interesting because just about all of these schools that were after him were offering me a scholarship to try to get me to talk him into going to their school," she said. Despite Branch McCracken's reputation for only offering a player a scholarship and the opportunity to play for "the glory of IU," even someone at Indiana offered Gloria a scholarship if she came to Bloomington with Don. But Gloria didn't want a scholarship. Instead of going to college, she went to work and started saving her money so that she and Don could get married as soon as possible. As it turned out, Indiana didn't need any extra incentives to land Schlundt. All they needed was Jim Schooley.

McCracken had a lot of scholarships to offer to the 1950 and 1951 recruiting classes because his 1949 recruiting class didn't pan out. Only one player from that class made it through all four years with the basketball team and graduated in 1953. That player was Jim Schooley.

In 1949, Schooley, a 6' 5" center, made a meteoric rise to fame in the Hoosier state when he led Auburn High School, a small rural school from northeast Indiana, to the Indiana state finals in Indianapolis, where he won the prestigious Trester Award for Mental Attitude.

After his outstanding senior season, Schooley fielded a variety of scholarship offers. Tulane's Cliff Wells, a former Indiana high school coach, was after Schooley pretty hard. Purdue's legendary coach Piggy Lambert, although he retired from West Lafayette in 1946, coached the Indiana all-star team that year and tried to convince Schooley to play for the Boilermakers. However, Schooley's high school coach, Keith Showalter, had played for Branch McCracken when McCracken coached at Ball State. After Schooley's senior season ended, Showalter took Schooley down to Bloomington for a meeting with McCracken and it was then that Mac first offered him a scholarship.

Schooley was interested in pursuing a career in science, so it was also arranged for him to visit the chemistry department and meet with faculty during his recruiting visit. He quickly learned that the chemistry professors were big sports fans and were willing to be flexible with Schooley's schedule so that he could be in a rigorous academic discipline like chemistry and still devote the necessary time to the basketball team. That was a big pull for Jim. He had wanted to go to college and study science for a long time before he became a star basketball player. Unfortunately, his father—who was a high school science teacher—died an untimely death when Jim was a sophomore in high school and that cast doubt on whether the family could afford to send Jim to college. As a result, Jim Schooley was more grateful for an athletic scholarship than the average college basketball player.

To help close the deal for IU, McCracken came to Auburn to visit Jim and his family. "He impressed my mother very much," said Jim. "He told my mother that I would be guaranteed a scholarship and that I could study chemistry and they'd try to make basketball not interfere with my studies. He created a very good impression for my mother, and for me, too."

Another factor in Jim's decision was that both his father and his mother had graduated from IU. His dad had earned a master's degree in physics and his mother had a bachelor's degree in English and Latin. Also, two of Jim's four older sisters had also gone to IU, and one of them was married and still living in Bloomington. All those factors combined to make Jim's decision to choose Indiana an easy one.

As a sophomore in the 1950–51 season, Jim joined the varsity and became the backup center behind IU's senior star Bill Garrett. McCracken loved Schooley's intensity and hustle. In practice, Schooley's job was to harass Garrett, who was called "Bones" by his teammates. "I would outwork him in practice," said Schooley, "and McCracken would say, 'Bones, Schooley is making you look bad!' And under his breath Garrett would say, 'This ain't no game.' He was not interested in practice, but in the game he was something else. He was very graceful and a very good player."

Schooley had hoped to succeed Garrett as IU's center the next season. Unfortunately, by the end of his sophomore year, he pretty much knew that his chances of ever becoming the starting center for Indiana were extremely slim. Ironically, he probably sealed his own fate when he helped McCracken recruit Don Schlundt.

At the end of Schooley's sophomore year, McCracken approached him about hosting an important big man he was trying to bring to IU. "Mac asked me if I would take care of Schlundt on his recruiting visit, so he stayed with me at the Beta [Theta Pi] house," said Schooley. "When a guy was recruited, you always set up a multiple date. You gave him a date and took him to a dance or something. [Schlundt] enjoyed that, although he was seriously in love with a girl back in South Bend named Gloria, whom he later married. He enjoyed his recruiting visit a lot, although he actually turned his ankle while we were shooting around when he was there, and he ended up with a crutch on Sunday of his recruiting visit. He was a very good prankster, so when he left on Sunday to go back to South Bend after the visit, I flopped on my bed because I was worn out from taking care of the big kid all weekend, and I really cracked my head because Schlundt had put his crutch underneath my blankets."

Gloria said that Schooley was a major factor in Don's decision. "I think Jim Schooley was probably the biggest draw for Don. Schooley befriended him and was like a big brother," said Gloria.

More than any other place he visited, Schlundt had really hit it off with the IU basketball players—especially Schooley. After his visit, Schlundt told McCracken that he would commit to IU if he could join the Beta Theta Pi fraternity and room with Jim Schooley. McCracken said that would be no problem, and he had his big man.

"After I visited Indiana, my mind was made up," Schlundt later said. "You couldn't ask for a finer coach or man than Branch McCracken."[6]

McCracken was predictably giddy about landing Schlundt. He told a professor at IU, "I've got this great basketball prospect who is also a fine scholar."

"How do you know he's a fine scholar?" the professor asked.

"Well, he's 6' 9" isn't he?" said McCracken.[7]

This time, Mac was not going to let another school sweep in at the last minute and steal his big man out from under his nose, as Phog Allen had done with Clyde Lovellette. McCracken enrolled Schlundt in summer school and had him come to Bloomington shortly after graduating from Washington-Clay.

While Schlundt was clearly Branch McCracken's top priority in the class of 1951—and the most coveted recruiting prize in the state since Clyde Lovellette—McCracken also landed a guard who was a bit of an afterthought at the time but who turned out to be a perfect fit on the championship roster Mac was building. The guard was Burke Scott and he was from a little town called Tell City on the Ohio River between Evansville and Louisville. Tell City was known for two things during those years—its furniture businesses and its sports. Despite its backwater location, Tell City's basketball team had already amassed fourteen sectional titles and was regularly ranked in the top ten in the state during the 1948–49 season when Burke Scott was a sophomore and his brother Dale was a senior.

Burke Scott came from a big family, with eight kids and a "big, tough, stern father," as he tells it. Burke's dad worked for General Electric. "I came from a very poor family, but we always had enough to eat and a few clothes on our back and everybody respected us," said Burke. It was also a very athletic family. Burke had four older brothers who played sports and they gave him a hands-on education. Burke's dad loved baseball and was a big St. Louis Cardinals fan, and Burke became a tough little baseball player at a young age. However, his older brothers Ross and Dale introduced him to basketball and that became his favorite sport.

Growing up during the Depression in Tell City, there were a lot of basketball goals in Burke's neighborhood, but not many basketballs. There was also a big group of kids his age and they all loved to shoot hoops. "We just roamed all over town playing basketball, me and my buddies," said Burke. "But I don't think any of us ever owned a basketball." Their favorite place to play was behind a small neighborhood grocery store, a block away from Burke's house. It had a nice hoop and kids would come from all over town to play there. Burke was just a little kid when he started going over to that court and he didn't get to play that much, and he could never practice to get better because he didn't have a ball of his own.

"All the guys would leave and they would take their balls home with them," said Burke. "So Mrs. Lennison [who owned the grocery store] called me into her house when I was about nine years old and said, 'I've got something for you.' And we walked through the house and out to the back porch where the basketball goal was and she said, 'Look in that clothes basket.' And there was a brand new basketball. I said, 'Oh my goodness, whose is that?' And she said, 'It's yours but it's always got to be put right back there after you get through using it.' So that was my first basketball. They were hard to come by."

With his own basketball to practice with, Burke Scott fashioned himself into a terrific ballplayer. He played basketball year-round, even in the muggy Tell City summers when only the die-hards ignored the heat and humidity to play pickup games. Fortunately for Burke, there were plenty of die-hards in his neighborhood.

"My neighborhood guys were all my heroes," Burke said. "They're the ones that taught me everything. There were like fifty-some boys in a block and a half in our neighborhood. It was a knockdown, drag-out [on the basketball court]. If you got knocked around, they just laughed at you and said, 'Get up and come on.' That kinda toughens you up a little bit."

Toughness was never a problem for Burke Scott. By the time he reached Tell City High School and made the varsity as a sophomore, he was known as a hard-nosed little hustler who didn't hesitate to throw his body on the floor. As a junior, he helped Tell City capture its fifteenth sectional championship. In the regionals in Evansville, Branch McCracken came down to recruit a player named Bill Fikes. Fikes had already decided to go to Vanderbilt, but McCracken's trip wasn't wasted because he was very impressed by what he saw from Burke Scott. He told Tell City superintendent Fred Fechtman, an IU basketball star from the 1930s, "Forget Bill, if he's going to Vanderbilt, I want that little dark-haired guard." Fechtman responded, "Well, he's just a junior." So McCracken said, "When he graduates I want him up at IU." After the regional ended, Fechtman told Scott, "I talked to the coach at Indiana University and he wants you to come to IU." Scott said, "Okay," but he didn't give it a whole lot of thought after that because he never heard directly from McCracken.

During Scott's senior year, Fechtman took him up to Bloomington to watch an IU game and afterwards took him into the Hoosier locker room to meet the players. Burke was especially impressed with IU star Bill Garrett, the Big Ten's first black recruit. Still, Burke didn't think of it as much of a recruiting visit—although Fechtman and Mc-Cracken did—because he didn't really get to sit down and talk to McCracken and a scholarship wasn't mentioned. Back in Tell City, Scott had a terrific season as a senior and led the Marksmen to yet another sectional championship. His reputation had grown to the point that a lot more college coaches started knocking on his door. John Wooden, only a few years into his new post at UCLA, invited Burke to come to Los Angeles for a visit and a tryout, but Burke decided he didn't want to go to college that far away. Another topflight coach, Ed Diddle from Western Kentucky—only ninety miles south of Tell City—pursued Burke especially hard. Diddle used an up-tempo offense and Burke had speed to burn, along with a reputation for being able to run all day.

By the time he graduated in the spring of 1951, Burke had decided to commit to Western Kentucky and told Coach Diddle he was coming down to Bowling Green that fall. In August, Burke had packed up most of his things when Fechtman stopped by his house one day.

Fechtman asked Burke if he was ready to go to college and Burke replied, "Yeah, I just about got everything packed."

"Well, Coach McCracken wanted to know when you were going to call him or come up," Fechtman said.

"Who?" Burke said. "I'm going to Western Kentucky down there to play for Ed Diddle."

"The hell you are!" Fechtman responded. He had Burke finish packing and then drove him up to Bloomington that day. About three hours after Fechtman had pulled into his driveway, Burke Scott was in Branch McCracken's office at IU calling Ed Diddle to tell him he was going to be playing for Indiana.

Next to Don Schlundt, the player McCracken coveted more than any other in the 1951 recruiting class was Paul Poff from New Albany. A good Catholic boy from southeastern Indiana just across the river from Louisville, Poff was one of the most popular players in the Hoosier state during his high school career, and he had been playing on winning teams since his days at Holy Trinity grade school.

In New Albany, his talent was first widely recognized when he was a junior high school center playing for one of the city's smaller schools. He led his underdog squad to the city title that year, including a stunning upset of the incumbent public school champion. Area basketball coaches told themselves to remember the name "Paul Poff."

When he moved up to New Albany High School, Poff planned to play football, basketball, and baseball, since he thought that's what all the best athletes did. However, his football experience didn't last long. At one of his early football practices the coaches had him hold a big padded tackling dummy. It was pouring down rain and the field was so muddy that he couldn't stay on his feet. Several big offensive linemen kept barreling into Poff and knocked him down three straight times. The fourth time, Poff sidestepped a lineman at the last minute and the guy went sliding through the field and thundered into the ground with a big splash. "Then the coach wanted to know what the hell I was doing," said Poff, "and I said, 'Coach, if I could have some solid ground under me, I know these guys couldn't make me fall down every time.'" After the coach started reading Poff the riot act, he said,

"I quit" and walked off the field. "He called me in the next day and gave me hell," Poff remembered. "Back then, they cursed you a little bit, and maybe whipped on you a little bit. But if you went home and told your parents, you just got more of it."

That was the end of Poff's short-lived high school football career. Things came much easier for him on the basketball court. In fact, he was so quick to impress on the hardwood that he made the varsity as a freshman and became only the second freshman in New Albany history to start a game. In his four years on the varsity, New Albany went 99-16, won three sectional championships, went to semistate three times, and made it to the 1950 state finals, where the Bulldogs fell to Lafayette Jefferson 41-39 in the state semifinals. The sharp-shooting Poff finished his New Albany career as the all-time leading scorer in school history (a record that stood for thirty years, until 1981). Poff and Don Schlundt were both leading candidates for Indiana Mr. Basketball, but the award ended up going to Tom Harrold, who led Muncie Central to the state championship that season. However, both Poff and Schlundt were named to the Indiana all-star team.

After Schlundt, Poff was the most widely recruited player in Indiana. He was pursued by coaching giants such as Phog Allen at Kansas, Adolph Rupp at Kentucky, Everett Dean at Stanford, and, of course, Branch McCracken at Indiana. Poff didn't show much interest in Kansas or Stanford, but since he lived just across the border from Kentucky, and Adolph Rupp had led UK to three NCAA championships in four years, many people thought Kentucky had a good shot at stealing Poff from the Hoosier state. "I can remember [Rupp's] assistant calling me on the phone," said Poff, "and he just said, 'You can travel around and see what everybody has to offer you, and then we'll top it.'" What Rupp didn't realize was that he didn't have much of a shot with Poff. "I wasn't a Kentucky fan," Poff said. "I remember reading the papers. As I can remember it, Adolph Rupp never lost a game. He'd always say, 'The team didn't come to play' or 'They didn't listen to me.' He didn't lose any games, the players always lost them. I never was a Kentucky fan. I wouldn't have gone there for hell or high water."

Paul Poff narrowed his choices to IU, Tulane, Vanderbilt, and

Detroit, where his older brother Walter Poff was already making his mark on the basketball team. After visiting all four schools, the choice came down to IU and Detroit. Privately, Paul was leaning toward IU, but he was also very close to his brother and the two of them had dreamed of playing together in college. Ultimately, he decided to join his brother in Detroit, but while his brother Walter went on to become one of Detroit's top players, Paul was unhappy in Detroit and quietly left the team during Christmas break. He wasn't even halfway through his freshman year and had not completed his first semester (which ended at the end of January for most schools back then), and he had a girlfriend back home and thought he was in love. He wished he had chosen Indiana, so he called Coach McCracken to see if there was still a chance that he could come to Bloomington on scholarship and play for the Hoosiers.

"It was a mistake that I went [to Detroit] in the first place," said Poff. "I only went there because of my brother. I should've gone to IU right off. That was the only school I really wanted to go to, down deep in my heart. . . . I was fortunate that McCracken still wanted me. So I came back and started at IU in February of '52."

When Paul Poff was a senior at New Albany during the 1950–51 season, the Bulldogs were one of the favorites to take home the state championship. However, New Albany was upset in the semistate by Evansville Reitz, a team New Albany had soundly defeated earlier that season. One of the Reitz guards Poff matched up against in that game was Phil Byers. Little did they know at the time since neither one of them was headed to IU on a basketball scholarship, but Poff and Byers would become buddies and key role players on IU's 1953 team.

Phil Byers grew up in Evansville, the son of a football coach. His dad, Herman Byers, was an IU alumnus who won three letters in football and was captain of the 1927 IU football team. Herman Byers eventually became the head football coach at Evansville Reitz, where, over a twenty-seven-year career, he compiled a record of 234-105-5 and won seven mythical state championships. Today, Herman Byers still ranks in the top twenty-five in all-time wins as an Indiana high school football coach.

Naturally, Phil Byers grew up playing football. In fact, basketball and football were pretty much the only sports he played as a kid. When Phil arrived at Evansville Reitz, his dad had already built a football powerhouse, while the Reitz basketball team was perennially mediocre, always living in the dual shadow of Evansville Bosse and Evansville Central, which had both amassed several trophy cases full of basketball hardware.

When Phil was a junior, the basketball team had another one of its mediocre seasons. But that team featured seven juniors, and all seven of them went to Indianapolis together at the end of the season to watch the 1950 state finals in Butler Fieldhouse. "We all kind of made a little bit of a vow to ourselves that we were going to be there the next year at the state tournament," said Byers, "and we made it. It was pretty neat." Reitz shocked their fans and basketball observers throughout the state by making it all the way to the final game in the 1951 state tournament before falling 60-58 to Muncie Central.

After their spirited Cinderella run, all seven of the Reitz class-mates who had banded together ended up going to college on athletic scholarships. Reitz's 6' 6" center Jerry Whitsell, who was the team's representative on the Indiana all-star team, went to play for Ed Diddle at Western Kentucky. Whitsell and Byers were invited by Phog Allen to come down to Kansas for a visit and a tryout, but they declined. Five of the Reitz players were offered basketball scholarships if they came to Alabama as a group. Almost all the Reitz seven had a standing scholarship offer at the University of Evansville. None of them was offered a basketball scholarship by IU coach Branch McCracken.

However, Phil Byers and two of the other Reitz players—Don Henry and Merle Reed—didn't pursue basketball scholarships. They were football standouts and all three accepted football scholarships to IU. Growing up, Phil Byers had attended a lot of IU football games— and a few IU basketball games—with his dad and was a big IU fan, and by the time Phil graduated from high school, his older brother George was already at IU on a football scholarship. "My dad was interested in seeing me play football up there and so that was one of the motivations for going to IU," said Phil.

As a freshman, Byers and his two Reitz teammates played both football and basketball and all three made an impact on both the freshman football team and basketball team. Byers, who was a tough, aggressive player, was impressive enough on the basketball court that he asked McCracken if he could switch his scholarship from football to basketball, and McCracken agreed.

"There were [some guys] on the football team that were a little rough around the edges," said Byers. "I didn't relate as well to that group as well as I did to the basketball group." The chemistry Byers developed with the guys on the basketball team—guys like Burke Scott, Paul Poff, and Bob Leonard—would become an important part of the synergy between the starters and the reserves during the 1952–53 season.

While Byers would end up becoming one of the key reserves as a sophomore on that 1953 squad, it was another one of McCracken's recruits from the class of 1951 who would end up being the sixth man on that team. That player was Dick White from Terre Haute Wiley, whom McCracken coveted for his versatility. The 6' 1" White was an excellent shooter, a solid rebounder, and a tough defender. He also had great composure on the floor and was a clutch performer.

White's older brother was also an excellent athlete and the two of them played a lot of sports together when they were growing up. They were both excellent baseball players and they both really liked football, even though they never played much organized football. They were big fans of IU football and idolized Hoosier football stars George Taliaferro and Pete Pihos. "We always fantasized about playing football—him throwing and me catching," said Dick.

Dick eventually played one season of football in high school before Wiley basketball coach Norm Conam talked him into focusing his energy on the hardwood. It ended up being a wise move because White became a terrific player for Wiley and was pursued by a variety of college coaches. Conam had played for Piggy Lambert at Purdue and so he took White up to West Lafayette for a campus visit, but he didn't put any extra pressure on Dick to become a Boilermaker. Notre Dame, Dartmouth, and Tennessee also heavily recruited White. And Ernie Andres, the IU assistant coach, followed White's high school career and invited White to come to Indiana on scholarship.

In the spring of his senior year, White had a meeting with Branch McCracken, who told him that Indiana had one of the top programs in the country, that Bob Leonard from Terre Haute was already there, and that they had an opportunity to have a very good team with all the players who had committed to Indiana in 1950 and 1951. "I had plenty of opportunities," said Dick, "but I wanted to stay close to home and Indiana had a good program—one of the best—so that's where I ended up."

McCracken also landed two other players from the class of 1951 to round out his recruiting class—Jack Tilly and Goethe Chambers. Tilly was a terrific player from Anderson High School who played on the 1951 Indiana all-star team with Don Schlundt and Paul Poff and was a widely sough-after recruit. He would end up playing well as a freshman at IU, but he had a tough time with his academics and left Bloomington after his freshman year.

Goethe (pronounced Gate-ee) Chambers was a big star at a small school in Union City, Indiana, a provincial little border town that straddled the Indiana-Ohio state line. Chambers had just forty-four students in his graduating class at Union City High School, but they had some good basketball teams.

Chambers's father was a physician in Union City and an Indiana University alumnus. Previously, he had served as a doctor in the Air Force and was stationed in California during World War II, so the family spent the war on the West Coast. "We lived right on the ocean and I can remember having to make sure there was no light shining out the windows at night," said Goethe. "I guess I was too young to understand that there could have been an invasion, but I was aware of the fact that there were precautions taken to safeguard people."

Goethe's father was a serious man who had never been involved in athletics, and he believed that athletics had dubious value for a young man. Nevertheless, the Chambers family supported Goethe's basketball career. His parents went to his basketball games and then waited for him by the fireplace at home so they could sit down with him and critique his performance afterwards. "I was never right," Goethe remarked. "My coach was always right."

As a husky 6' 4" center, Branch McCracken led the Hoosiers in scoring for three straight seasons, was an All-American in 1930, and finished his career as the all-time leading scorer in school history. (*Indiana University Archives*)

In 1938, McCracken returned to his alma mater to take over the head coaching job from his departing mentor, Everett Dean. The thirty-year-old McCracken had already enjoyed a successful eight-year coaching career at Ball State. (*Indiana University Archives*)

McCracken takes the game ball from Phog Allen after Indiana defeated Kansas 60-42 in the 1940 NCAA championship game. (*Indiana University Archives*)

After five straight winning seasons in Bloomington, McCracken took a leave of absence in 1943 to enlist in the U.S. Navy, where he became a lieutenant and served a tour of duty in the Pacific during World War II. (*Indiana University Archives*)

In 1946, Mac returned to Bloomington and resumed his role as
head basketball coach. Mac now had a full head of white hair,
an outward symbol of the inner toll that the war had on him.
(*Indiana University Archives*)

Bob Leonard (*Indiana University Archives*)

Don Schlundt (*Indiana University Archives*)

Dick Farley (*Indiana University Archives*)

Charlie Kraak (*Indiana University Archives*)

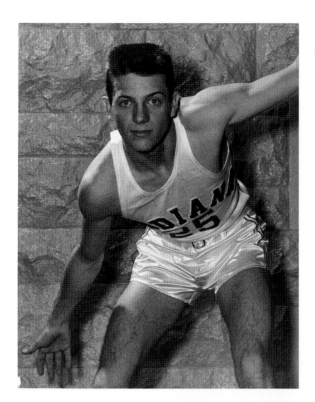

Burke Scott (*Indiana University Archives*)

Dick White (*Indiana University Archives*)

Lou Scott (*Indiana University Archives*)

Phil Byers (*Indiana University Archives*)

Paul Poff (*Indiana University Archives*)

Jim DeaKyne (*Indiana University Archives*)

Jim Schooley (*Indiana University Archives*)

The Gables was one of the most popular hangouts in Bloomington for both students and local residents. It was located on Indiana Avenue, across from the IU administration building. (*Indiana University Archives*)

Branch McCracken had not expected Bobby Leonard to be the leader
of the 1952–53 Hoosiers, but Leonard surprised him by stepping up
and becoming one of the greatest floor leaders in the history of college
basketball. (*Indiana University Archives*)

After years of suffering without a true big man, by the 1951–52 season
McCracken had two of them, Don Schlundt, left, and Lou Scott, right. (*Indiana
University Archives*)

Dick White, left, and Bobby Leonard, right, battled each other in the team's free throw contest on the day before the start of practice in the fall of 1952. (*Indiana University Archives*)

IU forward Charlie Kraak runs down a rebound in Indiana's season opener against Valparaiso. (*Indiana University Archives*)

Don Schlundt runs the break and reaches above the rim to tip in a missed layup from one of his teammates. Behind him, Burke Scott hustles down the floor. (*Indiana University Archives*)

Don Schlundt winds up for a hook shoot in the IU Fieldhouse. Schlundt practiced his free throws and his hook shot every day, all year around. (*Indiana University Archives*)

Bobby Leonard was a master sharpshooter from the outside. Here he releases a step-back two-hander, while Dick Farley (31) and Paul Poff (30) look on. Leonard was also one of the early pioneers of the jump shot in Indiana. (*Indiana University Archives*)

McCracken was always animated on the sidelines, as he was in this late-game huddle in IU's pivotal game against Minnesota on January 10, 1953, at the IU Fieldhouse. Dick Farley is on Mac's right and Bobby Leonard is on his left. (*Indiana University Archives*)

McCracken winces and runs his hand through his hair after an IU miscue in a road game as Jim DeaKyne and Jim Schooley watch the action on the floor. (*Indiana University Archives*)

The IU Fieldhouse featured a raised floor and the players sat along the edge of the floor during the game. Here, the IU players are at the bottom of the picture and the visiting team is at the top. The white-haired guy in the dark suit is Coach McCracken. (*Courtesy of McCracken family*)

McCracken gives a pep talk to the players during a practice in the IU Fieldhouse. (*Courtesy of McCracken family*)

The IU Fieldhouse after a game in 1953. (*Indiana University Archives*)

Nick Poolitsan, one of the biggest IU fans in Bloomington, serves one of his customers at The Gables, which was owned by his family. Nick also did his "Pick by Nick" prediction before every IU football and basketball game. (*Indiana University Archives*)

Coach McCracken addresses the crowd during a pep rally the day after Indiana's big win over Illinois in Champaign. (*Indiana University Archives*)

At the pep rally on March 1, IU students expressed their feelings about IU's rivalry with Seton Hall for the No. 1 spot in the Associated Press poll. (*Indiana University Archives*)

Goethe was a bona fide star by the time he was a 6' 3" senior forward. In one game that year, he scored sixty-three points against one of the top teams in Ohio in a Friday night game. The next night, Union City played a small school in Indiana and Goethe couldn't hit anything. At the end of the third quarter he was still scoreless and his coach turned to him and said, "You know, I think I'm going to do you a favor. Why don't you go take a shower, because I've never seen anybody play any worse than you've played tonight."

"And I was very happy to go," Chambers later remarked.

Despite that tough game, Chambers had a great senior year and was heavily recruited by many top basketball programs. He narrowed his choice down to Kentucky, Indiana, and Ohio State and visited all three schools.

"I visited Kentucky and met Adolph Rupp and was very impressed with him," said Chambers. "But I couldn't cross the river. I just didn't think that's what I wanted to do."

He also visited the IU campus and Bloomington and really liked the school and Coach Branch McCracken, and McCracken went to Union City to visit Chambers and his family. "He was a very big hit with my mother," remembered Goethe. "My mother was an ex-English teacher and a very staunch Republican. And Branch was a Republican."

Chambers's family definitely encouraged him to go to IU. However, Chambers initially decided to strike out on his own and go to Ohio State. He even moved over to Columbus, Ohio, shortly after graduation and enrolled in summer school. However, it didn't take long for him to have a change of heart. "I really didn't like the [OSU] coach," said Chambers. "He was not being completely honest with the way he approached practice in the summer. So I thought, 'I don't think I want to do this.' I called Branch and asked if I could still come to Indiana, and he said 'yes.'"

So McCracken actually lost his fifth recruit from his 1951 class, but then got him back shortly before school started in the fall. That gave Mac his five Indiana high school kids from the graduating class of 1951: Don Schlundt, Burke Scott, Jack Tilly, Dick White, and Goethe Chambers. Combined with his fabulous 1950 recruiting class,

Mac believed he had the material needed to build a champion. This core group would be bolstered by adding Paul Poff, Phil Byers, and a walk-on from the 1950 class named Jim DeaKyne.

Still, McCracken knew that talent alone wouldn't build a winner. In his 1955 book *Indiana Basketball,* McCracken wrote, "The important factors that mean the difference between a great ball club and an average one, even though the players are of equal ability, are the unseen assets that must be developed by the coach and his players during the years they are together. An outstanding team isn't built up merely during the basketball season. The spirit, understanding, and desire must be developed from the time a coach and his players first meet until the boys' playing days are over."[8]

McCracken knew that all the talent he amassed in the 1950 and 1951 recruiting classes simply gave him an opportunity for a championship contender. He knew that having all that talent would raise expectations, and he knew that landing all that talent gave him a significant responsibility—a responsibility to the kids to weld them into a cohesive unit, a responsibility to the university and the fans to give them a winning basketball team, and a responsibility to himself to put together the kind of championship ball club that he'd been trying to build since he had returned to IU at the end of World War II.

The end product was an unbridled success—the greatest team of McCracken's highly successful thirty-two-year coaching career.

BIG MAC AND THE
FIREWAGON

4

[Branch McCracken] was a very impressive individual, and
basketball was his whole life.
—SAMMY ESPOSITO

Looking at Branch McCracken, the first thing that came to mind was
not speed. He had broad shoulders, a squared, well-chiseled head with
a confident jaw, and a thick set of eyebrows that were furrowed with
intensity when he was anywhere near a basketball court. He stood 6'
4", but he seemed bigger than that, either because of his husky build
or simply because the coach carried himself with a resounding confidence and authority. Or maybe it was because his reputation preceded
him wherever he went in the Hoosier state. After all, he *was* Branch
McCracken, Big Mac, the Big Bear, the Sheriff. He was the anointed
basketball king of Indiana, which was arguably the basketball capital
of the world in the 1950s. Some folks would even have said that
McCracken was the most popular man in the whole state, with apol-
ogies, of course, to the governor.

As the head coach of the Indiana University basketball squad,
McCracken earned his acclaim by fashioning a hypersonic style of play
that overwhelmed opponents with its frenzy and its fury. McCracken's
boys snatched the ball off the backboards and threw it upcourt to

sprinting teammates who were always trying to outrun opponents for easy scores. On defense, the Hoosiers often pressed and trapped and hounded their opponents in every corner of the court to force turnovers that led to more easy baskets for IU. In the course of many games the Indiana team, which was in supreme physical condition, used these tactics to put so much pressure on their foes that many challengers simply wilted in exhaustion during the final minutes.

From the very beginning of the McCracken era, this breakneck style of play earned his Indiana teams the moniker of the "Hurryin' Hoosiers." It was completely fitting and it stuck. McCracken himself often referred to this brand of basketball as the "firewagon" attack or simply the "running game." The firewagon was definitely McCracken's favorite sobriquet, probably because of the image it evoked—a group of determined men who were united in purpose rushing frantically to fulfill their duty. On the basketball court, McCracken's boys were almost always in a rush.

However, if the Hurryin' Hoosiers appeared helter-skelter and out of control at times, the reality was just the opposite. McCracken had dissected the running game into the science of up-tempo basketball and he systematically drilled his players on all the principles and nuances of how to execute it to perfection. He schooled his teams on the full breadth of basketball fundamentals—from the body mechanics of a jump shot to the proper techniques of delivering a pass to the best methods of trapping an opposing player in the full-court press. Beyond that, McCracken also demanded the highest level of conditioning from every player, to the point that from the first day school started every September each of his players had to run the IU cross-country course every afternoon, six days a week, during the pivotal weeks before basketball practice officially began. That conditioning, as much as the running game itself, is what allowed the Hoosiers to overwhelm so many opponents and achieve so much success during McCracken's thirty-two-year stint as the IU head coach.

Still, even as McCracken became an ambassador for the game and conducted basketball clinics in more than twenty states as well as Europe and Japan, he always remained a country boy at heart—and a consummate Hoosier.

Thirty-five miles north of Bloomington—as a crow flies—sits a little speck of a town called Monrovia, with a population of fewer than seven hundred. Branch McCracken grew up on a farm just outside of there. Actually, it was barely even a farm, by most Indiana standards. Charles and Ida McCracken owned only twenty acres and that often wasn't enough to make ends meet and keep their nine children fed. The family lived in a little farmhouse with a big white barn out back. Since the farm didn't provide enough income to support the family, Charles also worked as a road contractor, at a time when mules were the primary power tools used for the job.

On June 9, 1908, Ida gave birth to Emmet Branch McCracken. He grew to become a tall, hearty fellow with a tough, ambitious demeanor. He loved animals and was well known in Monrovia for his aspiration to become a veterinarian, so almost all the people in the area simply called him "Doc" by the time he was a teenager. To his family, he was "Branch." Like all of his three brothers and five sisters, he had to find work from an early age to help support the family. Branch was employed as a farmhand and had to do a variety of hard labor, which helped him grow strong and develop a well-muscled physique.

When Branch wasn't working or going to school, he spent the little bit of leisure time he had left playing basketball—usually on Sundays. As a kid, he got his first taste of basketball when he and his brothers used an inflated pig bladder to shoot into a fruit basket. As they got a little older, the McCrackens built a makeshift basketball rim in the loft of their barn. Branch and his younger brother Bill would play ball with their neighbors, the Wooden boys. The back of the Woodens' farm butted up against the back of the McCrackens' farm, and Johnny Wooden, who went on to basketball fame as a player at Purdue and a coach at UCLA, was the same age as Bill and they were good friends. John's older brother Maurice was close to the same age as Branch.

"We played with a stuffed sock because we didn't have enough money to buy a basketball," said Bill McCracken. "We had some pretty rough games there in that old barn."[1]

The McCracken and Wooden boys all developed into good basketball players, but they never got to play much competitive basketball on the same team. When the boys were in elementary school, the Woodens moved a little farther south in the county and ended up feeding into Martinsville High School, while the McCrackens moved from their farm to a house in Monrovia while Branch was in junior high school, and he ended up going to Monrovia High School.

Branch's prowess on the court began to show itself even before he entered high school. As a sixth-grader, Branch made the eighth-grade team in junior high school and ended up playing three seasons on the eighth-grade squad. Then, as a ninth-grader he made the varsity at Monrovia High as a forward. By his tenth-grade year, in 1923–24, Branch and Monrovia began to make some big noise for a small school. That season Monrovia joined seventy schools from Indiana, Ohio, and Kentucky to play in the famed Tri-State Tournament in Cincinnati, and tiny Monrovia shocked several larger schools on the way to a runner-up finish. The Bulldogs finished the season 25-3. The next year they were even better.

With Mac bigger and stronger as a junior and taking on the role of the team's primary offensive weapon, Monrovia started the 1924–25 season by demolishing Gosport 75-8 and Cloverdale 65-18. Keep in mind that this was a low-scoring era when high-scoring teams were usually the ones that broke forty and the 1928 Indiana state championship game was a 13-12 thriller. The 1924–25 season also began a trend for Branch McCracken in which he often outscored the opposition entirely by himself. Monrovia went back to the Tri-State Tournament and won five straight games to capture the title, with McCracken winning the MVP. That victory made the Monrovia boys state heroes. They were hailed as "giant killers" and one reporter dubbed them the "Corn Stalk Boys." The Bulldogs won twenty-seven straight games before falling to Martinsville, the eventual state champ, 28-23 in the sectional finals. Monrovia finished the season 27-1.

The next season, Monrovia became the first school ever to win the Tri-State Tournament twice in row as the Corn Stalk Boys ripped through five straight opponents by a combined score of 180-50 (an average victory margin of twenty-six points) and McCracken was once again named the tournament MVP. Unfortunately, Monrovia fell to its nemesis, Martinsville, in the sectional finals for the fourth-straight season to finish the year 26-2. Johnny Wooden was a sophomore on the Martinsville team that year, and the Martinsville coach was the legendary Glen Curtis, whose younger brother Herb Curtis was Monrovia's coach and McCracken's early basketball mentor.

Branch's Monrovia teams went 78-6 during his final three seasons on the varsity and Branch McCracken became one of the biggest names in Indiana high school basketball. He was such a big name throughout Indiana during his high school career that Logansport, a city in north-central Indiana, had Branch come up to dedicate their new gym while he was still in high school. Meanwhile, the McCracken house had gotten so crowded that Branch didn't even have his own bedroom at home during his last two years of high school. Instead, he slept at the less crowded home of a family friend nearby.

Naturally, Branch was widely coveted by college basketball coaches. There weren't athletic scholarships in that era—college coaches basically guaranteed their top recruits a job that would pay for most of their college costs—so recruiting was not nearly the high-stakes, high-pressure affair it would later become. Nevertheless, McCracken was as heavily recruited as any player in his era. One day during McCracken's senior year, Pete Straub from the IU Alumni Association came to the McCracken farm to call on Branch. Straub was directed out back to a creek, where he caught site of the powerful 6' 3", 190-pound youngster wading in a storm-swollen stream using his powerful arms and agile hands to pluck out watermelons that were getting washed away by a flash flood. Straub saw that he had a bona fide country boy on his hands, and a very promising athlete. He made an appeal for Branch to go to IU.

However, someone else who was enamored with Branch was Butler University's Pat Page. Page coached both football and basketball for the Bulldogs, but football was his primary gig. In Branch Mc-Cracken, Page saw a player who was not only big, but also fast and had a great pair of hands and lightning-quick reflexes. Page watched Branch in a basketball game during his junior year and offered him an opportunity to come to Butler to play not only basketball but also football—even though Monrovia didn't have a football team and

Branch had never played a single down of organized football. Branch told Page to come back the next year because he was only a junior.

As it turned out, Page was hired the next season as the football coach at Indiana University. He came back to see Branch and offered him a chance to come to IU to play football, which also gave Branch the opportunity to play basketball for IU's up-and-coming young coach Everett Dean, who was known as a terrific leader and a fine midwestern gentleman. In the end, Branch didn't require a whole lot of persuasion. Indiana University was close to home and offered him a great opportunity to play two sports. Dean later said, "We didn't have any trouble recruiting Mac, although there were several other universities that wanted him. But he wanted to come to Indiana and he was a great player."[2]

McCracken not only became a great college basketball player, but he also proved Pat Page right by becoming a terrific college football player despite his inexperience on the gridiron. The Monrovian man-child became a starter at end—on both offense and defense—as a sophomore. The highlight of his football career came in Bloomington that first season when McCracken scooped up a fumble and returned it twenty yards for the game-tying touchdown in a 14-14 tie with Minnesota, the eventual Big Ten co-champion. On that famous play, McCracken had Minnesota's bruising All-American Bronko Nagurski breathing down his neck from start to finish, and Branch later said it was the fastest he ever ran in his life. In football, he went on to earn honorable mention All-American honors as a sophomore and an all-conference nod as a junior. Still, as good as McCracken was on the football field, he staged his greatest performances at IU on the hardwood, where he became one of the first great low-post power players in the Big Ten.

Freshmen, of course, were not eligible for varsity athletics, but during his first year on campus, McCracken quickly made an impression on Coach Dean and the other IU basketball players and made it clear that he had a chance to become a major contributor as a sophomore. "I loved the game of basketball, and I had enough confidence in myself that I thought I could make any team in the country," Branch said. "When freshman practice started there were a lot of boys who came out for basketball who had quite a reputation. Some of them were all-state in high school and I didn't know just how good they were going to be, but [after] the first scrimmage I knew right then that if they were good enough to play at Indiana University then I could make the team, too."[3]

On the other hand, Branch was not a natural scholar and so the older basketball players looked out for him and gave him hell when he missed class or wasn't doing his work. McCracken was eventually very grateful for that, and he never forgot it.

His sophomore year, McCracken joined the veteran-heavy varsity basketball team and immediately earned a starting spot at center. In the first Big Ten conference game of his career—and only the fourth game of the season—he scored twenty-four points against Chicago to set a new conference scoring record. That season the Hoosiers went 15-2, losing by only a point at Michigan and by three at Purdue, and shared the Big Ten championship with the Boilermakers. McCracken finished the year as the second-leading scorer in the conference.

That 1927–28 season was the winningest in school history at the time and made the IU basketball team a hot ticket. As a result, the IU trustees decided to build a fieldhouse with more seating than the 2,400-seat Men's Gym. An 8,000-seat arena was commissioned, and it was completed just in time for the 1928–29 season. As a coach, McCracken would later make the IU Fieldhouse one of the legendary venues of college basketball. However, his first two seasons in the Fieldhouse as a player were both gut-wrenching.

During McCracken's junior year, opposing teams began keying on him, and his scoring average dipped from 10.1 points per game as a sophomore to 8.7 as a junior. Both his field goal percentage and free throw percentage were down as well. He still finished second in the Big Ten in scoring for the second-straight year, and his friend and teammate James Strickland averaged 7.0 points per game and was named an All-American, IU's first since Everett Dean in 1921. Nevertheless, the highly touted Hoosiers struggled to an inexplicable 7-10 record and an eighth-place finish in the conference.

McCracken's senior year started out even worse as the team dropped its first four games of the season before pulling together and going 7-5 in Big Ten play for a fourth-place finish. McCracken's play was brilliant throughout the season as he averaged 12.1 points per game, but no other Hoosier averaged more than 4.6 points per game, and other teams simply focused on shutting down McCracken at the end of close games. As a result, the Hoosiers went 1-7 in games decided by five points or fewer and finished 8-9 overall. Despite the team's struggles, Branch won the conference scoring title, was a consensus All-American selection, and finished his IU career as the all-time leading scorer in conference history.

In 1989, Everett Dean remarked, "Mac was as good a basketball player as they are today. He had something that some of the big boys don't have: he was active and he had speed. He could handle himself well. And if any of the opposition got a little too rough with him, it didn't take long for him to get rough in return."[4]

Branch McCracken slipped a graduation cap onto his handsome young head and a gown over his broad shoulders in the spring of 1930 and proudly accepted his Bachelor of Science degree. Even though he was leaving college just as America was sliding into the Great Depression, he had a variety of career options to choose from. The Green Bay Packers offered him a professional football contract and the Fort Wayne Hoosiers of the fledgling American Basketball League were after him to play pro basketball. It wasn't easy to make a living as a professional athlete in those days. There were no guaranteed contracts. Players were often paid on a per-game basis and most of them also had day jobs.

By the time he graduated from IU, McCracken had already decided that he wanted to put his physical education degree to good use by becoming a basketball coach and a physical education instructor. Yet he wasn't totally ready to hang up his sneakers, so he planned to play pro basketball part-time. Before McCracken had even officially graduated, he was recruited to play an exhibition game for the Fort Wayne Hoosiers by Bruff Cleary, the team's promoter, who offered McCracken—one of the biggest names in the state at the time—a one-game exhibition payoff as well as a spot on Fort Wayne's roster the next fall. After the exhibition, McCracken approached Cleary about getting paid for the game, and Cleary handed Branch a check for $50, the one-game fee for top stars at the time. An awestruck McCracken told him, "I don't want to be paid for the whole season!"[5]

As the team's season approached that fall, the *Fort Wayne Journal-Gazette* reported, "The coming season should prove to be an exciting one for the Fort Wayne professional cagers. Branch McCracken, former Indiana University star, will be with the local American League club in its first game of the season. The probabilities are that he will be unable to become a regular member of the Hoosier squad this year, but some arrangements may be made whereby he can be called into service for part of the games at least."

McCracken's gig with the Fort Wayne Hoosiers turned out to be a good arrangement because he also landed the head coaching job at Ball State Teacher's College in Muncie—just eighty miles south of Fort Wayne. During McCracken's first year in pro ball, the Fort Wayne squad made it to the ABL championship series against Brooklyn, but lost in six games. However, fewer and fewer patrons could afford tickets as the Depression bore down on the nation and the world, and as a result the ABL folded at the end of the 1930–31 season. The next season, McCracken moonlighted with the Indianapolis Kautskys, and he later did stints with the Oshkosh All-Stars, the Dayton Metropolitans, and a pro team in Richmond, Indiana. Pro basketball had a reputation for being excessively physical during that era, with few fouls called, so McCracken fit in quite nicely. He turned into a terrific pro player even though he only played part-time as his coaching and teaching duties allowed. He learned a lot from the pro game and still enjoyed the competition, but coaching was always his top priority.

At twenty-two, he became the youngest head coach in college basketball when he took the Ball State job, where Paul Parker, another IU big man, had paved the way for him. The 6' 7" Parker was the captain of Everett Dean's first team at Indiana, and shortly after Parker graduated in 1925 he took over the coaching job at Ball State and put together an excellent 55-34 record in five seasons in Muncie. McCracken became his successor in 1930.

The assignment for McCracken at tiny Ball State, which had had a basketball program for only ten seasons, was made more difficult by the economic quagmire of the time. Kids would routinely come and go from college because of family financial problems during those lean years, which led to year-to-year roster fluctuation. Because McCracken was so driven to succeed, he aggressively investigated different styles of play to formulate his coaching philosophy and to find the right style for the talent of his Ball State team.

"I was as green as grass that first '30–'31 season," said McCracken. "My center was 24 years old and I was 22."[6] That center was senior Floyd Harper, an excellent pivot man who had already played some semipro ball by then.

John Brogneaux, who also played on that 1930–31 squad, said, "Mac was able to come in and command the respect of Floyd Harper. The age differential didn't hurt at all. McCracken was the leader and he was accepted as the leader. He was the coach and everybody knew it and we did what he asked us to do because we wanted to be successful."[7]

Success came quickly as Ball State won eight of its first ten games in Branch's first season as the Cardinals' coach and finished with a 9-5 record. The next season, McCracken was honored as the nation's Small School Coach of the Year. Despite those early accomplishments, McCracken was still experimenting with different styles of play, and his teams usually hovered around the .500 mark. In fact, during his first five seasons, his teams posted a respectable but mediocre 43-40 record. But then Mac took the program to another level during the next three years, going 13-7 in 1935–36, 13-6 in 1936–37, and a stellar 17-4 in 1937–38.

It was during that 1937–38 season that McCracken made an impression on the folks at his alma mater. Mac won the Small School Coach of the Year award for the second time, and even more importantly, he led his Cardinals to an upset win over IU at the beginning of that season. The Ball State–Indiana matchup took place in Muncie on December 11, 1937, and it was that game that served as the catalyst for Ball State's excellent season. The Cardinals actually went into the game 0-2 after season-opening losses to Notre Dame and the University of Indianapolis, while the Hoosiers were 1-0 after trouncing

DePauw in their season opener. But for the Ball State players and their fans, the IU game was the biggest game of the year. The two teams had been playing each other since the 1934–35 season and Indiana had easily won all three contests, including an eleven-point victory in Muncie during the 1936–37 season. This game would be different.

Everett Dean's Hoosiers came up to Ball Gymnasium, which was crammed to capacity with 3,200 spectators, and found themselves in a dogfight with the Cardinals from the opening tip. The two teams went into the intermission tied 21-21, but IU stormed out of the locker room with a 9-2 run to take a solid 30-23 lead. Then, McCracken's boys surged back with a 7-0 run of their own to tie the game at 30-30 midway through the second half, and the game was nip and tuck the rest of the way. McCracken had a little 5' 5" fireball of a guard named Rex Rudicel from Huntington, Indiana. He didn't look like much of a basketball player but the kid could light up a scoreboard—he ended up leading Ball State in scoring for three straight seasons. With less than five minutes to play, Rudicel converted a free throw that put Ball State in front 39-36 and sent the home crowd into delirious applause. But then Indiana's Jay McCreary stole the ball and scored to pull the Hoosiers to within one. Ball State's Ray Lackey responded by burying a one-hander from the baseline to put the Cardinals back up by three points with two minutes left, and Rudicel then sealed the win with another free throw to make the final score Ball State 42, Indiana 38. Ball State's two heroes, Rudicel and Lackey, fittingly shared game-high honors with thirteen points apiece, while IU junior Ernie Andres led the Hoosiers with eleven.

Following the game, the *Indianapolis Star* wrote, "Branch McCracken, former All-American center at Indiana, sent into action a team that was too good in the pinches for Everett Dean's Crimson squad." Another Indiana basketball reporter called Ball State's performance "forty minutes of flawless basketball."

The significance of McCracken's victory over his mentor was not lost on Indiana athletic director Zora Clevenger. That spring, Everett Dean made a surprise announcement that he was leaving Indiana to take the coaching job at Stanford, and when Dean met with Clevenger he also recommended a successor, a young up-and-comer he thought would be a perfect fit for IU: Branch McCracken. "I think Clev already had the same idea," Dean later stated. "He simply said that he couldn't agree with me more, and then he approached Mac."[8]

"Mr. Clevenger called me and wanted to know if I would be interested in the job at Indiana," McCracken said, "and I told him that I would, so he said, 'Well, if you want the job, it's yours.'" Branch then went to Dr. Lemuel Pittenger, president of Ball State, and explained that he had been offered the coaching job at Indiana. Pittenger, who was also an IU grad, asked Mac if he thought he could handle the job, and Mac replied, "Why, it's just basketball—the same as we're playing here." With that response, Pittenger recommended that he take the job. So in the summer of 1938, Branch McCracken returned to Indiana University. But when he returned to his alma mater, he didn't come alone. While McCracken gained valuable experience during his tenure at Ball State, he also gained something else that would be just as important to his career as a basketball coach—his wife Mary Jo.

The thing to understand about Lemuel Pittenger was that he was not only the president of Ball State, he was also Branch McCracken's father-in-law. When McCracken arrived in Muncie in 1930, Pittenger, who had been a successful teacher in his own right, quickly recognized McCracken's promise as a coach and teacher. Pittenger was also a sports fan and had been quite a baseball player in his youth.

However, as interested as Pittenger was in monitoring and nurturing the career of his new basketball coach, he was quite surprised when he learned that his daughter Mary Jo Pittenger had fallen in love with the new coach during McCracken's first year in Muncie, and that she wanted to get engaged to him.

Mary Jo recalled, "My father thought it was a very strange thing that in that little time I was saying 'yes' to [marrying] the new coach."[9]

Through her father's influence, Mary Jo had grown up an ardent baseball fan. Although she was born and reared in Selma, just outside of Muncie, she had never caught the highly contagious disease of Hoosier Hysteria. In fact, she didn't really know much about basketball and had little interest in it. And she had never heard of a former Indiana high school star and IU All-American named Branch McCracken.

When Lemuel Pittenger hired Branch McCracken in 1930, Mary Jo was teaching English and music at Muncie Central High School. She was a beautiful twenty-three-year-old young lady with a kind smile that could melt hearts. But underneath her gentle surface she was tough-minded, independent, and determined, traits that Branch McCracken also possessed. However, in many other ways, Mary Jo was quite the opposite of Mac. While he was still a country boy at heart and even spoke with a bit of a hillbilly twang, she was cultured, refined, and proper. While his idea of fun was talking basketball or hunting, she enjoyed plays, musicals, and orchestral music.

The two of them were introduced by the football coach at Muncie High School, who was a former teammate of McCracken's. One day, Mac was visiting his old pal at the high school and the football coach's car mysteriously wasn't working, so he asked Mary Jo if she would mind giving Mac a ride over to the Ball State gym. She agreed. "I had never heard of Branch and barely recognized the existence of basketball," Mary Jo later admitted.[10] Still, she didn't mind giving the ruggedly handsome young coach a ride, and the two of them shared a pleasant conversation on the way. Mary Jo thought, "He seemed to be a very nice person, but who wants to go around with a basketball coach?"[11]

While she was ambivalent toward Mac at that point, he was smitten with her. He called her that Saturday and said, "I'm going to referee a game up in Selma and I know you are from there, so would you like to go?"

"Well, there were a lot of people up there I still knew," said Mary Jo, "so I said, 'Sure.' After that he started to call quite a bit and he was absolutely disgusted with me because I didn't know anything about basketball. I never had heard of him before and what business was it of his to tell me everything that went on at a game anyway! For Christmas that year he bought me one of those Spaulding rules books and his picture was on almost every page! I thought to myself, 'Well, maybe he knows more about the game than I thought he did.' "[12]

Mac eventually won her over, and within a few months of first meeting Mary Jo, he told her that it might be a nice thing if they got married. She did a lot of thinking about it and decided that he was right.

When they broke the news to Dr. Pittenger, he was initially very concerned—and his concern wasn't only for his daughter. "When Mac and I were first engaged, my father called me into his office one day and asked me point-blank what qualifications I had to be a good coach's wife," Mary Jo said. "He told me that the university had a fine young basketball coach and he didn't want [Branch's] career to be impaired. So we sat there for four hours and discussed how I could help Mac in his profession. I honestly believe that my father was more interested in Mac's future than he was in his daughter's ability to be a wife."[13]

During that meeting, Dr. Pittenger also had another concern. "He asked me, 'What do you know about basketball?' And he had me right there," said Mary Jo. "I said, 'I don't know anything but I can learn and I'll bet you one month's salary that I'll know just as much as Branch McCracken does by the end of the season.' He said, 'I'll take that bet.' "[14]

Mary Jo probably walked away with her father's money from that wager because she quickly fashioned herself into a basketball aficionado. "I began to travel with Mac, asking questions of the coaches and players," said Mary Jo. "I found that everyone was eager to help me learn the game."[15] She not only learned the game and all its fundamentals and subtleties, but she also grew to become an impassioned basketball fan.

Branch and Mary Jo were married on December 20, 1931, a little over a year after Branch had first arrived in Muncie. Alone, Branch already showed great promise as a basketball coach. With Mary Jo, he had an extremely capable partner who could help compensate for his lack of refinement.

"Branch's background and athletic ability didn't lead to social graces," said Mac's friend Bill Unsworth. "She helped him in ways like that, and when it came to recruiting, boys would come many times with their parents, and Mary Jo was a charmer. Mothers and fathers would meet Mary Jo and they just felt like they could trust their son with Mary Jo and Branch."

Mary Jo's role began when Mac was at Ball State, as she tutored players, made home-cooked meals for the boys when they came over to see Mac, and helped entertain recruits and their families who visited the campus. However, her role expanded when Mac moved on to IU. There, she became a key advisor and handled many of the off-the-court affairs for Mac, who was under a lot more pressure to develop a winning program year in and year out. Mary Jo served as an unofficial academic tutor and a liaison to many of the professors on campus. She also acted as a personal counselor for many of the boys and played a crucial role in recruiting visits and in communicating with the players' parents at home and their girlfriends at IU.

Years later, when he retired from IU, Mac stated, "A lot people have given me credit for being a fine recruiter. Mary Jo did a fine job. She could sell the mother on why her son should come to Indiana University, and after the mother is sold [on] why the son should come, you've got a good chance of getting that boy in school. And my wife, Mary Jo, did a great job of selling mothers on Indiana University."[16]

From the start of his coaching career, Branch McCracken wanted his teams to run. What isn't widely known is where McCracken developed his affinity for the running game. It came from two sources—his IU coach Everett Dean and his experiences in professional basketball.

Coach Dean was known much more for his patterned, methodical approach to the game, but he was a well-rounded coach and his system also included an approach to the fast break that he occasionally used when the matchups favored it. As a player, Branch McCracken was quick for a big man and he would often outrace opposing centers down the court for easy scores. He loved to run and decided that when he became a coach he would do it a lot more often.

"I idolized Everett Dean and he had a great effect on me," said McCracken. "I wanted to be a lot like him and I wanted to become a very good coach. Everett was a very good fundamentalist and he used a fast break, which I loved, and I made up my mind when I was playing if I got out and got a coaching job that I was going to fast break the same as we had, only I was going to fast break more than we had when I played."[17]

When Mac arrived at Ball State that first year and played pro ball part-time with the Fort Wayne Hoosiers, he also had an experience that further influenced his commitment to the fast break.

"In those early days I was earning $1,200 a year and Branch was only earning $1,000 a year," said Mary Jo. "He didn't think that was right, so he would play for professional teams on the weekend to earn an extra $30 a night. One day we traveled up to Fort Wayne for a pro game and when we got there the guy who played center said he was too sick and weak to play. Well, [forfeiting] a game was unheard-of in [Indiana], so the rest of the players decided on a strategy. They told this guy to just plant himself at the top of the key and they would throw the ball down to him to then feed off to one of the others who were breaking for the basket. Up until this time the game was slow and the spectators would settle into the stands with some popcorn and watch. That night they saw an entirely new game. The action was fast and everyone was cheering and really getting into it. On our way home Branch talked about how much everyone had enjoyed the game. He was determined right then and there to develop that strategy into his team at Ball State. Later he brought it to IU and that's how they became known as the 'Hurryin' Hoosiers.' "[18]

All in all, there were several reasons that McCracken was enamored with the running game, which Mary Jo also explained. "Certainly, he loved for his teams to run," she said. "But he did that primarily because boys liked the running game and had fun playing it. It also was an exciting thing for the people to watch, and he wanted to promote basketball and draw the crowds."[19]

With Ball State as his basketball laboratory for eight seasons, McCracken developed what he felt was a sound, fully developed system based on the fast break—and he used it with great success over his final three seasons in Muncie, going 43-17. Mac's approach was to get all of his players in supreme physical condition, which he did by requiring them to run outside of practice, especially in the preseason, and then work them at a breakneck pace during practice to improve their stamina. Then he taught his players to always look for fast break opportunities from loose balls, defensive rebounds, missed free throws, and jump balls (which involved an actual jump between two players and were much more prevalent back then). Next, he drilled them on exactly how to execute the fast break—how the rebounder should throw the outlet pass to a player on the sideline, how that player should position himself to catch it and relay it upcourt, and how the other players should execute the "three-man rush" to attack the basket as quickly as possible.

Mac never saw his system as being particularly complicated or ingenious. He simply stated, "The idea was to get down there the firstest with the mostest."[20] McCracken firmly believed that if his team always got more field goal opportunities than their opponents, they would always have a good chance to win. He told his teams not to worry if they missed some shots while playing at this speedy pace. He told them to just make sure they got up more shots than their opponents. And Mac had student managers who closely tracked the shot charts to let him know how many shots his boys were taking in comparison to their opponents.

Of course, McCracken couldn't always have his teams run at an all-out pace. Sometimes he didn't have the players best suited for the running game, so he had to ease off the reins a little bit. However, by the time he left Ball State and came to IU, McCracken knew exactly the type of player he needed for the type of game he preferred to play.

"When he was out to recruit a boy, the first thing he checked was quickness," explained Mary Jo. "If they didn't have quickness and a lot of heart, they weren't what he was looking for, and he was very honest with coaches, the boys, and their parents. If he didn't think the boy would fit into Indiana basketball, he'd tell them, and suggest a school where they could probably fit in better."[21]

What Mac didn't realize when he took over the Indiana job in 1938 was that Everett Dean had already stocked the IU locker room with exactly the kind of thoroughbreds McCracken wanted to build his kind of team. As a result, Mac was able to fully unleash his running game right away. And Indiana basketball, the Big Ten, and the NCAA Tournament would never again be the same.

THE SECOND-PLACE CURSE

5

Branch was an excellent coach, and a wonderful man. . . . His teams were really well-coached and they really ran with an understanding of the fast break.

—PETE NEWELL

By 1938, the state of Indiana had already earned a national reputation as "the basketball state." That was mostly due to the Hoosierland's manic obsession with high school basketball, but several Indiana colleges had also established themselves as bellwethers of the collegiate game. However, the pre-eminent college basketball program in the Hoosier state at the time was not Indiana University. It was Purdue University, led by its Hall of Fame coach Ward "Piggy" Lambert. Indiana and Purdue were, of course, archrivals from the very first time they played each other in basketball in 1901. The intense rivalry had started in football a few years before and it immediately carried over to the hardwood.

Still, in 1938, you could only call it a basketball rivalry in the sense that statewide bragging rights were always at stake and both schools always circled the game on their calendars. Nevertheless, from a competitive standpoint, it had not been much of a rivalry up until that point. Through the 1937–38 season, Purdue had won twelve Big Ten championships, while Indiana had won only three (and Purdue was actually co-champion in each of those three seasons). Purdue had eighteen All-American selections, while Indiana had just six. And, worst of all, Purdue owned a 50-10 advantage over Indiana in the all-time head-to-head series.

Of all the things Branch McCracken would accomplish as the IU coach, perhaps none endeared him to the Hoosier faithful more than that he completely reversed this trend and took the IU program to such heights that it replaced Purdue as the pre-eminent college basketball program in the state—an honor that Indiana has retained ever since. For all the joys Mac got from his many victories and championships, there were few things he enjoyed more than beating the Boilermakers.

Branch McCracken's triumphant return to Bloomington in 1938 to take over the Indiana University basketball program was welcomed by many die-hard Hoosier fans. Like Everett Dean, McCracken was a former IU All-American who had made good in the coaching field at a small school and then returned home to coach his alma mater. McCracken was also one of the state's biggest basketball stars because of his outstanding achievements in high school, college, and the pros.

Despite having all that going for him, there was still a sizable contingent of IU fans who felt the Hoosiers needed someone older and more experienced than the thirty-year-old McCracken to lead the Indiana team in the wake of the departing forty-year-old Dean. Some of those critics had probably forgotten that Dean was only twenty-six years old when he first took over the job in 1924. Either that or they keenly remembered Indiana's mediocre record in the Big Ten before Dean's arrival and did not want to risk returning to mediocrity by placing the Indiana program in the hands of a guy who wasn't much older than many of the IU players—even if he had been an outstanding IU player himself and even if he had won a few games while coaching in the collegiate minor leagues.

McCracken went out and did the only thing he could do to quiet that type of criticism—he won. Dean left him with a young but extremely talented roster for the 1938–39 season. The elder statesman on the team was senior guard Ernie Andres, who had been an All-

American performer as a junior and had set a new Big Ten single-game scoring record by netting thirty points against Illinois. The two other experienced performers were senior forward Bill Johnson, the team's second-leading scorer behind Andres in 1936–37, and junior guard Marv Huffman, a tough-minded floor leader and returning starter. The rest of the rotation on McCracken's first IU team was made up primarily of sophomores. Luckily for Mac, they were probably the best class of sophomores that IU had ever seen up until that point.

That class included Bill and Bob Menke, Paul "Curly" Armstrong, Herm Schafer, Bob Dro, Chet Francis, and several other players who had been Indiana high school stars. When Everett Dean landed all nine of those recruits in 1937, it was the best recruiting class he had ever put together and arguably the best in IU history for that era. During his final season in Bloomington, that recruiting class was learning the ropes on the freshman team, so Dean never got the opportunity to coach them, but he did get an opportunity to see just how good this group was going to be. On one occasion, he had the freshman squad scrimmage the varsity to help the varsity better simulate a game situation. The youngsters did something that had rarely—if ever—been seen on the IU campus: they whipped their elders in the scrimmage.

When Dean decided to leave IU for Stanford, many of his top-notch recruits were understandably upset. Most of them had been wooed by out-of-state schools when they were in high school, and Dean had appealed to them to serve their home state by playing for IU. Then Dean himself jumped ship and left for California. And then, the gentlemanly, low-key Dean was replaced with the fiery McCracken, a fierce competitor who was wound about as tightly as any coach you could find. And even though McCracken was a disciple of Coach Dean, the players also had to adjust to a significant change in playing style. While Dean ran a methodical offense and a containment defense, McCracken had his teams push the ball up the floor much more often on offense, and he believed in an aggressive man-to-man defense that sometimes included a full-court press. McCracken also worked on converting his players from using only two-handed set shots to also using the one-handed shot (a precursor to the jump shot). He made them practice hundreds of one-handers. "No defense has ever been devised to halt this type of shooting," said Mac.[1]

Naturally, not all the Hoosier players took to McCracken's system as smoothly as some of the others. Seniors Ernie Andres and Bill Johnson had been teammates at Jeffersonville High School, where they played an up-tempo running game, so both of them took to Mc-Cracken's system without a hitch. Junior Marv Huffman was a hard-nosed competitor, so he and McCracken got along just fine. Then there were several sophomores who quickly distinguished themselves from that talented but crowded group. One was Bill Menke, a 6' 3" center with terrific foot speed and a set of tireless lungs. Another was Curly Armstrong, a solidly built 5' 11" forward with a brash demeanor and a terrific scoring touch. The other two major sophomore standouts were forward Herm Schafer and guard Bob Dro.

With that young nucleus in place and a new coach who still had to prove himself in the big leagues, the Hoosiers were a bit of an unknown entity heading into the 1938–39 campaign, although they certainly appeared to have the talent for an upper division finish in the conference. The big question was whether their inexperience—on the floor and on the bench—would haunt them during the rugged Big Ten season.

Indiana opened McCracken's inaugural season with six impressive double-digit victories over non-conference opponents, then won Mac's first Big Ten conference game as a coach with a 37-33 win at Michigan State to improve to 7-0. After a 45-38 setback at Ohio State—the conference favorite—the Hoosiers reeled off ten straight victories to up their overall record to 17-1 and their conference mark to 9-1. With two games left in the season, Indiana was being declared the hottest team in the country. It would be another decade until the weekly AP polls would rank college teams, but if there had been a poll during the final week of February 1939, the Indiana Hoosiers would likely have been sitting at the top of it.

However, there were still two games to play and both of them were on the road—at Purdue and at Michigan. IU dropped both games, 45-34 to the Boilermakers and 53-45 to the Wolverines, to finish 9-3 in the Big Ten and watch the conference title slip out of their hands and into the clutches of 10-2 Ohio State. That also gave Ohio State the opportunity to represent the Big Ten in the first annual NCAA Tournament. The Buckeyes finished as the runner-up, losing to Oregon in the national championship game.

With a 17-3 record and a second-place finish in the Big Ten, Branch McCracken won over most of the IU faithful. Of course, there were still a few naysayers who claimed Mac was in over his head, as proven by the team's collapse in the final two games of the season. For those who still doubted Mac's coaching ability because of his youth, that doubt was permanently put to rest with the Hoosiers' success the next season.

Heading into that 1939–40 season, IU returned its entire roster except for Andres, who had helped steady the youngsters, and Johnson, who had mostly been relegated to a reserve role as a senior. However, the Hoosiers added another excellent junior to their roster with the return of Jay McCreary, who had played his sophomore season under Everett Dean in 1937–38 and then took a year off school. The 5' 10" McCreary was a former all-state guard at Frankfort, which he led to the Indiana state championship in 1936 with a title game win over Fort Wayne Central, then led by Herm Schafer and Curly Armstrong, who were now McCreary's teammates at IU. An aggressive, tough-minded team player, McCreary fit in perfectly with the other Hoosiers and became the team's sixth man.

The 1939–40 Hoosiers once again zipped through the preconference schedule with a 7-0 record, including road wins at Nebraska and Villanova and a squeaker at Duquesne, one of the top teams in the nation. In the Big Ten, IU got off to a 7-2 start, with heartbreakingly close defeats at Minnesota and Northwestern. That put IU a game behind archrival Purdue (8-1) with three games to play. Indiana's hopes for the conference title were deflated with a loss to Ohio State on February 28, which, coupled with a Purdue blowout over Iowa, dropped IU two games behind the Boilermakers with only two games to play. The Hoosiers' next game was against Purdue in West Lafayette. Three weeks earlier, the Hoosiers had dealt the Boilermakers their only conference loss of the season with a 46-39 win in Bloomington. But Indiana had never swept two games from Purdue in the same season.

McCracken's pep talk to his team before that game was simple. He told them, "If you're not going to win, we're not going to the [postseason]."[2] On March 2, IU went into West Lafayette—where Indiana hadn't won in seventeen years—and dominated league-leading Purdue from the opening tip to the final gun for a 51-45 victory in front of a raucous, record-setting Boilermaker crowd of 9,150. IU closed out its season two days later with a twenty-one-point win over Ohio State in Bloomington, while Purdue clinched the Big Ten championship that day when they slipped by Illinois 34-31 in West Lafayette.

Surprisingly, the NCAA selection committee picked Indiana over league champion Purdue as the tournament's representative for the Midwest. Indiana's season record (17-3) was better than Purdue's (16-4), and the Hoosiers had convincingly beaten the Boilermakers twice. Purdue coach Piggy Lambert, who was not a big fan of postseason tournaments, agreed with the selection.

In 1940, the NCAA Tournament was called the "Tournament of Champions" because it featured the best team from each of the different regions across the country. For 1940 that included the University of Southern California, which was widely considered the top team in the country, and Colorado, which had already captured the NIT championship. The NCAA Tournament had an eight-team field and was divided into an Eastern Regional, played in Indianapolis, and a Western Regional, played in Kansas City. The winners of the two regionals would meet in Kansas City for what was dubbed the "World Series of Basketball." Indiana sailed through the Eastern Regional, beating Springfield 48-24 and Duquesne 39-30. Duquesne had lost only twice all season, once to Indiana and once to Colorado in the NIT finals, but in Indiana's 51-49 regular season win over Duquesne in Pittsburgh, the Dukes' crowd had mocked and ridiculed the IU players as a bunch of ignorant farm boys. The farm boys were ticked off by that kind of treatment and made a point to take it out on the Dukes in the rematch.

On the other side of the bracket, Kansas outlasted Rice 50-44 and then won a 43-42 thriller over USC. The next week, Kansas and IU squared off to decide the national championship at the Municipal Auditorium in Kansas City, which drew a capacity crowd of ten thousand spectators and enabled the NCAA to make a profit on the tournament for the first time. Since the game was being played only forty minutes from the Jayhawks' campus in Lawrence, Kansas, the Jayhawks wore the home white jerseys and the crowd was almost unanimously in favor of Kansas. In fact, as the two teams were standing on the sidelines before the game, there was an elaborate round of honors presented to the Kansas team. They even gave Kansas coach Phog Allen a set of golf clubs.

When the pregame ceremonies started, Jay McCreary turned to McCracken and asked him, "What the hell is going on?"

"I don't know," said Mac, "we're just going to have to go out and win the ball game."[3]

Once all the fanfare was over, IU's Curly Armstrong turned to his teammates, hitched up his shorts, and said, "Now, wasn't that something! Let's go out there and whip them before all their fans."[4] And the Hoosiers did just that.

The great strength of that Kansas team was its shooting. They had four terrific perimeter shooters—Don Ebling, Bill Hogben, Howard Engleman, and Bob Allen (the son of Phog Allen)—and the Jayhawks ran a patterned offense that focused on getting those four players open for set shots. McCracken's idea for shaking that up—which was recommended to him by USC coach Sam Barry, whose Trojans were defeated by Kansas in the previous round—was to full-court press the Jayhawks from the opening tip. Charged up by the home crowd, Kansas shrugged off the pressure early on and used their hot shooting to take a 10-4 lead. But then Indiana, desperate to take control, turned up the heat on their pressure defense and the Jayhawks buckled. Kansas started turning the ball over and had a difficult time setting up their defense as the Hoosiers raced all over the court for easy scores. IU went on a 28-9 run and led 32-19 at the half. Indiana continued to dominate the action in the second half and walked away with a 60-42 victory. Senior guard Marv Huffman, who usually focused on distributing the ball and leading the team (and averaged only 4.3 points per game for the season), scored twelve points in the title game and won the award for the Most Outstanding Player of the 1940 Final Four.

Afterwards, Phog Allen shook McCracken's hand and exclaimed, "Say, Branch, where did you dig up so many speed merchants? Your fast break ran us to death!"[5]

The college basketball world was awestruck and excited by the Hoosiers' style of play. A reporter from the *Kansas City Star* wrote, "On the sidelines were members of the National Association of Basketball Coaches and members of the Joint Basketball Rules Committee of the United States and Canada, meeting for the first time in history, and they were as astonished as the unschooled spectators at Indiana's breathtaking antics on the court."[6]

USC coach Sam Barry simply said, "I knew Indiana was fast, but not that fast."[7]

If Branch McCracken had held a preference for fast break basketball and the full-court press before the 1939–40 season, then his belief in it was completely solidified that night as McCracken's "Hurryin' Hoosier" basketball lit up the national sports scene.

IU returned its entire roster except for Marv Huffman for the 1940–41 campaign and naturally entered the season as the Big Ten favorite. McCracken decided to challenge his boys by taking them on a tough five-game road trip over the winter holiday. And he did something groundbreaking in the process. In order to save time, he had his team fly on an airplane for the road trip instead of taking a train. In a one-week stretch, IU played games against four of the top teams on the West Coast—Stanford, California, UCLA, and USC—and won three of them, including a 60-59 overtime thriller over Everett Dean's Stanford team in the first game of the tour. The only loss was a 41-39 defeat to Sam Barry's USC squad in the final game of the West Coast swing. IU then flew to New Orleans and played in the Sugar Bowl Carnival game against Kentucky on December 30, beating the Wildcats 48-45. Adolph Rupp, who had turned Kentucky into an SEC powerhouse during the previous decade, said after the game that McCracken was "one of the greatest young coaches in the nation."[8] It was one of the few kind statements ever shared between the two highly successful coaches, who would become bitter rivals over the next two decades.

After amassing a 7-1 record against impressive competition, IU got off to a solid 8-1 start in the Big Ten. However, during that stretch, Curly Armstrong, the team's senior captain and second-leading scorer, was declared academically ineligible for the final semester of his senior season because of a failing grade in Roman History. Without Armstrong, Indiana lost a showdown with Wisconsin, and the Badgers (11-1) ended up finishing one game ahead of the Hoosiers (10-2) in the conference race. Wisconsin also went on to capture the 1941 NCAA Tournament.

Despite graduating almost all his starting lineup and top reserves, McCracken had the Hoosiers challenging for the Big Ten title again in 1941–42. The Illinois "Whiz Kids" ran away with the conference crown with a 13-2 record, but McCracken's young squad tied for second with a 10-5 mark that included a 41-36 win over the Illini. IU started the next season by winning its first sixteen games, but dropped two of its final four games to finish 18-2 overall and 11-2 in the Big Ten. The Illinois Whiz Kids went 17-1 overall and a perfect 12-0 in conference play and relegated the Hoosiers to second place once again.

However, while the Whiz Kids were the most highly regarded team in college basketball that season and were the favorites to win both the NIT and NCAA tournaments, they never got a chance to play in the postseason. Three of Illinois's starters were drafted into the army at the end of the regular season and the Illini did not play in either of the postseason tournaments. The U.S. involvement in World War II was building to a crescendo and it would soon engulf the Indiana Hoosiers as well.

Branch McCracken's 1942–43 squad, which went 18-2 and was barely eclipsed by that legendary Illini team, featured only one senior and would have returned its top five scorers for the 1943–44 season. They would very likely have been the runaway favorite for both the Big Ten and NCAA championships, but that was not meant to be. In the spring of 1943, every member of the squad either enlisted in the U.S. armed forces or was drafted—including the coach.

With all his boys heading off to the war, McCracken did not want to be left behind. In his life as a basketball player and coach, Mac had never backed down from a fight, and he was not about to back down now that his country's future was at stake. At thirty-five years of age, Mac was not going to be drafted. He certainly could have maintained his cloistered and comfortable life at a quiet midwestern university. "He didn't have to go. He was too old," said Dave McCracken, Branch's son. "There was no question he didn't have to go, but he wanted to go badly because he felt it was his duty."[9]

On March 3, 1943, two days after Indiana's 41-38 loss to Purdue that ended the 1942–43 season, McCracken enlisted in the U.S. Navy. He was first assigned to the navy preflight school in Chapel Hill, North Carolina, where he started out by working as a coach and physical education instructor for the young men coming through the school. Because of his experience in handling pressure-packed situations as a ballplayer and coach, McCracken was selected to go through training in Chicago for a special relaxation program he was assigned to teach to the pilots. The navy was having a serious problem with pilots freezing up at the controls during extremely dangerous and highly critical flight missions. McCracken's relaxation training was very successful and he received high praise for his efforts from the navy and from many of the pilots who went through his program and then flew important missions in the war.

Nevertheless, Mac didn't want to stay in North Carolina. All the kids he was training were going off to serve overseas and Mac felt he should do a tour of duty as well. "He finally agitated his way to go out to the Philippines, because he felt that if everybody else was going, he should go, too," said Dave McCracken.[10] At the end of 1944, Lieutenant McCracken was shipped to the South Pacific to serve as an athletic officer and to continue providing his relaxation courses to pilots. He was stationed in the Philippines during the spring and summer of 1945 when General Douglas MacArthur made his crucial move to retake the Philippines and Corregidor Island.

McCracken wrote to his son Dave in a letter dated July 18, 1945, "A few weeks ago I went over to [Corregidor] and went through some of the caves. They are full of dead Japs. Some of the caves still have live Japs in them. I didn't go in those. . . . These places all took a bad beating when we came back in. I have been out here seven months and if I have to stay eighteen I have eleven more to go. Don't think I'll have to stay that long."[11]

A month later, America dropped atomic bombs on Hiroshima and Nagasaki, and on September 2, 1945, the Japanese officially surrendered. Shortly thereafter, McCracken was shipped back to the U.S. mainland, and on Saturday, December 1, 1945, he was officially released from active duty at the U.S. Naval Separation Center in Chicago. Just as the cold midwestern winter was sweeping in and a new basketball season was about to start, a war-weary Branch McCracken left the Windy City to return to civilian life in the Hoosier state.

He went from Chicago to Selma, Indiana, just outside of Muncie, where his wife Mary Jo and his eleven-year-old son Dave had been staying with Mary Jo's parents while Mac was serving in the Pacific. On December 11, 1945—ten days after McCracken was discharged— a story from Muncie, Indiana, hit the Associated Press news wire, reporting that McCracken was going to be visiting the IU campus the next day and meeting with Indiana University president Herman B Wells and athletic director Zora Clevenger on Saturday, December 15. In that report, McCracken said that he "doubted" he would return to IU to coach the team that season (the IU squad, which was being led by interim coach Harry Good, was already 2-0). However, the real bombshell in the AP report was that McCracken also said he "might not go back" to coaching IU at all, and admitted he had received head coaching offers from other schools.

The news that McCracken might not return as the IU coach spread through the Bloomington campus like wildfire and triggered great alarm among IU students and basketball fans. The editor-in-chief of the *Indiana Daily Student*, Dee Harrington, called an impromptu meeting with more than twenty student organizations and they quickly formulated a "Draft Back McCracken" movement to include a pep rally for the returning war hero and celebrated coach.

At 11:00 AM on Wednesday, December 12, Mac returned to Bloomington and visited the IU campus for the first time since leaving for his naval assignment in 1943. Wearing his blue naval officer's uniform, McCracken paid informal visits to several of his old colleagues. Newspaper photographers caught up with him at several points and snapped pictures of him shaking hands. When the pictures hit the papers the next day, many Hoosiers were surprised to see that Mac, who had had a full head of black hair that was touched with a few gray flecks on the sides when he left IU in 1943, now had predominantly silver hair with only a few hints of black on top. It was an outward symbol of the inner toll the war had taken on McCracken.

The first night Mac was back in town, a "Welcome Home" dinner was held in IU's Alumni Hall. More than eight hundred students, faculty members, and boosters crowded in for the event during which Mac spoke briefly about some of his navy experiences and his happiness about being back on the IU campus. He declined to comment about his future plans.

That Saturday he officially met with Wells and Clevenger to discuss his demands for a substantial increase in salary and the addition of a full-time assistant basketball coach. Saturday came and went without an agreement, so the three men agreed to meet again on Monday. On Tuesday morning, Zora Clevenger announced that Branch McCracken would return to Indiana University as a physical education instructor and head basketball coach at the beginning of the spring semester in February. He also announced that interim coach Harry Good would finish the 1945–46 season.

There was a palpable sense of relief and gladness in Bloomington.

If Mac's presence was commanding before the war, he now exuded a charisma that was larger than life, and his deep, twangy voice now boomed with even greater authority. As a returning war hero and one of the most respected basketball coaches in the country, his reputation now preceded him wherever he went.

Nevertheless, it took Mac a few years to build the IU basketball program back up to the elite level he had established before leaving for the war. During the first few postwar seasons, college basketball rosters took on an unorthodox flavor. They mixed the standard incoming students with an older cadre of war veterans who were either returning to school after serving in the military or taking advantage of the G.I. Bill to become the first in their family to get a college degree. The postwar years also witnessed a tremendous rising tide of interest in basketball on campus, as IU overflowed with record numbers of students. In Mac's first game back, the IU Fieldhouse had to be equipped with extra bleachers to meet the frenetic demand for tickets. Eventually, 9,300 spectators crowded in to watch the Hoosiers run and shoot their way past Wabash for an easy 69-46 victory.

Because of the number of men still returning from overseas posts in the armed forces, a wartime waiver was still in effect during the 1946–47 season, McCracken's first season back at the helm. This meant that McCracken could use freshmen on the varsity. A twenty-two-year-old freshman named Lou Watson, who had been part of the Allied forces that stormed Normandy, was an important part of the rotation and went on to have a terrific IU career. That season Mac also benefited from the return of Ward Williams and Ralph Hamilton from his highly successful 1942–43 squad. Hamilton served as captain for the 1946–47 team and had a sensational year that was capped off by his selection to the All–Big Ten and All-America teams. The IU team got off to a shaky start but straightened things out to finish 12-8 overall and 8-4 in the Big Ten, which put the Hoosiers in, where else, second place in the conference standings.

The next year, IU returned all of its top nine scorers except for Hamilton and was favored to win the conference. Unfortunately, the season turned into a disaster. The team never found any cohesion or rhythm, and nearly everything that could go wrong did. The team was 0-for-7 in games decided by five points or fewer, and the Hoosiers ended the season on a five-game losing streak to finish 8-12 overall and 3-9 in conference play, tied for last place with Northwestern. To Mac and the IU players, the season was pretty much summed up by one play—the "sit-down shot." It came against Purdue in the IU Fieldhouse in the next-to-last game of the season. With ten seconds remaining and the game tied 49-49, Boilermaker guard Howie Williams slashed to the basket and put up an off-balance shot that bounced off the rim. Howie fell on his fanny and the ball fell right into his hands. While sitting on the floor, he quickly flipped the ball back toward the basket. It went in and Purdue won 51-49 in front of a stunned Hoosier crowd. For Mac, it was his worst season in coaching up until that time and he had no explanation for it. "I thought we had what it takes [to win] in this league," said Mac, "and look what happened."[12]

Things got worse that summer. Indiana's top recruit, Clyde Lovellette, a bruising 6' 9" center whom McCracken was counting on to handle the pivot position in future years, had a last-minute change of heart and decided to go to Kansas. Lovellette had already committed to IU, but Kansas coach Phog Allen convinced Lovellette to come to Kansas for a visit, and once he was there Clyde decided to stay until school started. He never informed McCracken, who found out he had lost big Clyde when the story hit the news wire. That episode spoiled forever the previously cordial friendship between Allen and McCracken.

Also that summer, UCLA went looking for a new coach and the first man on their list was McCracken. UCLA was rumored to have offered Mac a $14,000 contract (about twice what he was making at IU) to come to California and build up the UCLA basketball program. McCracken nearly decided to take them up on their offer. He went to IU president Herman B Wells and explained that UCLA had made an offer he didn't think he could refuse. Wells reminded Mac that he had just signed a ten-year contract the previous fall and appealed to the coach to stay at IU and keep his commitment. Wells also said that IU would work on improving the financial terms of his contract (although he could not match what UCLA was offering). When push came to shove, Mac decided to stay at Indiana. UCLA was disappointed, but they asked him who he would recommend for the job. McCracken said they should hire his old pal John Wooden, who had just completed two successful seasons at Indiana State, where he led the Sycamores to an NAIA championship. UCLA did, of course, hire Wooden, and he eventually went on to have the greatest coaching career in the history of college basketball.

McCracken returned to the IU sidelines for the 1948–49 season and began the process of re-establishing his program among the Big Ten elite. Fortunately, Mac had an ace in the hole named Bill Garrett, who in 1947 had led Shelbyville High School to the Indiana state championship and was named Indiana Mr. Basketball. Garrett was the second-straight African American player to earn the Mr. Basketball title, following Jumpin' Johnny Wilson of Anderson in 1946. Wilson had hoped to play for IU, but the Big Ten coaches had a "gentlemen's agreement" that none of them would recruit black players, so Wilson was never offered a chance to play for the Hoosiers.

However, a group of alumni from Indianapolis, including several African Americans, approached Herman B Wells and told him that if McCracken would be willing to play Garrett, then they thought he would be willing to play for IU. Wells approached McCracken and Zora Clevenger about it. Mac said he would love to have Garrett, but that if IU took him they would probably have a difficult time scheduling games. Wells said he would make sure that wouldn't happen, because if any of the coaches or athletic directors made an issue out of it then he would bring pressure on them though the Council of Ten (a convocation made up of all the Big Ten presidents). Wells believed that none of the coaches or their schools would dare make a public issue out of it, and he was right. McCracken agreed to let Garrett join the team and—more importantly—to give the kid an equal shot at earning playing time. Rather than staging a fight against Garrett joining IU, most of the other Big Ten basketball teams began scrambling to land the best black basketball players they could find to join their teams. The color line in Big Ten basketball had been permanently broken.

In his first season in 1948–49, the 6' 3" Garrett did a little bit of everything—passing, rebounding, driving, shooting from the outside, and defending. His natural position was forward, but because of IU's lack of frontcourt size and depth, Garrett often had to step in and play center. The sophomore led IU in scoring at 10.0 points per game and the Hoosiers finished 14-8 overall and fourth in the Big Ten with a 6-6 record.

The next season, 1949–50, the Hoosiers were even better. Bill Garrett, Lou Watson, and Jerry Stuteville each averaged double figures in scoring—the first time three IU players had done that in the same season. Indiana roared through the preconference season with a 9-0 record, but in conference play, the Hoosiers were snakebitten by three narrow losses that included a two-point defeat to Michigan on a final tip-in, a one-point loss to conference champion Ohio State on two last-second free throws, and a one-point defeat at Iowa. Those three tough losses doomed IU to a 7-5 conference record and a third-place finish. Overall, the Hoosiers went 17-5. McCracken was pleased to have his IU team competing for the Big Ten title again, but he was still brooding over the loss of Clyde Lovellette. His team's biggest weakness that season was the lack of a big man to play the pivot, and Lovellette was the pivot man Mac had lined up to take over the position that season. He felt Clyde had been unjustly swiped away from him, and it didn't help that Lovellette averaged 21.8 points per game as a sophomore for the Jayhawks that year.

Still, McCracken didn't waste much time feeling sorry for himself. He went out in the spring and summer of 1950 and put together his best recruiting class ever—Bobby Leonard, Dick Farley, Pat Klein, Jack Wright, Charlie Kraak, Sammy Esposito, Ron Taylor, and Lou Scott.

Mac's 1950 recruiting class didn't include a blue-chip big man, but it did include a big guy, Lou Scott, whom McCracken thought he could transform into a solid center. Mac believed that having a big guy like Scott would at least keep Indiana from being exploited inside defensively and on the boards. The challenge was that it was going to take a lot of work.

Shortly after Scott graduated from high school, McCracken had him come to Bloomington for the summer, and he placed Lou Watson in charge of Scott's development. The twenty-six-year-old Watson had just graduated after an All-American senior season and was the newly appointed coach of the freshman team. Watson was a 6' 5" guard with a strong physique and a hard-nosed demeanor, both of which were honed during his stint in the army in World War II. In the first assignment of his coaching career, Watson had his work cut out for him. Big Lou Scott really had only two things going for him to help him become a Big Ten center—his size and his ambition to become a good basketball player.

Scott stood 6' 11" with his shoes on and had broad shoulders and long arms. He was quite thin, especially in the upper body, so as soon as he arrived in Bloomington he was fed a daily dose of milk shakes mixed with raw eggs to help him gain weight. Scott's greatest weaknesses for playing in McCracken's system were that he was not mobile and he lacked stamina. He also didn't have a lot of polished basketball skills. Lou Watson's job was to work with him all day, every day for six days a week and teach him everything he needed to know to be able to play in the Big Ten. Watson's primary tactic was to rough up the big kid, physically and verbally. Watson banged against him again and again to get him used to the contact, and he criticized him repeatedly for making mistakes that would cost him in a game. Watson second-guessed himself on a few occasions, wondering if he was being too hard on the kid, but in the end, the work that Watson put in went a long way toward turning Lou Scott into an effective Big Ten basketball player.

Scott roomed with Bobby Leonard, the other rookie who was staying in Bloomington in the summer leading up to their freshman year. While Scott was working on his game with Watson in the old Men's Gym during the daytime, Leonard was working in a stone quarry, a job McCracken had lined up for him. At night, both of them joined in the pickup games that were played in the Men's Gym, games that included the current varsity players who stayed around campus for the summer as well as former players who had come back for the summer to work on their degrees. It was hot up there (the gym was on the top floor of the building) and the games were predictably intense and physical, but the experience was invaluable for Scott and Leonard. When the freshman team began practicing in the fall, Leonard and Scott were two of the first players to grab starting positions in that intensely competitive group.

For the IU varsity entering the 1950–51 season, the situation was still the same—lots of talented players, but still no big man in the middle. Mac's best option was to once again play senior Bill Garrett at center, and Garrett stepped up and did a courageous job. He averaged 13.1 points per game and focused on using his athletic ability to outmaneuver bigger, slower opponents. He would cap off his landmark career by earning All-America and first team All–Big Ten honors, and he finished as the all-time leading scorer in school history.

Above all, he led IU to a stellar 19-3 record that season. The Hoosiers had started the season by going 7-1 in their preconference games, the only loss a 64-62 defeat at second-ranked Bradley, which had been the NCAA and NIT runner-up to CCNY the previous season and returned many of their top players. The Braves' Charley Grover hit the game-winner with fourteen seconds left on the clock to deliver the victory in Peoria, Illinois, on December 27. The Hoosiers held Bradley star Gene Melchiorre—who along with several teammates was later convicted of point shaving during the 1950–51 season—to just six points, and Melchiorre fouled out with six minutes left in the game. Bradley's win propelled them to the No. 1 ranking in the AP poll. If the fifth-ranked Hoosiers had upset the Braves in Peoria, they likely would have vaulted to the top spot.

The week after the Bradley game, Branch McCracken did something he hadn't often done in the past—he invited the freshmen to come down from the Men's Gym, where they practiced every day, and scrimmage the varsity on the floor of the IU Fieldhouse. It's unknown why McCracken did it. The freshmen had been playing well, and it's possible that he wanted to reward them by giving them a chance to play on the big floor against the varsity. He also may have wanted to take the freshmen down a notch by having the varsity dominate them and show them how much they still had to learn. And it's also possible that Mac was curious to see just how good his up-and-coming players were, and there was no better way to do it than to put them in a live competition with the big boys.

So Watson brought his freshman team down and McCracken set up a scrimmage with two twelve-minute halves. Watson's starting five featured Bobby Leonard, Sammy Esposito, Dick Farley, Charlie Kraak, and Lou Scott. They outsized the varsity in four out of five positions and after the first twelve minutes of play they had nearly a double-digit lead on the varsity, which was still ranked in the nation's top five teams at the time. McCracken turned to Watson and said, "Hey Lou, you take those guys back upstairs." McCracken had seen all he needed to see.

The varsity, undersized though it was, went on to post a 12-2 record in the Big Ten. When the Hoosiers completed their 68-58 victory over Wisconsin in Bloomington to finish their Big Ten schedule, they tuned into the radio to listen for the result of the Michigan State–Illinois game later that day. Illinois was 12-1 but they had to get by a gritty Spartan team in East Lansing in their final game. If Michigan State could win, IU would tie the Illini for the conference crown. Among the other teams in the conference, IU was the sentimental favorite at that point because of all the times McCracken's teams had finished second.

The Spartans very nearly pulled off the upset. They led Illinois by six points with four minutes left to play. "We were well ahead and Illinois had a great team," said Pete Newell, who was the first-year Michigan State coach at the time. "But Indiana had a damn good team and if Illinois loses that game then Indiana is the champion, and I thought, in fairness to Branch, I would stall the ball and they would have never caught us."

However, there was one hitch in Newell's plan. He started a senior guard named Jimmy Snodgrass in that game since it was the final game of his career. Snodgrass, who was usually a reserve, played well in the first half and did some good things in the second half, but he wasn't a very good ball handler under pressure. When Michigan State went up six with four minutes to go, Newell had his two starting guards—both excellent ball handlers—ready to check back in and start the stall, which would have let Snodgrass come out of the game and get an ovation from the crowd. However, before the regular guards could check back into the game, Snodgrass lost his man, who quickly scored. Illinois immediately set up a full-court trap and Snodgrass threw the ball away and Illinois scored again. By the time Newell got his starting guards back in there, the game was tied with a minute and a half to play. Illinois had all the momentum and went on to win 49-43 to finish 13-1 and claim the outright Big Ten championship. Illinois also made it to the Final Four, where they were barely nicked 76-74 in the national semifinals by eventual champion Kentucky.

Indiana, of course, finished second in the Big Ten. It was the seventh time in McCracken's ten seasons at IU that his Hoosier squad had finished second. The gut-wrenching part was just how close the team had come to finishing first during most of those second-place finishes. In most cases, one bad break had made the difference.

Entering the 1951–52 season, McCracken had the IU cupboard fully stocked with the kind of players he wanted and the talent he believed he needed to compete on a national level. In addition to all the terrific players from his 1950 class who were moving up to the varsity as sophomores, McCracken also had another fantastic recruiting class in 1951, headlined by Don Schlundt, the blue-chip big man Mac had been waiting for.

Because of the shortage of young men on college campuses due to the Korean War and the draft, a war waiver went into effect for the 1951–52 season, which meant that freshmen were eligible to play on varsity teams. For Don Schlundt, this meant a rare opportunity to make an immediate impact as a freshman. For Branch McCracken, it meant that he would get an extra season to develop his megatalented young recruit under the fire of varsity competition. For Lou Scott, who was originally recruited to succeed Bill Garrett at center, it meant that his shot at becoming the next great IU pivot man was greatly diminished. Still, Mac gave Scott every chance to beat out Schlundt for the starting center position on that 1951–52 squad. But while Scott was the better rebounder and defender, Schlundt was the more skilled and polished player, and a far superior offensive threat, and Schlundt won the starting nod.

In the opening game against Valparaiso on December 6, 1951, McCracken played six sophomores and one freshman, with mixed results. Mac's two big men struggled. Schlundt was 1-for-5 from the field and finished with six points and three rebounds. Scott was 0-for-4 from the field and also missed his only free throw and failed to grab a rebound. However, Mac started a pair of sophomores at the two forward spots and both of them played well. Dick Farley scored a game-high nineteen points and grabbed six rebounds, and the other forward, Bobby Leonard, scored nine points and collected five rebounds. Sophomore Charlie Kraak came off the bench to fill in at forward and center and added eight points and six rebounds. IU's two steady seniors, Sam Miranda and Bobby Masters, started in the back-court and scored ten and nine points, respectively. IU struggled to find consistency in the first half, but pulled away late to outlast the Crusaders 68-59 at the IU Fieldhouse.

In the next game, Schlundt and Scott bounced back with solid performances as both scored in double figures, Schlundt with a game-high sixteen points and Scott with eleven points and nine rebounds. Farley and Leonard chipped in fourteen and thirteen points, respectively, and IU blew out Xavier 92-69. With Schlundt, Farley, and Leonard taking on leading roles, the Hoosiers swept through the preconference schedule at 7-0, including victories over fourteenth-ranked and previously undefeated Wyoming, fifth-ranked Kansas State, and ninth-ranked Notre Dame.

Entering conference play, IU was ranked fifth in the country and was viewed as one of the most dangerous squads in college basketball. They were scoring points at an unbelievable pace, having already notched eighty points or more in four of their seven games. However, over the next two months, they would learn several tough lessons that would be very important for the next two years. The first was that no matter how well you play in the preconference season, it's always a different story when you get into Big Ten play—especially on the road. The second was that a team that is not unified will lose games it should win.

Indiana opened Big Ten play with a twelve-point win over Michigan, led by a terrific eighteen-point, nine-rebound performance from Leonard. Then the Hoosiers went on the road for four straight games. The first was a 73-72 loss at unranked Ohio State. Fourth-ranked IU led by seven points with six minutes to play but the Buckeyes surged back and won the game when guard Dick Dawe's desperation shot swished through the net as time expired. Then the Hoosiers got trounced 78-59 by undefeated, tenth-ranked Iowa in Iowa City. Schlundt had twenty points and eight rebounds, but gave up twenty-seven points and sixteen rebounds to Hawkeye star Chuck Darling. The Hoosiers then dropped their third-straight game by falling to second-ranked Illinois 78-66 in Champaign.

The young Indiana squad showed some fight by pulling out two big victories after that—an 82-77 win at Purdue, led by twenty-nine points from Schlundt, and an 82-69 pounding of Iowa that handed the high-flying Hawkeyes their first loss of the season. That gave IU a 3-3 conference record heading into the semester break, during which the Hoosiers took two weeks off from competition in order to focus on their finals.

McCracken always liked to schedule a non-conference game at the end of the semester layoff so his players could shake off the rust without risking a Big Ten loss. The layoff game usually pitted Indiana against a smaller school like Butler; however, for the 1951–52 season, IU had scheduled high-powered St. John's, which was ranked fifteenth in the country. The thirteenth-ranked Hoosiers continued to practice during the layoff and were pointing toward the showdown with the Redmen. St. John's was another New York school that was implicated in the gambling scandals of the time, but the Catholic university got off lightly because New York district attorney Frank Hogan was a devout Catholic and, either consciously or unconsciously, was not nearly as hard on the Johnnies as he was with players from other schools.

Although the IU team was gearing up for the big St. John's game, one of Mac's young players decided to bend the training rules the night before the game. On Thursday, January 31, two days before the St. John's game, Don Schlundt walked up to student manager Don Defur before practice and said, "Hey, what are you doing tomorrow night?"

"Nothing," Defur said.

"Mikan and the Lakers are playing the [Indianapolis] Olympians tomorrow night," Schlundt said. "Why don't we go up there for the game?"

"Okay, sounds fine to me," Defur excitedly said.

So the two of them went up to Indianapolis and watched the Olympians and the Lakers battle it out. George Mikan was Schlundt's hero and he was thrilled to see him play for the first time, even though the Olympians won the game 85-77.

On the way back to Bloomington, Defur and Schlundt stopped

at a little diner in Mooresville to get a milk shake and a hamburger. While they were eating, two little kids saw the towering Schlundt sitting there and came over to the table and said, "Who are you guys?"

Now, Schlundt knew he wasn't supposed to be out that night because Mac's training rules required that players be in bed early the night before a game. And while Schlundt actually followed the training rules more closely than most of his teammates, he hadn't wanted to pass up the opportunity to watch Mikan play.

So Schlundt smiled and told the kids, "I'm Lou Scott, and this is Sammy Esposito."

The next night, St. John's beat Indiana 65-55. Schlundt had eighteen points and seven rebounds, but gave up twenty-five points and ten rebounds to 6' 7" All-American Bob Zawoluk. Despite the storm clouds surrounding St. John's and other New York schools, the Redmen went on to have a fabulous season. The Johnnies made it all the way to the NCAA championship game, where they lost to Clyde Lovellette and Kansas.

A week after the St. John's game, when Don Defur came out on the floor for practice, Schlundt pulled him aside and said, "Remember those two little kids from Mooresville?"

Defur said, "Yeah."

Schlundt said, "Look down there under that basket." Defur looked and saw the same two kids sitting with their fathers watching practice. It turned out that their fathers both knew Mac because Mooresville wasn't very far from Monrovia.

"We're in trouble," Schlundt said.

Sure enough, at the end of practice, McCracken barked, "Defur and Schlundt, I want to see the two of you in my office." There, Mac bawled out the two of them, telling them unequivocally that they had better not pull a stunt like that again if they wanted to be part of Indiana basketball in the future. Schlundt was a model citizen off the court for the rest of his career.

After the St. John's game, IU went 6-2 to finish the conference schedule and post a record of 16-6 overall and 9-5 in the Big Ten, which landed Indiana in fourth place. During that stretch, another sophomore emerged as a major contributor. Sammy Esposito had battled senior Sam Miranda for a starting guard spot all season. Miranda, who was a terrific ball hander and outside shooter, held the spot for most of the season, but Esposito, who was one of the most dynamic natural athletes in the Big Ten, finally overtook him down the stretch. Esposito's breakout game came at Northwestern, where the Chicago native scored a game-high twenty-five points and triggered a big second-half surge that carried IU to a 96-85 win. After that, Esposito was the starter for the rest of the season and averaged 12.3 points per game over the final six games.

Ironically, Sam Miranda had also displaced a senior starter when he was a sophomore, but Miranda, who had always been a crowd favorite because of his flashy dribbling, took it pretty hard when he was replaced by Esposito. "Miranda was not easy with that," said Jim Schooley, who was a junior that season. "It kind of soured him a little bit."

Miranda's demotion in favor of Esposito was in many ways the final symbolic act in passing the torch of the IU program from the older group of players that had been part of the Lou Watson–Bill Garrett era to the new group of young players who obviously had an extremely bright future ahead of them. Unfortunately, throughout the season there was a natural tension on the team between these two groups, and most of it was because the young players were taking spots in the rotation that the older players felt they had earned over time.

"There were a number of seniors that got beat out for their positions," said Bobby Leonard, "and all of a sudden they weren't the big men on campus anymore. They didn't go for that."

"There were factions on the team at that time," said Schooley. "It just didn't have the camaraderie or cohesiveness. There was some discontent [from the seniors]."

The next season, the roster was even more crowded with talented players, but cohesiveness turned into one of the team's greatest strengths, and much of that change was due to the on-the-court leadership and off-the-court personality of Bobby Leonard and the selfless example of Jim Schooley with the reserve players.

PART TWO

THE RACE AND THE FREE
THROW CONTEST

6

No coach ever starts a game with a poorly inflated ball. And
no coach should ever start a ball game with poorly
conditioned players.

—Branch McCracken

When the IU players officially reported to campus during the third
week of September in 1952, there were three things they had to do:
(1) stop by Coach McCracken's office to let him know they were back
in town; (2) see trainer Spike Dixon down in the basement of the old
gym to get their gear for the season; and (3) start running.

From the time students returned to campus during the week of
September 15 until basketball practice officially opened on October
20, Mac expected his players to run the IU cross-country course and
run the steps of the football stadium every afternoon for six days a
week (they were allowed to rest on Sunday). Mac also expected the
players to discipline themselves to do the running without being reminded by anyone. Of course, Mac always knew if they weren't running or were loafing because he had friends throughout Bloomington
that informed him of nearly everything that went on with his players.
And, occasionally, he had the student managers time the players when
they were running the stadium steps just to keep them honest and to
give them a way to track their own progress.

Beyond observing the players' stamina once practice started and having the trainer check their feet for blisters, there was one major tactic McCracken used to tell whether his players had put in the work to get themselves in basketball condition. At the end of the preseason, Mac always staged a timed race on the cross-country course. All the scholarship players and the others who were trying out for a spot on the roster (what are called "walk-ons" today) had to participate in the race. When the players started running in the fall, they knew that the main goal they were working toward was to get in shape for the season, but the other goal was to make a good showing in the race. That was a quick way to prove to McCracken that they had a strong work ethic and the speed and stamina to handle his running game.

As critical as conditioning was to Mac, there were also other things he wanted his players to work on in the preseason. The big men would skip rope to improve their footwork and coordination. Players who needed to improve their upper-body strength did push-ups and worked with a medicine ball. Others did a little work with dumbbells and weights (although comprehensive weight training was not yet a common practice). But the most important thing next to running was free throw shooting. "I have always maintained that any individual with average coordination could be a good free throw shooter if he spent enough time practicing," stated McCracken. "To become a good free throw shooter takes a lot of daily practice."[1] Mac highly "recommended" that his players work on their free throws every day, so some of the players would shoot a hundred free throws daily. Don Schlundt was the most faithful free throw shooter. He regularly shot *at least* one hundred per day, and he rarely missed a day of shooting practice. It ultimately served him well because he got fouled a lot, and he went on to become the Big Ten's all-time career leader in free throws made (a record he still holds today by a wide margin). Like the cross-country race, there was also a free throw contest at the end of the preseason; however, the free throw contest was even more competitive because the winner got a coveted prize.

The Hoosier lineup for the 1952–53 team had been clearly envisioned since the end of the previous season. Sophomore Don Schlundt would obviously continue to hold down his spot at center. The forwards would be junior Dick Farley, the team's third-leading scorer in 1951–52 (behind Schlundt and Leonard), and junior Charlie Kraak, who played very well as the team's sixth man during his first season on the varsity. Those three gave the Hoosiers one of the tallest frontcourts in college basketball. Schlundt was 6' 10" with his shoes on, Kraak was 6' 6" in sneakers, and Dick Farley was 6' 4" when the Chuck Taylor All Stars were laced up. By comparison, many Big Ten schools of that era had centers that were 6' 5" or 6' 6" and forwards that were just over 6' 0".

In the backcourt, the Hoosiers were set with juniors Bobby Leonard and Sammy Esposito. The 6' 3" Leonard was a sharpshooter who had played mostly as a high-scoring forward as a sophomore since the Hoosiers were so deep at guard. However, moving him over to guard was a logical transition because of Leonard's knack for the outside shot and because working from the outside would give him more room to attack the defense with his slashing ability. Leonard and Esposito were also close pals and had great chemistry playing together.

Down the stretch of the 1951–52 season, the 5' 9" Esposito had emerged as one of IU's rising stars. He was lightning-quick, had great hands, and was very smart with the basketball. He was a terrific passer and could use his athletic ability to break down the defense and create shots for himself and his teammates. He was the quintessential "point guard" (although that term was not yet in use in the early 1950s). Unfortunately, "Espo" didn't come back to IU for his junior year. During the summer of 1952, he signed a $50,000 contract (a $17,000 signing bonus and $11,000 for each of his first three seasons) with the Chicago White Sox, which ended his promising career as a college athlete.

It was tough for Esposito to break the news to McCracken, but he waited until after he had already signed to tell Mac so that Mac couldn't try to talk him out of it. "I called him, because I was back home [in Chicago]," said Esposito. "We talked awhile and he wasn't happy. He knew we had a helluva chance to win it all. He wasn't very happy and I didn't blame him. . . . He told me I was going to be the captain of that ball club."

Later that fall in a speech to the Bloomington Kiwanis Club, McCracken said, "When we lost Esposito, I was down in the dumps. I counted on Sammy as my team leader this year." However, Mc-Cracken then explained what a terrific contract the White Sox had offered Sammy and said, "Can you blame a kid for taking that kind of money? I certainly can't."[2]

However, not having Esposito meant that the Hoosiers had to rely even more heavily on Leonard, who would need to take on more of the ballhandling and floor leadership duties rather than just being a scorer. And there was still the big question of who was going to fill the other guard spot in Esposito's absence. The two candidates with the most experience were returning lettermen Dick Baumgartner and Johnny Wood (the younger brother of Marvin Wood, who coached tiny Milan High School to the Indiana state championship the next year, 1954). Baumgartner and Wood certainly were not potential stars, but both had shown the ability to become solid contributors. They were also both seniors, so their maturity could potentially be an asset on such a young team. But, as luck would have it, both of them got drafted into the military before the basketball season even started.

The losses of Esposito, Wood, and Baumgartner meant that McCracken had no experienced guards returning for the 1952–53 season, and Mac would have to start an unproven player next to converted forward Bobby Leonard in the backcourt. Mac essentially had to find his fifth starter from among three juniors and four sophomores. The juniors were Ron Taylor, who hadn't played a minute as a sophomore, Jack Wright, a tough little player who missed his entire sophomore season because of back surgery, and Jim DeaKyne, a 6' 3" walk-on guard-forward who was a good shooter but not an experienced ball handler. The sophomores were Burke Scott, a quick, hard-nosed player who nearly got called up to the varsity as a freshman, Goethe Chambers, an outside shooting specialist, Dick White, a versatile guard-forward with a nice shooting touch, and Phil Byers, a football player who had played well as a guard on the freshman team. That fall, Byers came to Mac and asked him if he could switch his scholarship from football to basketball and focus all his time to working with the basketball team. McCracken agreed. There was also one other guard in the mix. Paul Poff was a terrific player who had transferred from Detroit in mid-semester the year before, but that meant he wouldn't be available for the Hoosiers until the start of the second semester in February.

The Hoosier frontcourt, in addition to having its starters more clearly set than the backcourt, also had a much clearer picture for its reserves. Farley and Kraak both had great stamina, so they usually stayed in the game unless they were in foul trouble. McCracken had Dick White and Jim DeaKyne to give them a rest when needed, and occasionally Mac inserted White or DeaKyne for Schlundt and moved either Farley or Kraak over to center to have a faster, more mobile team on the court. Schlundt's primary backup at center was big Lou Scott. During the 1950s, most colleges felt fortunate to have one effective player who was taller than 6' 6", but McCracken had the luxury of two. Scott stood nearly 7' 0" when he was wearing his size-sixteen sneakers, and he offered a perfect complement to Schlundt. While Schlundt's greatest strength was scoring ability, Scott specialized primarily in rebounding and defense. With Scott, White, and DeaKyne to fill in for an already stellar frontcourt, McCracken had an outstanding rotation there.

Mac also had a third-string center in 6' 5" Jim Schooley, the only senior on the team. Schooley came to IU as a big-name recruit, and as a sophomore he had been the backup to Bill Garrett. But the arrival of Lou Scott and Don Schlundt meant the end of playing time for Schooley, who outhustled and outworked all the other frontcourt players but simply didn't have the physical gifts to be an outstanding player. "I went to McCracken when my senior year started," said Schooley, "and I told him that I appreciated having the scholarship but I realized that I wasn't contributing a whole lot to the team, and I offered to give up my scholarship so he could bring in somebody else."

Mac replied, "You think you're not contributing, but you're a team leader. You keep these guys straight. You work as hard as anybody during practice and during the games. I told you it was a four-year scholarship and that's what it is. No way would I replace you."

In his Kiwanis speech that fall, McCracken paid special tribute to

Schooley by saying, "In my entire life I have never known a finer boy. He is the type of fellow that every parent wants his son to grow up with. If at any time I ever learned that Jim would not be able to finish school for financial reasons I would personally pay his expenses. I am only sorry that Jim has had to ride the bench for two years, but he has been a wonderful inspiration for the entire team. He has sat the bench like a true champion."[3]

Schooley's terrific team-first attitude ended up being an important example for the rest of the reserves on the 1952–53 squad, and it helped the team develop the kind of unselfishness and cohesion that IU had been missing the previous year. McCracken also held up Schooley as an off-the-court role model for the young players because he felt that some of them were a little too loose in their academic and social lives on campus. "Jim was a scholar," said Bobby Leonard. "Branch liked to use him as a role model. You go to class every day. You go to church on Sunday. Branch wanted us to follow some of the good habits that Jim had, and get away from some of our own bad habits."

Friday, October 17, 1952, was the day of the basketball team's big race on the IU cross-country course, which was located in a wooded part of campus north of the classrooms and campus buildings (today, this is the land where IU's Assembly Hall and Memorial Stadium are). Coach McCracken had the student managers spread out over the course at several key intervals to make sure that none of the players cut any corners or took any shortcuts. And he had the team's senior manager, Ron Fifer, run a timer at the finish line.

Some of the players couldn't stand the cross-country run, while others were intimidated by it. Don Schlundt, who was the most faithful at shooting free throws every day, was not as interested in the conditioning runs, nor was he as disciplined about running on his own because he found it to be extremely boring. "It just never made sense to him to get out and run and run and run," said Gloria Schlundt. "He hated running, and every year he came in last [in the race]."

Ron Taylor dreaded the race. He said, "The thing I hated the most was the cross-country run. I was not the kind of athlete those other guys were. I was afraid I'd come in last. If you weren't a runner, that [cross-country course] was really difficult. You don't have any teammates in that. We had a couple runners in my fraternity and they said, 'Look here Ron, just get out in front and don't let anybody pass you.' Of course, people passed me, but I didn't end up last."

Another player who was initially intimidated by the race was Burke Scott. As a freshman, he was mostly intimidated by the older players and held back to finish tenth in the cross-country race. Burke had not been a huge star in high school the way most of the other IU players had, and so he didn't have a big ego. However, he was one of the few freshmen who got to practice with the varsity during the 1951–52 season, and he performed well enough to gain confidence that he could not only earn some playing time as a Hoosier but could really help the team. With a starting guard spot up for grabs, Burke went all out as a sophomore and easily won the race.

Burke Scott crossed the finish line a full fifteen yards ahead of the second-place runner, Bill Dittus (a sophomore trying out for the varsity). Third place went to Jim Schooley, the only guy over 6' 1" to finish in the top eight. The order of the next group to cross the line was Jack Wright, Dick White, Phil Byers, Junior Phipps (a freshman guard), and Jim Fields (a sophomore trying out for the varsity). The next group finished in the following order: Dick Farley, Bob Leonard, Charlie Kraak, Goethe Chambers, Jim DeaKyne, Paul Poff, and Ron Taylor. Then came the three big guys. Dick Hendricks (a 6' 5" junior transfer who was trying out for the varsity and ended up sticking with the team for the season) finished just in front of Lou Scott, and then Don Schlundt came lumbering in a little bit behind those two.[4]

Some of the virtues of sportsmanship that McCracken regularly preached went out the window during the last part of the race. "It was a war coming up the last hill," said Goethe Chambers. "People were pushing and fighting and shoving. The only guys you didn't have to worry about were the real big guys because they finished about twenty minutes after everybody else was done."

After the race was over, the team went back to the Men's Gymnasium and had a free throw shooting contest. Actually, it was the tenth and final day of the free throw shooting contest. On each of those days, each player shot one hundred free throws and the student managers recorded the results and posted them on a bulletin board. Every player knew exactly how many free throws he had made and how many his teammates had made, so when it came down to the last day, it was clear which players were competing for the top spot. McCracken wanted all the players to show improvement over time and to finish the contest with a solid percentage going into the season. But Mac reserved a special prize for the guys that made the most free throws out of one thousand shot over those ten days. The players who finished first and second were treated to a dinner with Mac and Mary Jo, and the first-place winner always received an additional bonus as well. Some years it was a new suit. Other years it was a crisp $10 bill. Whatever it was, it was always something good, and the players coveted that prize for, if nothing else, the right to brag and taunt their teammates.

The final day of the free throw contest in the fall of 1952 came down to three competitors: Dick White, Jack Wright, and Bobby Leonard. Eventually, it came down to Wright and Leonard, and Leonard prevailed.

That year, McCracken, who was ordinarily extremely tight-fisted with his money, was feeling very generous. He and Mary Jo took Jack Wright and Bobby Leonard over to Nashville, Indiana, a little tourist town about twenty miles east of Bloomington. They ate at the Nashville House, a rustic-looking log cabin that served some of the best food in southern Indiana. It was also one of the more expensive restaurants in the area, but their meals didn't just include an entrée; they also included mashed potatoes, vegetables, fried biscuits with apple butter, and dessert.

Although Mac splurged by taking the boys to such a nice restaurant, he still wanted to keep the bill under control, so he told them, "Get what you want. We always get the chicken here." The chicken dinner was basically the least expensive dinner meal on the menu back then at $1.75 (today it costs about $18.00). "So I look at the menu," said Bobby Leonard, "and it came around to me and I was the last one to order. Everybody else ordered chicken. It got to me and I said, 'Give me a T-bone steak.' You should have seen the look on [Mac's] face! He was a tightwad and a T-bone steak was like $6.00." Mac glared at Bobby for a few seconds, but he didn't say anything, and he didn't have Bobby change his order. Mac probably hadn't realized it yet, but Bobby Leonard knew him very well, and the T-bone steak was simply an ornery gesture that Leonard knew would ruffle the uptight coach a little bit.

As annoyed as Mac may have been that night, as the season unfolded, Mac became extremely pleased to know he had a player on the floor who understood him so clearly. Mac may have lost the kid he had originally foreseen as the leader of his 1953 squad, but it opened the door for one of the best floor leaders in the history of college basketball to step forward.

On Monday, October 20, the 1952–53 college basketball season officially began. The Indiana Hoosiers met at 3:00 PM in the old Men's Gymnasium (where the varsity would practice until the basketball floor was ready in the IU Fieldhouse). Autumn rays of sunlight shone through the long cathedral-like windows in the Men's Gym and landed on a silver-haired mentor who was pacing back and forth and revealing truisms about what it takes to have a winning basketball team and explaining the expectations—both on and off the court—that he had for every boy who played for him.

The team had opened its first practice by working on one-handed and two-handed shots and layups. Then all the players took a seat on the floor and listened to Coach McCracken. Some of the boys sat with their hands draped over their knees, others leaned back on their hands with their legs stretched straight forward, and a few of them sat Indian style. But no matter how they sat, all of them listened closely. It was impossible not to with McCracken. He always spoke loudly and with lots of emotion and charisma. And if he got upset, his deep, twangy voice could rumble like a navy jet, so most of the players tried not to do anything that would upset him.

Mac forcefully reiterated the need to truly become a team, to communicate, to help each other. "He impressed that in order to win anything, one person can't do it," said Dick White. "It has to be a team effort with all working together. Branch was a pretty big star himself and I think that maybe he learned from that experience that you couldn't just concentrate on one or two players."

Bobby Leonard remembered McCracken driving home the point that it didn't matter how many points any one player scored. What mattered was how many games the team won. "He was very decisive in his presentation," said Leonard.

One of Mac's axioms was, "Basic fundamentals and team spirit are the two most important assets of an outstanding team." He also added, "Do the basic things right. Develop individual finesse. Have the proper desire for perfection both as an individual and as a unit and you have a good chance of developing a successful team."[5]

He capped off his speech by telling them that the secret to everything was to play hard, recalled Jack Wright. Mac said, "If there's a ball loose in the center of that floor or any place on that court, if you play for me you better lose some skin gettin' it."

After that, the players worked on a variety of passing drills—short passing, three-man crossover passing drills, and five-man crossover passing drills. Next came the start-and-stop dribbling drill, and the practice ended with Mac's patented fast break drill in which the big guys grabbed the ball off the boards, pivoted, and threw it to a guard on either sideline, who then threw the ball to the other guard or a forward in the middle of the floor. From there, IU executed the "three-man rush" with a ball handler in the middle and players filling the lanes on both sides of him, looking to get an easy score.

For the first several weeks of practice, it was these kinds of drills—for both offense and defense—that McCracken used over and over again. He wanted his team to be sharp on their fundamentals and up to speed on the skills they would need to run his system. "He just fundamentaled the daylights out of us," said Burke Scott.

At the end of each practice, the players also got a special treat—fresh-squeezed orange juice in Spike Dixon's training room. The players loved the fresh-squeezed orange juice (which wasn't as common or as easy to get back then) and it was available almost every day. McCracken and Dixon wanted to pump the players full of as much orange juice as possible because they believed it helped keep the players healthy and prevented them from getting as many colds.

On the day college basketball kicked off its new season, Kansas coach Phog Allen was not with his team in Lawrence, Kansas. Instead, he was in Chicago preparing a college all-star team to play an exhibition game against the Minneapolis Lakers, and he also gave a memorable speech at a sports luncheon in the Windy City. Allen used the speech as an opportunity to campaign for cleaning up college basketball, which was still licking its wounds from the CCNY and LIU scandals. As he often did, Allen railed against commercialism invading college sports. He stated, "There still is a lot of folding money being passed under the counter" to star athletes being recruited in major conferences. Because Allen felt that the NCAA had little power or skill to prevent this type of corruption, he recommended that a national commissioner be appointed to lead college athletics. "Such a man must be prominent and respected like J. Edgar Hoover," said Allen. "He must rule college sports like [Kenesaw Mountain] Landis ruled baseball. Give such a man two years to study the situation thoroughly and then let him go to work with an iron hand."[6]

In the weeks following Allen's pronouncement, the storm that hovered over college basketball ended up swirling around Allen's former protégé, Adolph Rupp. Earlier in the year, the NCAA had found Rupp and Kentucky guilty of violating subsidization and eligibility rules (paying players and using players who should have been ineligible) and the NCAA put the school on a one-year probation. The NCAA also fined the UK athletic department $100,000 (a huge sum at the time) and the SEC subsequently banned Kentucky from conference play for the 1952–53 season. Rupp and the UK athletic department then tried to line up a full season of non-conference games before the NCAA stepped in and asked all member schools not to schedule games with the Wildcats, effectively banning Kentucky from all collegiate competition that season. On November 4, 1952, less than two weeks after Phog Allen's speech in Chicago, the University of Kentucky announced that it would not appeal the NCAA's findings and that it would not schedule any games for 1952–53. However, in an act of defiance, UK officials said they would not take any disciplinary action against Rupp, who would remain the head coach and be fully paid for the 1952–53 campaign.

Kentucky had been the most successful program in college basketball in the postwar years, winning three national championships,
and they had the talent to be a major force again in 1952–53. Unfortunately, when Rupp's methods of building successful teams came to
light, Kentucky became a public symbol of everything that had gone
wrong with college basketball in the postwar years.

The official arrival of the new basketball season also brought dis-
cussion about important new rules changes in NCAA basketball, plus
a new scheduling format in the Big Ten that promised to produce an
undisputed champion.

One of the most important rules changes was that when a player
was fouled when not in the act of shooting, his team could no longer
waive off the free throws and simply take the ball out-of-bounds. This
rule (in an era where there was no shot clock) made it much more
difficult for the winning team to simply stall in the final minutes and
not allow the other team to get possession of the ball. Whenever a
player was fouled when not in the act of shooting, he now *had* to
shoot a free throw. The new "one-and-one" free throw format was also
added, although it worked the exact opposite of the way it works today.
If a player made the first free throw, then the opposition got the ball.
If the player missed the first free throw, the player was then awarded
a second chance (two years later, for the 1954–55 season, the rule was
changed so that the player was awarded a second free throw only if
he *made* the first free throw). The one-and-one and free throw rule
was only in effect during the first thirty-seven minutes of play. During
the final three minutes of regulation and any overtime periods, a player
was automatically awarded two free throws on non-shooting fouls. The
other exception was when a player was fouled in the act of shooting
and still made the shot, in which case the player was automatically
awarded only one free throw (called the "and one" rule). The overall
effect of these rules changes was to give teams that were behind in
the final minutes a better chance of staging a comeback by fouling at
the end of the game to stop the clock and regain possession of the
ball. This added some additional drama to the end of games for spectators.

There were also some rules changes dealing with intentional fouls.

If a player was intentionally fouled at any point in a game, that player was automatically awarded two free throws, even when a player was fouled in the act of shooting and made the shot. However, another rule change stipulated that all body contact after a dead ball was to be ignored by the officials unless it involved unsportsmanlike conduct. These new changes were intended to cut down on the kind of rough play that occasionally broke out in college basketball.

Another change was that an offensive player could freely touch the ball when it was on the cylinder. In 1944, it was ruled that a defensive player could not touch the ball when it was on the cylinder (now called "goaltending"), but it was unclear whether an offensive player could touch it until the new ruling came out before the 1952–53 season. This rule was helpful for teams like Indiana that had big men who could reach up and tip in shots that were bouncing around the cylinder. (Later, this was called "offensive goaltending," and in 1957 a new rule was passed that made it a violation.)

There are a couple other rules to keep in mind about college basketball in the 1952–53 season. The year before, a new rule was put in place to change all college games from two twenty-minute halves to four ten-minute quarters (for the 1954–55 season, it was changed back to two twenty-minute halves). Also, although the three-second lane violation had been in effect since 1944–45, the free throw lane was only six feet wide during this era (it was widened to twelve feet in 1956–57). This meant that low-post players such as Indiana's Don Schlundt could set up very close to the basket to battle for position. If a talented big man like Schlundt caught the ball just outside the lane, it was extremely difficult to stop him from scoring without fouling him.

Of the changes made for 1952–53, the one that most pleased Branch McCracken had nothing to do with fouls and free throws. The Big Ten decided to go to an eighteen-game round-robin schedule, and McCracken was thrilled. "This gives every team an equal chance," McCracken said. "No one can slip in the back door."[7] In other words, a lesser team could not win the Big Ten championship simply because it got a favorable draw in scheduling and a good team could not be denied the title simply because it got a tough draw. With every team playing every other team in a home-and-home series, the Big Ten champion would have to earn the title on the court. Of course, that also meant that each team would have to play eighteen conference games, which left few scheduling slots for non-conference opponents, and it also meant that conference play would have to begin in mid-December rather than in January.

During the first several weeks of practice, McCracken began to slowly ratchet up the intensity as the team moved from doing mostly drills and working on fundamentals to doing more all-out scrimmages that included long stretches of the fast break offense against the full-court press defense (one of McCracken's favorite methods for building conditioning).

Early on, junior Jim DeaKyne drew McCracken's ire by reporting to practice overweight. "McCracken wanted you to come into the season in shape," said Bob Howard, a sophomore student manager. "Jim came in heavy. He was thirty pounds overweight. So McCracken wouldn't let him take his sweatshirt or sweatpants off [during practice], trying to make him sweat it down. He wouldn't let him go rest either. He just worked him until he got that weight down where McCracken wanted it. It took at least a month before he could take his sweatpants off."

The other colorful issue during the early weeks of practice was a confrontation between Charlie Kraak and Lou Scott. Schlundt, Kraak, and Scott had a rebounding move they worked on over and over again in practice. They would go up and grab the ball off the board with two hands, bring the ball down so that it was right across from their upper chest, stick out their elbows to both sides, pivot with the elbows still sticking out (to keep opposing players from reaching for the ball), and prepare to make an outlet pass. Kraak was by far the best at this technique, and the best rebounder in general. "If the ball went on the backboard, it was his," said Goethe Chambers. "And in practice it was his. If you were in the way, he'd run you over. That's just the way it was." There wasn't anything malicious about Kraak. He was just big, well-muscled, and extremely determined to do his job as the team's leading rebounder.

"Chuck was a helluva physical specimen. Nobody fooled around with him," said senior manager Ron Fifer. "He could clear the backboards."

One day, Burke Scott was trying to sneak in and grab a rebound in practice and Kraak accidentally caught him right in the mouth with an elbow and knocked several of his teeth out. Kraak, who felt bad about hurting the little guard, leaned over and said, "Burke, you know you're not supposed to be under here."

Burke didn't hold any hard feelings toward Kraak. He knew it was an accident and that it was partly his own fault for fighting with the big guys for a rebound. In fact, Burke pointed to another guy as one to watch for physical play. Burke said, "The guy that was a mean machine was Lou Scott. He roughed up [Schlundt] every day in practice. He gave Don a hard time. Don had to work hard [to score on Lou]. We all knew that was helping Schlundt, and so did Mc-Cracken."

As the 1952–53 season began, Lou Scott had made enough progress that McCracken was experimenting with the idea of having a "double pivot" by playing Schlundt and Lou Scott at the same time. That meant that Lou was not only competing with Schlundt for minutes, but he was also competing with Charlie Kraak.

In one of the early practices, Kraak and Scott were battling for a rebound and Lou got hit by one of Kraak's inadvertent elbows. Lou wasn't happy about it and gave Kraak a shove, which led to a pushing and shoving match that was eventually broken up by their teammates.

Jim Schooley explained, "Lou was from a rough-and-tumble background and Charlie wasn't going to back down at all. But I think they became very good friends after that."

After practice, big Lou felt bad about the incident and went over to see Charlie at his fraternity house, and the two of them talked it out. "From that time on, he and I were close," said Kraak. In fact, the two of them remained close friends long after leaving IU.

As for the incident itself, Mac wasn't too concerned about it. Kraak said, "I think McCracken enjoyed it because it showed a lot of spirit."

Mac always preached good sportsmanship and good manners, but he also wanted his players to show aggressiveness and toughness on the court. Occasionally, when his team lost, Mac would grab the box score and look at the personal fouls. If a player didn't have any fouls— even if he scored a lot of points—Mac usually felt that the player hadn't given enough effort on defense, and he would let the player know it. Because the Hoosiers played so hard and aggressively, some opposing coaches accused McCracken of encouraging rough play. When asked about that, Mac quickly replied, "No, I don't!" Then, after a slight pause, he added, "But I don't discourage it!"[8]

In practice, McCracken was an undeniable taskmaster, both in the way he ran drills to demand his players master the fundamentals and in the way he made the players scrimmage at full speed for unmercifully long stretches of time. His reasoning with fundamentals was that he was always shooting for perfection from his players and wanted them to make perfection the goal for themselves. With scrimmages, he used extended, full-speed game conditions to maintain and elevate the conditioning of his players. Mac was fond of saying, "I have heard a lot of my players make this statement many times: 'The game is a lot easier than our practice.' We go on the theory that if a player can take the work in practice, he won't have any trouble going full speed the entire game."[9]

McCracken found a way to constantly push his players in practice without burning them out. In fact, many of his players have said they enjoyed the practices, and a lot of that had to do with Mac's attitude during practices. He was almost always very animated, engaged, and upbeat during practices. He completely threw himself into his task of developing basketball players and building a successful team, and his enthusiasm and energy were contagious.

Jay McCreary, a member of McCracken's 1940 championship team, stated, "The scrimmages were killers. We would start scrimmaging hard and quit two hours later, and wouldn't stop for anything—I mean nothing! We wouldn't even leave the floor for water. McCracken was a driver, but he drove himself. It was sort of an infectious thing. When the man ahead of you is driving, you don't feel so bad about working your fanny off. We did things to perfection. I mean, if we had a certain movement we had to go through, we went through it until we could do it in our sleep."[10]

One guy on the 1953 team who loved McCracken's practices—especially the scrimmages—was Burke Scott. "The harder he worked us, the better we liked it," said Burke. "We never complained. We never griped. We didn't ever think about when practice was going to be over." Still, even though Burke probably had better endurance than anyone on the team, there was one night after an intense scrimmage when he took a shower and lay down on one of the benches between the lockers for a quick rest and was so tired that he fell fast asleep and didn't wake up for more than an hour.

Phil Byers also had good memories from practices that season. "They were always positive and upbeat," he said.

Goethe Chambers said the players also got "a lot of praise" from McCracken when the Hoosiers executed what Mac wanted in practice. "He was quick to compliment and quick to criticize if you had it coming," said Chambers.

Jack Wright remembered that Mac could get very excitable. "You may make a nice play and he would come over and just almost lift you off the floor and say, 'Son that was a great play!' He'd really get into it. You'd think he was going to bounce you off the wall," said Wright. "And if you did something wrong he would come over and say, 'Now that's *not* the way to do that!' He always got your attention. . . . I was a little bit afraid of him because I knew he could come down hard. It was just like being afraid of your father and mother. . . . When he told you something on the basketball floor, he'd expect you to do that."

Whether they loved Mac's practices or not, all the players could admit how extremely difficult they were. "Practice was an absolute bear," said Bobby Leonard. "Practice was a monster because of the way Branch coached."

Ron Taylor remarked, "The practices were hard. We had an hour-and-a-half or two-hour practice and I was always beat afterwards. I was so tired I couldn't even eat. Every day was like that. He worked us hard."

Dick White reiterated that the practices were always tough, but he added that the way McCracken conducted practice was invaluable for developing the conditioning the team needed to run the fast break in games.

Once, when the team did a great job of flying the ball downcourt for a fast break but then missed the shot at the end, McCracken yelled out, "Boys! Boys! Boys! That's an awful long way to run and still not score."[11]

When one player helped out another player who was out of position defensively, McCracken yelled out, "You're operatin', you're operatin'. Now you're operatin' boys! Talk to each other. Help each other out. Talk! Talk!"[12]

During one practice, Burke Scott was racing upcourt on the fast break and threw the ball ahead to Charlie Kraak. Kraak was furiously sprinting ahead of the pack but not looking up for the ball, and Burke's pass hit him in the back of the head. Mac blew his whistle, threw his arms in the air, and bellowed, "Whoa, ho, ho! Kraak! You've got to know where the ball is at all times!"

Student manager Bobby Howard remembered a move that McCracken did on a regular basis. "[Mac] would get in the crouch position like a guard with his arms up," said Howard. "He'd yell out all the time, 'Hands up! Hands up!' He'd get out there in a crouch position and go left and then right like he was guarding someone. He would stop everyone and make sure they were all watching him. He'd say, 'This is the way to move your feet. Don't cross your feet. Be hunched down so you can go forward, you can go sideways, and you can go backwards.' "

Mac had the team focused mostly on intense scrimmaging by the middle of November. However, there was one skill he continuously drilled his team on throughout the season: shooting. Mac firmly believed that good fundamentals in shooting could turn a poor shooter into a reliable one and a good shooter into a great shooter, and McCracken was a stickler for getting his players to develop proper form and understand the nuances of how to put the ball in the basket. While his players worked on practicing various types of shots, Mac would pace back and forth in the gym and shout out various tips:

"Go straight up in the air!"

"Get spring in your legs!"

"Soft! Soft! Use a good, soft touch."

"Lay the ball up there, don't throw it."

"Expect the ball to go in every time you turn loose of it!"

"You miss one—shake it off—get the next one."

"Relax—I'll tie up [enough] on the bench for all of you!"[13]

Of course, Mac's favorite pet phrases always came in threes. In the games, his favorites were "Go! Go! Go!" and "Run! Run! Run!" During practice his favorite was "Hustle! Hustle! Hustle!"

At the beginning of a new season, Branch McCracken almost always played the devil's advocate when talking about his team's prospects. He would usually speak about his team's deficiencies and about the strengths of the other teams in the conference. So when Mac admitted that his 1952–53 squad could be pretty good and that they might "win a few games," it appeared that McCracken secretly felt he had quite a team in the making.

The biggest reason for McCracken's optimism was the improvement of Bobby Leonard, the team's MVP from the previous season. From Leonard's showing in the first month of practice, the transition from forward to guard looked like it was going to be miraculously smooth. In fact, Leonard looked even better at guard than he had been at forward because he was a much better ball handler and floor leader than McCracken had anticipated, and Mac was becoming very comfortable with the idea of having the ball in Leonard's hands.

Entering the season, McCracken said, "Leonard can be one of the best ball players I've ever had with added experience. Right now, he is the [team's] greatest shot."[14]

Mac's other key returnees—Don Schlundt, Dick Farley, and Charlie Kraak—had also improved as well, and were set to hold down starting spots. The fifth starting spot remained up in the air until a few days before the Hoosiers' opening game with Valparaiso on December 1.

The Hoosiers' greatest strength heading into the 1952–53 season was the ability to put points on the board. The previous season, IU had set a new Big Ten record by scoring 1,035 points (73.9 points per

117

game) in conference play, and they had led the Big Ten in field goal percentage by shooting .349. Individually, the previous school record of 302 points in a season, set by John Wallace in 1945–46, was shattered by both Don Schlundt (379) and Bob Leonard (319). The Hoosiers also had Dick Farley, who could have been the leading scorer on most of the other teams in the conference. For IU, Farley focused primarily on defense and rebounding, but could step up to score points in bunches when the occasion demanded it.

McCracken's two biggest concerns were defense and a lack of experience on the second team. On the defensive end, the big concern was with Schlundt. The other starters were all tough defenders, but Schlundt was laid back and not very aggressive, and Mac hoped that Schlundt could strengthen his defense after a year of Big Ten play under his belt. McCracken pointed out that as many points as Schlundt scored—he broke nearly every IU scoring record as a freshman—it was likely that he allowed opposing centers to score even more points against him because his defense was so weak during his rookie season.[15] To help keep opposing centers in check, Mac decided to use Farley or Kraak to defend them, especially if the big man was shorter than 6' 6". The Hoosiers' other main weakness was that few of its bench players had any significant experience, which made the second team unpredictable. The frontcourt had Jim Schooley and Lou Scott for relief duty, and the two of them had both seen some spotty reserve action in the past. The backcourt, however, had no experienced reserves and was definitely a major concern.

Mac was not a big fan of polls and team rankings, which had sprung up in the late 1940s. He was especially dubious about the value of preseason polls. At the beginning of 1952–53, he stated, "These pre-season polls are usually based on a team's performance the previous year. Look Magazine has us rated 12th in the nation, while Illinois is number one. . . . I'm glad that the Illini are at the top. It's the roughest spot."[16]

When asked what he thought of Indiana being in the twelfth spot, Mac simply replied, "That rating is alright now, but it won't satisfy me at the end of the season."[17]

More than three thousand freshmen arrived on the IU campus for the 1952–53 school year. One of them was a wide-eyed young fellow named Charley Cogan from tiny little Clinton, Indiana, which sat on the Wabash River about fifteen miles north of Terre Haute. Charley loved basketball. He loved to play it and he loved to watch it. Growing up, he was a devoted fan of IU basketball and of Indiana high school basketball. When he came to IU, he looked forward to watching Bobby Leonard play for the Hoosiers because Charley knew just how good Leonard was. Bobby had led Terre Haute Gerstmeyer to several convincing wins over Cogan's Clinton Wildcats.

Cogan wasn't nearly good enough to play basketball in college, but he signed up to play intramural ball at IU and registered for a physical education class that allowed him to play basketball and several other sports. Like most of his fellow freshmen, he was a bit overwhelmed at first by the size of the school and the masses of students, but eventually he made some new friends and happily settled into the rhythm of college life. He eagerly bought a Student Sports Card, which got him into all the home football and basketball games. By the beginning of November, the football team was already 1-3 in conference play and headed toward another losing season, and so students went to the football games for two reasons: to watch and listen to IU's award-winning "Marching 100" band and to start talking about the prospects of the IU basketball team, including who the starters might be and the team's chances in the Big Ten.

One day after playing basketball in his physical education class, Charley popped through the second-floor doors of the Men's Gym and scuttled down a set of metal stairs that went from the outside of the old gym and opened into the west end of the IU Fieldhouse. Once he got to the bottom, Charley looked up and saw something that stopped him in his tracks, then slowly drew him near. The cavernous IU Fieldhouse had a sawdust floor that stretched nearly the length of a football field. On this day, it was emptied of the mammoth bleachers that seated 10,000 fans during basketball season. However, what was happening in the middle of the Fieldhouse is what caught Charley Cogan's eye.

"Workers were putting sections of the [raised basketball] floor to-gether," said Cogan. "They were literally [in the middle of] it. There were still sections to be joined and put together. It just fascinated me to see something like that, because it never occurred to me that you could put a floor together. I had been to Butler Fieldhouse and places like that, but they were always permanent floors at ground level. Here was something that, to my surprise, was taken down at the end of basketball season and put back together before the next basketball season. It was a modern marvel to me."

As Cogan stood marveling at the varsity basketball floor being assembled, he realized there was a tall, burly man with white hair and a long topcoat standing next to him. Cogan said to the tall man, "Wow, I didn't know our basketball court was so huge!"[18] The man smiled at the awestruck freshman and told him he always enjoyed watching the floor come back together. He went on to talk about how great a place IU was for basketball. Cogan told him that he could hardly wait for the basketball season to arrive, then ran over to meet his friends, who were waiting for him at the exit.

As they walked away from the Fieldhouse on the way to their next classes, one of the friends said, "I didn't realize you knew such im-portant people, Charley."

Another friend quickly asked, "Did he give you any tips on how we'll do this season?"

Charley replied, "What are you guys talking about? We were just discussing the floor being put together."[19]

Charley's friends let him know that the guy he had been talking to was IU basketball coach Branch McCracken. Charley had never seen an IU basketball game before. He had only heard games on the radio and read about them in the newspaper, so he didn't know what Coach McCracken looked like. As it turned out, between two of his classes, Charley would regularly see Coach McCracken a couple of times a week walking across campus near the Jordan River, and when he passed by, Charley would typically nod or say "hello" and Mac always gave a friendly reply. Three months later, Charley Cogan and the IU coach would meet again.

Back in the IU Fieldhouse, Branch McCracken finished watching the basketball floor being reassembled with a sense of reverence and satisfaction, as if a great hand were reaching down from heaven and putting the pieces of the universe back in place, just where they should be. Another season of basketball was about to begin at Indiana University.

HERE WE GO AGAIN

7

To those who may be about to watch their first collegiate basketball season, we must explain at this time that the term "Hurryin' Hoosiers" means a McCracken-driven jet machine powered by 10 legs, steered by 10 keen eyes, and motivated by the desire of 5 fighting hearts to dethrone the University of Illinois.

—Herb Michelson, *Indiana Daily Student*

The issue of who was going to be IU's fifth starter, winning the spot that had been reserved for Sammy Esposito, remained up in the air until the final week of practice—the week of Thanksgiving. IU students had most of the week off and most of them went home for the holiday, but the Hoosier basketball players stayed in Bloomington. Their season opener against Valparaiso was the following Monday, the day classes resumed, so Branch and Mary Jo had the whole team over for Thanksgiving dinner at their tiny house on 801 South High Street. And since the campus was pretty much empty, many of the basketball players also came back for leftovers later in the weekend.

Going into that final week of practice, the competition for the starting guard spot had narrowed down to three players: sophomores Burke Scott and Phil Byers, and junior Jim DeaKyne. Scott and Byers were both hard-nosed defenders, while DeaKyne had a little more experience and was a much better outside shooter. By the weekend, McCracken decided to go with Burke Scott, who was a pesky and active defender but whose offense was a big question mark. It didn't hurt that Scott was the fastest and most athletic player on the team.

The year before, as a freshman, Scott nearly got a chance to play on the varsity. Don Schlundt ended up being the only Hoosier freshman who took advantage of the Korean War waiver and made the varsity, and he played with the big boys from start to finish. But Burke Scott and Jack Tilly had played so well on the freshman team that McCracken decided to call them up to the varsity in midseason. Unfortunately, the first day the two of them reported for varsity practice, McCracken told them, "You can forget it. You both flunked a class." Scott had flunked U.S. History and he was ineligible for the rest of the season, but he still got to practice with the varsity and got some valuable schooling from it. "I used to go to practice every day and guard [Sammy] Miranda while he practiced dribbling full court," said Scott, "and then Esposito would do the same thing. I learned to play pretty good defense that way."

Jack Tilly, who had been an Indiana all-star as a senior in high school, also got to practice with the varsity and played very well. However, he left school that spring and didn't return to IU for his sophomore year.

Burke Scott almost left IU that first year, too, although he nearly left much sooner than Tilly. During his first semester on campus, he wasn't sure if he wanted to stay in Bloomington. "I wasn't crazy about college," said Burke. "I wasn't crazy about being away from home." At one point, he basically decided he was going to drop out, but his father gave him a call.

"I heard you were quitting school," Burke's dad said.

"Yeah," Burke said.

"That's fine if you think you can come back here and find a job," his dad replied. "Just don't let me catch your little ass in the city limits."

That changed Burke's mind. "So I decided after him saying that, I thought I'd better stay at IU, and that was the end of that," Burke said. "The thought of quitting didn't enter my mind anymore."

During the rest of his freshman year Burke turned things around in the classroom and gained confidence on the court by holding his own against the varsity. McCracken even gained enough confidence in Burke as a freshman that he didn't mind singling the kid out to illustrate a lesson during one practice that a bunch of fans had come to watch.

"I remember one day there was a couple thousand people in there watching us practice," Burke remarked. "When I played in high school, our coach let us make some fancy passes, behind the back and all of that. McCracken didn't believe in that kind of stuff. So one day in practice I made a behind-the-back pass to somebody and he blew the whistle and he told all of the players to go to the side of the floor. He was showing off in front of those [fans]. So he got the student managers out there in the middle of the court and he got me, and he made me throw the ball about twenty-five times behind my back to one of the managers. Then he said, 'Are you getting tired yet?' And I said, 'No, not really.' And then he said, 'Let me tell you something. That last pass you made is the last one of those that you're going to make as long as you're up here with me.' So I never made another pass like that. And those people in the stands were about to go crazy. That's the kind of [coach] he was. He didn't mean a whole lot by it. He was just trying to prove a point and show off a little bit."

When McCracken penciled Burke Scott into the starting lineup at the beginning of the 1952–53 season, the speedy sophomore did not have the position completely locked up. There was a feeling that Byers or DeaKyne could still grab the starting spot if Burke didn't perform. However, Burke quickly closed the door on that possibility.

There was no chance that any of the Hoosiers were going to take the Valparaiso Crusaders lightly in the season opener on Monday, December 1 at 7:30 PM. Even though Indiana was undoubtedly favored to win the game, Coach Kenny Suesens's team was fully expected to give IU all it could handle. The year before, Valpo had come into the Fieldhouse and led the Hoosiers at halftime, but they couldn't keep pace in the second half as IU survived for a 68-59 win. The 1952–53 Crusaders were young and tall (with a front line that was 6' 8", 6' 3", and 6' 3"), and they were already 2-0 with a 104-68 win over Hope (Michigan) and a 62-50 victory over Concordia of St.

Louis. Valpo's big veteran center, Don Bielke, had scored a total of thirty-eight points in those two opening games and was expected to give Schlundt an early test to see how much the Hoosier pivotman had improved since his rookie campaign.

On the day of the Valpo game, the Indiana players began their regular game-day routine that they would keep throughout the season for home games. By 3:00 PM (when the players would normally be practicing), all the players were supposed to be in their rooms lying down to get a final rest. They had to meet at the Indiana Memorial Union at 5:00 PM sharp for the pregame meal with Coach McCracken. And when Branch McCracken said 5:00, he meant 5:00, or better yet 4:45. A player had better not be there at 5:01.

"Don't ever be late," remembered Bobby Leonard. "[McCracken] would not stand for being late for even one minute. . . . When he set a time for something you better be there on time." In fact, most of the players planned to arrive *at least* fifteen minutes early to any team activity, just in case there were any unexpected holdups along the way.

For the team meal, the Hoosiers always had the same thing: a glass of water (no ice), a five-ounce filet steak, a five-ounce baked potato (prebuttered), two pieces of dry toast with one pat of butter, and coffee or tea with milk and sugar.[1] A number of the players, especially several of the starters, were too nervous to eat much. Farley, Leonard, and Burke Scott didn't eat much at all. Farley was the worst. Off the court, he was normally a quiet, laid-back guy with an easy smile, but when it came time to play basketball, he was a bundle of nerves. He would get so worked up right before a game that he would usually vomit in the locker room, so he wisely didn't eat a whole lot at the pregame meal.

After they finished the meal, McCracken and the players walked out of the north side of the Indiana Memorial Union and across Seventh Street to the IU Fieldhouse to get dressed and start warming up. The players slipped on their cream-colored satin shorts and belts, as well as their close-fit cotton IU basketball jerseys which had "INDI-ANA" sewn across the front in raised block lettering. Next, the players took turns in the training room, where trainer Spike Dixon and his student assistants taped the ankles of every player. Then it was time to pull on their thick wool socks with a red band at the top (two or three pairs in some cases) and lace up their white Chuck Taylor All Star sneakers with red laces. Finally, they pulled on their red satin warm-up pants and their red satin warm-up jackets, which had a large white "I" sewn on the left side. Coach McCracken emerged in his customary navy blue suit with a white shirt and red tie, and he had on his classic black-rimmed glasses (which he didn't always wear during practice). Mac had just started wearing the glasses two seasons earlier and they gave him the look of a benevolent basketball professor, whereas without the glasses he looked more rugged and foreboding.

While the varsity was getting dressed and taped, out on the Fieldhouse floor the freshman team was having an intrasquad scrimmage, red vs. white, while the crowd filed in to take their seats in the bleachers. This was the regular routine between 6:00 and 7:00 PM.

A ticket to the game simply got you in the door at the IU Fieldhouse. There were no assigned seats, so you had to get there early to get yourself a good spot. The students usually took up one whole side of the giant wooden bleachers, and there were unofficial areas for each class. The seniors, of course, got the center court area. Different groups had their own clusters where they would sit together, and sometimes they even devised their own cheers. For example, fraternities, sororities, and some of the residence halls had their own clusters. The football players usually sat together, and they had their own cheer they loved to shout. It went like this: "Hoo-sa-saa! Hoo-sa-saa! Hit 'em in the head with a Koo-ba-saa!"

The Valparaiso game was packed, but it wasn't a sellout. There were about a thousand tickets available on game day and they sold for $1.50 each at the Fieldhouse ticket window. The public could also purchase season tickets for $16.50 for all eleven home games. On the day of the game, IU athletic director Paul "Pooch" Harrell announced that season tickets had been selling very well, right on pace with their usual numbers. There was a fear that ticket sales might decrease because, for the first time ever, ten of Indiana's eleven home games would be televised. WTTV in Bloomington had a new $85,000 mobile unit to transmit the games from the IU Fieldhouse, and the Valparaiso game was the only home game that would not be televised.

Once the freshmen finished their game and cleared the floor, the IU pep band struck up a loud and upbeat tune, and the IU players burst out of the locker room and jogged up to the court while the home crowd erupted into a stirring ovation. The band continued to play while the Hoosiers ran through their layup line, shot free throws, and practiced shots from inside and outside. And if the music wasn't loud or upbeat enough, the band director got an earful from McCracken to kick it up a notch. Mac wanted his boys fired up by game time.

When warm-ups were over, the starting lineup of the visiting Crusaders and Coach Kenny Suesens were introduced to cordial applause, and the starters lined up on the foul line across from their bench. Then, the IU starting lineup was introduced to frenzied applause and took their spot on the opposite foul line, and the biggest round of applause came when Coach McCracken was announced. Next, with both sets of starters still standing out on the floor and the coaches and reserves standing along the sidelines, a huge American flag was raised up from the middle of the floor to the rafters and a spotlight shone on it as the national anthem played.

Then, while an early snowfall covered the ground outside the IU Fieldhouse, the Hoosiers kicked off one of the greatest seasons in IU basketball history.

Valparaiso snatched the opening tip and the Crusaders struck first blood when guard Jim Howard buried a quick shot to give the visitors a 2-0 lead. However, Bobby Leonard didn't let that stand for long. He scored two quick baskets to put IU on top, and the Hoosiers never trailed again. IU took a 20-9 lead after 6:25 had elapsed, as Valparaiso focused its defense on Schlundt and the Indiana forwards and guards found room for easy scores. The Hoosiers dominated the defensive backboards in the opening ten-minute quarter and used that advantage to trigger fast break after fast break. At the end of the first period, IU led 23-14. Lou Scott replaced Schlundt for most of the second quarter and had three tip-ins to help push the Hoosier lead to 47-27 at the break.

IU came out of the locker room and the starters triggered an 8-0 run to open the second half and push the lead to 55-27, with Leonard scoring twice in that key stretch. McCracken experimented with some of his reserves for the rest of the period and the lead shrunk to 71-46 at the end of the third quarter. In the opening minute of the fourth quarter, Dick Farley fouled out of the game. But then Burke Scott and Bobby Leonard each drove the lane and scored to give IU a comfortable cushion. In the middle of the fourth quarter, Mac sent in Lou Scott and had both of his big centers in the game at the same time, which didn't last long as Schlundt fouled out at the 4:13 mark. Then Burke Scott took over down the stretch to finish off the visitors. Burkie had four field goals and a free throw in the fourth quarter, including a twenty-footer in the final minute that gave Indiana its final victory margin of 95-56. During that final quarter, senior Jim Schooley got in the game and scored on a tip-in, the first points of his collegiate career.

Bobby Leonard had triggered the IU attack all night and he finished with sixteen points and six rebounds. However, the surprise star of the game was Burke Scott, who finished with sixteen points, six rebounds, and six assists (assists weren't part of the official stats back then, but one newspaper reporter credited Burke with six assisted field goals). All in all, IU had six players in double figures. Don Schlundt had thirteen points, Charlie Kraak had thirteen points and twelve rebounds, Dick Farley had twelve points (on 5-for-7 shooting from the floor), and Lou Scott had eleven points off the bench. Jim DeaKyne and Dick White also chipped in five points apiece off the bench.

IU put up ninety-five shots from the field and hit forty-two of them for a .442 percentage (which was outstanding for that era) while holding Valpo to only sixty-nine shots. The Crusaders only hit sixteen, for a .232 shooting percentage. Even though they were the home team, the aggressive Hoosiers were called for twenty-nine fouls to only fourteen for the Crusaders. That put Indiana right on pace from the previous season, when IU led the nation in personal fouls with 644, or 29.3 per game (in fact, the Hoosiers were tops in the nation in fouls for two years in a row and had been in the top eight for five straight seasons). Indiana's ninety-five points against Valparaiso tied the Fieldhouse record set the previous season against Ohio State. The thirty-nine-point win also set a new record for victory margin in a season opener.

By all accounts, the Hoosiers looked great. They owned the backboards against a team with good size, they ran the fast break like they were in midseason form, and they had great scoring balance. Of course, McCracken still found a couple of soft spots. IU shot only eleven of twenty-two (.500) from the foul line, and IU's interior defense allowed Don Bielke to score a game-high seventeen points. And, as good as IU looked against Valpo, there was little time for pats on the back, because the Hoosiers' schedule was about to get a lot tougher.

Because of the expanded eighteen-game Big Ten schedule, IU had only four scheduling slots for non-conference opponents, and one of those was reserved for a midseason showdown with Butler. That left Indiana with only three games in December before the start of conference play. After Valparaiso, IU went on the road for two games against top-ranked opponents Notre Dame and Kansas State.

"You couldn't pick two stronger teams for us at this stage of the campaign," said Coach McCracken. "Notre Dame, one of the top teams in the Midwest, is hard to defeat on its home floor, and Kansas State was rated second in the nation in the [United Press] poll."[2]

In that preseason UP poll, the Hoosiers were ranked No. 8, and even received one first-place vote. Notre Dame was ranked No. 12 and Minnesota was ranked No. 17. The defending national champion, Kansas, was ranked No. 19. The No. 1–ranked team in the land—by a wide margin—was Illinois. The Fighting Illini were the two-time defending Big Ten champs and were coming off a strong third-place finish in the NCAA Tournament the previous season. They returned five of their first six players and had a squad with great size, speed, experience, and depth. According to most of the preseason polls and publications, they were the nearly unanimous favorite for the 1953 national championship. On Thursday, December 4, the same day the poll was released, an AP report came out of Chicago from the Big Ten coaches meeting. Not surprisingly, the basketball coaches selected

Illinois as the favorite to win the conference, with Indiana and Minnesota as the top challengers. And, although it led to some strange scheduling in December, most of the conference coaches expressed support for the eighteen-game round-robin Big Ten schedule, which they felt would produce an undisputed champion.

Following their Monday night victory over Valpo in the opener, the Hoosiers had all week to prepare for their Saturday showdown with Notre Dame in South Bend. Mac had them spend extra time working on their free throws after their poor showing at the line against the Crusaders, and he did some fine-tuning on defense, especially with Schlundt. Mac had assistant coach Ernie Andres work with Schlundt on moving his feet and keeping his hands and arms up. Andres kept drilling it into Schlundt that he could cause a lot of problems for other teams if he just kept active and used the right body mechanics. "I'd keep after him and after him," said Andres, "and a lot of times he'd look at me like he didn't want to shuffle his feet faster or lift up his arms. He was one of the first guys that big that could play. If he just moved a little and held his arms up, you can imagine how he'd cause some problems for the opposing offense."

On Saturday, December 6, at 10:00 AM, the Hoosiers hopped into a DC-3 and flew to South Bend for their 8:00 PM game with the Fighting Irish, who were itching to take on their cross-state rival. IU had beaten Notre Dame five straight times and the Irish hadn't won a game in the series since 1946. The 1952–53 Notre Dame squad returned several veterans, including 6' 5" senior center Norb "Gooch" Lewinski, the team captain, and 6' 5" junior forward Dick Rosenthal. They also had some talented newcomers and the home-court advantage (the previous five IU–Notre Dame games were played on a neutral floor at the Butler Fieldhouse in Indianapolis).

"Playing Indiana was always a thrill," said Dick Rosenthal, "and was probably always the number one game on our schedule. It was always a game that we tried to get up for."

This game had added significance. Notre Dame assistant coach Mickey O'Conner had contracted polio and was relegated to a hospital bed. In the locker room before the game, Coach John Jordan read his team a message from O'Conner: "Let me wish you luck in tonight's game. We are all aware that Notre Dame has not beaten Indiana since 1946, and my only desire is to see you end this famine tonight. Go on out there and win this one for me. I'll be pulling for you all the way."[3]

With five thousand fans packed into the tiny "cracker box" Notre Dame Fieldhouse—some having paid as much as $10 for tickets—the Fighting Irish tore out of the locker room and rushed onto the court to slay the eighth-ranked Hoosiers.

IU scored the game's first five points—on a pair of free throws from Schlundt and a field goal and a free throw from Leonard—and held the lead for much of the first quarter before the Irish pulled ahead 16-14 at the end of the first ten minutes. The game continued to seesaw until Notre Dame led 25-24 with six minutes left in the second quarter. That's when the Irish made their move. Gooch Lewinski got hot, buried six of eight field goals, and Notre Dame went on a 16-4 run to grab a commanding 41-28 lead at the half. McCracken tried to slow down Lewinski by replacing Schlundt with Lou Scott, but it didn't work. Lewinski scored on tip-ins, layups, hook shots, and even some long one-handers. He had nineteen points at the half and also helped the Irish completely dominate the boards in the first half, which grounded the IU running attack.

Lewinski scored nine more points in the third quarter to keep the Irish in front 57-50, but he also picked up his fourth foul and Indiana started to get its offense in gear. With Lewinski on the bench, Don Schlundt, playing in his hometown, went to work. After Schlundt scored a couple of quick ones to open the quarter, Bobby Leonard and Burke Scott started pounding the ball into him from different angles. Three minutes into the fourth quarter, Schlundt scored to tie the game at 59-59, then scored again to put IU ahead 61-59 with 6:30 remaining. After Indiana's 11-2 run, Notre Dame fought back and tied the game at 63-63, but Schlundt scored a field goal and a free throw to give IU a 66-63 advantage. During the Indiana run, Lewinski re-entered the game for Notre Dame, but he quickly picked up his fifth foul and returned to the bench without having scored at all in the fourth quarter. Then the Hoosiers upped the lead to four points at 69-65 with 1:30 remaining.

But Lewinski's replacement at center, Dick Wise, threw in an unexpected hook shot to cut the lead to 69-67. Next, Bobby Leonard was fouled and missed the first free throw but made the second to push the lead to 70-67. Reserve guard Jack Reynolds kept Notre Dame's hopes alive when he sliced in for a layup with fifteen seconds remaining to cut the Indiana lead to one point. As the Hoosiers brought the ball up the court on the ensuing inbounds play, Notre Dame's Joe Bertrand was called for a foul as he tried to steal the ball from IU forward Jim DeaKyne, who had helped trigger the fourth-quarter run with six points. Normally a solid free throw shooter, DeaKyne stepped to the line and missed both shots, setting the stage for one final dramatic play.

The rebound from DeaKyne's second free throw bounced into the hands of Notre Dame's Jack Reynolds, who turned and whipped a pass ahead to guard Junior Stephens at midcourt. Stephens then rushed the ball toward the Hoosier basket with two of his Irish team-mates filling the lane on either side. Notre Dame had a three-on-two fast break as the final seconds were ticking away. As Stephens reached the free throw line, two IU defenders held their ground, evenly spaced, ten feet away from the basket. Both of them figured Stephens was going to dump the ball off to one of his wing men and they were ready to stop them from scoring. But Stephens sensed them waiting for the pass and made the split-second decision to do the one thing they weren't expecting: he went right down the middle. Splitting the two defenders—who were a fraction of a second late in collapsing on him—Stephens went right at the basket and lofted a short little layup off the board and in with only two seconds remaining. The Notre Dame Fieldhouse erupted in a frenzy of joy and disbelief as the last two seconds ticked away without the Hoosiers even getting off a final shot. Fans spilled onto the court and paraded Stephens around on their shoulders to celebrate Notre Dame's stirring 71-70 victory.

In the locker room afterwards, the five Notre Dame starters, who had played almost the entire game, collapsed in exhaustion. Meanwhile, in the visitors' locker room, Coach McCracken was visibly irritated that his team had given away the game in the final minute, but for the sake of his young squad he tried to strike a positive note. "I was proud of the way they came back," Mac grumbled. "[Notre Dame] had us on the ropes in the second quarter, and they could have broken us wide open. But we came back, and we'll have to come back other times. Now I know we can do it. We didn't shoot very good. And we forgot a few things in the last minute. But it was a tough one and it was a toss-up. We did well to be in there after that slow start."[4]

The things the Hoosiers forgot in the final minutes were free throws and ball control. IU missed three of four free throws at the end that would have sewed up the victory, and the Hoosiers also didn't do a good job of controlling the ball and keeping it away from the Notre Dame defenders in the final minute. Some IU supporters were saying that if IU had had a ball handler like Sam Miranda or Sammy Esposito, they probably would have pulled out the win.

Still, IU nearly stole a road win in one of the toughest venues in the country (one of the things that made it so tough was that the Notre Dame band was situated right behind the visitors' bench, which meant the players couldn't hear anything the coach said during time-outs). IU was also badly outrebounded 49-37 by the shorter Fighting Irish squad, and the Hoosiers got little production from their two starting forwards, Dick Farley and Charlie Kraak, who combined to shoot 3-for-10 from the field. In fact, McCracken replaced Farley and Kraak with Jim DeaKyne and Jim Schooley for most of the fourth quarter. Despite all that, IU outscored Notre Dame 42-30 in the second half and controlled the game right up until Stephens's final basket.

Schlundt led the Hoosiers with twenty-three points (fourteen in the fourth quarter) and twelve rebounds, while Leonard scored thirteen, but shot only 3-for-17 from the field. Gooch Lewinski had game highs of twenty-eight points and thirteen rebounds for the Fighting Irish, while Dick Rosenthal added twelve points and nine rebounds.

After the game, the IU squad went out to eat at the Old Chinese Inn, a block away from the Oliver Hotel where the team was staying in South Bend. As everyone was finishing up their meal, Mac stood up and said, "About that game, there's nothing to be ashamed about. We came back like real champions. . . . Who would have ever thought that after being 16 points behind, we would charge right back? I want every man to analyze his mistakes. . . . That's what will make us great.

This Notre Dame outfit is tough on their home floor. I doubt if they've lost three or four games on that floor in the last five years, and they probably won't lose a single game at all there this year. It's better to lose a game now than to drop one over at Ohio State later. This defeat ought to make us mad, fighting mad [and Mac shook a fist as he said that]. It ought to make us determined not to lose another one. So let's pick up our heads. . . . It was a tough one to lose, but the cause is far from lost."[5]

McCracken and his Hoosiers had another full week to prepare for their next big road game against Kansas State on Saturday, December 13, in Manhattan, Kansas. Like the Fighting Irish the previous week, the Wildcats couldn't wait for their matchup with the Hoosiers. Kansas State, the Big Seven favorite, returned most of its roster from the team that had blown an eight-point lead to IU in the final minutes and lost 80-75 in overtime the year before in Bloomington. Overall, Indiana had defeated K-State three straight times, including a 58-52 win that spoiled the dedication game for the new Kansas State fieldhouse in 1950—the only loss the Wildcats had suffered in twenty-two games in the new gym. Kansas State also featured two former Indiana high school stars from Anderson in their backcourt, senior Bob Rousey and junior Gene Wilson. Both Rousey and Wilson had been Indiana all-stars, Rousey in 1949 and Wilson in 1950.

If all that wasn't enough motivation for Kansas State, there was also the fact that the Wildcats had come out flat in their season opener, barely edging out a badly overmatched Drake team 79-73 in overtime. Thus, coach Jack Gardner cracked the whip against his second-ranked Kansas State team heading into its big showdown with IU. The K-State–Indiana matchup was one of the most highly anticipated interconference college basketball games in the country during the preconference season, and it wouldn't disappoint.

While the Hoosiers were preparing for Kansas State, Illinois opened its season on Wednesday, December 10, with a 71-57 win over previously undefeated Loyola of Chicago. Illinois was powered by 6' 10" center Johnny Kerr, who broke loose for a game-high thirty-four points. That was Illinois's only preconference game before starting Big

Ten play against Michigan, although the Fighting Illini mixed in a couple of non-conference opponents later in December.

On Friday morning, the IU team flew from Bloomington to Topeka, Kansas, and then took a fifty-mile bus ride from Topeka to Manhattan, where the team worked out on the Kansas State floor that night. Before the team left Indiana, McCracken declared that he was sticking with the same starting lineup he had used in the first two games, and he said, "The boys are in good mental and physical condition. They really want to win this one."[6]

The game was expected to be a battle between two large and talented frontcourts. To match up against the Hoosiers' Schlundt, Kraak, and Farley, Kansas State sent 6' 6" center Dick Knostman, an All-American candidate, 6' 7", 240-pound forward Jack Carby, and 6' 5" forward Jesse Priscock.

At 8:00 PM on Saturday, December 13, a sellout crowd of 12,500 watched one of the first great college basketball games of the season. From wire to wire, the game was hard-fought and well played by both teams. The first quarter ended with Kansas State ahead 19-18, but the bad news for Indiana was that Don Schlundt picked up three fouls in the quarter and had to sit down with 3:30 left in the opening period. However, Lou Scott stepped up and played one the best games of his career at a key moment. At the 5:10 mark of the second quarter, Scott and Dick Farley scored on consecutive possessions to give IU a 37-30 lead—the largest lead of the game for either team. Big Lou scored eight points in the first half and IU led 44-38 with 2:01 left in the half, but Dick Knostman rallied the Wildcats on an 8-0 run to close the half, and they led 46-44 at the break. Knostman, one of the top returning scorers in the Big Seven, had twenty points in the first half.

In the third quarter, Lou Scott scored eight more points while holding Knostman to just a pair of free throws, but Kansas State clung to a 65-64 lead going into the final period. Schlundt returned for the Hoosiers at the start of the fourth quarter and keyed a 9-3 spurt to put IU back in front 73-68. Naturally, the Wildcats charged back. Guard Marvin Mills drove in for a layup and beefy forward Jack Carby, who was benched at the start of the game, made a free throw and then nailed a set shot to tie the score at 73-73 with 4:21 left.

Schlundt quickly made a hook shot to put IU back in the lead, but Knostman responded by drawing the fourth foul on Schlundt and burying a free throw to pull the Wildcats within a point. Forward Jim Smith grabbed an offensive rebound and hit a follow-up shot as Kansas State took back the lead 76-75 with 3:15 to go, and Knostman buried a baseline jumper to push the lead to 78-75. Then it was IU's turn for another spurt. Phil Byers nailed a clutch shot from the outside and Schlundt came back and swished a short face-up jumper to give IU a 79-78 advantage with 1:51 remaining. Bobby Leonard then made one of two free throws with thirty-two seconds left to put Indiana ahead 80-78. That was IU's final point and its last lead.

Kansas State worked for a quick shot and found guard Gene Stauffer on the baseline, where he calmly sank a one-hander to tie the game with fifteen seconds remaining. The Hoosiers rushed the ball up the court and got off a potential game-winning shot, but it missed the mark and the Wildcats rebounded with less than ten seconds remaining. Then, for the second-straight game, Indiana watched its chance at a valuable road win disappear with one final spectacular play.

The Wildcats' big forward, Jack Carby, dribbled the ball across the midcourt line, paused, looked up at the clock, and then, unpredictably, positioned himself for a two-handed set shot from forty feet away. As the clock ticked down to five seconds, Carby released a high-arching shot that sailed way above the backboard and looked as if it might soar over the entire basket. In the air, the ball had a slightly odd side-to-side spin to it, rather than a standard end-over-end rotation. When it finally descended from the rafters, the ball barely caught the upper right side of the backboard and then jumped to the left just enough to twist its way right through the net. The K-State crowd exploded with a rapturous roar as their Wildcats pulled out an 82-80 victory.

It was a poetic end to a highly entertaining game that sported fourteen ties and fifteen lead changes. Afterwards, Kansas State coach Jack Gardner said, "I guess we were just destined to win."[7] Of course, to Branch McCracken and the Hoosiers, it was almost too farfetched to believe that they could lose a second-straight game on a miraculous play in the final seconds. And with all the narrow scrapes with destiny that Indiana had suffered in the preceding years, "There was a feeling that 'Here we go again,' " said senior manager Ron Fifer.

But Branch McCracken was not superstitious. He had seen some good things out of his team that he believed could translate into a competitive run in the Big Ten. He also needed to make sure his young squad maintained its confidence in the face of two gut-wrenching defeats. In the locker room, he told his boys that they had showed improvement over their performance against Notre Dame. They played more consistently, they rebounded better, and they had much better scoring balance. He also told them that even though they had lost two tough ones in a row, playing competitive teams such as Notre Dame and Kansas State would benefit them much more in the long run than if they had simply racked up two easy wins over small schools.[8]

Mac also said, "The boys played a terrific ball game, but we were beaten at the free throw line."[9] Statistically, he was exactly right. Indiana scored thirty-two field goals, while Kansas State scored twenty-eight. However, Indiana was 16-for-20 (.800) from the free throw line, while Kansas State was 26-for-36 (.722). Indiana was whistled for twenty-five fouls, while Kansas State was called for only sixteen. In the pivotal second half, Indiana went to the free throw stripe only five times.

The Wildcats' Dick Knostman led all scorers with twenty-seven points. Dick Farley was the Hoosiers' high scorer with eighteen, while Bobby Leonard and Lou Scott added sixteen points each. Lou Scott also chipped in twelve rebounds, while Charlie Kraak posted eleven points and fifteen rebounds and Don Schlundt added ten points and thirteen rebounds in only seventeen minutes of play. Overall, IU outrebounded Kansas State 61-57. Still, the loss dropped Indiana to 1-2, the first time the Hoosiers had fallen below .500 since the 1947–48 season. Even Coach McCracken, who was always reticent about his teams' championship prospects, figured this team wouldn't be saddled with a losing record for long. However, he certainly could not have anticipated the type of winning streak this team was about to begin.

KISS IT GOODBYE

8

I was out there for one thing and that was to win a ball
game. I was the leader of the ball club so I'd get on guys
and try to keep them fired up. I've said a few things to
[opposing] players, too.

—BOBBY LEONARD

On Tuesday, December 16, the first Associated Press poll of the season
was released. Unlike the United Press, *Look* magazine, and others, the
AP did not release a preseason poll in 1952–53. They waited until the
games had actually started before ranking teams. The No. 1 team in
the AP poll was LaSalle, which had won the NIT the previous season
and had already started the 1952–53 campaign with a terrific 6-0 record. No. 2 was Kansas State, fresh off its big win over Indiana. No.
3 was Illinois, which had opened the Big Ten season the night before
with an easy 96-66 win over Michigan. Seton Hall, which was also
off to a 6-0 start, was No. 4, and Henry Iba's Oklahoma A&M Aggies
were No. 5. Notre Dame, the other team that had knocked off the
Hoosiers, was No. 7. The Hoosiers themselves were No. 19, despite
their 1-2 record. And the Big Ten's other ranked team was Minnesota
at No. 16.

After the Kansas State loss, Indiana had a week to prepare for the
start of the Big Ten season, which meant a pair of games on Saturday,
December 20, and Monday, December 22. The opener was against

the struggling Michigan Wolverines in the IU Fieldhouse, while the Monday game pitted the Hoosiers against the talented and always dangerous Iowa Hawkeyes in Iowa City.

Michigan was a team in transition, and it possessed a distinctly Hoosier flavor. The Wolverines' first-year coach, Bill Perigo, was an Indiana native from Lebanon and Delphi, and both of his assistants were also Hoosiers—Matt Patanelli from Elkhart and Dave Strack from Indianapolis. In his first season in Ann Arbor, Coach Perigo faced a daunting challenge in building a winning program. The previous two seasons, Michigan had gone a combined 7-21 and had been a regular second-division punching bag. Perigo immediately set out to turn the Wolverines into an up-tempo, fast breaking team, and he had a few Indiana high school players on the roster to help him. His team captain was 5' 8" guard Doug Lawrence from Fort Wayne, and he also had 5' 11" guard Ray Pavichevich from East Chicago and 6' 4" forward Ralph Kauffman from Elkhart. Perigo's Wolverines opened the season with wins over Marquette (80-72) and Pittsburgh (85-78), but had already dropped conference road games to Iowa (85-77) and Illinois (96-66) prior to their matchup with the Hoosiers in Bloomington.

However, for the Indiana-Michigan matchup, the IU Fieldhouse was not going to have the same atmosphere that the notoriously raucous arena usually had during Big Ten games. Since classes let out for Christmas vacation the day before the Michigan game, the arena was expected to be less than half full for the game, and the crowd would be made up mostly of older fans and alumni, rather than students. Another factor that was expected to keep some fans away was that WTTV was going to be broadcasting the game from the Fieldhouse using its powerful new mobile equipment. The telecast, which started a long-beloved tradition of IU on WTTV, would be sent over Channel 10 (later changed to Channel 4) to television antennas within an eighty-mile radius of Bloomington, including Indianapolis, Columbus, Terre Haute, and other cities. All in all, two million viewers were expected to watch the game, including some IU season ticket holders who planned to watch the Michigan game on TV simply for the novelty of the experience.

On Saturday, December 20, at 7:30 PM, a crowd of about four thousand gathered in the IU Fieldhouse. Normally, that might have taken some energy from the high-octane Hoosiers, but this team was so hungry for a win after two narrow defeats that no cheers or applause were necessary to help them shift their attack into overdrive. Since Michigan wanted to be a fast break team, IU came out and gave them the full clinic in run-and-press basketball. The Hoosiers struck first to grab a 3-0 lead, pushed it to 11-2, and then 22-9. They overwhelmed the Wolverines, who were bewildered by Indiana's pressing defense and by the speed and split-second coordination of Indiana's offense. IU repeatedly picked off Michigan passes and turned them into easy scores throughout the opening minutes of the first quarter. Once IU got into a rhythm early in the quarter, the Hoosiers started pouring in shots from every angle on the floor, and Don Schlundt took advantage of Michigan's 6' 4" center Paul Groffsky on the inside. By the time the opening ten-minute period had ended, Indiana led 41-18. Schlundt finished the quarter with thirteen points, including 7-for-8 from the free throw line. Burke Scott hit four out of four field goals and also buried his only free throw in the quarter. Bobby Leonard hit four out of five from the field. Charlie Kraak buried his only two field goal attempts and his only free throw. Overall, IU hit fifteen of twenty-three shots for a white-hot .652 shooting percentage. It was one of the most impressive stretches of basketball ever seen in Big Ten play, and it certainly didn't disappoint its television audience. Indiana's forty-one points also set a new conference record for points in a quarter. It was almost impossible to imagine a better start to conference play.

For the second quarter, McCracken removed all his starters and put a full lineup of reserves into the game to get valuable experience. Michigan's starters had much better luck against the IU second team, outscoring them 18-15, but Indiana still led 56-36 at the break and set a new conference record for most points scored in a half. Mac brought his starters back for the third quarter and this time they put the defensive clamps on the Wolverines, holding them to just six points while the Hoosiers ran up eighteen in the quarter, eleven of them from Schlundt.

In the fourth quarter, the starters returned to the bench and the reserves came in to finish the task. Michigan outscored the reserves again, 18-14, but IU still prevailed with a comfortable 88-60 victory. Schlundt led all scorers with twenty-four points on 8-for-12 from the field and 8-for-9 from the line in only twenty minutes of play. Ten different Hoosiers scored in the game and IU outrebounded Michigan 46-31.

Following the Saturday night win over Michigan, the IU team departed on Sunday morning for Iowa City, where the Hoosiers would face their first road test of the Big Ten season. Like Indiana, the Iowa Hawkeyes were 2-2 and both of their losses were close defeats on the road—a one-point loss at Oklahoma and a five-point loss at Wisconsin. The Hawkeyes were led by sophomore forward McKinley "Deacon" Davis, who ranked as one of the top scorers in the conference at 19.8 points per game. Davis, who hailed from Freeport, Illinois, was also one of the first African American players to join the Big Ten following Bill Garrett's arrival at Indiana in the late 1940s. Davis was a quick, talented, and versatile performer who posed a demanding challenge to the IU defense, which had not done a very good job thus far in holding down high scorers. However, the Iowa game would witness the emergence of an important weapon in the arsenal of the 1952–53 Hoosiers—the defense of Dick Farley.

At 7:30 PM on Monday, December 22, the ball tipped at the Iowa Fieldhouse. Indiana struck first when Don Schlundt tipped in an offensive rebound just thirty seconds into the game. Iowa answered when Deacon Davis buried a fifteen-footer to tie it. But then Bobby Leonard and Burke Scott scored back-to-back field goals and IU went up 6-2. IU clung to the lead for the rest of the period and finished the first quarter with a 23-21 advantage, but in the process looked like it was on the verge of having several of its best players slip into foul trouble.

The second quarter was the decisive period and it belonged to Bobby Leonard. The Iowa defense chose to sag in on Don Schlundt, which left Leonard plenty of room to roam out on the perimeter, and after he made several long bombs to start the quarter, his backcourt running mate Burke Scott started feeding him the ball. When the gun sounded at halftime, Leonard had drained seven of twelve shots from long distance (between twenty and thirty feet) and had already racked up twenty points. The Hoosiers had outscored the Hawkeyes 26-10 in the second quarter to take a formidable 49-30 lead into the locker room. In the third quarter, Indiana built the lead to 67-40 before the shell-shocked Hawkeyes could mount any kind of run. Iowa won the fourth quarter 24-20, but Indiana walked out of Iowa City with an impressive 91-72 victory.

Bobby Leonard scored a game-high twenty-seven points and also added eight rebounds, while Don Schlundt posted a workmanlike twenty-four points (12-for-14 from the line) and thirteen rebounds. But the most significant Hoosier performance didn't come from either of Indiana's two big stars. It came from forward Dick Farley, who had the defensive assignment on Deacon Davis. Farley utilized his long arms, big hands, agile footwork, and shrewd timing to deny shots to Davis and to make him work harder than usual for the shots he did get. Davis finished with thirteen points (almost seven below his average) on 3-for-15 shooting from the field. Meanwhile, Farley also contributed ten points and eight rebounds. Leonard and Schlundt grabbed the headlines with their big offensive performances against the Hawkeyes, but Farley's contributions were absolutely critical to the Iowa blowout. And although Farley had already been known as a solid defender, his performance against Davis showed he had the potential to become the Hoosiers' defensive stopper.

The next day, Tuesday, December 23, Illinois traveled to Minnesota for the first showdown between two of the Big Ten's three heavyweights. In front of an enormous crowd of 16,787 Golden Gopher fans, Minnesota upset Illinois 77-73, using their beefy front line to control the lane on both ends of the floor. They didn't give Illini star Johnny Kerr any room to operate inside and held him to just five points (he had been averaging 21.5 points per game). Minnesota also scored thirty-three points from the free throw line, while Illinois scored only nine.

When the Hoosiers returned to Bloomington from Iowa, they had almost a two-week break until their next game. The campus was practically empty since most of the students—except for a handful of international students—were home for the holiday break. However, there was no vacation for the IU players. They had practice every day to prepare for the rest of the Big Ten schedule. Part of being a college basketball player meant sacrificing the holidays with family and not having carefree time with friends during the holiday break, but at Indiana, it wasn't quite as much of a bummer because of the way Branch and Mary Jo treated the players like family. And for the 1952–53 squad, it wasn't so bad because the players had such a good time together.

The players spent Christmas Day at the McCracken house, where Mary Jo cooked a terrific dinner and the players got a chance to unwind and joke around—even with their coach, who was normally deadly serious. "As soon as practice was over and he was over all of his real seriousness, he was just a sweet old man," said Burke Scott.

During the rest of Christmas vacation, the players regularly came to the McCracken house for meals and some of Mary Jo's classic apple pie. "That was part of the reason you didn't mind staying in Bloomington while the rest of the students went home for the holidays," said Goethe Chambers. "Mary Jo made sure you had [good] food available to you."

"They ate everything in the house that Christmas vacation," remembered Mary Jo, "and decided that they might as well win the Big Ten and the NCAA. . . . Not only were those boys good basketball players, but they also truly liked and respected each other."[1]

One of the other IU traditions during the holiday break was that on New Year's Eve, Coach McCracken had all the players stay in the hotel in the Indiana Memorial Union building. One of the reasons he did that was because much of the campus was shut down on New Year's, but he also wanted to keep the players out of trouble. For the most part it was effective, but the players still had some fun playing cards and doing some wrestling and roughhousing. "You didn't get to sleep, I'll tell you that," said Goethe Chambers. "You'd get in pillow fights. It was kind of a good time to harass each other." The only big rule McCracken gave them was that they were not to leave the Memorial Union building. "I'd like to report that no one ever did, but I'd be lying," said Chambers.

While the players who wandered out of the Union on New Year's Eve may have thought they were slipping one by McCracken, he knew very well who the rabble-rousers were. The year before, when Don Schlundt was a freshman, McCracken had him room with student manager Ron Fifer on New Year's Eve. Mac told Fifer, "I'm going to have Schlundt room with you. You've got one job—keep him away from Leonard!"

After New Year's 1953, the Hoosiers had to prepare for a doubleheader on the road against Michigan and Michigan State. Mc-Cracken had the challenge of getting his team energized to play a Wolverine squad it had easily demolished in Bloomington two weeks earlier. The Hoosiers were heavy favorites but they had two things working against them—a two-week layoff and the fact that the game was being played in Ann Arbor.

When the ball tipped on Saturday, January 3, McCracken's worst fears were realized. Rather than looking intimidated, the Wolverines came out aggressive and determined to avenge their embarrassing defeat in the IU Fieldhouse. Michigan immediately went into its running attack just as it had done in Bloomington, but this time the Wolverines took better care of the ball and made their shots, and Indiana barely clung to a 25-22 lead at the end of the first quarter. However, Michigan center Paul Groffsky came out so aggressive in the first quarter that he picked up four fouls in the first six minutes as Michigan tried to rough up Schlundt to get him off his game. Their strategy backfired as Schlundt and Farley pounded Michigan inside during the first fifteen minutes of play. But then Farley got a cut over one eye at the midpoint of the second quarter and had to go to the bench. When he left, IU was up 41-36. Michigan closed the half on a 13-7 run to grab a 49-48 lead at the break.

The third quarter turned into a seesaw battle as the game was tied at 50, 57, 59, 63, and 66. Then Schlundt and Leonard combined for nine straight points to put IU ahead 75-66 heading into the final period. Michigan gamely fought back by opening the fourth quarter on a 7-2 run to pull within four points at 77-73. The Hoosiers took command again before the Wolverines surged back to within 88-84 in the final minutes. After Phil Byers sank a free throw to put IU ahead 89-84, Michigan failed to score on its next possession and then got desperate, trying to gamble for a steal. But Indiana moved the ball with confidence until they got it into the hands of Bobby Leonard, who held the ball deep on the right wing in front of the Indiana bench. As the clock ticked away, the Michigan crowd let out occasional spasms of cheers for its team to get the ball, still holding out hope for an upset of the fifteenth-ranked Hoosiers. Leonard wanted to let plenty of time tick away and then put the nail in the coffin, and he knew exactly which move to do it with.

When Bobby first came to IU as a freshman, he was exclusively a one-handed jump shooter—one of the first great ones in Indiana high school basketball. Two-handed set shots were still the standard at the time, and one-handed set shots (sometimes called "push shots") were gaining in popularity. The one-handed jump shot was still a bit controversial. Some coaches simply didn't like it, but Branch McCracken saw that the jump shot was the future and he taught it to his players. But he also didn't dissuade players from shooting one-handed or two-handed set shots if they were already proficient with them. He even convinced Bobby Leonard that there were times when a two-handed set shot could benefit him, especially on longer shots from beyond twenty feet. During Bobby's freshman year, McCracken had IU senior Bill Tosheff, who was a great two-handed shooter, teach Leonard one of his specialty moves—a short little feint with a step back into the two-handed shot. With Mac's help, Tosheff taught it to Bobby and Bobby practiced it over and over again. Eventually, Bobby added a bit of his own flair to the "two-handed step-back." Instead of shooting it strictly as a set shot, he got a little more lift with his legs, and he also developed an extremely quick release that made it difficult to defend. "It was a good thing for me," said Bobby. "It was another weapon."

With the seconds ticking away against the Wolverines, Bobby finally started his dribble. The Michigan fans got excited, hoping that their team would now have a chance to get the ball back. Leonard began to attack with the dribble. He jabbed one foot forward, leaned down like he was going to slash toward the basket, then quickly stepped back so that both feet were right next to each other. Then he told the Michigan guard who was defending him, "Kiss it goodbye," as he gathered the ball at his chest and went straight up with his two-hander from twenty-five feet. The ball arched high in the air and went straight through the net to give Indiana an insurmountable 91-84 lead. Leonard's teammates on the IU bench smiled and shook their heads after hearing him "call his shot." The Wolverines managed to net two quick baskets in the final minute to make the final score 91-88, but the result was never in doubt after Leonard's step-back two-hander.

Schlundt, despite getting roughed up by the aggressive Michigan frontcourt, scored thirty-nine points—almost all on hook shots and tip-ins. He was 11-for-22 from the floor and 17-for-20 from the line. Farley added fourteen points, while Leonard finished with eighteen points, including eleven in the final twelve minutes.

While Indiana was edging out upstart Michigan, Northwestern was busy pulling off the biggest upset of the young Big Ten season by beating Minnesota 71-65 in Minneapolis, on the same floor where the Golden Gophers had defeated conference favorite Illinois just eleven days earlier. That left Indiana alone atop the Big Ten with a 3-0 record, and Illinois, Minnesota, and Michigan State tied for second at 2-1.

Although trash-talking was not unheard-of in the Big Ten in the 1950s, many guys had never seen a ballplayer quite as cocky and brash as Bobby Leonard, who would talk to you throughout a game to get a psychological advantage. This was a decade before another midwesterner named Muhammad Ali would turn braggadocio into an art form and trigger a trend toward bragging and trash-talking in professional and college sports. If you asked any opposing Big Ten players or coaches what they thought about Bobby Leonard, one of the first words they would utter was "cocky." And many of them could share stories of things that Leonard said to them or that they had heard him say.

"Bob Leonard was a great leader. He was a cocky guy and he could back up anything he said," remarked Pete Newell, who coached Michigan State in the early 1950s.

"[Bobby] had so much determination, and a little bit of cockiness," said Johnny Kerr of Illinois, "but he backed it up with his good play. It's too bad that they didn't have the three-point line when we played. He would have probably set a record that nobody would have broken."

"He talked to everybody—anybody that would listen and some that wouldn't," said teammate Goethe Chambers. "If a player missed a shot by several feet, he would tell them, 'That's the best shot we've ever seen you take.'"

But Bobby didn't just talk to other players. He also talked to the refs. During the Michigan game that he clinched with his two-handed step-back shot, he got called for a technical foul earlier in the game for jawing with an official. However, when he talked to the refs, it wasn't always to give them hell. The Kansas State game in December that IU narrowly lost 82-80 was officiated by one Big Seven referee and one Big Ten referee. The ref from the Big Ten was Jim Enright, a rotund sportswriter from Chicago who was a showman and very flamboyant on the court. If he whistled a guy for hand-checking, he wouldn't just call a foul, he would make a big scene and say to the player, "I caught you! Keep your hands off of him. Cut it out!" Enright loved to talk with Bobby Leonard. The two of them almost always had a tense but friendly verbal sparring match whenever Enright officiated IU games. In the final minutes of that nip and tuck Kansas State–Indiana game, Enright made a key call that went against IU. Bobby was right there when he made the call. "Instead of being mad at him, I said, 'That was the right call.' From that time on, I had him," said Bobby. "That's what I used to do with the referees sometimes—kill them with kindness. Because if you challenge them all the time then you'd get a reputation as a referee-hater and they'd be all over you. That was just the psychology of the game—butter them up a little bit."

Coach McCracken loved Leonard's competitive spirit and that he always played so hard on the court. What drove McCracken crazy about Leonard was that the kid liked to play just as hard off the court, and keeping an eye on him and keeping him out of trouble caused McCracken fits on several occasions.

College basketball teams have had "training rules" since basketball became a competitive intercollegiate sport in the early 1900s. Depending on the coach, these rules sometimes function as simple guidelines, while at other times they are organized into a rigid set of team rules that, when broken, can lead to a player's being disciplined, benched, or even kicked off the team. In the 1950s, when a player didn't follow the rules it was called "breaking training."

Branch McCracken's approach to training rules reflected his personal down-to-earth philosophy as a pragmatic, churchgoing midwesterner. "Training is nothing more than good common sense living," stated McCracken. "An athlete should get at least eight hours of sleep regularly. No player can smoke or drink and expect to be at his best. Proper training is a matter of will power. There must be a proper understanding about training between the coach and the player. If so, it will be unnecessary to have any set rules. The player who has the desire to win and to be the best basketball player he possibly can, will train. Having a set of training rules will not ensure strict training and often will put the coach in a spot. The player must be sold on the importance of training for his personal good and for the good of the team."[2]

On the first day of practice, when Mac gave his speech to the players about his expectations, he talked about the general principles of training. He said that training was about developing good physical and mental habits. He told the boys to always get eight hours of sleep and to make sure to get plenty of rest after hard workouts. He said to eat sensibly and avoid overeating. He advised that they take care of any injuries or illnesses as soon as possible, with the help of the trainer. He told them to enjoy other activities as part of college life but not to overcommit themselves. He also told them to reduce stress and worrying as much as possible. He said that they needed to be in bed early on the night before a game. And he said that it was up to the players themselves to stick to training. He told them that a lack of training would show in their stamina and their level of play, and break-

IU ladies enjoyed the pep rallies as well. In the second row, second from the right, is Mary Jo McCracken. (*Indiana University Archives*)

In the Chicago Stadium locker room before their first game in the 1953 NCAA Tournament, the Hoosiers get last-minute instructions. From left to right: senior manager Ron Fifer, Don Schlundt, Charlie Kraak, Goethe Chambers, Phil Byers, Dick White. (*Indiana University Archives*)

Bobby Leonard
releases a jump
shot in IU's regional
semifinal game
against DePaul in
Chicago Stadium.
(*Indiana University
Archives*)

Don Schlundt launches a
hook shot against DePaul
in the NCAA Tournament.
(*Indiana University Archives*)

Bobby Leonard finishes
the fast break with a
layup against DePaul.
(*Indiana University
Archives*)

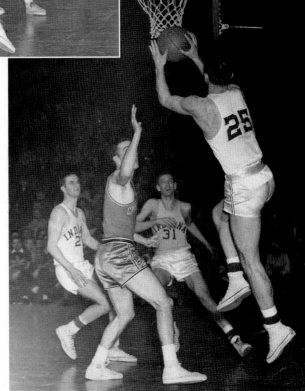

Burke Scott drives the baseline and
goes in for a score against Notre
Dame in the NCAA regional finals.
(*Indiana University Archives*)

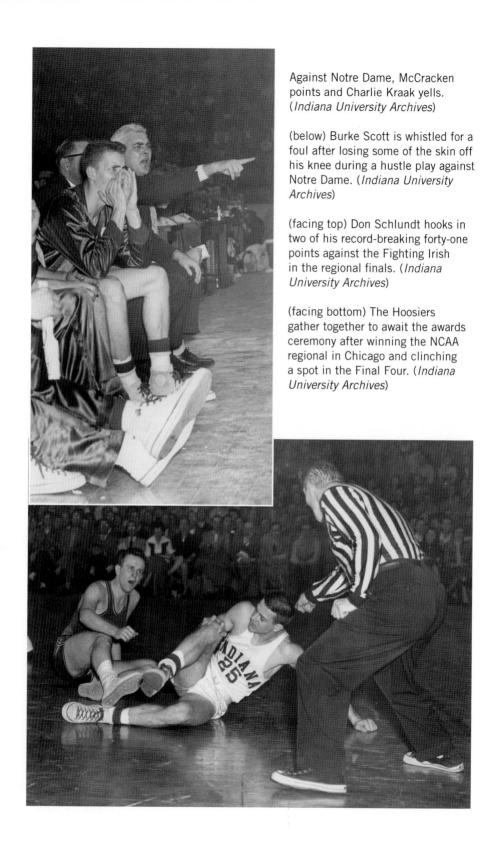

Against Notre Dame, McCracken points and Charlie Kraak yells. (*Indiana University Archives*)

(below) Burke Scott is whistled for a foul after losing some of the skin off his knee during a hustle play against Notre Dame. (*Indiana University Archives*)

(facing top) Don Schlundt hooks in two of his record-breaking forty-one points against the Fighting Irish in the regional finals. (*Indiana University Archives*)

(facing bottom) The Hoosiers gather together to await the awards ceremony after winning the NCAA regional in Chicago and clinching a spot in the Final Four. (*Indiana University Archives*)

McCracken hands
the NCAA regional
MVP trophy to
Don Schlundt.
(*Indiana University
Archives*)

Schlundt gets
mobbed by his
teammates after
receiving the regional
MVP award. (*Indiana
University Archives*)

In the Chicago Stadium locker room after the regional clincher against Notre Dame, the Hoosiers were all wearing smiles. (*Indiana University Archives*)

Dick Farley swoops in for a reverse layup, but is blanketed by LSU's Bob Pettit (50) in the NCAA semifinals in Kansas City. (*Indiana University Archives*)

Charlie Kraak
pulls up for an
uncharacteristic
jump shot against
the LSU Tigers.
(*Indiana University
Archives*)

Following Indiana's win over
LSU, Dick Farley shakes hands
with one of the Tigers while
Dick White gives the LSU player
a pat on the back. (*Indiana
University Archives*)

For the NCAA championship game, Indiana sent out the same starting lineup that had started each of the previous twenty-five games that season: forwards Charlie Kraak and Dick Farley, center Don Schlundt, and guards Burke Scott and Bobby Leonard. (*Indiana University Archives*)

Kraak goes up for a layup as IU forwards Dick Farley (31) and Dick White (41) and Kansas guard Dean Smith (22) position themselves for the rebound. (*Indiana University Archives*)

IU's Dick Farley drives down the lane past Hal Patterson and Dean Kelley, as Dick White (41), Allen Kelley (24), and Dean Smith (22) look on. (*Indiana University Archives*)

Don Schlundt scores inside over Kansas center B. H. Born, as Allen Kelley (24) watches. (*Indiana University Archives*)

IU fans, student managers, players, and coaches mob the floor just moments after the Hoosiers clinched a narrow victory over Kansas in the NCAA title game. (*Indiana University Archives*)

Branch McCracken and Bobby Leonard both get shoulder rides after Indiana captured the national championship. (*Indiana University Archives*)

A happy bunch of IU players stand in line as they wait for the postgame awards ceremony to begin in Kansas City. From left to right: Phil Byers, Goethe Chambers, Jim DeaKyne, Dick Farley, Charlie Kraak, Bobby Leonard, Branch McCracken, Paul Poff, Don Schlundt, Jim Schooley, Burke Scott, Dick White, Jack Wright, Ernie Andres. (*Indiana University Archives*)

Don Schlundt cuts down a part of the net in Kansas City. (*Indiana University Archives*)

The Hoosiers show off their plaques and Mac holds the national championship trophy. Front row (left to right): Dick Farley, Phil Byers, Burke Scott, Dick White, Don Schlundt. Back row (left to right): freshman coach Joe Thomas, Jim DeaKyne, assistant coach Ernie Andres, Goethe Chambers, Bob Leonard, head coach Branch McCracken, Charlie Kraak, Jack Wright, Paul Poff, Jim Schooley, senior manager Ron Fifer. (*Indiana University Archives*)

The IU players drive around the square in Bloomington as part of their championship motorcade. (*Indiana University Archives*)

Coach McCracken shakes the hand of a well-wisher during the motorcade on March 19, 1953. Behind Mac in the car are Goethe Chambers, Jack Wright, and Paul Poff. (*Indiana University Archives*)

IU students stand on the roof of the IU ticket office while waiting to welcome home the conquering heroes. (*Indiana University Archives*)

The Bloomington Chamber of Commerce presents a special plaque to Coach McCracken in honor of his many accomplishments. IU president Herman B Wells flanks McCracken for the presentation. (*Indiana University Archives*)

Mac and his starters pose for a picture with Ed Sullivan after the team appeared on the Ed Sullivan Show following its NCAA triumph. First row (left to right): Burke Scott, Ed Sullivan, Branch McCracken, Mary Jo McCracken. Second row (left to right): Don Schlundt, Bobby Leonard, Dick Farley, Charlie Kraak. (*Courtesy of McCracken family*)

McCracken was a strong believer in making sure his players finished their degrees and received their diplomas. These five players from Mac's pivotal 1950 recruiting class all went on to finish their coursework and receive IU diplomas. From left to right: Dick Farley, Charlie Kraak, Lou Scott, Jim DeaKyne, Bobby Leonard. (*Indiana University Archives*)

In 2003, the 1953 Hurryin' Hoosiers were honored at a game in Assembly Hall for the fiftieth anniversary of their NCAA title. (*Paul Riley, Indiana University Athletic Department*)

ing training would not only hurt them as individual players, but would also hurt the team.

Perhaps no player ever tested the boundaries of McCracken's approach to training more than Bobby Leonard. Bobby was a poor kid from Terre Haute who spent much of his teenage years running around the streets of that town. He was outgoing, good-natured, and tough, and he could make friends with just about anyone. He easily got to know a lot of good folks in Terre Haute as well as a few thugs and shady characters. When he arrived at Indiana University, he had already developed a few bad habits, and the freedom and open atmosphere of college helped him develop a few more. And, as an IU basketball player, he became instantly recognizable in Bloomington by students, alumni, staff, and townies, and that opened a lot of doors to different types of recreation.

When McCracken laid down the ground rules at the first practice of the 1952–53 season, he placed special emphasis on his players avoiding three things: smoking, drinking, and gambling. The first two were obvious because of Mac's belief that "smoking or drinking tears a player down faster than he can build himself up."[3] The third, gambling, he mentioned because, in light of the recent point-shaving scandals that had rocked college basketball, he did not want his players associating with gamblers.

"I think everybody knew that, for Bobby, those were three of his favorite occupations," said Jim Schooley.

However, since McCracken knew through his network of contacts just about everything that went on in Bloomington, that meant Bobby's indiscretions often landed him in hot water with his coach, especially during his first two years on campus.

McCracken explained his approach. "Training problems will vary in different communities. The city and industrial communities will often present much different problems than those of a rural community. The parents and the people in the community will play a very important part. In the smaller communities where everyone is very much interested in the success of the team and everyone knows each player well, the training problem is often much easier than it is in a big city."[4]

Leonard put it another way. "He had spies all over Bloomington," said Bobby. "He knew where you were all the time. . . . If you ever got a call from him when he was mad, you knew you were in trouble."

Bobby got several of those calls. One resulted from a report from the police that might have been much worse had it happened in a larger city. Bobby occasionally joined a private card game at The Gables, one of the most popular restaurants in Bloomington. The regular card game featured money on the table and involved some of the owners of The Gables and a few other local high rollers. "When they closed the restaurant [at night], they'd pull the blinds and there'd be a poker game in that front booth. I used to play there," said Bobby. One night, the Bloomington police decided to raid the card game and break it up by throwing a few guys in jail for a few hours as a harmless warning. However, when they came in, "I grabbed all the money in sight and put it in my pockets," said Bobby. The officers were shocked to find that IU star Bobby Leonard was one of the participants, but they didn't want to hurt the beloved IU team, so they just told the guys to break up the card game and headed back to the station.

When they came back and didn't have anyone to put in jail, the police chief asked, "Why'd you guys come back so quick?"

One of the officers explained, "When we came through the door, the first guy we grabbed was Bob Leonard. We couldn't have him arrested, so we just came back to the station."

But just because the authorities didn't throw the book at Bobby doesn't mean that McCracken didn't find out about it. "Branch knew right away," said Leonard. And that quickly resulted in a call from the fiery coach.

Another call came during Bob's sophomore year. Mac called him and said, "I want you in the office this afternoon at 3 o'clock." Bobby climbed the stairs up to Mac's office on the second floor of the old Men's Gym, knowing he was probably going to get chewed out. "I came in there and he was madder than hops because I'd been going down to the VFW [Veterans of Foreign Wars] slipping in the back entrance and playing quarter poker," said Bobby. "So when he got through with reaming me out, he stood up as I was walking out and said, 'I'm going to tell you something, son. If I ever have to call you back in this office again, I'm going to lock that door and only one of us is gonna come out.' And I looked right at him and said, 'I guess we both know who that would be, too.' And then I ran down the hall. . . . He loved it. He knew I was a renegade. He knew I was a free spirit."

Earlier that season, McCracken had already confronted Bobby about his extracurricular activities. "He had spies all over the place and they'd say, 'He's in here playing poker' or 'He's over here drinking beer' or whatever. . . . Branch called me and said 'This stuff has to stop.' "

McCracken also recommended something to help Bobby get himself under control. "Branch told me, 'You oughta get a religion. You *need* to get a religion.' Well, I started going [to church] with Nancy [Root], and Reverend McFall at the United Methodist Church baptized me."

Nancy Root was a fellow physical education major and sports aficionado in Bobby's class of 1954 at IU. The two of them met during their freshman year and started going steady on January 15. Nancy had an important influence that several people recognized, including Bobby's teammate Jim Schooley. "Bobby had a steady girlfriend named Nancy Root, who was a wonderful girl. She had all she could manage just to keep ol' Bobby going on the straight and narrow. I think she was working underground for Mac," Jim joked.

"Branch loved Nancy," said Bobby, "because he knew she had me headed in the right direction. . . . Anytime they wanted anything done by me, they got to Nancy. That's how they got it done."

"I was a controversial kid," Bobby admitted. "I was a wild kid, but I settled down."

He also added, "I was probably the best-conditioned athlete down there. I had the work ethic. Regardless of what I did or how much sleep I had or whatever, I was always ready [at game time]."

And after Mac issued his ultimatum to Bobby in his office, he never called him in there again. "From that time on, he and I had a great relationship," said Leonard. "He depended on me. He knew I was going to be there. He knew me."

After Leonard and Schlundt carried IU past Michigan on January 3, the Hoosiers traveled from Ann Arbor to East Lansing for their Monday night game against the Michigan State Spartans on January 5. The Spartans had not been expected to be a factor in the Big Ten race, but they had gotten off to a 2-1 start in conference play and during the preconference schedule they pulled off a shocker by defeating Kansas State 80-63 on December 20 in East Lansing (a week after K-State beat IU). Michigan State's third-year coach Pete Newell, who had led the University of San Francisco to the 1949 NIT championship and would later lead California to the 1959 NCAA title, had a solid lineup in East Lansing for the 1952–53 season. The roster included seven Indiana natives, led by 6' 1" forward Keith Stackhouse, who had been a member of the Indiana all-star team in 1950. Newell also had a solid 6' 8" center in Bob Armstrong and two excellent players he had plucked from New York City—6' 3" Al Ferrari, a high-scoring forward, and 5' 5" spark plug Ricky Ayala, a terrific little guard.

Indiana had averaged a gaudy ninety points per game in its first three Big Ten contests, so Newell's strategy was to slow things down, control the backboards, and limit Indiana's fast break points. And his team executed that strategy to near perfection—but only for one half.

The two teams traded baskets at the opening, with Indiana leading 14-12 just past the midpoint of the first quarter. But Dick Farley picked up his fourth foul while guarding Keith Stackhouse and had to go to the bench, and Michigan State promptly went on a 10-2 run and held a 22-16 lead at the end of the quarter. The other big story of the first quarter was the defense of Bob Armstrong on Don Schlundt. Armstrong limited Big Don to a single free throw in the opening ten minutes. Schlundt got things going in the second quarter, scoring twelve points, but Michigan State controlled the ball and dominated the boards to keep the Hoosiers in slowdown mode. At the half, Michigan State led 40-34.

Indiana didn't waste any time getting started in the second half. Dick White—starting in place of foul-plagued Farley—opened the half with an uncontested layup. Then Bobby Leonard came right back and sank a two-hander to put IU within striking distance. Bob Armstrong scored two field goals for the Spartans and gamely tried to keep them ahead. But Indiana pulled to within one at 45-44 and Schlundt then scored on a three-point play that gave the Hoosiers the lead. Meanwhile, Armstrong fouled out, which opened the floodgates for Schlundt. By the end of the third quarter, Indiana led 56-47. A minute into the fourth quarter they upped the lead to 59-47, which capped a 15-2 run in which IU took control and was never seriously threatened again.

The Spartans last gasp pulled them to 54-48 with four minutes left to play, but Indiana answered by pushing the lead to 68-58. Then the Hoosiers ran a five-man weave in the final two minutes to put the game away, 69-62. Schlundt scored twenty points in the second half to finish with thirty-three points and eleven rebounds. Leonard scored nine points in the second half to finish with thirteen, while Charley Kraak pitched in eight points and thirteen rebounds. Al Ferrari led the Spartans with twenty-two points (on 9-for-34 shooting from the field), but IU held Michigan State's other big scorer, Keith Stackhouse, to just four points on 1-for-10 from the field. In the second half, Indiana outscored Michigan State 35-22.

Schlundt's thirty-three points was huge for such a low-scoring game, and it gave him an average of 30.0 points per game after four games to lead the conference. It was also significant because Schlundt was physically challenged by the Spartans, who crowded him in the lane and swarmed him whenever his teammates got him the ball or he grabbed a rebound. Schlundt stood up under the pressure, and even made the Spartans pay when they got too close. "We used three men to guard Schlundt at various times," said Pete Newell. "All three came back to the bench with lumps on their heads big enough to hang their hats on."[5]

If the Spartans had pulled off a victory, they would have been part of a four-way tie for first in the Big Ten. However, the Hoosiers' win gave them three straight road victories and put the IU squad in an enviable position in the conference race. At 4-0, Indiana already had three road wins and sat alone in first place, with Minnesota and Illinois each tied for second at 3-1, and the Gophers and the Fighting Illini were scheduled for visits to the IU Fieldhouse on the next two Saturdays in January.

McCracken was thrilled to get out of Michigan with two wins. "All the boys deserve credit for our successful road trip," he said. "Schlundt scored so well that he's now leading the conference, despite the fact that two or three men were always guarding him. But part of the credit for his performance was due to the ability of the other boys in feeding the ball to him at opportune moments. . . . Leonard and Burke Scott were most valuable as ball handlers and playmakers. They fed the ball into the slot expertly. And Kraak proved himself to be one of the best rebounders in the Big Ten. . . . [Farley] did an excellent job of holding down Deacon Davis, and against Michigan State he stopped Keith Stackhouse cold, until he collected four fouls and had to be taken out.

"The Michigan game was much tougher than the Michigan State game," Mac added. "After beating Michigan by 28 points here in the Fieldhouse, the boys couldn't get steamed up for the game in Ann Arbor. Also, Michigan hit approximately 45 percent of its shots in the first half. That's enough to give any coach gray hairs."

Against the Spartans, IU committed a season-low sixteen fouls. When asked about that number, McCracken responded, "We decided to use a loose defense against Michigan State's slow offensive style and poor shooting record. We'll probably tighten up against Minnesota."[6]

The Golden Gophers were Indiana's next opponent on Saturday, January 10, when all the IU students would be back on the IU campus and prepared to return the Fieldhouse to the raucous venue that regularly made life difficult on visiting teams.

"Saturday's game with Minnesota is our first big test," said McCracken.[7]

SPEED VERSUS POWER

9

If I ever caught [Schlundt] in the corner and I had the ball,
I'd give it to him because I knew he was a dead-eye from
the corner. [The defense] wouldn't get near him until he
made two of three of them.

—Burke Scott

No team in the Big Ten presented a tougher matchup for Indiana
than Minnesota. Although Illinois was a better team than Minnesota,
Illinois was a lot like Indiana in its personnel and style of play. Minnesota was quite different. While the Hoosiers were tall and fast, the
Gophers had a beefy, rugged front line and they used a plodding attack
that relied on ball control to slow down and frustrate running teams
like the Hoosiers.

The previous season, Minnesota's 6' 6", 250-pound center Ed Kalafat had manhandled IU's Don Schlundt. In Minneapolis, the sophomore Kalafat held the freshman Schlundt to 1-for-12 from the floor
and seven points, while Kalafat rang up eighteen points and the Gophers won by thirteen. Things went even worse for the Hoosier rookie
in Bloomington. Kalafat abused Schlundt in the opening ten minutes,
scoring eighteen points in the first quarter alone (8-for-13 field goals)
and giving Minnesota a 24-13 lead. Kalafat finished with game highs
of twenty-six points and thirteen rebounds while Schlundt sat out
most of the game and finished with just two points and four rebounds.

Charlie Kraak and Lou Scott guarded Kalafat for the remaining three quarters and IU had to mount a determined second-half comeback to pull out the win in that game.

Minnesota also had an excellent coach in Ozzie Cowles, who was both an effective teacher of his basketball system and a terrific strategist during games. Like Branch McCracken, Cowles was a protégé of Everett Dean. Cowles had played for Dean at Carleton College, where Dean was the head coach for four years before returning to his alma mater, Indiana, to take over the basketball program in 1924. Cowles was actually much more like Dean than McCracken was. Like Dean, Cowles had a gentlemanly demeanor on the sidelines, was known as a master of defenses, and used a patterned offense that only occasionally took advantage of the fast break. McCracken, on the other hand, was explosive on the sidelines and his teams pushed the ball upcourt at every opportunity.

"[Cowles] was very conservative personally," said Minnesota guard Chuck Mencel. "He always dressed in a bow tie and a suit. He was not out there yelling and screaming. He was very calm and controlled. He had a very businesslike demeanor and appearance on the floor. . . . He was more defensive-oriented than offensive-oriented. We played a lot of changing defenses. We would change a lot between zone and man. On signal, we would change from one to the other. That was a pretty fundamental strategy for us. On offense, we would set picks and run when we could."

In 1952–53, Cowles was in his fifth season at Minnesota. He had previously led Dartmouth to seven conference titles and a run all the way to the 1942 NCAA title game, where Dartmouth lost to Everett Dean's Stanford team. In 1946, Cowles returned to the Midwest and took the head coaching job at the University of Michigan, and in his second season he led Michigan to an undisputed Big Ten championship, the school's first conference title in twenty-nine years. That also gave Michigan its first-ever berth in the NCAA Tournament. Although the Wolverines lost in the first round to Bob Cousy's Holy Cross team, Cowles hoped his team would get a decent reception when they returned to Ann Arbor and that he might get a decent raise on his $8,000 salary. However, the reception after the NCAA

Tournament wasn't what he was hoping for. "We'd been gone for a week, but no one seemed to notice," Cowles said. "A couple of days after we got back, Fritz Crisler [Michigan athletic director and head football coach] stuck his head in my office and asked me where I'd been. That was when I decided that Michigan was no place to coach basketball."[1] Later that year, the forty-eight-year-old Cowles resigned as Michigan's coach and returned to his home state to coach the University of Minnesota, which gave him a $10,000 salary. In his first season at Minnesota, he led the Gophers to a second-place finish in the Big Ten, the team's best showing in more than a decade.

Cowles's 1952–53 Gopher team had talent, balance, experience, and confidence, and they were a legitimate contender for the Big Ten crown. The Gophers returned their top two scorers from the previous season. At center, they had powerful junior Ed Kalafat, who was practically immovable because of his size and strength, but was also fairly agile and had a nice little hook shot. On the outside, Cowles had his other top scorer, 6' 0" sophomore Chuck Mencel, one of the league's top perimeter shooters. Like Don Schlundt, Mencel had gotten to play as a freshman because of the Korean War waiver, so he had already established himself as a Big Ten star. Minnesota also had two other double-digit scorers in 6' 3" guard Charles "Buzz" Bennett and 6' 3" forward Bob Gelle, the team's senior captain.

Minnesota had started its season with three relatively easy wins over Bradley, Xavier, and Nebraska. Then in their conference opener, the Gophers knocked off Illinois in Minneapolis, which gave the team a huge confidence boost. But after an easy home win over Michigan State, the Gophers dropped a non-conference road game to Marquette, then came back to Minneapolis and did the unthinkable—they dropped a home game to Northwestern.

Two days after the Northwestern loss, the Gophers bounced back by beating archrival Wisconsin in Minneapolis. That gave the Gophers a record of 6-2 overall and 3-1 in Big Ten play, but they had played their first four conference games at home and had to play five of their next seven on the road. The first game in that grueling stretch was against the conference-leading Hoosiers. A loss to IU would put Minnesota two full games behind Indiana, with a difficult string of road games still ahead, while a win against IU would automatically give Minnesota a share of first place.

Even though the Gophers hadn't won in the IU Fieldhouse in seven years, Minnesota came into the game with a palpable swagger and confidence. During the week of the game, they publicly bragged about how their interior defense had already shut down the league's top big men, holding Illinois's Johnny Kerr to five points, Michigan State's Bob Armstrong to eight points, and Northwestern's Frank Petrancek to six points. The Gophers knew that Indiana had been powered to four straight victories by performances of twenty-four, twenty-four, thirty-nine, and thirty-three points from Don Schlundt. They were confident that Schlundt would not have that type of performance against them and pointed to the job Kalafat had done against him the previous season. The Minnesota squad also felt it had already defeated the Big Ten's top team, Illinois, and that gave them the self-assurance that they could beat anyone. The Gophers obviously believed they were in an excellent position to steal a victory in Bloomington. They were nearly right.

The anticipation on the IU campus and throughout Bloomington had steamed to a rolling boil by the day of the Minnesota game. IU fans knew this was the Hoosiers' first big game of the year and that it would be a major indicator of just how good this IU team was. Many fans were starting to get their hopes up that this could be Indiana's year to win the Big Ten, but others reminded them that IU had been in this position many times before during the past decade and a half. Throughout the town, the debate raged over how Indiana would play Minnesota, whether Schlundt was ready to handle Kalafat, and which team would be able to dominate the pace of the game.

On game day, Saturday, January 10, the *Indiana Daily Student* reported, "The fellow that plunked a nickel on the counter for a cup of coffee would have probably shelled out a dime more for his talk over it. Comments on tonight's 'toss up' tilt between Minnesota and Indiana were about that much a dozen. It loomed in the air that maybe this was the year, and people were talking, talking, talking. . . . They've sold a lot of coffee for conversation on this tilt."[2]

At 7:30 PM, the college basketball spotlight turned to the IU Fieldhouse to see which of the two Big Ten heavyweights would emerge victorious from this battle royal. Whatever the outcome, everyone knew it was going to have major implications for the Big Ten race. No one knew it more than Branch McCracken and Ozzie Cowles, and the two coaches began a strategic chess match from the opening tip. Cowles flashed his defensive wizardry right away with a zone devised to keep Schlundt away from the basket. He created a triangle under the basket using center Ed Kalafat, forward Bob Gelle, and guard Buzz Bennett. Cowles had used a variation of this zone for part of the Illinois game, and it had worked well, but he ended up sticking with it from wire to wire against the Hoosiers. McCracken anticipated that Minnesota would clog the middle to try to neutralize Schlundt, so he pulled a surprise by starting Charlie Kraak in the pivot and moving Schlundt to forward, where he could operate from the baseline and show off a shot that few people outside of IU realized was part of his repertoire. McCracken also hatched a surprise on defense by having Dick Farley, rather than Schlundt, match up against Kalafat, the Minnesota man-child.

Schlundt grabbed the opening tip and Dick Farley put the Hoosiers on the board first with a quick field goal. Bobby Leonard followed that up with a free throw and Indiana was off to a 3-0 lead. But Gopher captain Bob Gelle scored seven points in an 8-1 run that gave the visitors an 8-4 lead. From there, the teams traded baskets until IU went on a run in the final minute of the first quarter to grab a five-point lead before Buzz Bennett scored for Minnesota to make it 20-17 at the end of the opening period. The grudge match continued in the second quarter, as both teams executed well and neither one could pull ahead of the other. Going into the locker room, Indiana clung to a 34-32 lead.

In the first half, both teams were effective in executing important parts of their strategies. Minnesota made it a half-court game by hustling back on defense and holding its own against the taller Hoosiers on the boards, which limited Indiana's fast break opportunities. Cowles's triangle-and-two zone defense also kept Schlundt out of the lane, where he had decimated previous conference opponents with his deadly hook shots. However, McCracken's strategy of moving Schlundt away from the middle had also proved effective, as Schlundt surprised Minnesota by facing up and burying four baseline set shots from eighteen to twenty feet to go into halftime with eight points. On the other side of the court, Farley kept Kalafat from getting anything easy and the Gopher center went into the half with eight hard-earned points of his own.

In the second half, both teams refused to give ground and continued to play well and with equal desperation. Both tightened down the screws another notch on their defense. And both made big plays and clutch shots down the stretch.

After Schlundt made a pair of free throws at the start of the third quarter to give Indiana a 36-32 lead, the Gophers went on a 10-3 run to take a 42-39 advantage. Minnesota pushed the lead to 47-43 before McCracken made a move that changed the complexion of the game. With 1:32 left in the third quarter, Mac inserted Burke Scott for Don Schlundt, who had already scored nine points in the period on three free throws and three more baseline shots. The substitution gave the Hoosiers a small lineup with Scott and Leonard in the guard slots, Farley and Dick White as forwards, and Kraak at center.

Burke Scott's hustle immediately re-energized the Hoosiers, and they suddenly started pressuring the ball harder and gambling for steals in the passing lanes. With a fast lineup on the floor, the Hoosiers carried their energy over to the offensive end and started racing the ball up the floor, which resulted in Leonard drawing two fouls and making two free throws. After the second free throw, Indiana went into a full-court press and Minnesota threw the ball away. Then Leonard drew the defense and dished to a wide-open Dick White, who confidently stroked a twenty-footer to cut the Gophers' lead to 48-47.

On its final possession of the quarter, Minnesota got the ball down the court and Chuck Mencel buried an outside shot, but the Gophers were called for a violation and turned it over again. Leonard streaked upcourt and pulled up for a twenty-four-foot shot that missed, but Dick Farley raced underneath to grab the offensive rebound and put in an uncontested layup just before the quarter ended to give IU a 49-

48 lead and all the momentum heading into the final ten minutes of play. During the short break between quarters, the IU crowd gave a raucous standing ovation to salute the Hoosiers for their 5-0 run to finish the third period.

Indiana controlled the opening tip in the fourth quarter. Burke Scott drove like he was going to attack the Gopher basket, then flipped the ball to Leonard, who was standing just left of the top of the key. Leonard gave a ball fake like he was going to shoot from twenty-two feet and drew two Minnesota defenders, which left Dick White wide open in the corner. Leonard quickly whipped the ball over to White, who sank an eighteen-footer that extended IU's run to 7-0 and put the Hoosiers ahead 51-48.

It looked like Indiana was ready to pull away and finish off the Gophers, but Minnesota's Chuck Mencel wouldn't let that happen. He put his head down and took the ball straight down the lane and scooped it in for two points. He was fouled on the play and converted the extra point to tie the game at 51-51. After several helter-skelter trips down the floor and several misses from both teams, Farley broke the tie with a pretty hook shot in the lane to put Indiana back in the lead at 53-51. A few minutes later, IU went up 56-52 after a free throw and a short jumper from Dick White, who scored five of the Hoosiers' first seven points in the fourth quarter.

But Minnesota doggedly kept fighting. Chuck Mencel hit one of two free throws to tie the game at 59-59 with under three minutes to play. Then Indiana, which still had a speedy, ball-handling lineup on the floor, began running its five-man weave to run some time off the clock. It worked to perfection, and after draining precious time off the clock, Farley broke free for a left-handed layup underneath to give IU a 61-59 lead. Minnesota answered again when Mencel stepped up and swished a clutch seventeen-footer to tie the game at 61-all with 1:19 remaining.

Indiana failed to convert on its next possession and then committed a foul that put Minnesota captain Bob Gelle on the line for two free throws with 1:13 remaining. Gelle sank them both to give the Gophers a 63-61 lead. Indiana raced the ball up the floor and Bobby Leonard aggressively drove to the basket, drawing a foul and barely missing a layup with 1:02 left to play. The foul was called on Mencel, his fifth, so the Minnesota sharpshooter was done for the night. Leonard missed the first free throw and made the second one, which left Minnesota with a 63-62 lead. IU immediately put on the press and Minnesota had a terrible time getting the ball inbounds. Farley deflected two inbounds passes, nearly coming up with a steal both times while knocking the ball out-of-bounds. When the Gophers finally did get the ball onto the court and into safe hands, the pressing IU defense had to scramble to set up a half-court defense. In the process, Indiana's Jim Schooley, who had come into the game two minutes earlier when Charlie Kraak picked up his fifth foul, lost his man on the inside. Minnesota's Buzz Bennett, the Gophers' leading scorer for the game, seemed surprised to find himself all alone under the basket, and he rushed a layup that banked too hard off the backboard and rolled off the front of the rim. Schooley had immediately realized his error when Bennett caught the ball, and he leapt to recover as soon as he saw Bennett's layup coming off the front of the rim. Schooley tapped the ball out to the free throw line, where Leonard snatched it out of the air and weaved between several Gopher defenders on his way down the court, where he was eventually fouled coming down the lane with only 0:28 left on the clock.

As was his custom, Leonard quickly stepped up to the line and fired his first free throw. When it bounced off the back of the rim, Leonard turned away and violently clapped his hands in disgust. A collective gasp went through the Indiana crowd. What if he missed the second one? With the entire IU Fieldhouse holding its breath, Leonard quickly fired again. The ball went up, landed softly on the rim, then rolled from the front to back and popped out. But the quickest rebounding hand was attached to the long, thin arm of Jim Schooley, who swatted the ball directly to Burke Scott standing outside the lane. Burke quickly grabbed it and uncorked a twelve-footer that hit the front of the rim and caromed into a crowd of big men. The rebound hit Dick Farley's hands but went straight through. Two Minnesota players grabbed for it, but they only popped it back into the air, and Jim Schooley then back-tapped it again toward the free throw line, where Burke Scott and Dick White both leapt in the air for it. Scott snatched it just before it reached White, came down just inside the free throw line, and took one dribble to his left, looking for space to create a shot. Two Minnesota defenders immediately collapsed on him, so he gave a head fake that drew both of them off their feet. As they flew toward him, Burke crouched down, pulled the ball into his gut, and gathered himself. He then leaned forward, ducked between the defenders, and rose into the air to release an eight-footer, with a third Minnesota defender stepping forward to contest the shot. The ball went straight at the glass backboard, hit dead-center in the middle of the white square behind the goal, then rolled all the way around the rim and dropped through.

Every voice in the IU Fieldhouse let out a holler and ten thousand spectators leapt to their feet. The Hoosiers led 64-63 but there were still eighteen seconds remaining, and it was Minnesota's turn to rush the ball up the floor to look for a game winner. The frantic Gophers got the ball safely upcourt and Ed Kalafat called for the ball near the top of the key. He got it and then dribbled to the middle of the circle, where he unloosed an arching sixteen-foot jump shot that hung precipitously in the air. When it harmlessly bounced off the rim, Bobby Leonard flew into the lane and ripped down the rebound. Leonard quickly flung the ball down the sideline to Dick White, who relayed it in one motion to a streaking Burke Scott, who flew straight toward the rim and dropped in two final points just before the final gun sounded. Indiana 66, Minnesota 63.

After dropping in his final layup, Burke Scott got mobbed by IU players, student managers, coaches, and cheerleaders. The mob was a collective mass of hugs, backslaps, and headlocks. After a few moments of jubilation, the players and coaches ran off the floor en masse, and as they jogged toward the locker room, the big meat hook of Branch McCracken was thrown around the shoulders of Dick Farley. As the players and coaches celebrated, the IU crowd went limp in a state of happy exhaustion. They knew their Hoosiers were now in a great position in the Big Ten race and had shown that they had what it takes to beat a very good team. Even a few of the most reserved fans had started wondering if this season might be different than IU's tough-luck second-place finishes in the past. This just might be Indiana's year, they admitted to themselves.

Branch McCracken was so thrilled to escape with a win that he sat around and chatted with reporters in the locker room long after the fans had filed out of the IU Fieldhouse. "We didn't give up; I'll admit I was scared when Bennett got that shot beneath the basket with only seconds to play," said Mac. "He was a half-a-step too far under the basket, or we'd of been done for. It was our toughest game. . . . Minnesota's zone was mighty good. We were pretty lucky to win this one. I didn't expect them to shoot that well from the outside."[3]

In the visitors' locker room, Ozzie Cowles knew that his Gophers had let a golden opportunity slip through their fingers, but he had a hard time feeling bad about it because his team had played so well. "We played a good ball game," said Cowles. "I thought we deserved to win. We played as well as we did against Illinois. Doing that on the road is pretty good. I figured we'd get Schlundt off the pivot, but I didn't think he would hit as well as he did from the corners. But the defense was worth the money all the way. We stuck to the zone all the way. Against Illinois we varied it. This was a little different— and maybe a little better."[4]

The Minnesota defense limited Indiana to mostly outside shots and took away almost all fast break opportunities by winning the battle of the boards 38-36 and hustling back on defense. As a result, Minnesota dominated the pace and got the half-court game it wanted. But Indiana shot 39 percent from the floor while the Gophers shot only 33 percent, and that was the difference in the ball game. Despite sitting out the final 11:28 of the game, Don Schlundt led the Hoosiers with seventeen points. He hit seven baseline jump shots from beyond fifteen feet and chipped in three free throws. He also collected eight rebounds. Dick Farley was brilliant with sixteen points (7-for-12 from the field) and ten rebounds, plus he held Ed Kalafat scoreless in the fourth quarter. Bobby Leonard struggled with his perimeter shooting in the second half but finished with fifteen points and five rebounds. He also did a terrific defensive job on Minnesota's top scorer, Chuck Mencel, holding him to only ten points on 4-of-17 from the field.

Burke Scott and Dick White each added nine points for the Hoosiers. White scored seven of his points in the second half to give IU a big boost off the bench. For Minnesota, guard Buzz Bennett came through with team highs of seventeen points and twelve rebounds, and senior captain Bob Gelle stepped up to contribute sixteen points. Kalafat finished with fourteen points (on 6-of-15 from the field) and eight rebounds.

While Indiana was barely outlasting Minnesota to improve to 5-0 in the Big Ten, Illinois chalked up a solid 71-61 victory over Wisconsin in Champaign. That put the Illini at 4-1 in the conference and all alone in second place. After IU finished off the Gophers, there were lots of people ready to look ahead to the monumental showdown the following Saturday when Illinois was set to come to the IU Fieldhouse. However, before that happened, the Hoosiers had to travel over to Columbus, Ohio, to play a mediocre Ohio State team just forty-eight hours after their grueling win over Minnesota. Since the Hoosiers had just gutted out a win over the Gophers and were looking forward to their bout against the Fighting Illini the next weekend, the Ohio State game had "letdown" written all over it. Nevertheless, there was one important factor that kept Indiana from looking past the Buckeyes.

The previous season, Indiana had traveled to Columbus riding an eight-game winning streak and ranked fifth in the nation. The Hoosiers were 1-0 in conference play after defeating Michigan in the IU Fieldhouse, and they were expected to have an easy time with the second-rate Buckeyes—even in Columbus. Things were going as planned as IU had Ohio State down by seven points with six minutes left to play in the game, but the Buckeyes made a spirited run to get back in the game, and then OSU guard Dick Dawe swished a buzzer-beater to give Ohio State a come-from-behind 73-72 victory. That started a three-game losing streak for Indiana, which then lost consecutive road games at Iowa and Illinois and dropped to 1-3 in the conference, virtually eliminating them from the Big Ten race before it had barely begun.

The sting of that loss to OSU still lingered for Bobby Leonard, Dick Farley, Charlie Kraak, and Don Schlundt. There was a sense that if they hadn't let that victory slip away in Columbus, they would have competed for the league crown in their first season on the varsity. Above all else, that memory kept the Hoosiers from taking the Buckeyes lightly, and it kept them from having a letdown after the emotional victory over Minnesota. Indiana's mindset was that it had worked too hard getting its cushion in the conference race to waste it by losing a road game against an OSU team that always played tough at home but was simply overmatched against the Hoosiers. IU had at least an inch advantage in height at every position, and at center, Don Schlundt had a towering five-inch advantage over Ohio State's Paul Ebert.

The two centers were battling each other for top scoring honors in the Big Ten, so the Schlundt-Ebert standoff was the most eagerly anticipated matchup of the game. The year before, Ebert had finished second in the conference in scoring with 21.4 points per game, while Schlundt had finished fourth at 17.4 points per game. This year Schlundt was off to a torrid pace in league play in 1952–53, leading the Big Ten with 27.4 points per game through five games, and Ebert wasn't far behind at 24.8. But once the game started on January 12 at the State Fairgrounds Coliseum, both of the big men were overshadowed. Indiana's full-court press kept the ball out of Ebert's hands, and when he did have it, he was hounded by IU's defensive ace Dick Farley, who held Ebert to just five first-half points. Meanwhile, Bobby Leonard was Indiana's dominant force on offense, as he staked IU to the early lead and refused to allow the Hoosiers to let down their guard.

In the opening minute, Leonard sank two quick field goals—one from beyond the top of the key and one from the baseline. That was the start of something big. The 6' 3" junior hit six of his first seven field goal attempts and the Hoosiers mounted a 24-8 lead after seven minutes. Ohio State made a little bit of a move to close it to 27-17 by the end of the opening quarter, but Indiana started the second quarter with a 9-2 run to take a 36-19 advantage, and Ohio State would never get closer than fifteen for the rest of the game. By halftime, IU's lead was 49-30 and the Ohio State crowd was stunned into a quiet disbelief. Clearly, there was not going to be a repeat of the previous season's upset.

By the end of the third quarter, the Hoosiers led 70-48. Schlundt had gone to the bench midway through the quarter and would not return. With most of the Hoosier starters retired to the bench for rest or because of foul trouble, Lou Scott and Dick White carried the IU second unit in the fourth quarter. Ohio State's Paul Ebert finally found some room to operate and scored a handful of futile baskets, but the Hoosiers prevailed with a surprisingly easy 88-68 win.

Leonard topped six Hoosiers in double figures with twenty-two points on 10-of-18 from the floor. Schlundt added fifteen points and nine rebounds. Lou Scott had twelve points and nine rebounds. Charlie Kraak contributed eleven points and eight rebounds. Burke Scott added eleven points, and Dick White chipped in ten. Paul Ebert led Ohio State with twenty-two points and nine rebounds, although Dick Farley contained him for the first three quarters.

Indiana shot 40 percent (35-for-87) from the field, while holding Ohio State to 31 percent (23-for-75). IU hit 18-for-23 (78 percent) from the line, while OSU was only 22-for-41 (54 percent). The Hoosiers won the battle of the boards 44-37.

While Indiana was running circles around Ohio State in Columbus, Illinois was busy trouncing Northwestern 83-58 in Champaign, and Minnesota was losing its second-straight heartbreaker, 76-74 at Wisconsin. The Big Ten was starting to look like a two-team race between the white-hot Hoosiers and the defending champion Illini. As the two teams prepared for their first confrontation of the season, the tension could not have been greater, and the stakes could not have been any higher.

THE GAME NEITHER TEAM
COULD AFFORD TO LOSE

10

On the court, it was heated [between Illinois and Indiana].
We had a lot of respect for each other. We played hard and
had some hard games.

—JOHNNY "RED" KERR, Illinois center

From the moment Indiana defeated Ohio State, the thoughts and
discussions of the entire team, the entire university, the entire town of
Bloomington, and practically the entire state of Indiana turned to the
subject of IU against Illinois. Much of the talk centered on how pivotal
the game was. In fact, the circumstances gave the game a perfect
urgency for both teams. It could not have been more perfect, even if
both teams had been undefeated in conference play. If that were the
case, Illinois could simply try to steal a win but could shrug it off if
they came up short because they would still have a return matchup on
their home floor to even the score. However, with Illinois at 5-1 in
conference play and Indiana at 6-0, the game became a must-win for
both squads.

For the Illini, a loss would drop them two full games behind the
Hoosiers, who had already won a surprising *four* road games in the
conference. An IU win over Illinois would also mean the Hoosiers
would have defeated both Minnesota and Illinois—their two top rivals
for the conference crown—in Bloomington. That would leave Indiana

168

undefeated at 7-0 and would mean that Indiana could potentially afford to lose at both Minnesota and Illinois later in the season and still win a share of the conference crown. Most of all, an Illinois loss in Bloomington would mean that the Illini would have little or no room for error for the rest of the season. They would have to depend on near flawless performances and spotless luck the rest of the way—and Big Ten teams rarely got a combination of those two. Plus, if Illinois was to have a shot at its third-straight undisputed Big Ten crown, then a loss in Bloomington would mean that the Illini would also need help from another Big Ten team to pull an upset or two over the Hoosiers. All in all, a loss would quickly turn Illinois into a long shot for the title.

For Indiana, a loss would be almost as devastating. It would drop IU into a tie with Illinois at 6-1 and would also breathe new life into contenders such as Michigan State and Minnesota. It would put the Hoosiers in a position where they would likely have to win a road game at Illinois or Minnesota—two of the most unforgiving venues in all of college basketball. Above all, because Illinois was still viewed as the class of the Big Ten, a loss to the Illini in the IU Fieldhouse would be a devastating psychological blow for Indiana that would all but prove that Illinois was the superior team. And, although it would simply tie the two teams at 6-1 in the race, it would potentially foreshadow the Hoosiers languishing in a familiar spot—second place—during yet another season in which they thought they had the talent to beat any team in college basketball.

When the Hoosiers returned from Columbus after annihilating the Buckeyes, their preparations for Illinois were quickly interrupted by bad news. In Columbus, Coach McCracken caught a "slight touch of the flu."[1] On Tuesday afternoon—the day after the Ohio State game—McCracken was confined to his bed at home and cancelled practice that afternoon. Still, Mac was expected to be back on his feet by Wednesday or Thursday. The bigger blow for the Hoosiers came the next day when Bobby Leonard was admitted to the IU Infirmary with a sore throat and a fever. Leonard was at first diagnosed with a bad cold, but the doctor feared it could turn out to be the flu and decided to keep Leonard in the infirmary overnight.

On Wednesday when Leonard was admitted, Dr. Bryan Quarles, the director of the Student Health Service, said, "His condition is not serious, but it could develop into influenza." Naturally, the question on everyone's mind was whether the illness was going to keep Leonard from being able to play in Saturday's game, but Quarles waived off inquires about the Illinois game by saying, "It's too early to predict his condition that far in advance."[2]

Leonard had to miss practice Wednesday afternoon since he was still confined to a bed in the infirmary. Meanwhile, the other sickly Hoosier—Coach McCracken—returned to the gym that afternoon and ran the team through its first preparations for the Fighting Illini. McCracken prepared his team as though they would be at full strength and refused to alter his game plan around the idea that Leonard would not be in the lineup.

The next day—Thursday—Leonard's illness was the top story in both the *Indiana Daily Student* and Bloomington's *Daily Herald-Telephone*. In the morning, when the *Daily Student* was published, the headline blared "Leonard May Miss Illinois Contest." For those who hadn't already heard the news about Bobby from campus gossip, the headline triggered gasps and shaking heads.

But then, the news from the infirmary on Thursday took a welcome turn. By Thursday afternoon, the headline of the *Daily Herald-Telephone* reported "Leonard Breathes Easier; So Does IU."[3] Earlier in the day, Dr. Quarles stated that Bobby was "quite improved." Quarles said, "We're not calling it influenza. It's not that serious. Bob has only a bad cold." For the second day in a row, Dr. Quarles was hit with the repeated questions of whether Bobby would be able to play on Saturday. This time, Quarles responded that it was a little too early to make "any definite statements." But he added, "Considering his improvement, Leonard should be able to play against Illinois."[4] Bobby was released from the IU Infirmary at noon and several hours later he reported for practice at the IU Fieldhouse, where he went through some light drills.

After his practice with the team, Bobby said, "I feel fine, just a little weak. I think I'll be ready to go Saturday—at least for part of the game."[5]

The entire city and campus collectively breathed a long sigh of relief knowing that Bobby was going to play, even though some still worried about his not playing at full strength. Still, once the news came that Bobby was going to make the game, the fans turned their attention from his health to IU's strategy against the Illini.

In many ways, the Indiana and Illinois teams were a mirror image of one another. They could both shoot the ball. They both loved to run the fast break and put a lot of points on the scoreboard (entering the game, Indiana was averaging 82.0 points per game for the season, while Illinois was averaging 81.9). Both possessed underrated defenses that were aggressive and physical. They featured two of the tallest teams in college basketball, both with starting lineups that averaged 6' 4" per man. And both teams were led by well-respected midwestern coaches who knew how to win ball games.

Like Branch McCracken, Illinois coach Harry Combes had the dream scenario of coaching at his alma mater. Prior to taking over the Illinois program from his highly successful mentor, Douglas Mills, Combes coached nearby Champaign High School to a phenomenal 254-46 record and the 1946 Illinois state championship. When Mills retired in 1947, Combes was the logical successor, and he quickly took the winning program Mills had built at Illinois and turned it into a national powerhouse. In his first five seasons, he led the Fighting Illini to Big Ten titles in 1949, 1951, and 1952. Illinois also finished third in the NCAA Tournament in each of those three seasons. Overall, during his first five seasons at the helm, Combes's Illinois teams amassed a 94-26 mark. That included a 7-3 mark in head-to-head competition against McCracken and his Hoosiers, including three wins in the IU Fieldhouse. And going into his sixth season in 1952–53, Combes had what was considered to be his best team ever, a team that was favored to win the Big Ten title and the NCAA championship.

Despite all the similarities between Combes's Illini squad and McCracken's Hoosiers that season, there was one area where Illinois held a huge advantage: experience. While Indiana featured a roster dominated by juniors and sophomores, Illinois usually featured four seniors in its starting lineup, and each of the four had earned letters during both the 1951 and 1952 championship seasons. They included center Bob Peterson, a 6' 8", 250-pound immovable force in the lane, high-scoring guards Irv Bemoras and Jim Bredar, and forward Clive Follmer. Those four guys knew how to take care of business in the Big Ten. They knew how to protect their homecourt, and they knew how to steal needed victories on the road.

But those four weren't the Illini's only weapons. Their big gun was 6' 9" junior Johnny "Red" Kerr. The tall, slender redhead was a product of Tilden Technical High School on the south side of Chicago. During his first three years of high school he focused on playing soccer, but then he grew eight inches and quickly drew the attention of the basketball coach. "The coach made me come out for the team my senior year," said Kerr, "and we won the city championship. So everything developed really fast for me." After leading Tilden to the top of the Chicago Public League, Kerr had plenty of college basketball programs knocking on his door. Indiana and Notre Dame both recruited him hard, but Kerr wanted to stay in the state of Illinois.

"Bradley was really my first pick," he said. "But Irv Bemoras called me and I went down and visited Champaign and fell in love with it. I changed my mind and that was it."

During his first season on the varsity as a sophomore in 1951–52, Kerr joined the defending conference champs and quickly established himself as Illinois's leading scorer and one of the top big men in the Big Ten. He also began developing a rivalry with a fellow 6' 9" big man who was also in his first season in the league—IU freshman Don Schlundt. Both big men were the leading scorers for their teams, but both were also surrounded by guards and forwards who could score. Both had slender, fragile-looking builds, and were often targeted for rough play by thicker opponents. But both had a mean streak and could mix it up with their opponents when they had to. And when they faced each other, it definitely got intense. Kerr was the more versatile and well-rounded player, but Schlundt was clearly the more prolific scorer, especially from the free throw line, where he made a lot more trips than Kerr.

During the previous season, the two of them basically had fought to a standoff. Schlundt outscored Kerr 23-18 in Champaign, but Kerr bested Schlundt 20-14 in Bloomington. Schlundt finished fourth in the Big Ten that first year with 17.4 points per game, while Kerr was seventh at 15.3 points per game. Entering the first Indiana-Illinois showdown in 1953, Schlundt was leading the conference with 25.3 points per game, while Kerr stood in sixth place at 16.3 points per game. The Schlundt-Kerr matchup was the key matchup of the game and the one that many IU fans felt would decide the contest. And, for the most part, they were right.

IU fans had anticipated that the Illinois game could be a big one, and it had been sold out since the end of December. It was as if everything the Hoosiers had done to that point in the season had been building toward this showdown with the Illini. And as game day approached, it seemed as if the question of whether Indiana was destined to relive the second-place curse or finally break through for a championship season would largely be answered on Saturday, January 17.

Those who couldn't get tickets could join what was expected to be a huge television audience that represented nearly every available television set within an eighty-mile radius of Bloomington. In the week leading up to the game, there were more than a few citizens who bought their very first set so they could watch the game live from their living room. On the Friday before the game, Hall Radio & Television in Bloomington ran a large ad in the *Daily Herald-Telephone* that was titled "IU Basketball on Station WTTV, Bloomington on Saturday Night." The ad read, "Still time to enjoy the basketball game tomorrow night on Arvin Television. And we mean enjoy it. Arvin's fine reception, easy tuning, and 'velvet voice' make it the finest television receiver available." Patrons were encouraged to visit Hall's at 1014 S. Walnut or call "The Store that Service Built" at 7311.

On Friday, with game day just twenty-four hours away, both coaches issued their final statements on the paramount importance of the contest.

"The team that loses this one tomorrow night is in a tough spot," said McCracken. "It would be particularly tough for us if we lose. . . .

The winner will be in the driver's seat, and it would require a couple upsets to move the leader out of first. But it has been done in the past. No team is safe in this league, you know."[6]

Harry Combes referred to the game as "the crossroads" for his team. "Either we have a potentially great team which can rise to the heights or we don't," said Combes. "Certainly, Illinois will have to play better than it has at any time this season to win."[7]

On the day before the big game, the atmosphere on the Indiana University campus was festive. It was an unseasonably warm Friday for January in southern Indiana, as the temperature topped out at sixty degrees that afternoon, and the Arbutus Queen Contest was held that night in the IU Auditorium. The pageant was one of the premier social events on campus during the winter, and in 1953 it held additional prestige because of a special visitor, Hoagy Carmichael, who crowned the queen at the culmination of the ceremony. Carmichael, a Bloomington native who was back in town for the first time since 1948, was an internationally popular songwriter and musician of the time, and one of Indiana's most famous citizens.

"Well, I've just had a great time being back," Carmichael said from backstage at the Arbutus Queen Contest; "Dunn Meadow used to be my playground."[8] Carmichael reminisced about running a lemonade stand on the corner of Indiana Avenue and Seventh Street and playing football in Dunn Meadow when he was a kid. In his typical Indiana drawl, he said, "I sure could tackle those big boys in football."[9]

Carmichael also talked about how he wrote his most famous song, *Stardust*, in Bloomington in 1927, shortly after he graduated from IU. "I was leaving the Book Nook over where it used to be and the tune just came to me." The Book Nook was a restaurant and soda shop that was the most popular student hangout in Bloomington in the 1920s. It was located in a row of stores on Indiana Avenue, right across the street from the IU campus. In the 1930s, it was turned into a diner and the name was changed to The Gables. By the 1950s, The Gables was by far the most popular hangout for IU students, including the basketball players. Meanwhile the Book Nook was reopened down the street on the corner of Indiana Avenue and Kirkwood Avenue. During Carmichael's college days in Bloomington, there was a piano in the Book Nook, so when he walked out of the Book Nook one night in 1927 and had a tune pop into his head, he sped back to the Book Nook to work out his song on their piano. However, when he got back he found the Book Nook locked, so he "pounded on the door until the owner opened up again and let me in so I could play it through."[10] *Stardust* was born.

Carmichael first recorded *Stardust* commercially in 1929. Later that year, lyrics were added and soon the wispy romantic song became one of the most popular tunes of the era. *Stardust* was a smash hit not only in English, but also in French, Spanish, and Japanese. Over the years, *Stardust* has been recorded more than two thousand times. Nearly all the great artists of Hoagy's time did a version of the song, including Nat King Cole, Frank Sinatra, Louis Armstrong, Dinah Washington, Bennie Goodman, Bing Crosby, Ella Fitzgerald, and many more. Modern artists such as Willie Nelson, Wynton Marsalis, and Aaron Neville have done their own versions of *Stardust*.

Of course, the popularity of *Stardust* was not lost on Hoagy's hometown. One of the most popular restaurants in Bloomington in the 1950s was the Stardust Cafe at 205 North Walnut, and on the day Hoagy returned for the Arbutus Queen Contest, the Stardust Cafe ran an ad in the *Daily Herald-Telephone* that simply stated, WELCOME HOME HOAGY CARMICHAEL.

Even though for most IU students, Hoagy Carmichael represented their parents' music, the fact that he was on campus for IU's biggest winter social event on the day before the biggest basketball game of the Big Ten season only heightened the excitement and added to the already electric atmosphere for the Illinois game.

By the time the game finally rolled around on Saturday night, the IU campus was primed and ready to pour its heart and soul into inspiring their Hoosiers to a big win in this critical showdown. They fully expected this much-hyped game to be hard-fought and well played, but what they ended up witnessing surpassed even those expectations. It was an instant classic.

Nearly ten thousand people crammed into the IU Fieldhouse for the Illinois game. Every seat in the gym was filled for what was undeniably the hottest ticket on IU's home schedule, but that didn't stop a few alumni and fans who didn't have tickets from finding their way into the Fieldhouse. Since there was no assigned seating, tickets were taken at the door, and anyone who had to go outside to smoke or meet someone had to go out through the pass-out gate, where they were given a pass to get back in later. Since there were influential alumni and friends of McCracken's who weren't able to get tickets to the Illinois game, senior manager Ron Fifer sent some of his younger managers through the pass-out gate several times and then let them back in through the locker room and collected the passes from them. Fifer then handed the passes over to McCracken, who passed them out to the ticketless alums, who then walked into the gym through the pass-out gate. The IU Fieldhouse featured huge bleachers on both sides of the court and both ends, behind the baskets. However, that left a lot of open space in the corners. For the Illinois game, that space was crammed full of people standing to watch the game, including many of Mac's ticketless alumni friends. Once the game got started, two hours wasn't long to stand for a game that was nip and tuck from the opening tip to the final gun, as neither team could ever open up a safe lead.

The Hoosiers struck first, jumping to a 5-0 advantage, but Illinois center Bob Peterson sank two straight hook shots to cut it to 5-4. A few minutes later, the score was tied at 8-8, and then Illinois grabbed its first lead at 10-8. Then IU went on an 8-0 run to pull back in front 16-10, but Illinois answered with a run of its own that was capped by Johnny Kerr's score on the inside to close out the first quarter with Indiana leading 19-18.

In the second quarter, both defenses got more active and started causing disruptions. The Illini defense was especially effective, holding the Hurryin' Hoosiers to just ten points in the quarter. IU had more turnovers (five) than field goals (three) in the second quarter and as a result went into the locker room trailing Illinois 33-29. Indiana's catalyst, Bob Leonard, scored just one point in the first half and definitely looked like he was feeling the effects of his illness, and Indiana's leading rebounder, Charlie Kraak, went down with a leg injury midway through the second quarter. Heading into the second half, the Hoosiers looked like a team in trouble.

The two bright spots in the first half for IU were that the Illinois forwards had been unable to control Dick Farley, who scored ten points, and Don Schlundt severely outplayed the large and talented Illinois front line. In fact, when IU student manager Bob Howard went into the Illinois locker room at halftime to deliver a copy of the first-half statistics, he overheard Illinois center Johnny Kerr complaining to Coach Harry Combes that the refs were letting Schlundt knock him all over the place. The Schlundt-Kerr battle got even more intense in the second half, and a couple other big men joined in the fray.

The second half opened with Illinois grabbing the tip and immediately driving the ball to the basket for a quick score to extend its lead to 35-29. IU's Bobby Leonard drew a foul and converted a free throw, then got called for a charging foul, and Illinois converted one free throw of its own to make it 36-30. The middle of the third quarter was then dominated by a fierce battle of the big men.

After Illinois converted the free throw from Leonard's charge, the Hoosiers came straight down and ran a play that dumped the ball to Schlundt. But Kerr had forced him into a tough position and Schlundt's shot hit the bottom of the backboard. After a jump ball and a violation from the Illini, IU got it back. From the top of the key, Burke Scott tried to feed it into Schlundt, but Kerr quickly stepped in front and stole the ball.

Bobby Leonard then drew a charging foul and hit the free throw to cut the lead to 36-31. Illinois brought the ball down and pounded it into Kerr under the basket, but his shot got swatted out-of-bounds by Schlundt. After the inbounds, Illinois got the ball back into Kerr, who made a nice spin move to free himself under the basket, but he hesitated before releasing the shot as he waited for Schlundt to commit. Schlundt held his ground and Kerr released an off-balance layup that Schlundt deflected, and it ended up as a jump ball. IU got the jump, then, in a bang-bang play, Dick Farley grabbed the ball, whirled around and fired a baseball pass up the sideline to Leonard, who collected it and weaved his way through traffic to the top of the key where he stopped and uncorked a high-arching twenty-three-footer that swished through the net to cut the Illinois lead to 36-33. Illinois quickly answered by coolly draining a nineteen-footer to push the lead back to five points at 38-33.

Indiana went back into Schlundt, who put his hip into Kerr and drew a foul under the basket. Schlundt missed the first free throw but made the second to put the score at 38-34. After missed opportunities on both sides, Illinois nailed another outside shot to open up a 40-34 advantage. The Hoosiers got the ball into Schlundt in good position and he backed Kerr all the way down, but when he turned to put the ball in the basket, Kerr was waiting for him and stuffed Schlundt's shot and recovered the ball himself.

After a Dick White free throw cut it to 40-35, Illinois opened up the game's largest lead when Irv Bemoras buried a twenty-footer from the top of the circle to push the Illini advantage to 42-35. IU worked the ball for a good shot and tried to lob over Johnny Kerr and into Schlundt, but Kerr leapt up and tapped the ball away for another steal. Then Illinois tried to get the ball into Kerr in the post, but Schlundt came around from behind him to deflect the ball, and Burke Scott came up with it. On the ensuing play, Schlundt slipped inside and posted up Kerr deep into the lane. Meanwhile, Leonard worked his way to the top of the lane, spotted Schlundt breaking free, stepped through the defense, and whipped a brilliant hook pass into Big Don. Schlundt gave a quick ball fake that drew Kerr's momentum, then softly laid the ball off the glass with his left hand while his right elbow cracked Kerr on the forehead and sent him reeling onto the floor with both hands clutching the top of his head. That put the Illinois lead at 42-37.

Over the next several minutes, Kerr missed two hook shots, IU failed to convert back-to-back fast breaks when Schlundt and Dick Farley missed layups, and Indiana hit two free throws while Illinois hit one to make the score 43-39. Then a different set of big men took up the battle. First, wide-body Bob Peterson came in to replace Johnny Kerr, then Lou Scott substituted for Don Schlundt.

Shortly after entering the game, Scott drew an offensive foul on Peterson and hit a free throw to draw the Hoosiers to 43-40. Then

Scott was called for a foul while trying to deny Peterson the ball, and Peterson converted a free throw to make it 44-40. At that point, Illinois had successfully answered every charge IU tried to make in the third quarter, but the Hoosiers finally grabbed some momentum on a key series of plays. It started when Bobby Leonard came down the floor and used a pick from Dick Farley to create enough space for a beautiful step-back twenty-two-footer that swished through the bottom of the net. As Leonard's shot went through the hoop, a whistle blew and the ref pointed to Bob Peterson, who had been battling with Lou Scott for position under the basket. Peterson exploded when the ref pointed at him and got nose-to-nose with the ref to state his displeasure. Then he swung around and planted an elbow in the chest of one of his teammates who was trying to pull him away and proceeded to storm back to the Illinois bench, looking like he was ready to hit something. He wouldn't even look at IU's Dick Farley, who was trying to calm him down as he stomped back to the bench. When he reached the bench, he took out his frustration on an innocent water bottle. Meanwhile, Scott stepped to the line and hit the free throw as IU pulled to within a point at 44-43. That capped an 8-2 Indiana run, which turned the game back into a nail-biter.

Both teams had trouble putting the ball in the basket during the final minutes of the third quarter. Illinois strung together three points and Bobby Leonard drilled a long thirty-footer to cut the Illini advantage to 47-45 at the close of the period.

Johnny Kerr outjumped Lou Scott for the tip at the opening of the fourth quarter, but Illinois was called for a violation and IU was awarded the ball. The Hoosiers patiently worked a play on the left side of the floor, then Dick White set a beautiful screen to free up Bobby Leonard for an open twenty-five-footer that he calmly swished to tie the game at 47-47. A few moments later, IU had a chance to take the lead after stopping the Illini and then racing the ball upcourt on a fast break, but the ball came to a hustling Lou Scott at the end of the break and he bobbled it out-of-bounds.

Over the next several minutes, both defenses dominated and both offenses sputtered, and neither team could score. Then Leonard hit Scott posting up on Kerr. Scott made a surprisingly quick spin and went right around Kerr, but when he stopped to gain his footing on the other side of the basket he slipped and nearly went down as two Illinois players converged on him. Scott flipped the ball back to reserve guard Phil Byers, who sank a little eight-foot jumper from the baseline to give Indiana a 49-47 lead, IU's first lead since the second quarter. It didn't last long.

The veteran Illini wasted no time getting the ball into Kerr, and he banked in a fifteen-foot hook shot to tie the game. With 7:18 remaining in the game, Indiana called a time-out. After the defenses had dominated the action during the second and third quarters, the two high-powered offenses finally got hot down the stretch. After the time-out, Indiana got the ball to Farley on the right wing and he faked right and drove left, went right across the lane, and laid the ball in with his left hand to put IU back in front 51-49. However, Johnny Kerr answered again. Illinois delivered the ball to Kerr just inside the free throw line. He faced up and faked Lou Scott off his feet and drilled a twelve-foot jumper to tie it again.

IU grabbed the lead right back when Dick White grabbed a long rebound from a Bobby Leonard miss and swished a seventeen-footer to put Indiana up 53-51. After several empty trips from both teams, Bobby Leonard drove to the basket and drew a foul. He hit the first free throw and missed the second, which left IU ahead 54-51. Leonard then broke up an Illini play and stole the ball, and the Hoosiers started working the clock for a good shot. They got it inside to Dick Farley, but he was double-teamed and passed to Don Schlundt, who shot a face-up fifteen-footer that swished through the bottom of the net, and Indiana suddenly found itself with a 56-51 lead.

Illinois's Jim Bredar nailed a clutch twenty-footer to cut it to 56-53 and then Bredar immediately drew a charging foul on Burke Scott. Bredar missed the first free throw but hit the second, and the IU lead was down to 56-54. Next, Burke Scott drew a foul on Jim Bredar (a "makeup" call by the referees), but Scott missed both free throws. After both teams hit one of two free throws, the score was 57-55. The Hoosiers took control with under three minutes remaining when Leonard took the ball from the top of the key and drove all the way to the basket and scored to put IU ahead 59-55.

Once again, Illinois answered by going into Kerr, who took the ball in the post and spun across the lane, releasing a running hook shot with Don Schlundt all over him. The ball hit the rim and popped out, banked against the backboard, and fell softly through the net, making the score 59-57 with 2:35 remaining. Bobby Leonard answered by taking the ball and driving to the basket again. This time he drove to the wing, then pivoted and raced down the baseline. He went all the way under the basket and scooped the ball up and under from the other side, and it rattled around on the rim and then bounced off, but Don Schlundt jabbed a hand up from underneath and tipped the ball in to push IU's lead back to four points.

Bredar brought the ball up and tried to get Illinois quickly back within two by driving to the baseline and uncorking a twenty-footer. It missed, but Irv Bemoras darted inside Dick White on the other side of the floor and snatched the rebound and laid it in to cut the lead to 61-59. The Hoosiers immediately went into their trusted five-man weave in an attempt to run time off the clock and run the opponent in circles until the Hoosiers could open up an easy score underneath. But the plan backfired when Burke Scott collided with Irv Bemoras. Both players went down and the ball squirted out-of-bounds. The whistle blew and both players—while still lying on the floor—jerked their heads toward the ref to see what the call was. The ref pointed toward Scott and motioned for an offensive foul as Scott turned his head away in disgust.

With a minute and a half left to play, Bredar stepped to the stripe and lined up the first free throw using his characteristic underhanded style. He let it fly and it hit the back of the rim and dropped through. He calmly measured the second one the same way and let it fly. It bounced twice on the rim, hit the backboard and dropped in to tie the game at 61-61.

The Hoosiers came down and whipped a couple of quick passes around. Then Bobby Leonard called for the ball in the corner, forty feet from the basket, standing right in front of the Indiana bench, with 1:21 left to play. After waving his teammates away, Bobby stood relaxed with his feet shoulder-width apart and the ball clutched in the middle of his chest with his elbows pointing straight out while Jim

Bredar stood fifteen feet away with his hands on his knees. The scene hardly changed for the next fifty seconds, and then, with thirty seconds left, Leonard began feigning drives and faking passes in various directions. With just three seconds left, Leonard collected himself, crouched low, and unleashed a two-handed forty-footer that brought Bredar flying at him. The ball went on a high, arcing path that drew every eye in the building. It was soaring on target, but when it reached the basket it hit the flat part of the rim behind the goal and bounced harmlessly away. The timekeeper put another five minutes on the clock, and this classic Big Ten battle went to overtime.

On their first two possessions of OT, the Hoosiers tried to get the ball into Schlundt, but both times Kerr deflected the ball away. Illinois struck first by scoring on a fast break, but after that score, Indiana threw the ball ahead to Don Schlundt, who beat Johnny Kerr down the court and laid the ball in the basket uncontested to tie the game at 63-63. But Jim Bredar didn't waste any time getting the lead back for the Illini. He brought the ball up the floor, blew by Leonard, and drove to the baseline, where he pulled up and buried a ten-footer. That put Illinois up 65-63 and gave the Illini their first lead since the start of the fourth quarter.

Indiana got the ball into Schlundt in good scoring position, but he missed a hook shot and Illinois grabbed the rebound. The Illini then went into a stall to run some time off the clock. During the stall, Kerr caught the ball on the wing and dribbled it out to midcourt. Schlundt tried to test Kerr, who was a good ball handler for a man his size. Going for the steal, Don swiped at the ball and was whistled for his fifth foul. While Schlundt took a seat on the bench, Kerr hit the front of the rim on his first free throw and than rattled home the second to give Illinois a 66-63 advantage.

Bobby Leonard came down and quickly launched a twenty-footer with Bemoras all over him. The shot hit the rim and bounced over the back of the backboard, and Leonard fiercely clapped his hands together in frustration as the ball was awarded to Illinois. The Hoosiers immediately went into their full-court press defense. The Illini broke the press and got the ball into the frontcourt, but Clive Follmer tried to drive into the lane and Dick White reached in and knocked the ball loose, and Follmer fouled him trying to get it back. White, an excellent free throw shooter, didn't hesitate at all. He stepped to the line and swished two straight free throws to cut the lead to 66-65.

After the second free throw, IU went back into its full-court press and forced a turnover. The ball ended up in the hands of Phil Byers, who was fouled driving to the basket. With the weight of this pivotal game hanging on his sophomore shoulders, Byers's first free throw went in and out. He stepped back, put his hands on his hips and dropped his head, as if to give himself a stern little pep talk. It worked. Byers's second free throw bounced around the rim and fell in to tie the game at 66-66.

The Hoosiers again went into the full-court press, but this time Illinois used an unconventional weapon to break it. Johnny Kerr came back and caught the ball in the backcourt and dribbled it all the way down the floor against IU's Jim Schooley, then pitched it out to Irv Bemoras, who flipped it to reserve guard Morris Sterneck, who tossed it out to Jim Bredar, who stood just inside the midcourt line in the center of the floor with 1:33 left on the clock. Bredar clutched the ball at his waist, then leaned back and relaxed as Bobby Leonard faced him ten feet away. It was a complete reversal from the end of regulation, as Bredar stalled for a final shot, but Bredar didn't take the shot himself. Instead, when the clock ticked to under thirty seconds, Bredar tossed the ball to Bemoras on the wing. Bemoras stood with the ball held high over his head and surveyed the scene, with Dick White closely eyeing him from a defensive stance. Then, with five seconds remaining, Bemoras brought the ball down, took one dribble toward the top of the key, and released a leaning twenty-two-foot jump shot. As the ball hung in the air, Bemoras's momentum carried him into Dick White, who collided hard into the right side of Bemoras and could have easily been called for a foul. White crashed to the floor while Bemoras regained his balance and quickly followed his shot, which caromed hard off the backboard and didn't touch the iron. Dick Farley snatched the rebound, spun around, and threw the ball ahead to Bobby Leonard, who tried to get off a long heave before time expired, but the gun had already sounded. It was on to double overtime.

Lou Scott won the opening tip from Johnny Kerr at the start of the second overtime and IU went to Dick Farley on the wing. Farley drove in and made a nifty spin move to free himself for a little hook shot in the lane, but it went in and out and Kerr got inside position on Scott for the rebound. Then Illinois patiently ran a play to free up Kerr, who got the ball at the free throw line, faced up on Scott and swished a fifteen-footer that put Illinois back in front at 68-66.

Back on the other end, Dick White attacked the basket and tried to score on a reverse layup, but Kerr used perfect timing to leap up and swat the ball out-of-bounds. But on the inbounds play, Leonard gamely stepped up and buried a twenty-five-footer to tie the game at 68-68 with 4:05 remaining.

Illinois came down and settled for a long jump shot that was short of the rim, and Lou Scott went up and plucked it out of the air. Then Indiana ran its five-man weave and Leonard paused near midcourt to let a little time tick away. Both teams were still scrapping with everything they had, but they were also wearing out. Around the 3:00 mark, Leonard made his move, drove to the left side, faked the shot and then fired the ball inside to Scott, who had good position on Kerr. Scott turned into the lane and shot a ten-foot hook that hit the right side of the rim and popped out, but Dick White streaked past his man from the wing to grab the offensive rebound and was fouled on the follow-up. White swished the first free throw but hit the front of the rim on the second, and IU had a one-point lead at 69-68 with 2:48 left.

Next, the Illini got the ball to Kerr deep in the lane, but he missed a short hook shot. Illinois got the offensive rebound and missed the follow-up from short range. Then things got physical in the scramble for the rebound and Kerr was whistled for fouling Lou Scott as referees and players separated the two of them to avoid an altercation. Scott stepped to the line and missed the first free throw badly, as the ball bounced hard against the back of the rim. But the second free throw hit nothing but net and Indiana went up 70-68 with 2:13 on the clock.

Once again, Illinois worked the ball around until they could get it to Kerr in good position. They got it to Johnny on the left side of the free throw line. He bobbled the ball and nearly lost it, but as soon as he got his hands firmly around it he put his head down and drove to the baseline, where he jump-stopped and pump-faked to get Scott off his feet. When Scott didn't fall for the fake, Kerr had to shoot a little fadeaway shot with Scott all over him. He tried to bank it and the shot looked good, but it bounced off the rim and Bobby Leonard darted in and blocked out the smaller Jim Bredar to grab the rebound. Leonard then took the ball the length of the floor before passing it back out to Phil Byers, and the Hoosiers began a game of keep-away by running their five-man weave again. Indiana called a time-out and then went right back into the weave. Bemoras finally fouled Dick White while going for the steal with 0:50 left.

After he was fouled by Bemoras and knocked off balance, White jogged toward the Indiana bench as he regained his stride, and he nonchalantly bounced the ball in the air with his right hand. If there weren't ten thousand spectators in the arena you wouldn't have known whether he had just called his own foul in a pickup game or whether he was about to go to the line with a chance to put away the team that was the favorite for the Big Ten and NCAA titles that season. As the sophomore stepped to the free throw stripe, he looked like the calmest man on the court. There was no tension in his shoulders and he looked totally oblivious to the fact that so much was hanging on his two charity shots. He didn't hesitate at all. He just looked like a kid shooting a shot he had practiced thousands of times before as he buried the first one to put IU up 71-68. Then he backed off and turned toward Bobby Leonard, who leaned in to say a few words. As Leonard spoke, White reached around and patted his leader on the back of the head, as if to say, "Don't worry, I got this one, too." Then he took one deliberate dribble and sank the second free throw—72-68 IU.

The Hoosiers didn't go into the full-court press, but immediately fell back on defense—except for one man. Dick Farley hung back and harassed the passer, and when the Illinois passer panicked and over-looked the wide-open Irv Bemoras on the other side of the floor to quickly lob the ball into Jim Bredar (who almost always brought the ball upcourt for the Illini), Farley used one of his long arms to reach out and steal the ball just before it reached Bredar. Farley then tossed the ball out to Leonard and the Hoosiers went back into their keep-away act for several moments until Bemoras hammered Farley with 0:05 remaining. Farley used his relaxed, underhanded free throw style to rattle in two more points and give Indiana an insurmountable 74-68 lead.

Bemoras hustled down and stopped, pump-faked White off his feet, and swished a ten-footer just before the buzzer to make the final score 74-70. But before the ball even hit the floor, pandemonium broke out in the IU Fieldhouse as players, cheerleaders, student managers, students, and even a few staff members swarmed in celebration at center court. In contrast to that scene, Johnny Kerr walked past with his head bowed while Branch McCracken shook hands with Harry Combes on the sidelines. Combes ran his fingers through his hair and followed Kerr back to the locker room. After shaking Combes's hand, McCracken slowly turned and walked down the sidelines, looking down at the floor. He never looked at the midcourt celebration but doggedly paved his way toward the steps at the end of the floor. He was a tired man who obviously knew how close his team had come to defeat, how important the game was that they had just won, and yet how far they still had to go to accomplish their goal. McCracken had been much closer than this to a Big Ten title and had it snatched out of his grasp before, so there was no way he was going to start celebrating after a win on January 17—even a win against the two-time defending Big Ten champs. As McCracken reached the stairs to leave the floor, he was joined by the rest of his team, who saw him heading for the locker room and took their cue that it was time to depart. His players slapped him on the back and there were a lot of arms thrown around Mac's broad shoulders, but his expression never changed. It was an important win, an absolutely pivotal win, but it was still only one win. And it was still only January 17.

Long after Mac and his boys cleared the floor, the IU Fieldhouse continued to resound with shouts and cheers. The crowd was jubilant, although emotionally exhausted, just as it had been the previous week after the Minnesota game. "It was great, wonderful!" bellowed IU president Herman B Wells after the game. Col. Raymond Shoemaker, dean of students, struck the other chord. "I'm going home to take some sleeping pills," he said.[11]

Since the Illini and the Hoosiers were both known for their running attacks, the showdown had been widely expected to be a shoot-out. When the first quarter had ended with the score 19-18 in IU's favor, it looked like the two teams were just getting warmed up for their usual hot-paced, high-scoring affair. However, the next two quarters had turned into a slog, with Illinois holding a 29-26 edge in the second and third quarters. Over that two-quarter period, neither team could get its fast break moving, but it wasn't because of the ineptitude of the offenses. It was because of the stinginess of the two defenses. The players on both teams had desperately hustled back on defense to break up or slow down every running opportunity, and that had turned this grudge match into a half-court struggle. That struggle continued during the first part of the fourth quarter, but then Indiana had started to get hot and looked like they might pull away. Not surprisingly, the veteran Illini kicked their game up a notch and met the challenge, as the two offenses regained their form and fought a seesaw battle that lasted until the Hoosiers took control in the final minutes of the second overtime.

After the final gun sounded and the mirthful spectators finally left the IU Fieldhouse, the stat sheet told the story of the Hoosiers' victory. Indiana shot just 31 percent from the field, but held Illinois to 25 percent. IU outrebounded Illinois 48-39, and the Hoosiers made thirty free throws while the Illini made only twenty-two. What kept Illinois in the game was that they put up a lot more shots—ninety-five by the Illini to seventy-one by the Hoosiers—and shot a much better free throw percentage—85 percent on 22-for-26 for the Illini to 68 percent on 30-for-44 for the Hoosiers.

The game's leading scorer was Don Schlundt with twenty-two points on 8-for-17 from the field. He also collected a team high eleven rebounds and helped hold Johnny Kerr to just 6-for-30 from the floor and fifteen points. Kerr also finished with ten rebounds.

While Schlundt was the top point-getter, the game's top perform-ers were Irv Bemoras and Bobby Leonard. Bemoras was the spark plug that powered the Illini to their biggest lead of the game in the third quarter, and his shooting (7-for-19 from the floor and 7-for-7 from the line) was one of the key factors that kept Illinois in the game. He finished with twenty-one points and ten rebounds. Meanwhile, Leonard practically willed the Hoosiers to the victory in the second half. He took care of all the ballhandling, orchestrated the half-court offense like a maestro, and saved all the big shots for himself. After netting only a single point in the first half, he scored seventeen points in the second half and the two overtimes to lead IU to the victory. Dick Farley added sixteen points and eight rebounds, and Dick White came off the bench to score ten, including eight of eleven free throws—nearly all of them at critical junctures. For Illinois, Jim Bredar added a gutsy seventeen points and Bob Peterson chipped in nine points. Illinois forward Max Hooper was the game's high rebounder with twelve. However, the defense of Farley, Kraak, and White held Hooper and five other Illinois forwards without a single field goal.

After the game, Illinois coach Harry Combes soothed his wounds at an Italian restaurant in Bloomington. Despite Illinois's gut-wrench-ing defeat, Combes was surprisingly upbeat when he talked about his team's performance with reporter Jack Powell of the *Champaign News-Gazette*.

"This is a better [Illinois] team than last year," Combes said. "It's better than the 1951 bunch. In my mind, it's better than the Whiz Kids [the great Illinois team from 1943]. It's a team that I think would do well in NCAA competition. I think they had set the NCAA [championship] as their goal."

Then Combes lifted his fork from his dinner, pointed it at Powell's notebook, and spoke another important epiphany about his team. "Put this down . . . I'm going to be surprised if they win. Everybody is after these kids, because they've won before."

Next, Harry summed up the meaning of the loss to Indiana. "Il-linois has never had a worse defeat—a defeat that meant so much—than this one. This may mean the end of our kids' championship chances. And I feel terrible. I never saw a team so ready to play. They gave it everything, and still lost. I thought it was our best game of the year.

"Don't take anything away from Indiana. Somebody had to lose, and it was us. It was tough to lose, sure, but Indiana is a great basketball team and it [has] lost tough ones over the years, too. I'll never forget the way the rest of those boys on the Indiana team turned to Leonard and Schlundt in the second half and just as much as said: 'You score for us.' They fed those two the ball, and they shot. Leonard took some bad shots, but he did it for the team. And the other players didn't mind. They counted on him to carry 'em through, and he did. And that Farley, what a ballplayer he is. He scores 10 points in the first half, he hurt us badly on the boards, and he's good defensively. He's their most valuable player.

"That's a great basketball team, and I'm not going to take anything away from them. We've still got a chance, just a bare chance, and we can't lose another one. I don't know whether we are up to that."[12]

CENTURY MARK

11

Almost everybody I knew in college served in the military.
You assumed you would either get drafted or most male
students were commissioned through the ROTC, either
through the Air Force or the Army. You just assumed that
you would. It didn't make you a hero, it was just something
that was taken for granted. It was the duty a man owed to
his country, or it was going to happen to him whether he
liked it or not.
—Martin Weissert, IU Class of 1955

On Monday, January 19, two days after IU won its critical victory over
Illinois, America opened a new chapter in its post–World War II history with the inauguration of Dwight D. Eisenhower as its new president. It was only the second time a president had been inaugurated
in front of a national television audience, and Eisenhower's inauguration was watched by seventy million Americans—half the nation.
Eisenhower's 1953 inaugural speech didn't contain any memorable
one-liners like John F. Kennedy's inaugural speech eight years later in
1961, but Eisenhower's rhetoric was a stirring testimony of the mindset of a nation still grappling with the angst of an unstable world and
yet also feeling the rising optimism of a new prosperity and peace. It
enunciated the values of the time and set them in perspective to the
timeless ideals that have defined the United States.

Eisenhower said, "The world and we have passed the midway
point of a century of continuing challenge. We sense with all our
faculties that forces of good and evil are massed and armed and op-

posed as rarely before in history. . . . Since this century's beginning, a time of tempest has seemed to come upon the continents of the earth. Masses of Asia have awakened to strike off shackles of the past. Great nations of Europe have fought their bloodiest wars. Thrones have toppled and their vast empires have disappeared. New nations have been born. For our own country, it has been a time of recurring trial. We have grown in power and in responsibility. We have passed through the anxieties of depression and of war to a summit unmatched in man's history. . . . In the swift rush of great events, we find ourselves groping to know the full sense and meaning of these times in which we live. . . . How far have we come in man's long pilgrimage from darkness toward light? Are we nearing the light—a day of freedom and of peace for all mankind? Or are the shadows of another night closing in upon us?

"... At such a time in history, we who are free must proclaim anew our faith. This faith is the abiding creed of our fathers. It is our faith in the deathless dignity of man, governed by eternal moral and natural laws. This faith defines our full view of life. It establishes, beyond debate, those gifts of the Creator that are man's inalienable rights, and that make all men equal in His sight. This faith rules our whole way of life. It decrees that we, the people, elect leaders not to rule but to serve. It asserts that we have the right to choice of our own work and to the reward of our own toil. It inspires the initiative that makes our productivity the wonder of the world. And it warns that any man who seeks to deny equality among all his brothers betrays the spirit of the free and invites the mockery of the tyrant . . .

"The enemies of this faith know no god but force, no devotion but its use. They tutor men in treason. They feed upon the hunger of others. Whatever defies them, they torture, especially the truth. . . . The faith we hold belongs not to us alone but to the free of all the world. . . . So we are persuaded by necessity and by belief that the strength of all free peoples lies in unity; their danger, in discord. To produce this unity, to meet the challenge of our time, destiny has laid upon our country the responsibility of the free world's leadership . . .

"We must be ready to dare all for our country. For history does not long entrust the care of freedom to the weak or the timid. We must acquire proficiency in defense and display stamina in purpose. We must be willing, individually and as a nation, to accept whatever sacrifices may be required of us. A people that values its privileges above its principles soon loses both. These basic precepts are not lofty abstractions, far removed from matters of daily living. They are laws of spiritual strength that generate and define our material strength. Patriotism means equipped forces and a prepared citizenry. Moral stamina means more energy and more productivity, on the farm and in the factory. Love of liberty means the guarding of every resource that makes freedom possible—from the sanctity of our families and the wealth of our soil to the genius of our scientists. . . . No person, no home, no community can be beyond the reach of this call. We are summoned to act in wisdom and in conscience, to work with industry, to teach with persuasion, to preach with conviction, to weigh our every deed with care and with compassion. For this truth must be clear before us: whatever America hopes to bring to pass in the world must first come to pass in the heart of America."

Back on November 4, 1952, Eisenhower, a moderate Republican, had won a predictable and decisive victory over Democrat Adlai Stevenson. Eisenhower was still a national hero after leading the successful Allied invasion of Nazi-occupied Europe in World War II. With 55 percent of the popular vote and a 442-89 landslide in the Electoral College, he easily swept by Stevenson in the presidential election.

When Eisenhower became the first Republican to occupy the White House in twenty-four years, no one in the state of Indiana was happier about it than Branch McCracken, who was a staunch Republican himself. Like much of the nation at the time, McCracken was not a fan of outgoing Democrat Harry Truman. Although basketball was by far McCracken's favorite subject on virtually any occasion, politics was usually second on the list. IU athletic director Paul "Pooch" Harrell was also a strong Republican, and when Mac and Pooch weren't talking sports, they were often reinforcing each other's conservative political views.

However, Mac wasn't overzealous about his political beliefs, and he took a good-natured stance when debating with students and colleagues who held different political opinions. In fact, the senior manager of IU's 1952–53 squad was Ron Fifer, a very active and outspoken member of the Young Democrats on campus. Despite Fifer's political affiliation, McCracken had handpicked Fifer to be the team's senior manager that year even though Fifer was not actually one of the top students in line for the job.

The way it worked for the student manager jobs on the basketball team was that there were four freshman managers, usually rotated among the different fraternities and campus organizations, three sophomore managers, two junior managers, and one senior manager. Each year was a weeding-out process until each class got down to a single senior manager, who had several important responsibilities with the team. Chief among those responsibilities was acting as the team's business manager on the road and serving as the official scorekeeper for home games. In general, the senior manager also served as a de facto personal assistant to the head coach.

Fifer had started his college career at IU Southeast (in New Albany) as a freshman. As a sophomore he transferred to the main IU campus in Bloomington and got one of the posts as a freshman student manager. As a junior he served as a sophomore manager, which would have likely been the end of the road for him, but instead he leapfrogged the two junior managers to get the senior manager job for the 1952–53 season. "Branch decided he didn't like the two junior managers he had to choose between and so I got the job," said Fifer.

The senior manager had a desk in the alcove just outside the office McCracken shared with Ernie Andres in the old Men's Gymnasium, and Fifer spent a lot of time at that little desk. "Every hour that I wasn't in class, I was spending time in the basketball office," Fifer said, "and so I got to be very close to Branch and he was very good to me."

Still, their divergent political views naturally led to plenty of hot debates. "Branch and I used to get in political arguments all the time," said Fifer. And Pooch Harrell also gave Fifer plenty of grief about his liberal political views. Once when Fifer, who handled all the team's cash on the road, turned in the basketball team's expense report to Harrell after a road trip, Harrell growled, "Damn, I can tell you're a Democrat. You're a deficit spender."

One of Eisenhower's most important campaign promises in 1952 was that he would make a speedy assessment of the Korean War (known at the time as the "Korean Conflict") and would work quickly to bring an end to the stalemate that had bogged down the war since the middle of 1951 and helped fuel Harry Truman's unpopularity. Many Americans took Eisenhower's words as a commitment to find a resolution to the conflict and bring home the U.S. troops. Eisenhower proved he was serious about the situation when he traveled to Korea on November 29, 1952—less than a month after his election victory and more than a month and a half before his inauguration.

The situation in Korea weighed heavily on the minds of IU students, including the members of the basketball team. The Selective Service was scooping up healthy young men in large numbers during that era. Every male had to register with his local draft board, and with Korea and other postwar hot spots needing troops in the early 1950s, the draft boards were always after hardy young men with backgrounds in athletics. What kept the members of the IU basketball team—and other male college students as well—from being drafted was *not* that they were enrolled at a university, but that they were enrolled in an ROTC (Reserve Officer Training Corps) program. At Indiana University, there were two options: Army ROTC and Air Force ROTC. "As long as you were in the ROTC program, you were pretty much exempt from the draft or getting taken out of school and sent to Korea or anywhere else," said Charlie Kraak, who had a cousin who was killed in Korea as an army infantryman. However, part of the deal with an ROTC program was that you also had to serve a two-year term in the military after you graduated from college, so nearly all male college students had that hanging over them in the early 1950s.

The foreword of IU's 1953 *Arbutus* yearbook clearly enunciates the atmosphere of the times:

" 'Don't tense' is *the* expression of the hour. It is the college Joe and Jane's own—developed after three long years of growing up in a scared, unstable world. Phrases such as 'Frustration of the times,' 'futility of the future' now sound acutely trite to the college student. He feels silly being described as desperate, emotionally insecure, depressed. He's tired of melodramatics and he's developed a stage technique of brilliant understatement. Worn out with talk that arrives nowhere, he has stopped talking.

"Not overly optimistic, yet not appreciably pessimistic, he tries to formulate tentative plans for the future, realizing that he must knit loosely to allow for alterations. Girls want to learn something useful, practical—a major that can procure a job while their men are at war. Fellows want to get their education behind them, serve their term in the army, get out and then start building a future.

"When asked how he feels about the war and the times, a college student's first impulse seems to be, 'Do I have any feelings?' He seems to have solved his uncertainty by variations of the philosophy, 'wait and see.'

"His mind has reconciled itself that there is a war, the end of which is not in sight. The fellows have to go, fight, and perhaps never come back; and the girls have to wait and occupy their minds with a job. When he comes back, that is the time the student expects to make some real plans. That is what everything hinges on . . .

"Although the war and the upset are important to him, the coke date at 2:30, the committee meeting at 7:00, his date for the formal next week end and the grade he made on his Physics test occupy most of his thoughts. He has been graphically shown by three shaky years that it is perhaps best not to try to look too far into the future. He has decided the best thing to do is to 'play it cool,' 'don't tense' and take things as they come."[1]

Forty-eight hours after their big win over Illinois, the IU basketball team had to travel to West Lafayette for a game with Purdue. Following up its triumph over the Illini with a showdown against the Boilermakers was both a blessing and a curse. On one hand, there was little chance that the Hoosiers would have an emotional letdown against their archrival. On the other hand, after nail-biting, energy-sapping victories over Minnesota and Illinois on two straight Saturdays, IU was running on empty, and the Boilermakers, who were floundering at the bottom of the conference, were undoubtedly going to be fired up. Handing the Hoosiers their first conference loss would have provided the ultimate bright spot in what was turning out to be a disappointing season in West Lafayette.

Unlike Indiana, Purdue hadn't played on Saturday, so the Boilermakers were much better rested heading into the Monday night matchup. Purdue had lost its previous game to Notre Dame 71-55 in the Purdue Fieldhouse, and the Boilermakers were struggling with a 2-7 record for the season, but there were plenty of IU basketball fans who nervously expected Purdue to give IU a tough time—especially in West Lafayette.

Apparently, not all Purdue fans felt the same way. On game day, the *Indianapolis Star* reported, "For the first time in many years, the Indiana-Purdue game at Lafayette tonight is not a sellout . . . fans must think the game is in the bag for Coach Branch McCracken's crew. To be sure, the Hurryin' Hoosiers are heavy favorites but when Indiana and Purdue lock horns anything can happen."[2]

The *Lafayette Journal and Courier* took a much more pessimistic outlook in its game-day coverage: "With the 'Hoosier Flyers' out there 'winging it,' tonight's game at the Purdue fieldhouse against the league's cellar occupants takes on the aspect of an exhibition."[3] However, the *Journal and Courier* also took the opportunity to get in a few well-placed shots against the Hoosiers. The opening shot was: "The first Indiana University basketball championship in Big Ten history appears almost assured. . . . All other conference schools have won at least one undisputed league title, but Indiana has staggered through half a century without gaining such an honor."[4] This assertion wasn't completely true. Newcomer Michigan State had never won an undisputed conference crown either. It also didn't take into account Indiana's three *shared* championships and innumerable second-place finishes. But the *Journal and Courier* didn't stop there. It also pulled Purdue's favorite trump card: "The Boilermakers, who have plunged to 'doormat' ratings in the Big Ten only in the last decade, still hold a wide all-time margin over Indiana, 58 wins to 29."[5] What the *Journal and Courier* failed to mention was that the Hoosiers had won eight straight in the series, including five straight in West Lafayette.

The trip to West Lafayette was one of the few road trips in which the Indiana team didn't fly. Instead they took a bus from Bloomington and eventually picked up U.S. Route 52 into Lafayette. Because the Hoosiers were taking the bus, they also took a larger traveling team than normal. Instead of taking twelve players, the Hoosiers took fifteen to Purdue, and they also took an extra student manager—John Heiney, one of the sophomore managers. The team left Bloomington at around 9:30 AM, stopped for lunch at Crawfordsville around 11:30 AM, and pulled into the Fowler Hotel in Lafayette around 2:00 PM. Game time was 7:30 that night.

The big question mark going into the game was whether IU's Charlie Kraak would be healthy enough to start and play at full strength. Kraak came out of the Illinois game with a bump on his right knee that had limited his action against the Illini. In the day between the two games, Charlie went through a light workout with the team, but his status was still undetermined leading up to game day. If Kraak couldn't start, most of the speculation centered around Dick White's taking his spot at forward in the starting lineup.

Purdue coach Ray Eddy had better news on the injury front. His starting sophomore guard Denny Blind, who had been an Indiana all-star from Lafayette Jeff in 1951, had recovered from a leg injury and was set to return to action against the Hoosiers.

When the ball tipped, both Kraak and Blind were on the floor and ready to go to battle. The Boilermakers came out with unbridled hustle, grit, and aggressiveness and turned the first half into a typical IU-Purdue grudge match that belied the teams' current standings in the conference. Thirty seconds into the game, IU led 4-0 on two free throws and a field goal from Don Schlundt. But Purdue quickly struck back with four straight points of its own to tie the game at 4-4. Several minutes later, Purdue forward Jack Runyan scored to put the Boilermakers ahead 13-12. IU tied it at 14-14, but Purdue center Glen Calhoun sank a hook shot to give the Boilermakers a 16-14 advantage. All told, the first quarter featured five ties and five lead changes before Purdue came away with a surprising 19-18 lead.

The Boilermaker advantage didn't last long. Just ten seconds into the second quarter, IU's Dick Farley scored to regain the lead for the Hoosiers. IU then monopolized the lead for most of the quarter until Calhoun scored to give Purdue a 35-34 edge in the final minutes.

However, that was the Boilermakers' last lead of the game. Indiana made a final spurt to take a 41-38 lead into the locker room at half-time.

One of the key elements of Purdue's first-half strategy was to foul Don Schlundt every time he got the ball in scoring position. This was effective in slowing the game down and keeping the Hoosiers from kicking their running game into high gear, but it was only moderately effective in slowing down Schlundt, who was held to a single field goal in the first half but scored twelve points on free throws and got most of Purdue's big men in foul trouble.

As usual, Bob Leonard was the Hoosiers' catalyst in the second half. He scored early in the third quarter to put IU ahead 44-38, and it looked as if Indiana was ready to pull away, but Purdue kept hanging on. With three minutes remaining in the third quarter, the Boiler-makers pulled back to within three points at 55-52. Then Leonard and IU finally broke free with a 10-0 run to close out the quarter, a stretch in which Calhoun fouled out for Purdue. Indiana's lead was 65-52 heading into the fourth quarter and the game was essentially over.

While Indiana played mostly its reserves in the final quarter, Purdue kept fighting and matched IU point-for-point in the quarter to make the final score 88-75. In addition to Calhoun, the Boilermakers also lost two other centers—Bob Vanderpool and Bill German—because of fouls. All told, Purdue committed thirty-nine fouls, while Indiana committed twenty-nine. The Hoosiers ended up shooting a grand total of fifty-five free throws, making forty-two of them. Schlundt was 16-for-20 from the line and finished with a game-high twenty-six points. Leonard, who scored just one point in the opening thirteen minutes of the game, triggered IU's offense in the second half and finished with twenty-one points. Burke Scott chipped in fourteen points for the Hoosiers, and Lou Scott and Phil Byers came off the bench to score seven and eight points, respectively. Denny Blind led the Boilermakers with fourteen points, and all five Purdue starters scored in double figures.

For the Boilermakers, it was one of their best performances of the season, but they were simply outgunned by the Hoosiers in the second half, and Purdue's aggressiveness ran its course when several of their top players got into foul trouble in the third quarter.

Although the Hoosiers had cruised to victory after their big run at the end of the third quarter and McCracken called off the dogs in the fourth quarter, it would be a mistake to think that the rivalry had lost any of its usual rancor and intensity. It would also be a mistake to think that beating the Boilermakers wasn't important to Mac, who had beaten Purdue only once during his playing career and had repeatedly watched Purdue dominate his alma mater after he graduated. Mac was keenly aware of the hot streak he had going against IU's archrival. As the Hoosiers filed back into the locker room after the game, McCracken exclaimed, "Well, we beat those sons-of-bitches for the ninth time in a row!"

There wasn't a soul in Bloomington who was happier about the Hoosiers' big wins over Illinois and Purdue than Nick Poolitsan, one of the owners of The Gables, a wildly popular student hangout famous for its hamburgers, sodas, and ice cream. The Gables was located on Indiana Avenue, right across from the Administration Building (now called Bryan Hall). Even more important was that next to Bryan Hall was the IU library (now called Franklin Hall), the epicenter of campus activity.

One of the time-honored rituals of that era was the "Coke date" or study date in which a guy would ask a "co-ed" (girl) to go study at the library and then afterwards they would walk across the street and get a Coke or a milk shake at The Gables, one of the diners that became an emblem of America in the 1950s. It had a jukebox, booths for two or four, and a counter where patrons could be served directly by Nick Poolitsan, a friendly little Greek man in a white button-up shirt with a bow tie and a white apron. Nick had a completely bald head but with short-cropped, jet black hair around the sides and back, and bushy black eyebrows. He wore black-framed glasses and a warm, grandfatherly smile.

There were plenty of IU faculty, staff members, and townies who frequented The Gables, but Nick Poolitsan's primary patrons were IU students, and he knew that and embraced it. Nick even let some of the regular students keep a "tab" when they couldn't pay. A longtime graduate student in the medical school named John "Hap" Dragoo once ran up a huge tab. Hap, who also moonlighted as a tutor for the athletic department during the late 1940s and early 1950s, knew that his tab was getting out of hand and so one day he went into The Gables and asked Nick to give him the total. When Nick added it all up, it came to $93.41. Hap said, "Okay, I'll be right back." He went across the street to the Administration Building and took out a student loan for $93.41, then took the check across the street and signed it over to Nick. That night, Hap got a full meal on the house.

Poolitsan also decorated the walls of The Gables with photos and memorabilia from IU basketball and football. Behind the counter, he suspended a large white sign from the ceiling that said "Pick by Nick" across the bottom in block lettering. One side of the sign had a large red megaphone with an Indiana "I" and the other side had a football player running the ball, and in the middle of the sign was a box where Nick would slip a large index card before every IU football and basketball game with his prediction for the score. Now, Nick was a pure homer—and obviously proud of it—because he always picked IU to win. As a result, Nick usually took a beating during football season because the Hoosiers were perennial cellar-dwellers in the Big Ten. Nick always fared better during basketball season when McCracken's boys took over the spotlight. The Hoosiers made Nick look especially brilliant with their wins during the 1952–53 season, but the highlight of Nick's picks that season came with his Illinois and Purdue picks on January 17 and 19. Nick predicted a 78-74 win over Illinois (74-70 was the final) and an 89-73 victory against Purdue (88-75 was the final).

The Purdue victory was Indiana's eighth-straight win, and it improved the Hoosiers' season record to 9-2 and their Big Ten mark to 8-0. Second-place Illinois remained two full games behind at 6-2 after grinding out a 76-64 win at Michigan State, a game that left the Spartans at 4-3 and tied with Minnesota for third place in the conference. The only other Big Ten team with a winning record in league play was Wisconsin at 5-4. Although there was a long way to go in the eighteen-game Big Ten schedule, it was essentially a two-team race between the Hoosiers and the Illini.

On Monday, January 19, the new Associated Press poll was released and it reflected a major shake-up as a result of games over the weekend. The nation's previous No. 1 team, Kansas State, took an 80-66 lashing from its archrival Kansas on Saturday, and as a result, the Wildcats dropped all the way to fourth in the poll while the Jayhawks jumped up to ninth. The new No. 1 team was Seton Hall, which was 18-0 and the only undefeated team remaining among the major colleges. It was the first time in school history that the Pirates had ascended to No. 1. Meanwhile, with its impressive victory over Illinois, Indiana jumped from No. 6 to No. 2, while Illinois dropped from No. 4 to No. 6. The Washington Huskies jumped up to No. 3 (from No. 5) and rounding out the top five was LaSalle, which had been ranked No. 1 back in December and was No. 3 the previous week before suffering a key loss. The only other Big Ten team represented in the poll was Minnesota at No. 19. The complete poll looked like this:

1. Seton Hall
2. Indiana
3. Washington
4. Kansas State
5. LaSalle
6. Illinois
7. Oklahoma
8. North Carolina State
9. Kansas
10. Fordham
11. Tulsa
12. Western Kentucky
13. Seattle
14. Louisiana State
15. California
16. Notre Dame
17. Oklahoma City
18. Eastern Kentucky
19. Minnesota
20. Manhattan

Later that week, another set of national rankings was released—the Litkenhous Difference-By-Score Ratings, or "Litratings," which were established in 1934 by Fred Litkenhous and Edward Litkenhous, a Vanderbilt professor, as a scientific way to rank sports teams. In the Litratings, Indiana shot to No.1. The top fifteen were:

1. Indiana (88.5)
2. Illinois (87.7)
3. Washington (84.2)
4. LaSalle (82.9)
5. Kansas State (82.4)
6. Minnesota (82.1)
7. Michigan State (81.2)
8. Notre Dame (79.9)
9. Oklahoma A&M (79.3)
10. California (78.8)
11. Wisconsin (78.8)
12. Seattle (78.6)
13. Kansas (78.3)
14. UCLA (78.1)
15. Iowa (77.9)

Not everyone was happy about Indiana's being ranked so high and getting so much national attention. A columnist for the *Indiana Daily Student* wrote, "It's nice to be No. 2 in the country, but not midway in the season. The University of Kentucky is the only team we can remember that could stay that high up and win consistently."[6] IU fans keenly remembered the 1951 Hoosier squad that was ranked in the top ten all season and rose as high as No. 3 at the end of January but was edged out by Illinois for the Big Ten title and never played in the postseason. There was still a fear in Hoosierland that Lady Luck might have another cruel twist of fate up her sleeve.

After the Purdue game, the Hoosiers—and the rest of the Big Ten—had a two-week layoff to focus on final exams. During this era, the first semester at Indiana University ran from mid-September to the end of January, and the second semester ran from the beginning of February to the beginning of June. During the league-enforced hiatus between semesters, the basketball players could focus on preparing for their final exams and could attend all their exams without having to reschedule them around the basketball schedule.

After playing Purdue on Monday, January 19, the Hoosiers didn't have another game until Monday, February 2, when they hosted Butler. They didn't have another conference game until Saturday, February 7, at Northwestern.

Even though they weren't playing any games during those two weeks, the IU squad practiced daily and basked in the warm glow of media attention as a result of their red-hot 8-0 start in the Big Ten. An Associated Press photographer came to campus for a photo shoot and captured several photos that made the rounds on the AP wire. One of the prominent photos showed McCracken standing with his hands in his pockets in front of a basket in the IU Fieldhouse with Don Schlundt and Lou Scott on opposite sides of the basket. Both of the big men had a basketball raised high in their right hand, looking as if a simple flick of the wrist was all it would take to score. The other prominent AP photo had McCracken kneeling at center court, in front of the red "I" with Schlundt and Scott kneeling on one side of him and Jim Schooley and Bobby Leonard kneeling on the other side.

During the break, the newspapers were also astonished when they started adding up the season statistics and projecting the number of offensive records the Hoosiers were on track to shatter. The *Bloomington Daily Herald-Telephone* wrote, "Of course, the Big Ten is playing an 18-game schedule this year for the first time, compared with a 14-game card for the 1951–52 season. This fact naturally would account for many of the new records that will go into the books. But, Indiana, at its present pace, still would collect many new marks, even in a 14-game schedule."[7]

As a team, the Hoosiers had scored 900 points and were easily on pace to break their single-season scoring record of 1,621 points from the previous season. They also had 655 points in Big Ten play and were on pace to shatter their conference mark of 1,035. Don Schlundt was shooting .452 from the field and .807 from the line—blistering numbers for that era. Don had already broken several records at that point in the season. The seventeen free throws he made against Michigan set a new Big Ten record. The year before, he had set a new school record with a total of seventy-six free throws in league play. He had already broken that with eighty-two free throws in eight games during the 1952–53 season, and he was within easy striking distance of the conference record of 100 free throws set by Iowa's Chuck Darling. With thirty-nine points against Michigan, Schlundt had also broken the school record of thirty-five points he set against Purdue as a freshman. Both Schlundt and Leonard were on track to blow away the season record for field goals (eighty-six) in conference play that Leonard had set the year before. Leonard already had fifty-four field goals and Schlundt had fifty-nine, and there were still ten games left to play in the regular season. Schlundt, who was averaging 25.0 points per game in conference play, even had an outside chance at becoming the Big Ten's all-time leading scorer—by the end of his sophomore year.

The game immediately following the semester break had not been kind to the Hoosiers during the previous two seasons. During the 1950–51 season, the Hoosiers emerged from the break with a 13-1 record, ranked No. 3 in the country, and leading the Big Ten with a 6-0 record. Their first game after the break was against Minnesota, the team the Hoosiers had beaten in the final game before the break, but IU had to travel to Minneapolis for the contest after the break, and the result was disastrous. IU lost 61-54. Nine days later, Indiana suffered a loss at Illinois, and the Illini went on to win the conference title by one game over IU.

McCracken actually preferred to schedule a non-conference game right after the break (usually in the IU Fieldhouse), so that his teams could work their way back into form without sacrificing a conference game. Mac went back to that strategy in the 1951–52 season, but it didn't work out very well as St. John's came into Bloomington on February 2 and soundly defeated the young Hoosiers 65-55.

St. John's was also a stronger opponent than what IU normally faced after the semester break. McCracken often scheduled a small school, usually Butler, and that was the team the IU squad faced after the break in 1953. That Butler team had gotten off to a dismal 2-4 start but had won eight of their previous nine games—and four straight—heading into their showdown with Indiana. Butler's 10-5 overall record included six games against Big Ten schools, with wins over Purdue, Ohio State, and Michigan.

Butler had played four games during the time that the Hoosiers enjoyed their semester break, so the Bulldogs were expected to be much sharper. Plus, as the *Indiana Daily Student* put it, "Coach Tony Hinkle, in his twenty-fourth year as head coach at Butler, is the dean of Indiana coaches, and he will not be frightened by Indiana's impressive record and high national ratings. His well-reputed 'Hinkle system' is unique in the Midwest, and still survives in spite of the obsoleteness of the 'set-pattern' type of basketball."[8] Butler was widely expected to give the second-ranked Hoosiers a tough game.

Back on January 17, Hinkle sat with Purdue coach Ray Eddy in the south press box at the IU Fieldhouse and watched the Hoosiers pull out their double-overtime victory against Illinois. If Hinkle was impressed by IU's performance that night, he must have been overwhelmed by the way his Bulldogs ended up getting manhandled two weeks later on the same floor.

The game started well enough for Butler, which quickly jumped out to a 4-0 advantage on two baskets from tiny 5' 9" guard Jim Crosley. Butler surprised Indiana by trying to run with the Hoosiers, and it worked, if only briefly. The Bulldogs led 9-3 after the first three minutes in the IU Fieldhouse, which was only partly full because many of the students were home on semester break (there were no classes that week). However, by the 5:40 mark, IU grabbed a 12-11 lead when Bobby Leonard hit from long distance. That was part of a 24-11 IU run, which put the Hoosiers up 27-20 at the close of the first quarter. Schlundt scored eleven points in the opening quarter and Leonard racked up seven.

IU's hot streak got even hotter in the second quarter. The Hoosiers held Butler scoreless for the first four minutes while IU poured in baskets from every angle. Indiana started with an 18-4 run to open the quarter, which, combined with their 24-11 run to close the first quarter, amounted to a 42-15 run and a 45-24 advantage. The Bulldogs played the Hoosiers even for the rest of the quarter, but still trailed 60-39 when the gun sounded to end the half. In addition to the scoring of Schlundt and Leonard, the other big story of the first half was Dick Farley's defense on Butler's top-scoring forward Keith Greve. Greve normally averaged seventeen points per game, but Farley held him to a single free throw in the first two quarters.

Butler changed tactics in the second quarter, as they went back into their control game and succeeded in turning the contest into a half-court game. At that point, the Hoosiers buckled down and started pounding the ball into Schlundt on nearly every possession. After Burke Scott scored IU's first three points of the third quarter, Schlundt put on an inside-scoring clinic, as he notched seventeen straight points for IU. The Hoosiers led 80-51 at the end of the third quarter.

Then Schlundt retired to the bench for the fourth quarter with thirty-three points to his credit, and the suspense seemed to be gone from the game. However, the IU fans continued to eye the scoreboard and cheer on IU's mix of second- and third-string players when they came in. The Hoosier faithful were sitting on the edge of their seats to see if this was going to be the night their boys would finally break 100 for the first time in school history.

With 2:45 left to play, Lou Scott buried a hook shot to give Indiana a 96-53 bulge, and the IU crowd sensed that the moment was at hand. Reserve guard Jackie Wright then nailed a little running hook shot and the Hoosiers were on the precipice of the century mark. The crowd was practically bursting with anticipation. At the 2:14 mark, Wright drew a foul and stepped to the line. Wright was one of the Hoosiers' best free throw shooters, and although he had logged very little court time so far during the season, he was like a seasoned veteran on the line. He calmly nailed the first one, then nailed the crucial second one as well, and the IU Fieldhouse erupted as if Wright had just hit a game-winner. The electronic scoreboard, which only had a place for two digits, rolled over from "99" to "00" as Branch McCracken stared up at it, grinning and shaking his head, as if even he was amazed by what his boys had accomplished.

"I don't like to run up a large score against a beaten team," said McCracken afterwards, "but there was nothing I could do about it. ... Everybody was hitting."[9]

Butler never quit. The Bulldogs still made a final run after the Hoosiers hit 100 and the final score ended up 105-70. In addition to

Schlundt's thirty-three points (9-for-21 from the floor and 15-for-16 from the line) and ten rebounds, IU also got terrific performances from three sophomores: Burke Scott had fifteen points and seven rebounds, Dick White had thirteen points and seven rebounds, and Phil Byers chipped in eleven points. Dick Farley finished with seven points and eleven rebounds and held Butler's Keith Greve to a paltry six points on 2-for-13 from the field.

With the Butler game under its belt, the IU squad prepared to return to conference play against the only two Big Ten teams it had not yet faced—Northwestern and Wisconsin. On Friday, February 6, the Hoosiers took the train to the Chicago area and set up camp in the North Shore Hotel in Evanston for their Saturday game against the Wildcats in the newly built, 18,000-seat McGaw Fiedhouse. Under first-year coach Waldo Fisher, the Wildcats were only 4-7 in league play, but they were a dangerous and streaky team. They had already defeated Minnesota in Minneapolis and had lost to Iowa by a single point in Iowa City, yet they had also suffered lopsided losses to Illinois and Wisconsin. Earlier in the week, Northwestern had lost 72-69 to Minnesota in Evanston. The most difficult thing about preparing for the Wildcats was that opposing teams didn't know which team would show up, the one that beat Minnesota up north or the one that got run out of the gym in Illinois.

One advantage IU didn't have against Northwestern—as they did against most teams—was a major height advantage. The Wildcats had a pair of centers, 6' 8" Frank Petrancek and 6' 10" Hal Grant, who could match up against Don Schlundt and Lou Scott. The Wildcats also had comparable height at the forward and guard positions. Where Northwestern didn't match up with Indiana was in the scoring department. While IU was averaging 83.8 points per game, Northwestern was scoring just 69.9. And Northwestern's top two scorers, Larry Dellefield at 11.1 points per game and Larry Kurka at 11.0 points per game, were barely averaging more that IU's third-leading scorer, Dick Farley, at 10.6 points per game—let alone Schlundt at 23.3 points per game and Leonard at 16.4. Naturally, the numbers didn't add up too well for the Wildcats, but Northwestern almost always played well against Indiana. In the all-time series, the Hoosiers held only a 28-25 edge, even though the Wildcats had collected just two conference titles and were a perennial second-division finisher.

For the first three quarters on February 7 in the McGaw Fieldhouse, the Indiana squad came in and simply outclassed Northwestern. But then something extremely unusual happened: the Hoosiers suddenly forgot how to score. By midway through the fourth quarter, the Wildcats found themselves with a chance to knock off the Big Ten's top dog.

No. 2 Indiana started the game in typical fashion, jumping out to a 20-13 lead at the end of the first quarter, with Don Schlundt carrying much of the scoring load. By halftime, IU upped the lead to 44-30 and appeared to be comfortably on the way to its tenth-straight win overall. In the third quarter, Northwestern started to heat up, scoring twenty-four points, but Indiana easily matched that and went one better with twenty-five, and the Hoosiers led 69-54 going into the final ten-minute period. The end result looked academic, but, for the first time all season, things started unraveling for Indiana.

The Hoosiers went scoreless for the first four and a half minutes of the fourth quarter, while Northwestern rode the hot hands of Larry Kurka and Frank Petrancek, who combined to put thirteen unanswered points on the board and cut the lead to 69-67. Schlundt finally broke the scoring drought to push IU's lead back to four, but Kurka answered, and by the midway point of the quarter, Indiana's lead was down to 71-70. Schlundt and Northwestern's John Biever traded baskets to make it 73-72. At that point, it was clear that the game was going to be a dogfight until the end, and the Wildcats had momentum and the home crowd on their side.

The Hoosiers were badly in danger of buckling, but instead they pulled together. Schlundt buried a pair of free throws and Leonard canned a field goal to give IU a five-point lead. The Wildcats kept coming, but the Hoosiers answered every charge. When it wasn't Leonard or Schlundt, it was Charlie Kraak, Dick Farley, or Dick White coming up with a big play. The boys in the cream and crimson stayed focused and unified and refused to give up the lead. The Wildcats scratched and clawed, but were never able to pull ahead. When the final gun sounded, it was Indiana 88, Northwestern 84.

Schlundt led all scorers with thirty-two points (on 12-for-21 from the field), his fifth thirty-point performance of the season. Leonard and White had thirteen points apiece and Kraak and Farley each scored eleven. Kurka led Northwestern with twenty-two, while Petrancek added sixteen. Like many previous Hoosier opponents, Northwestern also had its leading scorer handcuffed by Dick Farley, who held Larry Dellefield to just six points on 2-for-8 from the field.

The Northwestern game wasn't pretty. The start of the fourth quarter featured Indiana's worst stretch of basketball thus far in the season, but it was also a defining moment for the Hoosiers. And this Hoosier squad defined the moment with teamwork and tenacity.

With its undefeated conference record still intact, Indiana returned home the day after the Northwestern win to prepare for a Monday night showdown with the Wisconsin Badgers squad that nearly knocked off Illinois in Madison on Saturday night. Wisconsin led late in the game but faltered at the end as Illinois escaped with a 65-61 victory. Wisconsin had used its zone defense to effectively bottle up the Illini's Johnny Kerr and Bob Peterson, and the Badgers were expected to use the same tactics to clog the lane against Don Schlundt. On offense, the Badgers employed a set offense that methodically worked for its shots. As a result, McCracken fully expected the Wisconsin game to be a low-scoring slog.

Wisconsin coach Bud Foster was one of Mac's closest friends in the conference. The two of them played professional ball together in their younger years and maintained a mutual respect and friendship throughout their successful coaching careers. Foster's Badgers had won the NCAA championship in 1941, the year after McCracken's Hoosiers first won it in 1940. However, the Badgers also derailed Indiana's conference title hopes in both 1941 and 1947, and they led the all-time series with the Hoosiers 34-19. On the other hand, McCracken held a 7-6 advantage in his thirteen games against the Badgers as IU's head coach.

Knowing that Wisconsin would look to use its zone to put the squeeze on Schlundt, Mac believed that the key to the game for his Hoosiers was how well they shot from the outside. Bob Leonard and Dick White were his top two marksmen, but for the Wisconsin game McCracken also had a new sharpshooter to unveil in the form of 6' 1" guard Paul Poff. Since Monday was the first day of the new semester, McCracken was now free to use Poff, who had transferred to IU from the University of Detroit at the midpoint of the 1951–52 school year. Poff had been an Indiana high school superstar, leading New Albany to a 99-16 record during his years there as well as two trips to semistate and one trip to state. Because of that, he was well known to IU fans and his addition to the team was highly anticipated.

Unfortunately, with the new semester starting the day of the Wisconsin game, McCracken not only had an addition to his roster, he also had a subtraction. At around 5:00 PM in the IU Fieldhouse—two and a half hours before game time—workers were unpacking the programs for the evening's Big Ten grudge match. On the cover of that program was a feature on Lou Scott, including a photo of him dribbling the ball and a description that opened, "Fans who have watched the transformation of 6-10 Lou Scott from an earnest but raw and unpolished sophomore to a highly-capable junior who is at home in the fastest of company marvel at the improvement the Chicago 20-year-old has accomplished. Lou is in that category of a 'manufactured' player, the product of coaching and desire. When he entered Indiana University he had little to recommend him except exceptional height and the ambition—accompanied by a willingness to work—of becoming a great basketball player. . . . Long hours of extra practice and tutelage under Coach McCracken, coupled with Lou's unflagging effort to improve, have brought him much closer to his goal."

While those programs were being sorted, stacked, and prepared to be distributed to 10,000 Hoosier fans that night, the news was being delivered to Coach McCracken that Lou Scott had failed a conditional exam in history. Lou therefore flunked his history class for the first semester and was ineligible to play basketball for the remainder of the season. The sometimes combustible McCracken took the news with evenhanded composure, but he knew losing "the Horse" (as the team called Scott) was going to hurt. Scott had been relieving Schlundt during long stretches in many games, especially during the second quarter and at the start of the fourth, which allowed Schlundt to stay fresh and gave McCracken a loaded gun when he needed it at the end of the game. Scott had also performed admirably when he was in the game. At 7.4 points per game, he was the Hoosiers' fifth-leading scorer. Against Kansas State and Ohio State, Big Lou had stepped in when Schlundt got into early foul trouble and scored sixteen and twelve points, respectively. Losing him meant that Schlundt would have to log more minutes and that Mac was going to have to relieve him with 6' 5" Charlie Kraak, 6' 3" Dick Farley, or 6' 5" Jim Schooley.

It was against physical teams like Wisconsin that Indiana would miss Lou Scott most acutely—not only because of his size, but also because of his toughness. The boys from the dairy state didn't have Indiana's height, but they had some big inside players who knew how to throw their weight around. Starting center Paul Morrow was 6' 7" and 208 pounds (roughly the same weight as Scott, who was three or four inches taller), and Morrow was backed up by a pair of 6' 6", 200-pound reserves named Daniel Folz and Robert Weber. Morrow averaged 14.7 points per game, which tied him for the team lead with forward Dick Cable, but Cable was leading the Badgers in scoring in conference play with a 14.3 average while Morrow averaged 12.9. As a result, Cable drew the unwelcome assignment of being defended by Dick Farley.

As expected, Wisconsin opened the game in a tightly packed zone defense. Morrow repeatedly fronted Schlundt to deny him the ball, and when Don did manage to get it, additional Wisconsin defenders immediately collapsed on him. The strategy worked brilliantly in the opening minutes as Schlundt was roughed up and held scoreless. As the officials allowed the Badgers to bang Schlundt around, it didn't take long for McCracken to lose his temper. He got extremely animated with the refs and his antics got more pronounced each time Schlundt was hammered without getting a call. Still, the Badgers led 8-3 after three minutes and IU had yet to score a field goal. Schlundt didn't score at all until he sank two free throws to tie the game at 10-10 with just four minutes left to play in the first quarter. Then, almost a minute later, Schlundt scored IU's first field goal of the game to put the Hoosiers up 12-10. Bob Leonard finally found the range on a long jumper just before the end of the first quarter to give IU a 16-11 advantage.

It wasn't just the Badgers' defense that proved rock-hard. The Hoosiers gave Wisconsin fits as the Badgers tried to execute their set plays. Indiana's speed and quickness disrupted passes and didn't allow any Badger to get an open look at the basket, which led to a lot of miscues and errant shots. In the second quarter, both defenses continued to dominate the action and neither offense could find much of a rhythm, but Schlundt and Leonard started to find a few gaps and they triggered a 10-3 run that gave the Hoosiers a 37-25 lead at the intermission. Both Schlundt and Leonard racked up twelve points in the first half.

The start of the third quarter was a repeat of the start of the game as Wisconsin locked down IU. The Badgers opened the second half on a 9-2 run and narrowed Indiana's lead to 39-34. But then Leonard and Schlundt went back to work, scoring on a mixture of field goals and free throws. By the end of the third quarter, IU led 50-39 and Wisconsin never threatened again. The final score was 66-48 in a defensive struggle that wasn't pretty to watch but proved again that the Hoosiers could win even when they didn't get the kind of fast pace they preferred. IU also showed off its defensive prowess, holding Wisconsin to an anemic .189 field goal percentage (14-for-74), and its rebounding dominance, outboarding the Badgers 46-30.

Dick Farley turned in his usual defensive trick, holding Wisconsin's scoring ace Dick Cable well below his season average with just five points on 1-for-5 shooting from the field. Cable eventually fouled out in the fourth quarter. Schlundt led all scorers with twenty-five points (9-for-22 from the field and 7-for-8 from the line), but without Scott to back him up, "the Ox" had to play the entire game until checking out with just forty seconds left on the clock. Leonard finished with fifteen points. Paul Morrow topped the Badgers with fourteen points but was just 4-for-20 from the field. Charlie Kraak was the game's top rebounder with fifteen boards, and Leonard and Farley also grabbed ten each for the Hoosiers. In his first action as a Hoosier,

Paul Poff chipped in two points and two rebounds. At one point, the crowd held its breath when Poff unleashed a high-arching thirty-footer that bounced in and out. It was clear that the Hoosier faithful were pulling for Paulie.

The win improved Indiana to 10-0 in conference play. Illinois remained two games off the pace by slaughtering Michigan 92-62 in Ann Arbor. Minnesota, which was without Chuck Mencel because of an ankle sprain, fell out of sight in the race by losing to Ohio State 81-71 and dropping to 8-5 in Big Ten play. Michigan State grabbed sole possession of third place at 7-4 with a 60-48 win over Iowa.

The weekly Associated Press poll kept 22-0 Seton Hall at the top of the heap, with Indiana a steady second, and Washington rising quickly at No. 3. Illinois was No. 5. However, for the second-straight week, the United Press poll of college coaches disagreed and placed Indiana at No. 1 and Seton Hall at No. 2. The season's dynamic was swiftly changing for the Hoosiers. As the *Indiana Daily Student* put it, "You're No. 1 . . . And they all want to get you."[10] The hunter had now become the hunted.

A KNIFE IN WISCONSIN

12

I can say, honestly, Mac never asked a professor for a grade
for a basketball player. If he started that, it would have been
something any player could have asked of him. It would have
ruined all we were attempting to do.

—MARY JO MCCRACKEN

When Lou Scott was lost for the season because of his grades, it wasn't
just a blow to Coach Branch McCracken and the IU squad, it was
also a blow to Mary Jo McCracken, the team's unofficial head tutor
and guidance counselor. As a former English and music teacher with
a razor-sharp intellect, a tough-minded demeanor, and a warm midwestern charm, she was perfect for the job—and she took it very
seriously. Branch McCracken believed there wasn't a better English
tutor to be found anywhere, and he used to say, "If you can't learn
from Mary Jo, then you might as well forget it."

The athletic department had a handful of hired tutors—mostly
graduate students—who could help players with various subjects, but
when members of the basketball team were really having a hard time
with their classes—and Coach McCracken always knew when they
were having trouble—then they were assigned to work with Mary Jo.
A player would take his books over to the McCracken house and
spend several hours poring over the problem subject with Mary Jo,

who almost always found a way to help the player through it, or she would find a specific tutor to give additional instruction.

One of the students she spent a lot of time with was Bobby Leonard, who was clever and had an abundance of street smarts but was not well-versed academically. "I was a kid who never planned to go to college and wasn't very prepared when I got there," said Leonard. "[Mary Jo] had her hands full, helping me. But as long as you were prepared to work and give it your best effort, she would hang with you, through thick and thin. I had a great deal of trouble with English literature. She tutored me and tutored me and tutored me for a big test one time, and the morning of the test, I overslept—big time. She was a lovely, lovely lady, but she could get mad too, and boy was she mad at me. I finally convinced her that I was just too tired, I didn't mean to oversleep. I was sorry. And so she turned right around and convinced the professor that he ought to give me one more chance to take the exam. That's what kind of battler she was for you."[1]

Although she was very good at it, Mary Jo hadn't envisioned that role for herself. "When Mac and I went to Bloomington, I told him we wanted to be known as the coach and his wife. I wanted to be Mrs. McCracken to the players, and we would have our own home life," said Mary Jo. "So one day, there I was in our home in Bloomington on a rainy afternoon. Dave [their only child] was a baby and I was down on my hands and knees scrubbing the floor. I had dinner cooking in the oven and Dave was riding on my back pretending I was his horse when I heard the kitchen door open and looked around. There was Mac with a couple young men and he said, 'Mary Jo, this is Curly Armstrong and Herm Schafer, a couple of our basketball players. Curly is having trouble with his English and I want you to help him, and what do we have to eat!'

"So the first thing I did was tell all three of them to go back outside and clean off their shoes because I had just scrubbed the floor. Then Herm and Mac had dinner and I helped Curly; and when we finished, the food was all gone, so I had to cook Curly a hamburger. That was the end of our own separate home life," said Mary Jo. "From then on I was more or less a second mother to every player we had.

I'd do the tutoring, and when they had personal problems, they'd come to me and ask me to help explain things to Mac and we'd get things worked out."[2]

Mary Jo also made a point to get to know each player's steady girlfriend or wife. Sometimes Mary Jo would even gather together all the young ladies as a group, and other times some of the young ladies would come to the McCracken house alone to talk through their problems, ask her for advice, or even cry on her shoulder. Don Schlundt got married after his sophomore year, and his wife Gloria said, "If the guys were off on a basketball trip, [Mary Jo] would take us to dinner. That wasn't every trip, but she would keep in touch with us. She would subtly tell us what to do and what not to do. She strongly suggested things." One of the more subtle things Mary Jo suggested was that the ladies be careful not to "wear out" the guys before a big game. That was a topic of humor among the girls.

Above all, what Mary Jo's active presence and unwavering concern created was an atmosphere in which all the players and the people closest to them were part of the McCrackens' extended family. The approach Branch and Mary Jo took with the players was best summed up when Mary Jo later said, "All those boys Mac and I borrowed for four years from their parents to play basketball for Indiana . . . [they] truly became part of our family."[3]

Of course, being part of Branch McCracken's family at IU also brought certain responsibilities with it, especially regarding academics. Mac said, "That's the big thing, helping my boys get through school, making them go to class and get their degrees. Shaming them into it sometimes, or just plain giving them hell until they did what they had to do and got through school and into whatever field they chose. And I wasn't about to let up on them. They had to do their best or, by God, they'd hear from me. They were my boys and they were going to do things right."[4]

As a result, when one of the players—such as Lou Scott—ran into problems or suffered setbacks, the McCrackens felt the pain in the same way parents feel it when one of their kids suffers a setback or a slipup. In Lou's case, he decided to stick it out at IU, get his studies in order, and prepare himself for another shot during his senior year.

The Horse continued to work out with the team. He practiced hard and accepted his role as a foil to Schlundt by trying to make Don work harder for his shots in practice than he'd ever have to work in games.

The Hoosiers came out of the Wisconsin game mired in an offensive funk. For five straight quarters—the final quarter of the Northwestern game and all four quarters against the Badgers—IU ran a rhythmless offense and shot the ball poorly. While averaging a strong .383 shooting percentage for the season, Indiana hit just .265 against Wisconsin. Turning that trend around was not going to be easy against IU's next opponent, the third-place Michigan State Spartans, who were the class of the league defensively. In the first matchup in East Lansing, Michigan State hung with the Hoosiers all the way and became the first team that season to hold IU under seventy points, as the Hoosiers prevailed 69-62.

Once again, the Indiana–Michigan State matchup would feature the league's top offense against its best defense. Indiana's offensive cold spell continued in the first quarter against the Spartans. In fact, it got worse.

Schlundt hit an early free throw to give IU a 1-0 lead in the Saturday night contest at the IU Fieldhouse, but a field goal from Michigan State center Bob Armstrong and a free throw from forward Al Ferrari put the Spartans ahead 3-1. Michigan State quickly built that lead to 8-4 and then kept the advantage for the rest of the first quarter, finishing with a 15-13 lead. IU shot a chilly 3-for-16 from the floor in the opening quarter, as Farley, Kraak, and Schlundt missed a flurry of open shots.

In the second quarter, the Hoosiers' offense finally started to thaw out. Schlundt tipped in a basket on the opening sequence to tie the game, and a few moments later Schlundt scored again to put IU on top 17-15. Then the two teams played tug-of-war on the scoreboard for the rest of the quarter before Don Schlundt sank two free throws to put Indiana ahead 29-27. Just before the half came to a close, Al Ferrari buried one free throw for the visitors to cut it to 29-28. All in all, the first half featured nine ties and five lead changes.

With the start of the second half came a clash of strategies between Branch McCracken and Michigan State coach Pete Newell. Mac wasn't content with a slowdown tug-of-war. That was Michigan State's game, and the Spartans had used it to beat some good ball clubs already that season. So Mac sent his attack dogs into the full-court press in the third quarter to try to make Michigan State quicken its pace. Newell responded by telling his players to pull the ball up at half-court and run through its possession offense even when they cracked the press and had an opportunity at an easy shot. The result was devastating for the Spartans.

Schlundt scored on a put-back at the opening of the third quarter and then nailed a hook shot and suddenly Indiana led by five. Then Leonard nailed a long bomb and Farley tipped in a shot. Meanwhile, Michigan State battled the Hoosier press and failed to score a field goal for the first 4:34 of the second half. By that time, Indiana had already raced to 38-29 lead. The Hoosiers outscored the Spartans 18-8 for the third quarter and owned a 47-36 lead heading into the fourth against a Michigan State team that was not at its best when playing from behind.

Al Ferrari returned for the Spartans in the fourth quarter after sitting out all the third with four fouls, but he fouled out with 6:49 left in the game. IU started the fourth quarter on a 10-5 run and built its lead to 57-41 to put the game out of reach for Michigan State. Schlundt checked out at that point with twenty-seven points, but he re-entered the game when Farley fouled out, and scored three more to finish with a game-high thirty on 10-for-24 from the field, 10-for-11 from the line. He also collected twelve rebounds and played some of his best defense of the season as IU won 65-50. Leonard chipped in fifteen points, including several long ones that helped soften up the defense for Schlundt inside. Charlie Kraak also had a big game with ten points (3-for-7 from the field and 4-for-5 from the line) and a game-high thirteen rebounds. Center Bob Armstrong led the Spartans with sixteen points (6-for-20 from the field) and eight rebounds. Forward Al Ferrari, who led Michigan State with twenty-two points in the first matchup against Indiana, got the Dick Farley lockdown treatment and spent most of the night in foul trouble. Ferrari, a Brooklyn native who normally averaged 12.7 points per game, finished with just five points and attempted only two field goals.

Indiana still didn't light up the nets against Michigan State, as the Spartans outshot the Hoosiers .333 (16-for-48) to .306 (19-for-62). However, IU was much better from the line, 27-for-35 (.771) to 18-for-34 (.529), and Indiana outrebounded Michigan State 39-22.

Illinois continued to keep pace with Indiana by beating Iowa 80-63 in Champaign. Illinois still had a hope of catching the Hoosiers. The Illini had already played most of their toughest road games: at Minnesota, at Indiana, at Michigan State, and at Wisconsin, while Indiana still faced three major road challenges: at Wisconsin, at Illinois, and at Minnesota. Illinois needed to beat Indiana in Champaign and also needed at least one other team to knock off the Hoosiers. On paper, Wisconsin and Minnesota were the best hopes.

On the Monday after the Michigan State win, Indiana was set to play Wisconsin in Madison. It was the second consecutive Monday night game with the Badgers, but this time it was being played in the daunting Wisconsin Field House.

On the day before the game, IU traveled to Madison and got set up at the beautiful Edgewater Hotel on Lake Mendota. In that gorgeous and serene setting, the Hoosiers were able to step away from the pressures of the Big Ten race and the fact that they were preparing for their most critical game since the Illinois win. Lake Mendota was frozen solid, so several of them wandered around the lake. Dick Farley, Jack Wright, trainer Spike Dixon, and a few others saw some men ice-fishing out on the lake and decided to take a walk out to see them. About halfway through this leisurely stroll, the group realized that the fishermen were a lot farther away than they had originally thought. Spike Dixon had had polio when he was younger and walked slowly and with a noticeable limp (if a player ever went down on the court, he usually had to wait for a moment while Spike limped out to take a look at him). By the time the guys realized how far out on the ice they were, Spike was struggling to keep going. So Dick Farley and Jack Wright each threw one of Spike's arms over their shoulder, and they carried him back to the hotel. The players certainly didn't mind helping Spike, who always worked so hard to keep them fit on the court and worked to keep them out of trouble off the court.

At 8:00 PM on February 16 in the Wisconsin Field House, 12,500 raucous Badger fans gathered to see if their squad could do what no other Big Ten team had accomplished so far that season: beat the Hoosiers. By virtue of its valuable homecourt, fifth-place Wisconsin was given an excellent shot at stopping IU's hot streak. And not only was the entire dairy state rallying around the Badgers, but the entire state of Illinois was pulling for them as well.

The first quarter was every bit as competitive as expected, and it was just as physical as the first meeting between the Badgers and the Hoosiers a week earlier. However, this time both teams were much more effective on the offensive end. There were five ties in the first quarter and neither team could wrestle the momentum away from the other. The quarter ended with IU ahead 22-21 after Burke Scott drove in for a layup shortly before the gun sounded. The second quarter was nearly identical. Twice Wisconsin had a four-point lead, but the Hoosiers ended the half with a narrow 39-38 advantage.

The big story of the first half was the battle between the two big men. Wisconsin's Paul Morrow got off to a blazing start, hitting six of eight field goals and two of two free throws to score fourteen points in the first eight minutes of the game. Don Schlundt responded to the challenge by collecting twenty-one points by the intermission, but he also collected three fouls.

Schlundt opened the third quarter by drilling a fifteen-footer to give IU a 41-38 lead. But then disaster struck for the Hoosiers. After hitting his one-hander, Schlundt almost immediately picked up his fourth foul and had to leave the game, and the Wisconsin Field House erupted in delight. Badger fans knew that Schlundt was the primary cog in the Hoosier offense and that IU no longer had Lou Scott to back him up, and they sensed that Wisconsin now had the opportunity to take over the game. That is what made the events of the rest of the third quarter so shocking.

McCracken made the surprise move of going to a small lineup, rotating 6' 3" Dick Farley over to center. Over the next eight minutes, Farley and Charlie Kraak used beautiful interior passing to combine for three baskets, Leonard buried three long bombs, and Burke Scott went coast-to-coast for a flashy layup. To the astonishment of the home crowd, the Hoosiers suddenly led 56-48 as the third quarter ticked away and Schlundt remained stationed on the Hoosier bench. The quarter finally closed with IU leading 59-52.

Things only got worse for the Badgers at the start of the fourth quarter, as their two starting forwards—Dick Cable and Tony Stracka—both fouled out in the opening minutes. Then Schlundt returned midway through the quarter for the Hoosiers and scored on a tip-in to give IU a 69-61 lead with four minutes left to play. A minute later, the score was 71-63 as the game reached the three-minute mark. At that point, the Hoosiers were firmly in control, but they nearly gave the game away in the final minutes.

The first blow came when Farley picked up his fifth foul by hammering Morrow with 2:42 left on the clock. The Badger center stepped up and hit both free throws to cut the lead to 71-65. From there, the Hoosiers went into their patented stall with the five-man weave. In addition to running the clock, IU was also looking for a defensive breakdown that could lead to an easy score. An opening developed, but IU missed the shot and three follow-up opportunities before Burke Scott drew a foul. Scott hit one free throw to give IU a 72-65 advantage with 1:25 to play.

Wisconsin then drove the ball up the court and found 5' 8" reserve guard Ronnie Weisner, who buried a twenty-five-footer to cut the lead to five points. Then senior guard Charlie Seifert swiped the ball from Burke Scott and drove in for a layup as the IU lead disintegrated to just 72-69 and a hysterical roar spread through the Wisconsin Field House.

The Hoosiers brought the ball upcourt and held on to it until Dick White, one of Indiana's most reliable free throw shooters, was fouled with just sixteen seconds remaining. Then the unthinkable happened. White missed both free throws, then jumped into the fray to rebound his second miss, and as he did he was called for a foul on Wisconsin's Morrow with fourteen seconds remaining.

Badger coach Bud Foster called a time-out and had 6' 6" Bob Weber and 6' 7" Dan Folz check into the game. Foster's strategy was to have Morrow make the first free throw, then intentionally miss the second and have Weber and Folz try to tip it in or grab the offensive rebound.

Morrow, who had already scored twenty-nine points in the game and was almost solely responsible for keeping the Badgers in it, threw a wrench into Foster's strategy when he missed the first free throw. The backup strategy appeared to be that if Morrow missed the first one, then he would also miss the second one and Weber and Folz would try to go for the tip-in and draw a foul in the process. However, Morrow then made the second free throw—apparently by accident. That gave Morrow a game-high thirty points for the night, but it also essentially locked up the game for the Hoosiers, who played keep-away in the final seconds and ran out the clock for a 72-70 victory.

Turnovers and missed free throws nearly cost Indiana the game in the final minutes, but the Hoosiers' magnificent third-quarter run with Schlundt on the bench gave them enough of a cushion to withstand Wisconsin's final charge.

IU broke out of its shooting slump by hitting .358 (24-for-67) against Wisconsin, which shot 23-for-72 (.319). The Hoosiers outrebounded the Badgers 41-36—not nearly as lopsided as the 46-30 margin the week before. Charlie Kraak had a game-high fifteen rebounds to go along with twelve points. Schlundt finished with twenty-five points and fourteen rebounds, despite missing most of the second half. Dick Farley added eleven points and six rebounds. Bobby Leonard had fifteen points, but that didn't come close to measuring his contribution to the win. As the *Wisconsin State Journal* wrote, "The standout for Indiana was not Schlundt with his 25 points but Guard Bob Leonard who tallied 15 and who still would have been a standout if he hadn't scored anywhere near that total."[5] Leonard did a masterful job of feeding the ball into Schlundt in the first half, and orchestrating the Hoosier offense while Schlundt was on the bench in the second half.

Branch McCracken liked routines. When his teams traveled throughout the Big Ten he often liked to stay at the same hotels and eat at the same restaurants year-in and year-out. As a result, he usually got to know local folks in the cities and towns where the other Big Ten universities were located. In Madison, McCracken had a favorite steakhouse, which was owned by a family of six brothers, and that was where he took the Hoosiers after their big road win over the Badgers that increased their conference record to 12-0.

The team had a nice dinner. Their spirits were predictably high after a big win. However, before the night was over, one of the team's little road habits got them in trouble. Whenever the team traveled, many of the players made a habit of picking up little souvenirs and trinkets at the hotels and restaurants they visited, ranging from match-books at fancy restaurants to top-of-the-line towels at some of the hotels.

"There was a hotel up in Minnesota that had great, great towels," said Jim Schooley. "They were almost as tall as Schlundt. It was not unheard-of to go home with a towel or two."

The steakhouse in Wisconsin served its meals with beautiful pearl-handled steak knives. A few of the players decided it might be a good idea to make souvenirs out of those knives. However, as the team was leaving the restaurant, one of the owners came up to McCracken and whispered something in his ear. McCracken, visibly angered, got the attention of his players and told them all to line up and face him. Mac said, "Alright, some of you guys have got steak knives because they're missing six of them, and I want to know who's got 'em!" While he was talking, the person he was looking at more than anyone else was Bobby Leonard.

"I knew damn well by the look in his eyes that he thought it was me," said Leonard. "He just *knew* it was me."

"Leonard's the first one he would've picked out—absolutely, without a question," said Phil Byers.

There was a slight pause after McCracken made his initial de-mand, so Mac threatened to search their gym bags and make the boys empty their pockets. At that point, several players sheepishly pulled out steak knives to hand over. But McCracken's gaping stare was fixed on only one player—Jim Schooley. This, of course, was the same Jim Schooley who was Mac's golden boy. Mac would regularly tell the other players to go to class like Schooley, to go to church like Schooley, and to stay out of trouble, just like Jim Schooley. Mac could hardly believe what he was seeing when Schooley handed him a pearl-handled steak knife.

"Mac was flabbergasted. He said, 'Why, Jim, I'm surprised at you. I thought you would be the last guy that would steal a knife from a restaurant,' " said Schooley. "And Leonard was practically rolling on the floor. He thought that was the funniest thing."

Other players besides Schooley also produced stolen steak knives, but theirs were simply collected and given back to the owner. McCracken didn't pay much attention to them because he was so aghast at discovering Schooley as one of the culprits, and he was busy reading the riot act to the team's only senior.

"I took the heat," said Schooley. "It was out of character for me."

"McCracken couldn't believe Schooley," said Byers. "He could have believed Leonard and probably a lot of other guys, but no way he would have thought Schooley would have done it."

Nevertheless, the incident didn't have a long-term effect on the relationship between Mac and Schooley. "Mac didn't bear a grudge. He was just trying to keep us straight," said Jim.

By winning a major road test against one of the Big Ten's upper division teams in one of the conference's toughest venues, the Hoosiers set themselves up perfectly for the stretch run in the Big Ten race. With the Wisconsin win under its belt, IU was 12-0 in the Big Ten with just six games remaining, four of which were home games against second-division teams. The other two were road games at Illinois and at Minnesota. Assuming the Indiana team could take care of business at the IU Fieldhouse, the Hoosiers could afford to lose its two road games and would still be assured of at least a tie for the conference crown with Illinois (that was the most popular prediction for the race). That scenario assumed that Illinois would win all of its remaining games, but if the Illini slipped at all, then the undisputed crown would belong to the Hoosiers. And if the Hoosiers could win their remaining home games and also knock off either Illinois or Minnesota, then the crown would definitely belong to IU. The Hoosiers held their destiny in their own hands.

While students, newspaper columnists, and fans loved to discuss those kinds of scenarios, Coach McCracken did not operate that way. Mac never looked past the next game. He never counted a victory before it happened, and never conceded a loss. He lived and died by preparing his team for its next opponent, in this case the Ohio State Buckeyes on February 21 in Bloomington. Unfortunately, Mac's preparations for the game were limited because he ended up in Bloomington Hospital for most of the week after coming down with the flu. But he was discharged on the Saturday afternoon before the game and was cleared to roam the sidelines against OSU.

The IU-OSU game was predictably being billed once again as a battle of the league's top two scorers, Don Schlundt and Paul Ebert. For Indiana, the biggest challenge Ohio State posed was psychological. The Hoosiers had already defeated the Buckeyes by twenty points in Columbus, so they were widely expected to easily trounce them again in Bloomington. On one hand, that made it difficult for the IU squad to get fired up for the game. On the other hand, the Indiana team was also closing in on the Big Ten title and so the pressure was mounting to keep winning—or, more accurately, the pressure was mounting to *not lose.*

Trainer Spike Dixon sensed the pressure the players were facing and wanted to do something to help lighten up the atmosphere, so while the players were on the floor for warm-ups before the game, he went into the locker room and wrote a message on the blackboard that the players would see when they came back in for their final pep talk. Spike wrote a simple one-liner that was a popular slang phrase that students on campus regularly bantered back and forth with each other. Spike thought it would be appropriate for the moment and hoped it might help the team stay relaxed.

As the players filed back into the locker room and caught a look at the blackboard, a few chuckles started to break out. Then a few snickers erupted. Within a few minutes, the guys were smiling and elbowing each other in the ribs. What Spike Dixon wrote on the board was "DON'T NOT TENSE." The actual saying was simply "DON'T TENSE," but Spike's mistake broke the ice and got everyone smiling and joking. So Spike ultimately accomplished what he wanted, even though he did it by accident.

"He tried to write an inspirational message and screwed it up," said Jim Schooley. "But what it did was really cut the tension a lot. Everybody was laughing."

The players picked up the phrase and started saying it to each other. For example, to Dick Farley someone would say, "Hey Farls, don't not tense!" Or to Don Schlundt someone would say, "Hey Ox, don't not tense!" And, of course, they quoted it back to Dixon for weeks.

After all the buildup in the locker room, the Ohio State game itself didn't bring a whole lot of tension. IU quickly jumped to a seven-point lead in the opening minutes, then slacked off a bit and let the Buckeyes back into the game. Ohio State was leading 21-19 before Farley hit a twelve-footer to tie the game at 21-21 at the end of the first quarter. The Hoosiers shifted into a higher gear in the second quarter, outscored the Buckeyes 24-11, and went into the locker room with a 45-32 advantage.

Indiana opened the third quarter with a 9-1 run in the first three minutes to take a commanding 54-33 lead, and the game's result was mostly mathematical after that. Even though the Hoosiers down-shifted their intensity after taking that twenty-one-point lead, they were still ahead 67-50 at the end of the third quarter. Early in the fourth quarter, McCracken turned over the guard and forward slots to reserves while leaving Farley in the game to get some additional experience at center. When Farley finally checked out at the 3:21 mark, IU was ahead 81-59. Ohio State closed on an 8-0 run to make the final score 81-67, which made the game look closer than it was throughout most of the second half. The Hoosiers' play was not sharp against Ohio State, but they used several strong runs to build a lead that the Buckeyes couldn't match.

The showdown between the league's top scorers was anticlimactic. Don Schlundt fell just short of his season average with twenty-four points (8-for-20 from the floor, 8-for-11 from the line) and also collected twelve rebounds. Paul Ebert was held to six points in the first twenty-five minutes by Dick Farley, but then Farley left the game after picking up his fourth foul and Ebert started getting better looks. He finished with thirteen points (4-for-20 from the field, 5-for-10 from the line) and twelve rebounds. Leonard added sixteen points for IU and Farley chipped in sixteen points and ten rebounds. Charlie Kraak pulled down a game-high fourteen rebounds as Indiana beat the Buckeyes on the boards, 52-44.

The real excitement came thirty minutes after the game was over. By that time, the crowd had cleared out of the Fieldhouse, the players had showered and changed into their street clothes, and a small group had gathered around the press box, which featured a Western Union telegram station. The group was anxiously following the regular Western Union updates from the Illinois-Iowa game in Iowa City. Every few minutes, Western Union manager Ralph Suhrheinrich would read the updated score to his rapt audience.

While the players had been showering and dressing, the updated scores started spreading from one person to another from the press box all the way back to the locker room. As it became clear that the Illinois-Iowa game was going down to the wire, more and more players, student managers, and others started gravitating toward the bleachers in front of the press box. The tension mounted as the clock ticked away and the outcome hung in the balance. The message came that with a minute left, Iowa had a one-point lead.

Then Suhrheinrich received the final score and read it aloud: Iowa 67, Illinois 62. Immediately, the "Hoosier netters rocked the fieldhouse with a spine-tingling cheer equaling those, it seemed, of the 10,500 that watched the game here minutes before," reported Bruce Temple of the *Louisville Courier-Journal*.[6] The players yelled, whooped, and hollered as Dick Farley, Charlie Kraak, and Phil Byers led the cheers. When McCracken was asked his opinion of the news, the venerable coach said, "That cured my flu."[7]

The Illinois loss at Iowa left the Fighting Illini at 10-3 in conference play, a full three games behind the 13-0 Hoosiers, with five games left in Big Ten play. That meant the Hoosiers could clinch the title outright by simply winning their final three home games. Meanwhile, the Illini would need to win all five of their remaining games and would also need a couple of their Big Ten compatriots to knock off the Hoosiers in order to give Illinois a share of the title.

For Illinois, their run of consecutive Big Ten championships looked like it was coming to an end. For the Hoosiers, the pressure of the Big Ten title chase was clearly lifting as they closed in on the championship. On the Monday after their win over Ohio State, the Hoosiers hosted Purdue, and the IU team that showed up for that game was obviously a much more relaxed and unburdened team than the one that had played sporadically against the Buckeyes.

Purdue was expected to employ the same strategy it had used to hang with Indiana in West Lafayette—use an overly aggressive defense to disrupt the Hoosiers, especially Schlundt, and try to lure them into committing fouls in return. The IU squad knew that the Boilermakers would love to be the team that brought Indiana's Big Ten hot streak to end, and if they did, the Hoosiers knew that they would never live it down in their home state. That was all the motivation the Hoosiers required.

In an unforeseen move, Purdue coach Ray Eddy decided to go for broke. He abandoned his aggressive defense and told his team to use its speed to try to surprise and outrun Indiana in the IU Fieldhouse. To say the move backfired would be a colossal understatement. The result was that the Hoosiers came out for warm-ups before the game to run their usual layup line, but instead of stopping at game time they simply kept running it for the next two hours.

Indiana put on a clinic of razor-sharp offensive execution throughout the first quarter. When the Hoosiers weren't converting point-blank shots on the fast break with split-second precision, they were using crisp ball movement and touch passes to slice up the Boilermaker defense for easy scores. Burke Scott drove the length of the floor for one layup, then converted two more as the recipient of a pair of brilliant passes from Bobby Leonard. Bobby buried several long ones, while also repeatedly setting up the four other starters for open opportunities. Kraak and Farley both did a terrific job of setting up Schlundt, who gladly exhibited his usual hot hand.

After 3:09 elapsed, IU's lead was 10-4. A few minutes later, it was 18-7. By the end of the first quarter, it was 37-14. A few minutes into the second quarter, it was 47-18. At that point, McCracken summoned Schlundt and Leonard to the bench and told his team to lighten its foot on the gas pedal. Purdue discovered a little life at that point, and by the end of the first half, the Boilermakers had *cut* the lead to 61-35. Indiana shot a sizzling 14-for-29 (.483) in the first quarter, and an even hotter 23-for-47 (.489) for the opening half.

McCracken came back with his starters at the beginning of the second half, but they didn't stay in for long—at least not all of them as a group. In the third quarter, Schlundt mostly worked as a rebounder and defender, rarely looking for a shot, and he checked out of the game with 2:29 remaining in the third quarter. Leonard and some of the other starters had already retired to the bench by then. Purdue was so far behind at that point that the Boilermakers had to keep running and gunning just to make the score look respectable. The Hoosier reserves came in and outgunned Purdue 26-21 in the third quarter, which brought the score to 87-56.

Then, with 8:59 left to play in the game, Dick White fouled out, and the IU students started chanting for McCracken to put Schlundt back in the game, knowing that Big Don was on the cusp of breaking several records. Surprisingly, Mac obliged and sent Schlundt back into the game to join a group of IU's second- and third-team reserves. He also turned Schlundt loose to play his usual game, and the Ox picked up ten fourth-quarter points to finish with a game-high thirty-one. Mac summoned him back to the bench at the 5:56 mark, with IU leading 98-66.

The other star of the fourth quarter was Paul Poff, who played just as many minutes in the game as IU's starting guards and finished with thirteen points. Poff canned a forty-foot two-handed shot that brought the Hoosiers to 100 and revved up the home crowd to a fever pitch, then came back and buried another field goal. Farley, who re-entered the game for Schlundt, sank the next basket to give IU a 104-68 lead and break the Big Ten's single-game scoring record (103), which Iowa had set in 1944. The carnage finally came to an end when

IU's Jack Wright scored just before the buzzer to give Indiana a 113-78 victory.

The number of scoring records set by Indiana's startling outburst was still being researched and calculated by Big Ten statisticians for several days after the game. The Hoosiers clearly shattered the Indiana, Big Ten, and IU Fieldhouse scoring records for most points in a game. Records were also set in field goals, free throws, shot attempts, scoring in individual quarters, and more. Don Schlundt's thirty-one points gave him 367 points in fourteen conference games to set a new Big Ten record, breaking the record of 364 by Iowa's Chuck Darling during a fourteen-game season. Schlundt also increased his career total during the Purdue game to 822 points, to surpass Bill Garrett's career mark of 792. With a handful of games still left in his sophomore year, Don Schlundt was now the all-time leading scorer in IU basketball history.

To their credit, Purdue fought tooth and nail to the final buzzer, especially guard Denny Blind, who finished with a team-high nineteen points on 7-for-15 from the field and 5-for-7 from the line. Forward Jack Runyan and center Glen Calhoun added thirteen points apiece for the Boilermakers. Indiana had six players in double figures, led by Schlundt's thirty-one. Leonard scored sixteen, despite playing even fewer minutes than Schlundt. Farley had fifteen, Burke Scott and Paulie Poff had thirteen each, and Charlie Kraak scored ten. Once again, Kraak was the top rebounder as he pulled down seventeen boards. Schlundt grabbed fifteen, and overall IU outrebounded Purdue 61-34.

Scoring records weren't the only things that got broken during the Hoosiers' win over the Boilermakers. The day after the game, the *Daily Herald-Telephone* ran a sidebar article to its game report. The headline of the article read, "Burned Up! IU Cagers Too Hot For One TV Set." The article reported:

"Coach Branch McCracken's attempt to slow down the scoring in last night's IU-Purdue game came too late for at least one television set in Bloomington.

"McCracken was readying a crop of subs early in the second quarter, with IU already in front of the Riveters by 41-14 in slightly more than eleven minutes.

"Mrs. Maude Pettit, of the Allen Building, was watching the game via television—and her set was dutifully recording the scoring. IU's Burke Scott slipped into the free throw circle, potted a one-hander, and that was too much!

" 'Poof!' went the television set and a room full of smoke testified what had caused it. Firewagon basketball resulted in a call to the local fire department.

" 'That set survived both political conventions and a lot of other sports events in fine shape, too,' Mrs. Pettit lamented."[8]

The win over the Boilermakers improved Indiana to 14-0 in the Big Ten and 16-2 overall. Including the four wins at the end of the 1952 conference season, the Hoosiers had won eighteen straight games in Big Ten play, the conference's longest streak in forty years, when Wisconsin had won a record twenty-three straight between 1912 and 1913.

On the night of the Purdue game, IU nearly clinched a tie for the conference crown when Minnesota came within a pair of free throws of upsetting Illinois in Champaign. Minnesota led 82-81 in the final minute, but Illinois's Jim Bredar was fouled and sank both free throws in the final seconds to salvage an 83-82 win for the Illini.

Earlier that day, the latest polls were released. The top 10 in the Associated Press poll were:

1. Seton Hall
2. Indiana
3. Washington
4. LaSalle
5. Kansas
6. Louisiana State
7. Oklahoma A&M
8. Western Kentucky
9. Kansas State
10. Illinois

Seton Hall was still undefeated (26-0), but the Hoosiers, who had already bypassed them in the UP poll, were steadily gaining on them in the AP poll as well. Seton Hall received thirty-two first-place votes while Indiana got twenty-six, and overall, Seton Hall collected 632 points, while Indiana got 620.

That his undefeated Pirates were losing ground at the top of the AP poll despite winning all their games was disturbing to Seton Hall coach John "Honey" Russell, and he made his feelings known when he saw that Indiana was on a course to overtake the Pirates in the poll.

"Ordinarily a thing like this might make a team tight, conscious that they're being rated week in and week out the best in the country," said Russell. "But not these boys. I think, if anything, the poll has helped them. They believe they're No. 1 and every time they go out they're determined to prove it. No jitters on this club.

"We think we are as good as any team in the country. Our boys have grown up. We don't think we'd give quarter to anybody, and that includes Indiana.

"I can understand why Indiana is picking up ground, though. People think they're playing a tougher schedule. Nothing, of course, is further from the truth.

"It's just that Big Ten reputation. The Big Ten basketball teams get by on the reputation built up in football. Actually, I think we've played a tougher schedule and if Indiana had played the teams we did their record wouldn't be as good as it is."[9]

Russell clearly stuck his foot in his mouth on a couple of issues. The first was that Big Ten basketball was essentially overrated and derived much of its prestige from the reputation of Big Ten football. The second, more mysterious charge was that his team played a tougher schedule than IU. That assertion was difficult to back up since the Seton Hall slate was filled with small schools and basketball lightweights such as King's College, St. Francis, Scranton, Muhlenburg, and others.

When Russell's comments hit the news wire, they prompted a variety of derisive responses, especially in the Hoosier state. Columnists in Indiana newspapers fired off diatribes and mocking editorials. There were open letters written to Honey Russell and articles that compared the schedules of Seton Hall and Indiana.

When Coach McCracken was asked about Russell's comments, he

said, "Seton Hall must have a fine team. But we think we are good, too. I don't care to comment about the record of anybody else. We are happy with our own."[10]

McCracken also added, "I would compare Indiana's basketball schedule with any in the United States. It is as tough as they come. And as far as Big Ten basketball living off the reputation of Big Ten football is concerned, I think every coach in the conference would agree with me that it just isn't true. This league has been producing good [basketball] teams for a long, long time."[11]

THE CLINCHER

13

You can put it down in your little black book that Indiana is going to give any and all comers a rough time in the NCAA Tournament. . . . There's no reason why Indiana can't win it all. . . . The feeling here is that this is the best Big Ten champion in several years.
—*Champaign-Urbana News Gazette,* March 1, 1953

Indiana's road games were not televised during the 1952–53 season, so IU students and fans had to follow those games on Bloomington's WTTS radio station or Indiana University's FM station, WFIU. That wasn't a big deal because radio was a much more established media than television at the time, and sports fans had been listening to college basketball games and other sporting events on the radio for decades. On campus, students gathered together to listen to the road games in the common rooms of their dorms or fraternity/sorority houses, or in the main lounge of the Union Building.

Still, the writing was on the wall. Americans saw that television was the future and the rush to buy television sets was a cultural phenomenon in the early 1950s. In the 1952–53 season for the first time, all of IU's home basketball games, except for the opener against Valparaiso, were shown on TV, thanks to the equipment upgrade at Bloomington's WTTV television station. The games on WTTV were sponsored by Chesty Potato Chips (or, more specifically, Chesty Foods, Inc.) of Terre Haute, and Chesty made a name for itself that lasted for decades in the Hoosier state by sponsoring those memorable early broadcasts of IU games.

For many alumni and IU fans, being able to watch the Hoosiers play on TV was a strong motivator to buy a television set. The ones who did have a TV got to see a great show during the winter of 1953, as the Hoosiers played extraordinary basketball in the IU Fieldhouse, including a pair of classic thrillers against Minnesota and Illinois and a record-breaking romp against Purdue. That these games were televised during such a magical season made the 1953 Hoosiers statewide celebrities in a way that far exceeded the popularity of Indiana teams and players in previous decades. Indiana folks throughout the state—especially in central and southern Indiana—felt like these Hoosiers were *their* Hoosiers, because they got to watch the IU squad play every week on TV.

In addition to the home games, there was also one road game that was televised that season—the Illinois game in Champaign on Saturday, February 28. Ever since the Indiana-Illinois double-overtime cliff-hanger in Bloomington, the rematch in Champaign was anticipated as the league's game of the year and potentially the game that would decide the Big Ten title—or at least whether Indiana would win the championship outright or share it with Illinois. However, when Illinois lost at Iowa, the complexion of the race changed. Barring a total collapse, Indiana was virtually guaranteed the undisputed title even if the Hoosiers lost at Illinois and at Minnesota. Nevertheless, the Hoosiers and the Illini were the class of the league and two of the top teams in the nation, and their fantastic battle in January was one of the greatest games in the history of the conference, so Big Ten basketball fans still anticipated the rematch simply because of the excitement of watching the conference's two titans going to war once again.

Although it wasn't a must win, it was a litmus test for Indiana. A win would clinch the undisputed Big Ten championship IU had been chasing for five decades. A win would also unequivocally establish the 1952–53 Hoosiers as the Big Ten's best team. A loss—especially if Illinois handily defeated Indiana in Champaign—would shed doubt on Indiana's true place at the top. Sure, the Hoosiers would likely win two of their remaining three games and would still capture the outright conference crown, but there would naturally be nagging doubters who would have claimed that the Hoosiers benefited from a few fortunate breaks in key games that awarded them the championship over an equally talented Illinois team. On the other hand, a win in Champaign would silence such thoughts forever and would cement the superiority of Indiana's team over the powerful Illini. Branch McCracken knew it. The IU players knew it. Even the IU students and fans knew it. That's why the game still meant so much in Hoosierland and why Indiana wanted to win it so badly. During the week leading up to the game, students on the IU campus would shout back and forth to each other, "Beat Illinois!" The title was so close they could taste it, and clinching it in Champaign would provide the ultimate exclamation point.

To televise the game, Bloomington's WTTV station got involved in a "fantastically complicated" arrangement to transfer the broadcast from Champaign-Urbana to Bloomington, according to WTTV station manager Robert Lemon.[1] The transmission would not follow a straight line from southern Illinois to southern Indiana, because there was no cabling to carry the signal between the two cities. Chicago's WGN-TV television station held the exclusive rights for broadcasting Illinois games, so Bloomington's WTTV entered into a special deal with WGN-TV and Cincinnati's WKRC-TV to televise the game.

The signal would be sent by WGN-TV from Champaign to Chicago, as usual, but then it would be piped over to Toledo, Ohio, via special coaxial cable that was rented for this occasion. From Toledo, the signal would be transferred to Cincinnati, and WTTV would use its microwave relay station in Bloomington to pick up the game from WKRC-TV, which was also broadcasting the game throughout the Cincinnati area. The transfer was extremely expensive, but fortunately Chesty Foods stepped up and sponsored the arrangement. The one thing that didn't go as planned was that Cincinnati's WKRC-TV had to reschedule its regular CBS programs to make room for the game, but it was not able to reschedule the Jackie Gleason Show, which meant that viewers in Cincinnati and Bloomington would be forced to miss the first thirty minutes of the game. The tip-off was at 7:30

PM, but the Jackie Gleason Show wasn't over until 8:00 PM, so Indiana fans in Bloomington would have to rely on WFIU radio for the play-by-play of the first thirty minutes of the game. WTTV promised to periodically interrupt Jackie Gleason with updates of the score of the game.

Once all three stations joined in the broadcast, the game was expected to be seen by five million viewers.

Huff Gymnasium on the University of Illinois campus was not like most of the other basketball arenas in the Big Ten. Most of the big state schools had built fieldhouses during the 1920s and 1930s and upgraded them by the 1950s to seat at least 10,000 spectators. Huff was an old-style gym that seated fewer than 7,000, even when fans crowded into every nook and cranny. The *Indiana Daily Student* called Huff "the crackerbox of all crackerboxes" and a "flea bin of a basketball ampitheatre—a cozy little establishment where there are more spectators on the court than players."[2]

Fans crowded along the sidelines to form a human out-of-bounds line in the Huff Gym and they used their proximity to the court to rev up the Illini while jeering opponents as they ran by. And Illini fans were known to occasionally use more than just words to attack opposing teams. In 1951, an Illinois supporter was accused of trying to trip up Indiana's Bill Tosheff, and Tosheff ended up in a heated exchange with the fan. On another occasion, an Illinois fan was accused of putting a lit cigarette down the pants of a Hoosier player who was lining up to inbound the ball.

That kind of treatment made opposing teams hate to come into Huff, and Illinois used that intimidation factor to compile a pristine record in Champaign. Leading up to the Indiana game, the Illini had won thirty-two straight games at Huff and had lost only three games there in five years. During those five seasons, the Illini had lost only one Big Ten home game—80-66 to Indiana on February 27, 1950. The group of eight seniors and juniors that made up the core of Illinois's 1953 squad had already been part of a couple of great championship runs and had never lost a Big Ten game at Huff during their remarkable tenure. For an Indiana team that had already risen to every challenge and defeated every team in the conference, winning a game at Huff was the ultimate challenge.

When the game started at 7:30 on February 28, it looked like the two teams were simply continuing their January 17 seesaw battle in a new venue. Illinois center Bob Peterson struck first blood when he scored on a put-back. A few moments later, Indiana lost possession and the Illini were streaking back for another score when the Hoosiers stole the ball and threw it ahead to Schlundt for an uncontested basket to tie the game at 2-2. Then Illini forward Clive Follmer drove to the basket and scored to put Illinois back in front 4-2. IU forward Dick Farley answered by driving past two Illinois defenders on the baseline for a layup to knot the score at 4-4. Then the Hoosiers, led by Bobby Leonard, took over.

Schlundt sank a free throw to give IU its first lead at 5-4. As competitive as the opening minutes were, the Illinois faithful would have been stunned to learn that their team would never lead again. Indiana used a 10-3 spurt to open up a 14-7 lead.

Bobby Leonard had missed his first two long bombs for IU, so the Huff crowd started chanting "Shoot Leonard!" whenever he brought the ball upcourt. They figured that if they could goad Leonard into firing away from the outside, they wouldn't have to worry about him feeding it into Schlundt on the inside. It seemed like a sound strategy until Leonard sniped three baskets, each coming during a chant and resulting in audible groans from the crowd. After the third one, they changed their tune. Cries of "Don't let him shoot!" rang out when Leonard dribbled up the floor.[3] Bobby buried a forty-five-footer just as the gun sounded to end the first quarter, but the refs conferred and decided to waive off the shot, saying Leonard hadn't released the ball before time expired. Even some of the home fans were surprised by that call, but they were relieved because it kept the IU lead at 21-13 heading into the second quarter.

IU's three big guns did the damage on the offensive end in the opening quarter, as Schlundt scored nine points and Leonard and Farley each scored six, but the determining factor for the Hoosiers was their relentless aggressiveness and energy. The Indiana players hustled all over the court, tipped passes, came up with nearly every loose ball, and hawked the steps of every Illinois player.

Still, the Illini were a veteran ball club and they weren't going to be easily rattled. In the second quarter, they stepped up their game and scratched and clawed to keep up with the Hoosiers. With a pair of field goals from Schlundt and a Farley free throw, Indiana quickly opened up a 26-14 advantage. But then Illinois bounced back with an 11-3 run, which included three straight field goals that cut the Hoosier lead to 29-25, and the Huff Gymnasium crowd exploded into a fervor. IU took a time-out and Bobby Leonard came into the huddle and erupted on his teammates. "He said, 'Give me the ball' and he used a few choice words," said Jack Wright. "He said, 'Just give me the ball. They're not going to beat us.' "

After the time-out, Leonard immediately came down and buried a pull-up eighteen-footer. After IU hit a free throw, Leonard came down and buried another long shot. Don Schlundt hit a field goal, and then Jim DeaKyne, a little-used sub who was filling in for foul-plagued Charlie Kraak, hit a shot, and all of a sudden IU was back up by double figures at 38-27.

With four minutes left in the half, Schlundt picked up his third foul and had to be pulled from the game. Farley moved over to center for the Hoosiers and the Illini smelled an opportunity. With Schlundt on the bench, the Illinois frontcourt triggered a 10-5 spurt to finish out the half and trim the deficit to 43-37 going into the locker room.

The good news for the Illini was that they had been thoroughly outplayed for most of the half, their star guards Irv Bemoras and Jim Bredar hadn't scored a field goal, and yet they were only down six points at the break. With Schlundt in foul trouble for Indiana, and Bemoras and Bredar bound to heat up, Illinois was still in good position to grab a win. The Illini also had their usual home-court magic to count on in the second half to help get them over the hump.

In the other locker room, the Indiana team knew it should have gone into the half with a double-digit lead, and the Hoosiers knew they had let the Huff crowd get re-energized by letting Illinois back into the game in the closing minutes of the half. The Hoosiers had dominated Illinois during key stretches of the first half and were confident they could beat this team on its home floor. They desperately did not want Illinois to carry over its momentum from the end of the first half and get the Huff crowd worked up into another frenzy that would be difficult to overcome. The Hoosiers wanted a knockout blow to stagger Illinois and hush the crowd, and the stroke they landed was nothing short of devastating.

IU charged out of the locker room in a blistering fury. Before Illinois could gather itself, Farley broke free for an uncontested layup. Burke Scott sliced in for a layup of his own. Bobby Leonard drove the lane and scored. Then Jim DeaKyne caused heads to start shaking when he cocked the ball behind his head and buried a long two-hander. When Schlundt hit a free throw a few moments later, Indiana capped a 9-0 run to start the third quarter. The stunned Illinois faithful gaped at a scoreboard that showed their team down 52-37.

For the rest of the quarter, Leonard orchestrated an Indiana offense that pounded the ball into Schlundt on nearly every possession, and he delivered again and again. When the smoke cleared, Indiana had outscored Illinois 30-19 in the third quarter, with Schlundt scoring seventeen of the IU points, and the Hoosiers held a 73-56 advantage going into the final period.

Indiana also scored the first three points of the fourth quarter to open the lead to 76-56. The lead continued to hover at twenty points for the next several minutes, then IU began to ease off the gas pedal and protect the ball. Illinois responded by going into a full-court press, but the Hoosiers, who worked against the press every day in practice, easily cut through it for several wide-open layups. With six minutes left in the game, Indiana went into a full stall with its five-man weave and limited its shots to open looks at point-blank range.

As the minutes ticked away, the Indiana bench broke out into smiles. The players kept turning toward McCracken, waiting for him to acknowledge that his first Big Ten title as a coach was a done deal. But Mac remained stone-faced and kept shouting instructions until the final gun sounded, and the scoreboard read Indiana 91, Illinois 79. The triumphant Hoosiers then mobbed their white-haired mentor and lifted his husky 6' 4" frame onto their stout shoulders and carried him all the way to the locker room while serenading him with a chorus of whoops and hollers. Even the dispirited Illinois fans respectfully applauded McCracken as his boys carried him off the floor.

No team had ever scored ninety-one points against Illinois at Huff. The only team that had reached that number against the Illini was the high-powered 1951 Kansas State squad, which scored a 91-72 win over Illinois that season in Manhattan, Kansas, and eventually went on to a runner-up finish in the NCAA Tournament, where Kentucky upset Kansas State in the championship game.

Indiana certainly could have pushed its point total much higher if it hadn't backed off during the final minutes of the fourth quarter. The IU scoring spree was powered by its big three—Don Schlundt, Bobby Leonard, and Dick Farley. Schlundt finished with thirty-three points on 9-for-21 from the field and 15-for-19 from the line. He single-handedly outscored the two Illinois big men, Johnny Kerr and Bob Peterson, 33-28. Kerr had nineteen points (on 9-for-26 from the field) and Peterson had nine. Schlundt also had the best rebounding game of his career. The official scorers at Illinois didn't keep track of rebounds, so the official number of Schlundt rebounds was not recorded, but he dominated the glass even though he was in foul trouble for much of the game. Leonard had twenty-three points on 10-for-25 from the field. His long bombs at pivotal junctures repeatedly killed Illini runs and kept them from building any sustained momentum.

Dick Farley missed only one shot all night. He was 8-for-9 from the floor and 3-for-3 from the line. He finished with nineteen points, but his value went far beyond that. He used his uncanny basketball instincts to always be in the right spot for a loose ball or to block out and do whatever was needed to help out a teammate on offense or defense. Surprisingly, the Illinois game was actually not one of Farley's best games defensively. His primary assignment, forward Clive Follmer, had a sterling performance with twenty-one points on 9-for-16 from the floor. However, he was the only bright spot for Illinois. Jim Bredar and Irv Bemoras, the highly lauded Illini backcourt, were harassed into a combined 5-for-34 shooting performance. Bredar finished with four points while Bemoras had seventeen, most of them coming from the line, where he was 11-for-13.

The boldest stroke McCracken made in the game was to call on

seldom-used 6' 3" junior forward Jim DeaKyne—a former walk-on—
to replace Charlie Kraak at the start of the second quarter. DeaKyne
came in, rebounded well, and buried two shots, each during a critical
IU run, and he finished with five points. The only other reserve
McCracken used in the game was guard Paul Poff, who helped IU
control the ball and break the Illinois press in the fourth quarter. The
game was one of the best McCracken had ever coached. He pulled all
the right strings in motivating his team and selecting and timing his
substitutions, but when it was over, Big Mac didn't want any of the
credit.

After his players deposited him in the locker room after his celebration ride, an energized McCracken whipped off his navy blue suit
coat and tossed it aside. Then he turned and looked around at his
players and said, "When the chips are down, you got the stuff!"[4]

McCracken normally refrained from complimenting his teams
during the season. Instead, he constantly challenged them to iron out
the wrinkles in their game, and he generally saved his praise for when
the season was over. But after the Illinois game, Big Mac simply could
not contain his joy. He said, "I never praise you fellows and sometimes
you must think I'm pretty hard. I criticize and tell you where you do
the wrong things, and leave the praise to your mothers and sweethearts
and friends. But tonight I'll have to say that you're the greatest team
in the country."[5]

Then Mac broke from another one of his regular customs—the
one in which he rarely talked about any game except the next game.
Ever the psychologist, Mac wanted to set a new challenge for his
Hoosiers now that they had just climbed the conference's mountain-
top. He closed his postgame speech by saying, "Now, let's get 18
straight. . . . Remember, you're never satisfied."[6]

After that, a small group of photographers and people close to the
basketball program were allowed in the locker room to join the celebration and document it. Mac walked around to shake hands and slap
backs. To the players he kept saying over and over again, "Isn't this
great? Isn't this a wonderful thing?"[7] To the reporters, he kept saying,
"The boys did it."[8]

Meanwhile, the IU players were smacking each others' backs,

punching each others' arms, and just grabbing a hold of each other and yelling with delight. And every once in a while, they threw an arm around the shoulders of a teammate to pose for the photographers.

Trainer Spike Dixon supplied the refreshments for this party by passing around his fresh-squeezed orange juice and some quartered oranges. When the noise settled down a notch, Mac and the players were finally able to answer the reporters' questions and provide some retrospect on the victory and the championship.

"They hustled all the way," said McCracken. "They hustle in every game. Yes, in every practice. Give them the credit. I don't care if you don't mention my name."[9]

"This is the greatest thing which ever happened to me," said Charlie Kraak. "I don't imagine Illinois can realize how badly we wanted this one. They've had so many."[10]

Don Schlundt didn't stop smiling from the time the final gun sounded. When reporters told him that he had scored thirty-three points, the "Ox" was surprised he had gotten that many, and he admitted that Johnny Kerr was pretty tough. Schlundt answered questions about how he had stepped up his game since IU lost Lou Scott. In the six games since Scott was declared ineligible, Schlundt had averaged twenty-eight points per game and three times had broken thirty. "I play loose now," said Schlundt. "There's nobody tall enough to come in and I have to avoid fouls. Branch had me change."[11]

Bobby Leonard said, "This is as good as we've played all season. We had to play well to beat Illinois like we did. That's a good team, right through the eighth man, and I never expected we'd get so many points. But everything clicked."[12]

McCracken backed up Leonard's analysis. "I didn't expect to win as handily as we did. I don't believe any coach figures any game to be easy, certainly not Illinois," said Mac. "Frankly, I was scared to death. But like Bob said, we played extremely well."[13]

Then Illinois coach Harry Combes paid a visit to the IU locker room to congratulate the Hoosiers. "The best team won," he told them. "Thanks Harry," said McCracken.[14]

Once the atmosphere settled down, it was time for the players to get the tape cut off their ankles and jump into the showers. Many of them suddenly remembered that they had family and friends waiting outside the locker room, so they got dressed in a rush. Meanwhile, Bobby Leonard sat and slowly unlaced his shoes. "There's only one guy I wish was around right now," he stated.[15] He didn't have to say another word for everyone to know that he was thinking about his buddy Sammy Esposito.

The first guy dressed and ready to head out to the bus was Jim Schooley. "Schools" leaned up against one of the stadium turnstiles and waited for his teammates to say their goodbyes. As he did, an *Indiana Daily Student* reporter came up to him to grab one last quote. He asked Schooley, the emotional leader of the second team, what he thought about Jim DeAKyne coming off the bench and playing so well. Schools smiled and said, "Everybody comes through for the Bear."[16]

On the 170-mile bus ride back to Bloomington, the mood turned reflective. "You know, I don't feel any different," said Bob Leonard. "We're champions, but I still feel the same."[17] Dick Farley agreed that he didn't really feel any different either. Coach McCracken, who was still glowing with pride, looked at them with a knowing smile. Someday they would understand how difficult and how special it was to have accomplished what they had done.

Leonard may not have felt any different, but he did feel more strongly than ever about his teammates. "They're the greatest kids in the world, the greatest bunch of guys I've ever known," he said. "I've never seen such a great bunch of kids."[18]

Before leaving the Champaign-Urbana area, the bus stopped at a little diner, where the team was going to pick up a meal. When the bus rolled to a halt, McCracken bellowed out, "Sophomores!"[19] In standard IU tradition, the basketball team's sophomores filed off the bus to go get the take-out food—fried chicken and french fries, in this case—then came back on and delivered it to the rest of the team.

When Don Schlundt finished his chicken, he started singing the IU fight song. "Indiana, Our Indiana," he intoned. And the answer came back from his teammates, "Indiana, we're all for you." Then Schlundt sang, "We will fight for the Cream and Crimson." And the teammates responded, "For the glory of old IU." In the middle of the bus, Phil Byers quickly took up the role of conductor and directed the choir of players to continue their performance of the fight song. No one would have mistaken their singing for a genuine choir, but McCracken urged them to keep it up.

Once that died down, Leonard sneaked back and whispered something to the choir members. Soon they broke into a rendition of "Someone's in the cellar yelling hooray for Branch," in honor of their mentor.

After that, most of the people on the bus dozed off, but Leonard, Farley, and Kraak sat up front near McCracken and listened as Mac reminisced about his days as a player at Monrovia High School and all the classic showdowns in the Martinsville sectional. Mac was in the type of lighthearted mood the players rarely ever saw because he was such a high-strung guy and because he so acutely felt the pressure to win. On this bus trip, Mac even admitted to the boys that during high school he often skipped school to go hunting, which drew a lot of laughs and head shakes.

As the bus rolled back into Indiana, the conversation turned to the Illinois game. They went through all the great plays as well as the miscues. They talked about the shots they made and the ones they missed. They talked about the strange time clock in Huff Gym. "Never could understand that clock," said Charlie Kraak.[20] They talked about Leonard's shot at the end of the first quarter that should have counted. And they laughed about the pitiful-sounding gun that was used to signal the end of each period. "Sounded like a cap pistol," said Ron Taylor.[21] The others agreed.

A hush settled over the bus as they made the final leg of the journey past Greencastle and Spencer. McCracken talked quietly with Spike Dixon, Burke Scott drifted around looking for a water jug, and Bob Leonard opened his fourth bottle of ginger ale. As the bus scooted by Ellettsville, they all peered outside at the blustery snowstorm that was blanketing southern Indiana. And when they finally rolled into Bloomington in the early hours of the morning, the deserted town was enshrouded in white, and that eerie silence that can only be heard during a big snowstorm had settled over the scenic IU campus. It was as if the campus itself had dressed up in its very best and was now bowing in reverent silence before its newly crowned king.

Shortly after the Hoosiers returned to Bloomington in the pre-dawn hours on Sunday, March 1, the Sunday morning newspapers hit the stands and saluted the Hoosiers' victory.

Bert Bertine of the *Champaign-Urbana Courier* wrote, "The king is dead, long live the king. A new king, a mighty king, of Big Ten basketball was crowned in Huff gym Saturday night. Indiana, respond-ing to the challenge of Illinois in its own gym, shattered the tradition of home floor invincibility by crushing the Illini, 91-79, and thus con-vincing one and all of its right as successor to Harry Combes' club as undisputed champions."

Indianapolis Star sportswriter Charles Beal, Jr., wrote, "Indiana literally shot the eyes out of the basket last night, hitting a tremendous 41 per cent of its shots. The Hoosiers settled the issue in the first three minutes of the second half and played a mighty heady game the rest of the way to outclass Illinois."

"Indiana has won many a 'big' game in the past," wrote George Bolinger of the Bloomington *Daily Herald-Telephone*, "including the one that brought a national championship in 1940. But it is highly doubtful that any IU victory was ever more thoroughly enjoyed than Saturday's rout of the Illini on their own floor."

Vic Rensberger of the *Indianapolis News* wrote, "Big Mac had built a succession of fast, high-scoring teams, often of championship caliber, but fate always had brushed aside their grasp for the chalice. Great as those teams were and cherished as is their memory in the minds of Hoosier fans, they must now yield in esteem to the team which kept winning game after game through a long schedule until the race was decided. Miraculously regaining their balance when they teetered on the brink of defeat, doggedly clinging to precarious foot-holds when the inspired rushes of keyed-up opponents threatened to sweep them off balance, these now Merry Macs of 1953 gained mo-mentum as the season progressed and finally knocked the crown off the old champion's head right in the throne room itself. Never has an Indiana team run with more devastating swiftness, moved with more sure-handed quickness or shot with more deadly accuracy than did this one Saturday night."

Champaign-Urbana News-Gazette columnist Jack Prowell wrote, "Indiana waited a long time for an undisputed Big Ten basketball champion, but when it finally got one, it came up with one of the all-time greatest. It has to be great. How else can you rate a team which has not lost in 15 games in one of the toughest conferences in the country? If ever an All-American guard performed in Huff gym, it was Bob Leonard Saturday night. His long shooting was sensational, and if an Illinois guard came out after him, he would drive all the way or stop part-way for a jump shot. How can he be stopped? Illinois admitted it didn't know. And if Don Schlundt isn't the best center in the Big Ten, then where can you find one any better? He proved himself to doubting Illinois fans Saturday night. . . . This is a well-deserved championship for Indiana. Everyone in the league, except Illinois—which was still in contention—must have been unconsciously pulling for the Hoosiers to win. Even at Illinois, maybe there is the feeling now, 'If we couldn't win, Indiana sure deserved it. It's had to wait a long time.' "

By Sunday afternoon, the Hoosiers were back in the IU Field-house for practice to prepare for their Monday night encounter with Northwestern in Bloomington. At practice, McCracken asserted, "We aren't thinking yet about the NCAA championship. We just want to win those last three Big Ten games."[22]

Mac's one testy moment in the locker room the night before came when a reporter asked him if he expected a letdown from his team now that they had clinched the championship. "Never," McCracken said in a stern voice. "Not with these kids. They have too much hustle."[23]

While McCracken's Hoosiers were preparing for Northwestern in the gym, student organizations were preparing for an impromptu pep rally that night to celebrate Indiana's breakthrough Big Ten championship. Col. Raymond Shoemaker, dean of students, wasted little time in signing off on the idea, even though it was planned for 10:30 PM Sunday night. Female students normally had a 10:30 PM curfew on

Sundays, but Shoemaker extended that to 11:30 so the ladies could participate too.

More than four thousand students lumbered through the snow and swirling winds to the IU Fieldhouse to celebrate with their team, and most of them arrived long before 10:30 to get a good seat for the pep rally, which included the full band and all the cheerleaders. Col. Shoemaker kicked off the festivities with a few words. As he walked up to the microphone, several students yelled out, "No school Monday! No school Monday!"[24] Shoemaker didn't consent to that but he said a few words extolling the team, then gave the floor to several faculty members and guests, who spoke of the virtues of the 1953 Hoosiers. The students soon got restless and started chanting, "We want the team! We want the team!"[25] They soon got them, as Coach Mc-Cracken and the IU players came out in street clothes and lined up between the two free throw lines. They spent a long time standing and smiling as the crowd exploded into a lengthy ovation to honor the champs.

Coach McCracken, dressed in a light brown suit, was the first to take the microphone. "Our basketball team is the finest in the country," he admitted. "Last year they set a goal for themselves to win the Big Ten. Now, I've set a goal for them—to win the next three conference games for 18 in a row, and then win the NCAA." Then he explained why the team had accomplished so much. "They're a fine team because they are for each other [and] they have the desire to win."[26]

Next, the Hoosiers' lone senior, Jim Schooley, stepped forward to talk for his teammates. He started by saying, "I know I can speak for the seniors on the team when I say . . ." but he was immediately cut off by a roar of laughter from McCracken, the players, and the crowd. Schooley continued to charm the audience as he explained that IU's success was built on a foundation of teamwork and togetherness and not by the accomplishments of just one or two players. "It is the wonderful team spirit," he said, "with all the members working together all the time, that has brought victory."[27]

The crowd then gave a warm cheer to Mary Jo McCracken, who stepped up and shared a few eloquent words and also enjoyed a good jest with the audience about whether Big Mac was the boss in his house. Finally, Col. Shoemaker read a message from the convocation's most conspicuous absentee, IU president Herman B Wells, who was confined to his bed with the flu. The message from Wells said, "It would be my misfortune, due to illness, to miss one of the important events on our campus. I would be there regardless were it not for a direct order from my doctor. I do want all of those present to know how overjoyed I am with this Illinois victory which gives to those fine young players and their coach the Big Ten title. Through their individual play, teamwork, sportsmanship and spirit, they have brought high honors to our university."[28]

On Monday night against Northwestern, which was 5-10 in conference play, the Hoosiers opened the game looking like they would easily prove McCracken right about avoiding a letdown. The opening minutes looked like a victory lap for the team that had decimated Illinois in the second half just two nights earlier. IU jumped out to an 11-0 lead and held Northwestern without a field goal for the first seven and a half minutes of the game. By the end of the first quarter the score was 22-10. The Wildcats spent all their energy trying to shut down Schlundt with double and triple coverage, and Leonard and Farley made them pay by shredding the Northwestern defense for easy scores. Indiana looked like it was on track to cruise to another high-scoring blowout. But then the Hoosiers got sloppy.

In the second quarter, Northwestern's reserve center Harold Grant, a 6' 10" sophomore, surprised everyone in the gym—including his own teammates—by abusing Don Schlundt and Indiana's interior defense for sixteen points on 8-for-14 shooting from the floor. Meanwhile, Schlundt didn't hit his first field goal until he scored inside with just twenty seconds remaining before halftime. Going into the intermission, IU's lead had shrunk to 39-36.

In the locker room, the players prepared for McCracken to come in and go berserk on them because they had played so poorly after their hot start. Instead, the Bear walked in with a stony and scornful expression on his face and slowly walked around the room, staring each player in the eyes as he walked by. "He never said a word," said

Ron Taylor. "He just glared at everybody. There was not a sound." Finally, one of the student managers popped his head in the door of the locker room and said, "It's time." McCracken whirled around, pointed a finger at the locker room door, and yelled, "Go get 'em!"

Not surprisingly, Bobby Leonard was the first to answer Mac's call, as he buried an early basket, and IU also hit a free throw to quickly push the lead to 42-36. However, the Wildcats knew they had a chance to make history by ending Indiana's famed winning streak. While the Hoosiers got off to a hot start in the second half, Northwestern matched them shot for shot. Then the Wildcats knotted the score at 53-53 and took control in the final minutes of the third quarter to snatch away a 58-54 lead as the period came to a close.

The first eight minutes of the fourth quarter were disastrous for Indiana. Schlundt continued to be ineffective. Dick Farley and Burke Scott fouled out. Then Bobby Leonard followed those two to the bench with two minutes left in the game when he picked up his fifth foul by accidentally tripping up Wildcat center Harold Grant. At that point, Northwestern led 74-67 and had all the momentum in their favor. When Leonard took a seat on the bench, IU fans started to resign themselves to an upset—but the Hoosiers weren't through yet.

Led by Dick White, IU scratched its way back into the game at the free throw line. White buried two free throws to cut the lead to 74-69. Then Schlundt drew a foul and converted both free throws to make it 74-71. Larry Kurka sank a free throw for Northwestern to up the lead to 75-71, but White then sank two more free throws to make it a 75-73 game with 1:18 left to play. Larry Dellefield appeared to shoot down IU's rising hopes with two free throws of his own to put the Wildcats back up by four, but White came through again by sinking a field goal from the wing to keep Indiana within two points at 77-75. Next, Northwestern's Frank Ehmann hit two free throws, but White got the ball, drew yet another foul, and made his fifth- and sixth-straight free throws to make it 79-77 with 0:45 remaining on the clock.

Northwestern held the ball and tried to run out the clock, but Larry Kurka couldn't turn down a wide-open shot. As he wound up to release his overhead shot, IU's Paul Poff came flying at him and tipped the shot. A scurry for possession ensued and a jump ball was called between the two players. Poff controlled the tip and IU raced the ball up the floor and flipped it into Schlundt, who got hammered by Northwestern forward Rob Lebuhn with fifteen seconds left. Schlundt nailed both free throws to tie the game at 79-79, and Northwestern's desperation shot in the final seconds was way off the mark as the contest was forced into overtime.

Although the IU comeback had thrilled the home crowd, the Wildcats still hadn't spent all of their momentum. Larry Dellefield buried a hook shot to give Northwestern an 81-79 lead at the start of overtime. Charlie Kraak tied the game at 81-81 with an acrobatic tip-in of a wild shot. But shortly after that, Kraak was whistled for his fifth foul at the 3:30 mark. That left Indiana with Schlundt and four reserves—Dick White and Jim DeaKyne at the forward spots and Paul Poff and Phil Byers in the backcourt.

John Biever and Frank Ehmann each converted a free throw to put Northwestern back in the lead at 83-81. Schlundt tied it with a layup on the inside, and Rob Lebuhn answered for the Wildcats. Jim DeaKyne, who had entered the game for Kraak, tied the game at 85-85 with a jumper from the top of the key. Then IU got the ball back and Dick White came through with another huge shot as he buried a long one to give IU its first lead since the third quarter at 87-85. Next the two teams traded one free throw apiece to make it 88-86. When Northwestern got the ball, John Biever, a fast little guard who had given the Hoosiers fits all night, dribbled through the IU defense and scored on a drive to tie the game at 88-88 with forty-six seconds left to play.

The Hoosiers then planned to run out the clock and take one last fateful shot. Paul Poff took the ball and stationed himself on the left wing, forty feet from the basket. Northwestern allowed him to stay there but not come any closer. When the clock ticked under ten seconds, Poff began to coil himself. Northwestern's Rob Lebuhn ran toward Poff but didn't jump at him or deflect the ball, apparently to avoid a foul. With seven seconds left, Poff unleashed a high-arching two-handed set shot that hung in the air for a soundless eternity. On the opposite wing, Dick White tracked the ball on its towering flight.

Underneath the basket, Don Schlundt darted toward the hoop to prepare to tip in a miss. As the ball finished its descent, Schlundt jumped up to meet it, but the ball zoomed straight through the hoop, hit the bottom of the net, turned the basket inside out, and caromed off the airborne Ox.

Four seconds were left on the clock, but Northwestern failed to get off a final shot before the gun. The Hoosier players and fans rushed the court, threw Poff onto their shoulders, and paraded him around the floor to the adoring cheers of an ecstatic home crowd. Poff's picture-perfect shot made the final score Indiana 90, Northwestern 88. Somehow the Hoosiers had pulled out another miracle—and they had done it with four of their five starters on the bench in the decisive final minutes. After the opening quarter, the expected letdown had indeed come, but surprisingly, IU didn't conquer it with the starters who had powered them to sixteen straight Big Ten wins and seventeen straight overall. Rather, the Hoosiers did it with a handful of reserves who stepped up and earned their stripes.

Going into the 1952–53 season, "I think [McCracken's] biggest concern was reserves," said assistant coach Ernie Andres. With Don Schlundt, Bobby Leonard, Dick Farley, and Charlie Kraak, Mac knew he had four outstanding players who complemented each other very well. And early on, Burke Scott distinguished himself as the ideal fifth man for that team with his speed and defense. Throughout the course of the season the starting lineup was the same in every game, and the five starters logged most of the minutes on the court. However, when McCracken *did* call on his bench, the second team routinely stepped up and provided remarkable performances. They weren't called on often, but they delivered when needed at key junctures in several pivotal games. That was one of the most important factors in IU's extraordinary run during the 1953 Big Ten season—although it went deeper than that the reserves had several game-saving performances. It was more about the tight partnership between the starters and the reserves on that IU team.

"When you went in, [the starters] treated you like you were one of the first five. And it was that way off the court, too," said Paul Poff. "We never had any ill feelings about anything. I felt fortunate because I was the one that came in mid-stream. I felt, heck, they might get mad because here an outsider is coming in. Somebody like Phil [Byers], he would have played more if I hadn't got there. . . . What makes a championship is players that gel and play as a team. They accepted me when I came in like I was there from the beginning. That's the way that team was. We were one for all and all for one."

"We had a strong bench," said Burke Scott. "I could go out and try to steal the ball as much as I wanted to. If I got in foul trouble, I knew there were guys sitting on the bench that were just as good as I was."

Bob Leonard commented, "We had a great bench. I didn't even look at it as a 'bench' because those guys could have started anyplace else. We had 10 guys that could play. [Mac] could make a substitution and we wouldn't miss a beat."

In addition to coming into the game to put out a fire or provide a spark, the second team also played a pivotal role in practice. That role was twofold. First, they functioned as the scout team by learning the plays of the Hoosiers' next opponent and running through those plays to help prep the starters for what to expect during the game. Second, McCracken liked to keep his squad in condition during the season by having the first and second teams scrimmage against each other for long stretches with both teams running a full-court press against the other. Those practices were extremely intense and competitive.

"I didn't start, so I was on the scout team," said sixth man Dick White, "so we would always prepare our first five for the next game. That was sort of a fun role to play. . . . I think we worked hard at that [and embraced it]. . . . You have to, or it doesn't do anybody any good."

"The reason [the starters] were so good was because the second team made them what they were," said Paul Poff. "That's what we told them when we weren't in the game. We'd say, 'The only reason y'all did well was because you had to play a better team in practice.' "

Charlie Kraak admitted, "The second team played hard in practice.

They gave us all we could handle. It made them better and it made the team better. So they were valuable, even though the statistics may not show much."

That they respected each other on the court and hung out together off the court didn't mean that the all-out full-court scrimmages weren't heated and didn't get rough.

"You get guys hanging on you so long and guys would get upset with each other," said Bob Leonard. "Guys would get the ball stolen from them with full-court pressure and it would upset 'em. There were times in practice when things got tough. We were a tough bunch. It was heated, no question about it, and Branch wanted to keep it that way. That's the way he liked it. He'd work ya."

That the team was so unified and tightly knit that season also didn't mean that all the bench players were perfectly happy. They simply found a way to get past the disappointment of not getting to play more and focused most of their energy on what was good for the team, even when it involved quiet sacrifice on their part.

"I felt a little sorry for some of the [bench] players that I thought should have gotten more playing time," said Charlie Kraak. "Nobody's really happy sitting on the bench. I went through that for three years in high school so I knew the feeling. It would have been different perhaps if we would have had losing seasons. We had such great seasons that it was pretty hard to be disgruntled because you were going to be part of it, whether you were sitting on the bench or you were on the court. When you win . . . that makes everyone happy. You don't get much dissension."

One of the players who wasn't part of the regular rotation and saw very little playing time that season was Jack Wright. Coming out of high school, Wright was even more celebrated than Bobby Leonard, who was in the same recruiting class. The sharpshooting Wright was one of McCracken's most highly targeted recruits that year, but when he arrived on campus and started scrimmaging against his fellow freshmen, Wright quickly realized that the college game was different. "It was a little bit of a surprise for me when I started playing against those guys," said Wright. "It was a different level for me, even though I'd been playing against good ball players in the North Central Conference and I had led the North Central Conference in scoring." Then Wright injured his back at IU and had to miss his entire sophomore year to have surgery and recuperate. When he came back, he wasn't yet at full strength and Bobby Leonard and Burke Scott had established themselves as the starting guards and Phil Byers and Paul Poff stepped up to grab spots as the first two guards off the bench.

Wright said, "Every place I ever played basketball I had started and done well. So I was sorta disillusioned—not that I didn't have lots of enthusiasm for the other guys. After I came back [to IU from the back injury], my high school coach asked McCracken how I was doing and [Mac] said, 'He's about 75 percent, but I would carry that guy [on my team] if he was in a wheelchair. He's got more enthusiasm than anybody on the team.'"

Even though he wasn't playing, Wright still loved the game and wanted to see IU do well, so he focused on firing up his teammates, cheering them on, and competing against them in practice. "We had a good rapport," said Wright. "I didn't do any bitchin' or anything like that. That's why we won it, because we were all together on the same page. But we had some tough practices. Leonard and I, I don't know if we ever settled who was the best shot."

The other reserve player who privately had a difficult time sitting on the bench was, ironically, the one who set the best example for the rest of the reserves. When Jim Schooley came to Indiana, there were tremendous expectations that he could become one of IU's next big stars. As a high school senior, the 6' 5" big man carried tiny Auburn High School to a miraculous run through the Indiana high school tournament, including a major upset of Jack Wright's highly ranked New Castle team in the semistate in Muncie. Schooley used his terrific shooting touch to take Auburn all the way to the state finals in Indianapolis, and there he won the coveted Trester Award for Mental Attitude. He narrowed his college choices primarily to IU and Purdue and chose the Hoosiers because of his family ties to Indiana and because of his respect for McCracken.

However, in college, Jim quickly discovered that he didn't have the same height advantage that he enjoyed in high school, and he wasn't nearly as athletic as most of the other college players. During his sophomore year, Schooley was IU's backup center behind spectacular senior Bill Garrett. The next season, Don Schlundt, Lou Scott, and Charlie Kraak joined the IU varsity, and Schooley's chances of earning a spot in McCracken's rotation of big men had all but ended.

"My role with the team turned into somewhat of a nanny type of position," said Jim Schooley. "I remember calling a [players-only] meeting [during the 1952–53 season] and telling the guys that they had to concentrate on the team and on keeping their grades up so that they could play. Otherwise, they would be letting everybody else down. . . . I was hardest on Leonard. He swung pretty wide in terms of his social life."

That was the role McCracken wanted Schooley to play with the young IU squad during his senior year. He wanted Schooley, who was an outstanding student and an upstanding citizen, to be a mentor and role model and, because of the admiration he had for Mac, Jim embraced that role—even though it had its tough moments. When IU was on its big winning streak, nobody was happier for the team and for McCracken than Jim Schooley. However, there was also a part of Jim that was a little dispirited. As Indiana grabbed victory after victory and it looked like the Hoosiers would finally get their first undisputed Big Ten title and McCracken would finally get his first as a coach, Schooley couldn't help but feel a little depressed that he wasn't an integral part of making that dream come true. As a result, after a few of the final victories in Bloomington, when the crowds had dispersed and all the players had gone back to their dorms and fraternity houses, Jim Schooley walked alone in the quiet of the Bloomington night with his head hanging a little low and a strange mixture of joy and despair running through his mind. His basketball career was rapidly coming to an end with an abundance of team glory but with very few personal accomplishments on the basketball court.

"The hardest part in my personal case was being on the bench," Schooley admitted. "I wasn't used to being on the bench. I knew these guys were better players than I was and there was no way Mac could justify playing me, but after a game although we were happy to win and the crowd was happy and all of that, I would sometimes walk around town and mope because I didn't get to play. And I think that was probably the hardest part for me. I felt I wasn't contributing, and as a result I'd try to contribute in other ways. When I did get to play I would rebound as hard as I could and play as hard as I could, but I was not to be confused with a guy of the caliber of those guys I was playing with. So I felt bad about that."

Nevertheless, in the locker room and on the court, Jim Schooley's attitude was exemplary. Because Jim Schooley, who had been such a big star in high school, was willing to sacrifice his own personal glory for the glory of the team at IU, the other bench players followed his lead and were willing to do the same. Like Schooley, they bought into Mac's team philosophy. Branch McCracken often said, "*We* win games or *we* lose games." No McCracken team—and few in the history of IU basketball—ever bought into that philosophy more wholeheartedly than the 1953 Hoosiers.

"It's really *teams* that win," said Ron Taylor, "and that team had great chemistry. There weren't any jealousies that I ever saw or ever heard of. We just wanted to play basketball and do well."

"That 1952–53 team was remarkably cohesive," stated Jim Schooley.

"It was fun to be with those guys," said Dick White. "We jelled pretty well. There didn't seem to be any factions or anything like that going on. It was a great experience."

"That ball club was probably the biggest family ball club that IU's ever had," said Bob Leonard. "We were like brothers. We didn't have anyone going out on their own. . . . We had a great deal of respect for each other, we had a great deal of respect for Branch and our coaches, and we loved the university. It was like a puzzle and it all fit together."

After vaulting to the Big Ten championship with a victory over Illinois on Saturday, the Hoosiers jumped into an undisputed spot at the top of all the national polls on Monday. The final national poll the Hoosiers had to conquer was the Associated Press poll. IU had sat in second place behind Seton Hall for six straight weeks. However, while Indiana clinched the Big Ten title in Champaign, Seton Hall's twenty-seven-game winning streak came to an end on Sunday when the Dayton Flyers upset the Pirates 71-65 in Dayton. The Flyers were

13-14 on the season before the Seton Hall game, but the previous season the Flyers had played in the NCAA Tournament and had also gone to the finals of the NIT.

Even before the Dayton loss, New Jersey–based Seton Hall had already decided to bypass the 1953 NCAA Tournament to play in the NIT and was already awarded the No. 1 seed in New York City's classic postseason tournament. The combination of the Pirates' loss and the Hoosiers' monumental win made IU a landslide pick for No. 1 in the AP poll. And, naturally, IU maintained its top spot in the UP poll and the Litkenhous ratings.

Seton Hall slipped to No. 3 in the AP poll, which was released during the day on Monday, March 2. That night, the Pirates lost to the Louisville Cardinals 73-67 in Louisville to fall to 27-2 for the season. Seton Hall was not the only team that slipped in the AP poll. Washington fell from No. 2 to No. 4 after getting its twenty-one-game winning streak snapped by Idaho. Kansas dropped a spot to No. 6 after getting blown out 79-58 by Oklahoma A&M, which clung to the No. 7 spot because it also got upset by Bradley that week. LaSalle popped up to No. 2 after a pair of victories against overmatched foes, and LSU jumped up to No. 5 after clinching the SEC title. The breakdown of the AP top ten was:

1. Indiana

2. LaSalle

3. Seton Hall

4. Washington

5. Louisiana State

6. Kansas

7. Oklahoma A&M

8. Kansas State

9. Western Kentucky

10. Illinois

Entering the final weekend of the regular season, the conference champion Hoosiers prepared for one last Saturday–Monday Big Ten doubleheader before launching into the NCAA Tournament. After the Illinois win, McCracken had clearly set the team's sights on finishing the conference season with a perfect 18-0 record. IU would have to earn it. On Saturday night, they would play Minnesota at Williams

Arena, where the Gophers had blown out the Hoosiers in recent years, and on Monday, the Hoosiers would play host to Iowa, which was the hottest team in the Big Ten other than IU.

When the Indiana team flew up to Minneapolis for its March 7 game against the Gophers, there were two extra passengers—Mary Jo McCracken and "Hap" Dragoo. For Mary Jo, it was her first road game in a while.

"I went to the Notre Dame and Kansas State games," said Mary Jo. "When we lost by only one and two points, the boys came and said, 'You can't go to any more away games.' So that was it for a while. The boys agreed I could go to Purdue, and when that turned out okay, they decided to 'take a chance on Northwestern.' Of course I had to agree with them that if things got to looking bad I'd leave and outjinx any jinx I might have on their playing."[29]

When the team nearly coughed up a double-digit lead in the fourth quarter at Northwestern, the team again got cold feet about having Mary Jo come to road games. As result, she didn't travel with them to the Wisconsin or Illinois games. However, after IU clinched the Big Ten title, the players changed their tune.

"By the time of the second Minnesota game, with seventeen straight victories, they decided, 'Okay, we're in,' and they let me go to Minneapolis."[30]

The other guest who joined the team on the trip to Minneapolis was Hap Dragoo, a Ph.D. student in anatomy who tutored many of the basketball players and also developed a close friendship with many of them that lasted long after their IU days. Hap was a big basketball fan. He had played basketball in high school and tried out for the IU team when Harry Good was the coach during World War II, but he didn't get much of a look from Good. In 1948, Hap made the transition to graduate school in anatomy and got a job tutoring physical education majors for the athletic department (the flunk-out course in physical education was the anatomy class taught by "Ma Strong"). Hap also worked a maintenance job in the IU Fieldhouse and ran a paper route delivering the *Indianapolis Times* in Monroe County. Sometimes one of the players would ride along with Hap and help deliver the newspapers and "we'd do a little studying along the way," said Hap.

A few times, McCracken rode along to chat and check up on the progress of his boys.

Mac liked Hap, appreciated the help he gave to the athletes, and trusted him. In fact when Bobby Leonard got in some trouble during the second half of his sophomore year, McCracken called and asked, "Hap, how much room you got over there where you're living?" When Hap replied that he had some space, Mac said, "Bobby Leonard is going to be moving in with you this weekend." Leonard ended up living the rest of the spring and summer with Hap, and the two of them became good friends. In the fall, Leonard moved out and moved into a new fraternity house, but then Burke Scott and Paul Poff moved in with Hap for the 1952–53 season. Scott and Poff were the only two players on the team who weren't in a fraternity.

When Hap came with the IU squad for the Minnesota game, he wasn't just along for the ride and a free chance to watch the team. "I took my sack of bones and a couple books and tutored the troops en route, and while we were there, and on the way home," said Dragoo. Hap's "sack of bones" was a collection of human skeletal bones that the physical education majors had to be able to identify and memorize for anatomy class. Hap helped them by devising an elaborate series of mnemonics, which many of the players remembered long after they had forgotten most of the other details they had studied in college.

After beating Illinois at Huff Gymnasium, the task of taking down the Gophers in Williams Arena didn't seem quite as daunting a task as it once did for the Hoosiers. Most people thought Minnesota would use its ball-control game to keep the score close, but that the superior Hoosiers would ultimately come home with yet another win. And why not? IU looked like an unstoppable freight train with a full head of steam.

At that time, no team in the conference would have been happier to derail the Hoosiers' winning streak than Minnesota. The Gophers were trying to salvage a disappointing season in which they had felt they had an excellent shot at the Big Ten crown but made some early missteps in league play that put them behind in the race and they never recovered. A win over IU would help Minnesota end the season on a high note and help the Gophers catch Michigan State for third place in the conference.

Minnesota still carried a little bit of a grudge against Indiana that stemmed from a 1951 game in the IU Fieldhouse in which Indiana made a mockery of the Gophers' stalling tactics and zone defense by stalling out long periods of the second half in a 32-26 victory. Two weeks later, the Gophers had returned the favor in Williams Arena by conquering the Hoosiers, who had previously been undefeated in league play. That loss eventually cost Indiana a share of the 1951 Big Ten title. The next season when IU's freshman sensation Don Schlundt arrived, the bulky Gophers prided themselves on manhandling the lanky center and holding him far below his season scoring average.

During the 1951 and 1952 seasons, the two teams had split a pair of rough-and-tumble and extremely competitive games. The first contest between the two in 1953 had been no different as Indiana pulled out a sensational three-point victory on two Burke Scott scores at the very end. The rematch on Saturday, March 7, in Minneapolis was just the same as the Hoosiers and the Gophers battled ferociously from wire to wire and produced another classic that would go down as one of the best Big Ten games of the season.

Lifted by the red-hot shooting of Bobby Leonard, IU opened with a tremendous surge and grabbed an 11-3 lead with 4:45 left in the opening quarter. While Minnesota collapsed on Don Schlundt, Leonard hit four of his first six shots and looked like he might single-handedly shoot down the Gophers. But Minnesota never flinched. The Hoosiers still led 14-9 with 2:47 left in the first quarter, but Minnesota rattled off seven straight points to grab a 16-14 lead at the end of the period. Then the Gophers scored eleven more unanswered points to start the second quarter, increasing the lead to 27-14. All told, Indiana's scoring drought lasted 7:50 and Minnesota put together an 18-0 run. Starting with a Dick Farley free throw that finally brought an end to the dry spell with 4:57 remaining in the half, Indiana mounted a final rally to cut the Gophers' lead to 33-25 at the break.

When the third quarter opened, Minnesota roared out of the

locker room and quickly erased the progress IU had made just before the half, as the Gophers built their biggest lead of the game—fourteen points—at 45-31. The record crowd of 18,114 in Williams Arena was going berserk at that point. Minnesota was patiently working its offense and all five players were scoring. And on the other end, the Gophers were simply clogging up the middle and daring the Hoosier guards and wing players to shoot from the outside. After Leonard's early streak, neither Leonard nor any other Hoosier found the hot hand, and with Gophers hanging all over Schlundt and Farley on the inside, the Hoosier offense sputtered. However, Minnesota coach Ozzie Cowles had gone with his starting five for the entire game, and midway through the third quarter they started running out of gas. That was right about the time that a sense of urgency started to set in for the Hoosiers.

IU strung together a 16-8 run to close the third quarter and cut the lead to 53-47 entering the final period. Then the Hoosiers started the fourth quarter on a 5-1 run to pull within two points at 54-52. The rest of the fourth quarter was a high-stakes game of tug-of-war as the two teams traded baskets. Indiana finally pulled even when Dick Farley was fouled away from the ball and hit the free throw to tie the game at 63-63 with 3:01 remaining. If Farley had gotten fouled just one second later, he would have gone to the line for two free throws (all fouls within the 3:00 mark were automatically two shots) and he would have had a chance to give Indiana its first lead since the opening quarter. Instead, he tied the game, and Minnesota went into a long, highly effective stall. Twice the Gophers attempted shots and twice they missed, got their own rebound, and pulled the ball back out again. IU nearly got possession when Dick White tied up Minnesota guard Chuck Mencel, but it was called a jump ball and on the ensuing tip the Gophers got the ball back again.

While the final minute wound down, Mencel held the ball near midcourt and the Hoosiers stayed clear of him and the other Gophers to avoid drawing a foul. At that point, IU was essentially conceding Minnesota one final shot, and predictably, it was Mencel who prepared to take it for the Gophers. Cowles had just recently called Mencel "the best outside shot in America." When the clocked ticked down to five seconds, Mencel made his move. With Williams Arena hushed to a taut whisper, he darted toward the top of the key, rubbed off IU guard Paul Poff on a pick from a Gopher teammate, veered right, stopped on a dime, and elevated. Over 18,000 sets of eyes watched the ball leave Mencel's fingertips, softly arc toward the basket with a perfect backward spin going end over end, and then swish through the back of the net.

For the first time in almost three months, the Indiana Hoosiers had lost a basketball game.

Ironically, Indiana's 65-63 loss to the Gophers had an ending nearly identical to IU's last loss, an 82-80 defeat at Kansas State on December 13, when Jack Carby sank his towering thirty-five-footer at the buzzer to beat the Hoosiers. Between those two bookends, the Hoosiers were undefeated for eighty-three days.

The Minnesota loss not only ended Indiana's shot at an undefeated conference record, it also brought the high-flying Hoosiers back down to earth. The IU players had gotten to the point where they felt damn near invincible after beating Illinois in Champaign and then escaping from certain defeat against Northwestern in the final minutes. But when the Gophers beat the Hoosiers—their third loss that season on a last-second shot—it took a little bit of the swagger out of IU's step and made the players feel vulnerable again. When Mencel's shot went up, the feeling among most of the IU players was, "Oh no, not again."

Nevertheless, the loss ended up serving a sobering purpose for the young IU squad. "That was probably the best thing that happened to us," said Bobby Leonard, "because we were getting pretty cocky."

The humbled IU squad returned home after the Saturday night loss in Minneapolis and started preparing for Monday night's regular season finale against Iowa, which came into the IU Fieldhouse riding a six-game winning streak.

With the Big Ten title already wrapped up, the Hoosiers' home finale was also a celebration for the families of the Indiana players. The parents of each player were invited to attend the game. They were treated to a pregame banquet hosted by Mary Jo McCracken in

Alumni Hall at the Indiana Memorial Union, and then all of them were introduced and honored by the crowd in the IU Fieldhouse prior to the game. Many of the players' parents knew each other well because they regularly came to the IU games. For example, Dick Farley's mother, father, his two older brothers, and their wives all drove up from Winslow for every game in Bloomington, and also went to several of the away games. Don Schlundt's parents and his fiancée drove down from South Bend for every home game and went to all the away games that were within driving distance of northern Indiana. Naturally, both of those families came for the banquet and the Iowa game, and at least one of the parents of all the other IU players attended as well.

One player whose parents did not usually attend the games was Bobby Leonard. However, for this occasion, his mother and his sister Darlene made the trip from Terre Haute. It ended up being the only game that Leonard's mom got to attend during his college career, and his dad never got to see him play live. "My mom and dad weren't sports people," said Bobby. "They were so busy trying to make a living that basketball wasn't No. 1. . . . My dad used to watch the games on a television at a local bar about two blocks from where we lived. He kept up with it that way. They didn't come down [to Bloomington] and watch games like some of the players' parents did."

The game that Hattie Leonard did get to see her son play was controlled by Bobby and the Hoosiers from start to finish. It wasn't one of their sharpest performances of the season, but IU played well enough to easily defeat the red-hot Hawkeyes. And Hattie got to see Bobby hit several of his patented long-range bombs.

At the opening, Iowa led 2-1 and then 4-2, but Leonard soon scored to tie the game, and Don Schlundt hit to give IU the lead, and the Hawkeyes never pulled ahead again. The Hoosiers led 21-15 at the end of first quarter. Iowa mounted a determined charge in the second quarter with a 7-0 run that pulled the Hawkeyes to a slim 24-23 deficit, but Indiana finished the half on a 14-4 run of its own to take a 38-27 advantage into the locker room. Bouncing back from his season-low performance of thirteen points against Minnesota, Schlundt already had twenty points in the first half against Iowa.

Schlundt scored a field goal early in the second half but then had to go to the bench after picking up his fourth personal foul with 6:36 remaining in the third quarter and IU leading 43-31. Still, with Dick Farley at center, the Hoosiers streaked to a 59-41 lead by the end of the quarter to put the game safely in hand. At the start of the fourth, McCracken removed the rest of his starters except Farley, who came out a few minutes later.

For the home crowd, the highlight of the game came in the fourth quarter. Back on February 25, the *Indiana Daily Student* had printed an article that expressed the sentiments of a vocal faction of the IU crowd. That sizable group of students cheered heartily for IU's lone senior, Jim Schooley, whenever he entered a game. Most of them had come to Indiana around the same time as Schooley and had expected him to be a basketball star at IU, and the fact that he didn't turn out to be a star didn't diminish their devotion. That he didn't have the speed or the athleticism or the shooting skills to even crack the starting lineup only charmed them more, because whenever Schooley did get in the game he hustled and played so hard, and when he wasn't in the game he was constantly clapping his hands and whistling and firing up his teammates. He may not have been a starter, or even a member of Mac's regular rotation, but to the IU students, he was a star. The *Indiana Daily Student* article was titled "Whistle Spills Red's Bucket (Poof for Poff)" and it told how the students had chanted "We want Schooley! We Want Schooley!" during the second half of the Purdue blowout. McCracken obliged them by putting the redheaded senior in the game.

Shortly after entering the Iowa game, Schooley was fouled and went to the free throw line. When he hit a free throw, the crowd erupted as if IU was taking the lead for the first time. Schooley simply cracked a small grin as he backpedaled down the court. However, a free throw wasn't enough for the crowd. They wanted to see Jim score a field goal, something they had never seen in the IU Fieldhouse. In the season opener against Valparaiso, Schooley was credited with a tip-in, but actually a crowd of IU players—including Schooley—had batted the ball around and it went in the basket. Ron Fifer, fellow senior and official scorer at home games, credited the basket to

Schooley. Jim also scored a bucket against the Hawkeyes in Iowa City on December 22, and then he almost gave the crowd their wish against Purdue. Schooley got the ball down low, pivoted to his left and let go of a little jumper that banked off the glass and hit nothing but net. The Fieldhouse exploded again, but their joy quickly faded as a whistle blew and Schooley's basket was waived off and a foul was called, sending Paul Poff to the free throw line.

Thus, when Schooley entered the game in the fourth quarter against Iowa in the season finale, the IU students knew this was their last chance to see "Schools" get a basket, and the *Indiana Daily Student* article only widened his circle of admirers. With IU leading 63-48 in the middle of Jim's final quarter in the IU Fieldhouse, the Hoosiers worked the ball around until Phil Byers swung it out of the corner to Jim DeaKyne on the wing and DeaKyne quickly whipped it into Schooley at the high post. Schooley caught the ball with his back to the basket. An Iowa defender slid down from the top of the key to pressure him, but he quickly pivoted away from the double-team and went straight up into the air to launch a twelve-footer that banged the back of the rim, then the front of the rim, and then slipped through the net. The moment it went in, the IU crowd exploded into one of the longest and loudest standing ovations ever heard in Bloomington. Mary Jo McCracken called it the "greatest ovation ever given to a player, in appreciation of the leadership, sacrifice, and determination Jim gave from the bench."[31] Then, with less than a minute remaining in IU's 69-61 victory, McCracken summoned Schooley to the bench and the fans erupted for "Big Red" one last time.

PART THREE

A RECORD NIGHT
IN CHICAGO

14

It wouldn't have mattered if a guy was 7' 3"—Schlundt could score on anybody. He wasn't just a low post player. He could pull out to the top of the circle and beat you. He could shoot the ball.

—Bobby Leonard

The Iowa victory to finish off the regular season gave the Hoosiers a record of 19-3 overall and 17-1 in conference play. Many Big Ten basketball commentators and columnists were hailing it as the greatest single-season team performance in league history. IU's dominance and consistency over a full eighteen-game round-robin schedule was what impressed them most. Every other team in the conference had a hard time sustaining its focus and its level of play for a full eighteen games, and every team in the upper division of the Big Ten—except IU— lost at least a game or two they really should have won. In fact, the league's coaches and athletic directors were so unhappy with the eighteen-game schedule that before the season was even over, they voted to go back to a fourteen-game slate for the 1954 season, which made IU's 17-1 conference mark look like it might live forever as a standard of excellence. As it turned out, the Big Ten went back to a round-round schedule two decades later and another Indiana team set the new standard with two straight 18-0 seasons. However, next to that incredible undefeated streak notched by the 1975 and 1976 Indiana teams, the 17-1 mark of the 1953 Hoosiers (shared by the 1993 Hoosiers) still reigns as the next-best single-season performance in league history.

Despite the Minnesota loss during the final weekend of the regular season, Indiana retained the No. 1 position in the final AP poll of the regular season, although the Washington Huskies, who finished their season 27-2, were coming on strong in second place, only twenty-two points behind the Hoosiers in the poll. The top ten were:

1. Indiana

2. Washington

3. LaSalle

4. Seton Hall

5. Kansas

6. Oklahoma A&M

7. Louisiana State

8. Kansas State

9. Western Kentucky

10. Oklahoma City

Other notables were Illinois at No. 13, Notre Dame at No. 17, Minnesota at No. 22, and DePaul at No. 26.

The IU players didn't care so much about the rankings. The best thing about the Iowa win for them was that they could finally set their sights on the NCAA Tournament. Ever since they had clinched the Big Ten title in Champaign, the team had been ready to take the next step and go after the NCAA championship. Coach McCracken worked hard to keep his boys focused on the final three Big Ten games, but Indiana was not sharp in any of those three games. Against Northwestern, IU got outgunned from the field for only the third time all season and by the biggest margin—.394 for the Wildcats to IU's .314. The Hoosiers' shooting continued to struggle against Minnesota as IU shot just .321. And IU—which had dominated the backboards against almost every opponent during the season—got manhandled on the boards in Minneapolis as the Gophers outrebounded the Hoosiers 45-38. Although IU easily defeated Iowa, the Hoosiers were sloppy with the ball at times and still not up to form, shooting .347 from the field. Thus, many of the "bar stool coaches" at The Gables and various diners and watering holes throughout Bloomington were anxious about the Hoosiers' prospects going into the NCAA Tournament. The big question was, "Could IU get back to the form it had shown against Illinois in Champaign?" Some argued that when it comes to a high level of basketball, you can't simply turn it off and then turn it back on. Others felt the Hoosiers would easily bounce back once they had something to play for again. Nearly everyone agreed that if the Hoosiers *could* get back to the form they had showed at Illinois, they could whip any team in the country.

The most daunting obstacle for the top-ranked Hoosiers in the NCAA Tournament was No. 2 Washington, the Pacific Coast Conference champion, led by All-American senior Bob Houbregs. During the season, the 6' 8" center had averaged 25.0 points per game, shot an astonishing 54 percent from the field, set a new conference record with forty-nine points against Idaho, and led his conference in scoring for the third-straight year. By the end of the season, Houbregs was the consensus National Player of the Year. He was known as the most accurate hook shot artist in the country, and if there was any player in the nation that could match IU's Schlundt shot-for-shot, it was Houbregs.

No. 4 Seton Hall and its All-American center Walter Dukes decided to play in the NIT instead of the NCAA Tournament. Unfortunately, that cost basketball fans a chance to see a matchup of Dukes against fellow All-Americans Houbregs and Schlundt. Walter Dukes wasn't quite the scorer that Houbregs or Schlundt were, but the seven-footer from Rochester, New York, was a tremendously agile athlete for his size. He was the first of a series of great African American centers in the 1950s. During the 1952–53 season, he averaged twenty points and twenty rebounds per game and set a new NCAA single-season record for rebounds (734) that lasted more than two decades (and still remains the record for Division I players).

No. 3 LaSalle, which was the defending NIT champion (and had defeated Walter Dukes and Seton Hall on the way to the 1952 NIT title), also decided to play in the 1953 NIT. A new ruling from the NCAA had declared that only teams that did not play in any other postseason tournaments (not counting conference tournaments) were eligible to play in the NCAA Tournament. That rule went into effect for the 1952–53 season and it meant that LaSalle and Seton Hall could not compete in the NCAA Tournament. No. 9 Western Kentucky was the only other top ten team that opted for the NIT.

Because of the point-shaving and dirty recruiting scandals that came to light during a series of investigations in 1951 and 1952, college basketball was suffering from a terrible black eye and a sagging reputation among the general public. The investigations had unearthed point-shaving scandals and/or recruiting improprieties in all four NCAA championship teams between 1948 and 1951. The NCAA probably breathed a sign of relief in 1952 when Phog Allen's Kansas Jayhawks won the NCAA title. Allen had long been one of the most outspoken critics of gambling on college athletics and had predicted an impending scandal long before the point-shaving fiasco ever came to light. Still, even with the Kansas win in the 1952 tourney, the NCAA was under intense pressure to clean up the college game. As a result, NCAA officials came up with a program of "de-emphasis" that was aimed at "keeping college sports in perspective." On the other hand, interest in the NCAA Tournament was surging among college students and sports fans. To deal with these two conflicting forces, the NCAA made two major changes to the 1953 tournament. First, they expanded the field from sixteen teams to twenty-two teams to accommodate more automatic berths for conference champions, more sites for games, and more opportunities for fans to attend games. Second, they moved back the dates of the tournament games and shortened the time between the regionals and the NCAA finals. That meant that the first-round games opened on March 10 and the championship game was played on March 18—a remarkably short turnaround. The NCAA explained that the new changes were put in place for "proper control of postseason competition . . . shortening of the basketball season . . . and encouraging the organization of formal conferences."[1]

The 1953 tournament was organized into two divisions—East and West. There were four first-round sites—Philadelphia, Pennsylvania, and Fort Wayne, Indiana, in the East, and Seattle, Washington, and Palo Alto, California, in the West. The winners of the first-round games moved on to the regionals to play one of the ten conference champions that earned a first-round bye. In the East the bye teams were Indiana, LSU, Wake Forest, and Pennsylvania. In the West the bye teams were Washington, Wyoming, TCU, Oklahoma A&M, Kansas, and Oklahoma City. The four regional sites were Chicago, Illinois, and Raleigh, North Carolina, in the East, and Corvallis, Oregon, and Manhattan, Kansas, in the West. The Final Four was in Kansas City, Missouri.

For the Hoosiers, the road to Kansas City started in Chicago.

The day after Indiana beat Iowa in the IU Fieldhouse, the Hoosiers found out who their first NCAA opponent would be when DePaul edged Miami of Ohio 74-72 in Fort Wayne. DePaul earned one of six "at-large" berths in the 1953 NCAA Tournament, which were primarily reserved for independent teams that did not belong to a conference. The Blue Demons, coached by the crafty Ray Meyer, won their first-round game on a jump shot by Ronnie Feiereisel with just three seconds left in the game. In the other first-round game in Fort Wayne, Notre Dame crushed Eastern Kentucky 72-57 and earned a trip to Chicago for a date against Pennsylvania, the Ivy League champion.

Back in Bloomington, the Hoosiers were getting ready to set out for the Windy City. A group of Bloomington businesses called the "East Side Merchants" organized a dinner banquet on Tuesday, March 10, as a send-off for the team, which was scheduled to take the Monon train to Chicago the next day at 11:18 AM. The chairman of the banquet was Charlie Poolitsan, one of the owners of The Gables, which supplied the meal featuring T-bone steak and shrimp cocktail. It was Poolitsan who presented a special gift to Coach McCracken, trainer Spike Dixon, and the thirteen players who would make the trip to Chicago. A beautiful travel bag was presented to each of them, with the name of each individual engraved on a gold plate attached to the luggage. Poolitsan reported to the audience that he had no trouble finding local businesses to sponsor bags for the fifteen team members. The following list is of businesses that sponsored bags for individual team members:

Von Lee—Branch McCracken

Wible and Adams—Spike Dixon

Sunshine Cleaners—Burke Scott

Block's Barber Shop—Dick Farley

Claude Bartlett's Grocery—Charlie Kraak

Nathan Hale—Bobby Leonard

The Chatter Box—Don Schlundt

Home Bakery—Jim Schooley

Curry Book Store—Jim DeaKyne

Varsity Pharmacy—Goethe Chambers

Varsity Barber Shop—Phil Byers

The Gables—Jack Wright

Ferguson Drive Inn—Paul Poff

The Gridiron—Lou Scott

Leonard's Cafe—Ron Taylor

Earlier that day, the Hoosiers held one final practice in the IU Fieldhouse. Before practice ended, Bobby Leonard walked up to junior manager Don Defur and asked him if he could stay after practice to rebound the ball while Bobby got in some extra shooting practice. Defur said, "Of course. Fine." Leonard was known to stay after practice to shoot or work on a particular aspect of his game. One night earlier in the season, an IU senior named Jack Gilbert walked into the IU Fieldhouse to watch the last forty minutes of practice. He stayed and watched as everyone else headed to the locker room except for Bobby Leonard and Charlie Kraak, who stayed for another twenty minutes. They practiced length-of-the-floor baseball passes to each other. One player would run and the other would throw a one-handed baseball pass all the way to the other end, which would be caught and converted for a layup. Then the players would switch places and run it again and again.

But on the day before the Hoosiers were set to leave for the NCAA Tournament, Bobby Leonard had a different look in his eye. After the rest of the players filed out and only Leonard and Defur were left on the floor, tenacity started to flow out of every pore of Bobby Leonard's body. "I'd throw the ball back to him," said Defur, "and he'd just slam that thing into the hardwood as a dribble and say, 'D, we *got* to win this. We got to win. [dribble] We got to win. [dribble] We got to *win!*' I've never seen anybody with more determination to do something than Bob had [that day]."

If there was one person whose determination matched Bobby Leonard's, it was Branch McCracken. Mac didn't make it to the Hoosiers' send-off banquet on Tuesday night because he went up to Fort Wayne to personally scout the first-round teams that were feeding into the NCAA regional in Chicago. In the first game, Mac got to watch the two teams that were vying for a shot at his top-ranked Hoosiers. DePaul dominated Miami of Ohio in the first half and took a twelve-point lead into the locker room. But the feisty Redskins fought back and tied the game in the third quarter, and it was nip and tuck the rest of the way until DePaul won it with a jump shot in the final seconds. In the second game, Notre Dame made quick work of Eastern Kentucky. The Irish looked like they could beat just about anyone and were a legitimate threat to make a run to the Final Four.

In watching DePaul, McCracken was able to confirm what the statistics hinted at—that the Blue Demons' two primary threats were backcourt mates Ron Feiereisel and Jimmy Lamkin. Over the course of the season, those two combined to average forty points per game, and when they both got hot at the same time, the Blue Devils were very tough to beat. The pair combined for forty-two against Miami in the first round. Going into the Indiana game, Feiereisel needed only eight more points to become the second-leading scorer in DePaul history—trailing only the great George Mikan.

When asked about his team's improbable success during the 1952–53 campaign, DePaul coach Ray Meyer heaped praise on his two guards. "Just look at Ron Feiereisel and Jim Lamkin," said Meyer. "They bagged 45 points against Notre Dame . . . and 77 in two games against LaSalle. Feiereisel played against LaSalle with a temperature of 102.5 and still scored 14 points. You can understand an opponent's consternation at discovering our offense is built around the guards. We had to do it that way. We're mighty short on material, you know. Our regular center, Russ Johnson, never even played in high school!"[2]

Even though Indiana had the Blue Demons badly outsized and overmatched in the frontcourt, there was plenty of concern that DePaul could launch a legitimate upset bid. History showed that the Blue Demons would put up an excellent fight. In fact, DePaul was a notorious spoiler of Big Ten championship teams. Previously, the Blue Demons had played ten Big Ten title winners or eventual title winners and had won nine of those games, with the only loss coming in 1938 to Purdue. DePaul also held a 3-2 series advantage against Indiana, which included an 81-43 Hoosier massacre in Chicago Stadium in 1944, led by a stadium-record thirty-seven points from George Mikan.

The other concern was that Coach Ray Meyer was one of the country's best coaches and he always had his team well prepared for big games. The Chicago native and former Notre Dame star had taken over the reins at DePaul in 1942 and led the Blue Demons to a 197-83 record, four NIT appearances, and one previous NCAA appearance in 1943. During the 1952–53 season, Meyer's Blue Demons had already upset a trio of highly ranked teams in LaSalle, Oklahoma A&M, and Notre Dame, so they were not going to be in awe of Indiana.

The Hoosiers arrived in Chicago on Wednesday afternoon, March 11. On Thursday, the IU squad had a full workout in Chicago Stadium. The "Madhouse on Madison"—named because of its location on Madison Street and its raucous fans—played host to the NCAA regional. That essentially gave DePaul a home-court advantage because the Chicago-based school regularly played several games each season on the Chicago Stadium floor, and the Blue Demons could count on a partisan home crowd that would include many of its students. However, IU was expected to have excellent representation at the game. In addition to many Chicago-based IU alums, the Hoosiers got support from more than a thousand students and fans who took the train from Bloomington to Chicago on game day, Friday, March 13. As it turned out, so many Bloomington fans bought train tickets that the Monon train system had to lengthen its usual number of coach cars to accommodate them all. It turned into a late night for those Hoosier fans. Notre Dame and Pennsylvania played the first game at 7:45 PM and IU and DePaul had the second game at 9:45. Back in Bloomington, the game wasn't televised, so students and fans had to huddle around the radio to listen to the broadcast from WFIU or WTTS.

In the regional opener, the Fighting Irish used a huge fourth-quarter burst to overcome Pennsylvania 69-57, so the IU squad knew who was waiting for them in the regional finals if they could get past DePaul in the semifinals, and the Hoosiers relished the chance for a rematch against one of the three teams that had beaten them on last-second shots.

McCracken's strategy for beating DePaul was to put Farley on Feiereisel and Leonard on Lamkin, and Mac told the team that they had to hold the high-scoring Feiereisel-Lamkin duo to a combined total of thirty-two points or fewer. McCracken's other defensive plan was to use a shifting man-to-man that, similar to a zone defense, was aimed at closing off the middle and forcing a team to shoot mostly long outside shots. Mac's teams usually employed a standard man-to-man or a sliding man-to-man, so the shifting man-to-man was a surprise tactic.

However, before the Hoosiers started their quest for an NCAA crown, McCracken had one thing he wanted to clear up. He walked into the locker room before the DePaul game and declared, "Well, the word's out that I'm going to retire after this season if we win the championship." Then Mac turned to Charlie Kraak and said, "Charlie, how many NCAA championships does Rupp have?" alluding to Kentucky's head coach. Kraak responded, "Three." And then Mac confessed, "I'm not retiring until I've got more than that son-of-a-bitch."

Don Schlundt was used to being double- and triple-teamed by opponents. He was used to getting roughed up and bumped around, especially from the brawny giants that played for Big Ten teams like

Minnesota and Wisconsin. Don was even used to taking a few cheap shots once in a while, like the whacks he often took to his thigh brace. And for his part, Don was known to crack a few skulls with "inadvertent" elbows when he turned to pivot for a shot or grab a rebound. That was his way of saying "back off" to an overly physical opponent, and Don played that part with such perfect subtlety that he was rarely ever called for a foul on a play in which he landed an elbow.

However, even Don was surprised by the raw, savage strategy DePaul used against him. Coach Ray Meyer decided not to have his normal center, Russ Johnson, attempt to guard Schlundt. Instead, Meyer used 6' 4" junior forward Daniel Lecos and assigned him to simply beat up and provoke Schlundt. As one newspaper reporter wrote, from the opening tip Lecos "elbowed, pushed, held, kicked, clawed, and vocally insulted" Schlundt.[3] On the other end of the floor, Lecos was hardly involved in the offense at all, so it was abundantly clear that he was only in the game for one purpose.

Fueled by the rugged treatment of Lecos on Schlundt, the game featured a lot of fouling and rough play in the first half. The battle was especially brutal on the boards, where both teams tenaciously wrestled for every rebound. That battle quickly caught up with the Hoosiers, as top rebounder Charlie Kraak picked up three fouls in the first quarter and had to retire to the bench. Still, even with Schlundt being handcuffed by Lecos and Bobby Leonard shooting a chilly 4-for-18 in the first half, the Hoosiers led 20-16 at the end of the first quarter and upped the lead to 42-33 going into the intermission. The game had been tied at 27-27 midway through the second quarter, but IU rallied on 15-6 run led by Leonard, Dick Farley, and Dick White, who filled in for Kraak.

IU finally started to find its rhythm in the third quarter. Schlundt came out of the locker room and hit a hook shot and then a free throw and Leonard buried a jumper to give IU its biggest lead of the night at 47-35 with 8:55 left in the third quarter. Then DePaul hatchet man Lecos fouled out halfway through the third quarter and Schlundt, who had only nine points at that point, started to hurt the Blue Demons on the inside. But DePaul's two big guns—Ron Feiereisel and Jim Lamkin—also started turning up the heat in the third quarter, and they were able to turn what looked like an IU blowout into a nip and tuck battle heading into the final ten minutes.

Indiana led 62-55 at the end of third and upped the lead back to double figures at 65-55 in the opening minutes of the fourth. But then DePaul rattled off a 7-0 run to cut the lead to 65-62 on a hook shot from center Russ Johnson with 6:30 left to play. Minutes later, the IU lead was still three points at 69-66. Hoosier starters Kraak, Farley, and Burke Scott were all in foul trouble at that point and the Blue Demons looked poised to overtake the nation's No. 1 team and pull off the upset. But with Leonard and Schlundt leading the way, Indiana scraped together a 5-0 run to go up 74-66 with three minutes remaining. The Hoosiers held steady at 80-73 with 1:05 left, and 82-75 with just forty seconds remaining. Then things got a little hairy. The never-say-die Blue Demons went into a desperate full-court press—the kind the Hoosiers practiced against every day—and were able to come up with several aggressive steals that IU players felt should have been whistled as fouls. However, DePaul ran out of time and its final charge ended with a long two-handed shot from Feiereisel in the waning seconds to make the final score Indiana 82, DePaul 80.

Feiereisel led all scorers with twenty-seven points on a highly efficient 9-for-14 from the field and 9-for-12 from the free throw line. His backcourt mate Lamkin scored fifteen on 6-for-20 from the field and 3-for-4 from the line. Of course, their combined total of forty-two points was ten points above the limit McCracken had set for his team. Dick Farley and Burke Scott were in foul trouble for much of the night and that considerably weakened the IU defense.

Schlundt led the Hoosiers with twenty-three points and Leonard finished with twenty-two, but neither of them had a great night shooting the ball. Schlundt was 5-for-16 from the floor and 13-for-17 from the line. Leonard was 9-for-30 from the field and 4-for-9 from the line. Dick Farley finished with twelve points and Dick White added ten off the bench. Against DePaul, the Hoosiers still did not recover the shooting touch that had abandoned them since the Illinois game two weeks earlier. IU shot just .321 (26-for-81) from the field, while allowing the Blue Demons to shoot .397 (27-for-68).

McCracken was not happy afterwards, especially about the Hoosiers turning the ball over in the final minutes and nearly giving up a seven-point lead in less than thirty seconds. "We made a lot of mistakes—too many mistakes," said Mac, shaking his head. "It's fortunate you can make [that] many mistakes and still win in this kind of tournament."[4]

With Indiana's end-of-the-season struggles continuing and Notre Dame suddenly surging, IU looked vulnerable heading into the regional final. Even though the top-ranked Hoosiers were expected to be a strong favorite on paper against Notre Dame, there were plenty of commentators who expected Indiana to get all it could handle and more against the Irish. What they didn't realize was that as soon as the Hoosiers had seen the NCAA bracket, they had been hoping for a rematch with Notre Dame in the regional final. And as it turned out, a showdown with the Irish was just what the Hoosiers needed to snap out of the doldrums.

IU coach Branch McCracken and Notre Dame coach John Jordan were good friends. Of course, that didn't mean they wanted to beat each other any less when their teams played. In fact, the opposite was true. Much like IU's Bob Knight and Purdue's Gene Keady three decades later, McCracken and Jordan wanted to beat each other so that they had off-season bragging rights.

With Purdue suffering through a downswing in its basketball program during the late 1940s and early 1950s, Notre Dame was actually Indiana's most competitive intrastate rival. And although the rivalry didn't have the long history of the IU-Purdue series, the competition was every bit as intense. For example, after Indiana beat Illinois and rose to No. 1 in the national rankings, Notre Dame athletic director Ed Krause sent a friendly telegram to McCracken to remind him which Indiana team had earned bragging rights that season. The telegram read, "Congratulations on being the No. 1 team in the nation. We all voted for you. However, remember, Notre Dame is still No. 1 in Indiana."[5]

When it came time for the surprising rematch in the NCAAs, there were no sneak attacks or surprise strategies. Both teams knew each other and their personnel. Both coaches knew the tendencies of the other. And everyone from both schools knew how badly the teams and their fans wanted to beat each other and earn a trip to the NCAA finals. The teams were fairly evenly matched. Their records were similar—Indiana at 20-3 and Notre Dame at 19-4. And they were playing on a neutral floor. The game itself was about just throwing the ball up and seeing which team came out on top a couple of hours later.

After both teams won their Friday games, they turned around the next night and came back to Chicago Stadium for the regional championship game on Saturday. The third-place game kicked off the action at 7:45 PM, as Pennsylvania won a 90-70 slaughter over DePaul, which looked like it hadn't recovered from its intense game with the Hoosiers the night before.

The IU–Notre Dame game kicked off at 9:45 PM with the Irish breaking quickly out of the gate. Led by seven quick points from guard Junior Stephens, Notre Dame jumped to an 8-4 lead three minutes into the game. The Irish still led 10-7 at the midpoint of the first quarter, but Bobby Leonard recognized that Notre Dame center Norb Lewinski was playing behind Don Schlundt and the Irish weren't aggressively double-teaming the big sophomore, so Leonard started to methodically work the ball into Schlundt on every possession, and Big Don tied the game at 11-11 with two free throws. Irish forward Dick Rosenthal hit a free throw to put Notre Dame back on top 12-11, but Schlundt scored his second field goal of the game to give IU its first lead at 13-12. Leonard kept feeding the big guy, including several nifty passes that set up Schlundt perfectly for easy scores, and Schlundt kept scoring again and again until IU had built a 25-18 lead at the end of the first quarter. Schlundt had amassed an amazing eighteen points in the opening quarter on 5-for-8 from the field and 8-for-8 from the line.

Notre Dame's Lewinski picked up three fouls by the end of the first quarter trying to stop Schlundt's onslaught, so the Irish sent in 6' 9" sophomore Dick Wise at the beginning of the second quarter to try his hand at slowing down Schlundt. But when the second quarter opened, the rest of the Hoosiers started getting more involved in the scoring. IU built its lead to 36-23 halfway through the period, then Notre Dame scratched its way back. Still, when the gun went off at halftime, IU led 42-32. Schlundt had scored Indiana's final ten points of the second quarter and ended the first half with thirty points.

The Hoosiers came flying out of the locker room and went right back into all-out scoring mode, with Schlundt and Leonard taking turns doing the damage and Charlie Kraak and Burke Scott chipping in. Halfway through the third quarter IU led 57-40. At that point, McCracken started removing starters Leonard, Scott, and Dick Farley, who were all in foul trouble. With a reserve-dominated lineup, the Hoosiers finished the third quarter with a 62-48 lead. But Notre Dame kept chipping away at the lead and inching its way back into the game during the fourth. Finally, the Irish cut the lead to 71-63 as the three-minute mark approached, prompting McCracken to quickly put his starters back into the game. They responded by almost immediately pushing the lead back to twelve points, and they stalled out the final two minutes with their five-man weave to clinch a decisive 79-66 victory.

When Don Schlundt finally came back to the bench near the end of the game, he sat down next to Coach McCracken, who asked him if he knew how many points he had scored. Schlundt had no idea. Mac leaned over and held up four fingers on his right hand and one finger on his left hand—forty-one. That scoring outburst not only earned Schlundt regional MVP honors, but it also set a new IU single-game record (breaking the record of thirty-nine Don had scored against Michigan earlier in the season) and it set a new Chicago Stadium record as well, breaking the record of thirty-seven set by Don's idol George Mikan against the Hoosiers back in 1944.

Mac got to do the honors of presenting Don with the MVP trophy at midcourt after the game. As he handed off the trophy, Mac told the audience, "Don is just a 20-year-old sophomore, so if he works real hard he might become a pretty good basketball player someday."[6]

In addition to Schlundt's forty-one, Leonard scored eleven, and if they had been keeping track of assists Leonard would have likely been in double figures in that category as well. Burke Scott added ten and Charlie Kraak scored eight. Notre Dame was led by Norb Lewinski and Dick Rosenthal, who each scored nineteen, and Junior Stephens, who finished with fourteen. As a team, the Hoosiers finally broke out of their shooting slump, hitting at a .403 percentage (25-for-62), while holding Notre Dame to .311 (23-for-74).

After the game, the IU players squeezed back into the tiny Chicago Stadium locker room, which *Indiana Daily Student* reporter Herb Michelson said was "the size of at least two or three telephone booths."[7] The players didn't seem to mind as they threw their arms around each other and posed for newspaper photographers. Then McCracken started in on his usual postgame cigarette and summed up the game using his standard style of repeating himself. "It was a great way to come back after that battle last night," said Mac. "It was a great way to come back after that grueling game last night. . . . It was a great comeback after that battle last night."[8]

The players kept chiming back and forth to each other, "Two down, two more to go!"[9] Everyone was dead tired. Don Schlundt draped his long legs across one of the benches and leaned back for a well-earned rest. McCracken admitted, "I'm so tired I can't stay on my feet."[10] The only player who still seemed to have any energy was Bobby Leonard, who continued to whoop it up and slap backs. He also bragged about the news that his high school, Terre Haute Gerstmeyer, had won the semistate in Bloomington, and he declared that the Black Cats were going to win state.

Even as tired as they were, it was easy to tell that the Hoosiers had found their swagger again.

When the team returned to the hotel after midnight, McCracken turned to senior manager Ron Fifer and said, "Meet me in the lobby at 6 o'clock tomorrow morning." Fifer naturally said, "Okay." However, Ron was not an early riser by nature, and he knew that if Mac said "6:00" then it meant he would expect Fifer by 5:45—and Mac himself would be down there waiting for him by 5:30. So Fifer dragged himself out of bed early the next morning and made it down to the lobby before 6:00 AM. Mac was sitting there waiting and said, "Come outside with me." The two of them walked outside of their hotel in downtown Chicago. Because it was so early on a Sunday morning, the streets were completely empty and the city was devoid of its normal sounds of cars and trains and busy people hustling by. Instead, it was unusually quiet. McCracken walked out into the middle of the empty street, with Fifer trailing close behind, and he looked up between the tall buildings. He saw only a blue sky with a few stars still twinkling as dawn was breaking over the Windy City. "Well, it looks like it's gonna be okay," said Mac. That meant McCracken was ready to fly out of Chicago that morning. It meant that Fifer had to start making the arrangements. The Hoosiers' next NCAA game was less than seventy-two hours away. It was time to go to the Final Four. It was time to go after the national championship.

KANSAS CITY CORONATION

15

It comes down to one thing. Winning is all there is, because losing is heartbreak hell. It's not only heartbreak for you as a player or a coach, it's heartbreak for all the fans. It's no good.
—BOBBY LEONARD

The 1953 NCAA finals were like a once-in-a-decade prize fight, but with four heavyweight champions, one standing in each of the four corners of the ring. Based on the rankings, it was one of the most top-heavy NCAA Final Fours ever. It featured four of the nation's top seven teams from the final AP poll, including the top two—Indiana and Washington. The other two were No. 5 Kansas and No. 7 LSU. Each of the four teams featured an excellent center who had led his conference in scoring: Indiana's Don Schlundt led the Big Ten at 25.1 points per game, LSU's Bob Pettit led the SEC with 24.2 points per game, Washington's Bob Houbregs led the Pacific Coast Conference with 25.4 points per game, and Kansas's B. H. Born led the Big Seven at 18.4 points per game. Beyond that, the 1953 NCAA finals also featured four of college basketball's best stories.

On the day before the finals began, the Associated Press explained the anticipation and the expectations: "Kansas is defending champion, Indiana is No. 1 in the latest Associated Press poll, LSU has the season's best winning record [24-1], but towering Washington is the favorite to crash through to the title. Coaches assembling here for their annual meeting and rules conferences generally regard the Pacific Coast champions, with their great shooter Bobby Houbregs, as the team to beat."[1]

Nearly everyone was bullish about Washington because Houbregs had dazzled the college basketball world in the NCAA regionals at Corvallis, Oregon. In the regional semifinals, he scored forty-five points to break the single-game NCAA Tournament scoring record set by Clyde Lovellette a season earlier, then came back the next night and scored thirty-four points in the Huskies' 74-62 win over Santa Clara in the regional finals. That gave the senior center an average of 39.5 points per game for the tournament heading into the Final Four. People expected Houbregs to do for Washington what Lovellette had done for Kansas the previous season—carry the team all the way to the title. In fact, Houbregs was only fifty-two points away from also breaking Lovellette's record of 141 points in the tournament. However, what the college basketball world would eventually discover during the 1953 finals was that Lovellette—even though he bore the same type of scoring burden as Houbregs—was surrounded by a much better stable of teammates.

The few Lovellette teammates who remained from the Jayhawks' 1952 championship team were set to quickly get a firsthand look at Houbregs because Kansas and Washington were matched up in the semifinals on one side of the Final Four bracket, while Indiana and LSU were set to square off on the other side.

For Indiana, having all the attention focused on Washington wasn't such a bad thing. It meant that even though Indiana was carrying the burden of being the top-ranked team in the nation, the Hoosiers were flying surprisingly low under the radar and were even being cast in the underdog role while Washington claimed the headlines as the favorite going into the Final Four. That Indiana still had so much youth—only sophomores and juniors had played in the Hoosiers' first two tournament games—and that they had struggled to beat DePaul appeared to be the two main factors working against them. Plus, with Houbregs being the national player of the year and coming up with such phenomenal performances in the regional, he and Washington had quickly become the story of the tournament.

However, the college basketball world at the time was overlooking two things. The first was the level of competition Washington played against during the regular season and the postseason. During the regular season, the Huskies certainly didn't have to regularly battle the kind of teams that Big Ten, Big Seven, or East Coast teams had to face on a weekly basis. And even in the NCAA Tournament, Washington's two wins were over No. 14 Seattle and unranked Santa Clara—both solid teams, but neither of them on the level of Notre Dame, DePaul, or Pennsylvania. Also overlooked was Indiana's sensational record against teams outside the Midwest. At the time, IU held an all-time mark of 46-11 in intersectional play, which included a 20-3 record against the South, 13-1 against the West, and even a 13-7 mark against traditional powerhouses in the East. And during McCracken's term as head coach, IU's record was even better, as Mac's teams were 23-3 against teams from other regions. Indiana was at the time the all-time leader in winning percentage in NCAA Tournament play with a perfect 6-0 record. Yet no one seemed to be focused on whether McCracken and Indiana could maintain their spotless NCAA mark. The general perception seemed to be that the young Hoosiers were still a year away from reaching their peak on the national stage. But McCracken and his team didn't think like that. They felt they were the best team in the country, and now they had the golden opportunity to prove it against the nation's top competition. Next year was next year. Indiana's time was now.

Kansas City, Missouri, served as the host of the 1953 Final Four, and the Kansas City Municipal Auditorium was the tournament site. The 10,500-seat arena was an ideal location at the crossroads of America and was one of the NCAA's favorite venues during the tournament's first two decades. For Indiana, the Municipal Auditorium also held great nostalgia because it was the site of IU's 60-42 victory over Kansas in the 1940 NCAA championship game.

Normally, the NCAA finals would have taken place a week after the regionals, but in 1953 the time between them was shortened as part of the NCAA's "de-emphasis" plan. As a result, after the Friday-Saturday regionals, the NCAA finals were played on the following Tuesday and Wednesday, leaving just a two-day break in between. That meant the regional winners could waste little time traveling from their regional sites to Kansas City.

The Hoosiers were the first team to arrive on Sunday afternoon, March 15, as they flew straight from Chicago on the morning after beating Notre Dame. During the flight, senior manager Ron Fifer— a hard-core Young Democrat—talked about the fact that former president Harry Truman now had an office in the Kansas City area, and Fifer was wondering if it would be possible to visit President Truman. As the team got off the plane, Coach McCracken turned to Fifer and only half-jokingly said, "Now Fifer, I do not want you taking any of my boys around that son-of-a-bitch Truman." For the next several days, the running joke at lunch was that several players would ask Fifer, "When are we going to see Truman?" Little did they know, their chance would come soon enough.

As soon as the team got settled into the Continental Hotel, the grand old building that was going to host all four teams for the finals, McCracken called Fifer in his room and said, "We're going to be deluged with people wanting tickets and wanting rooms. I want you to go out and rent every hotel room you can find." So Fifer went around Kansas City and made reservations under false names and put down a bunch of deposits. Over the next couple of days, Mac would call Fifer and say that a certain person had arrived in Kansas City, and Fifer would direct them to a hotel and tell them the fake name the reservation was under.

During the course of the year, there were a number of well-to-do alumni who occasionally attended road games. "We would give them tickets and they would give Branch money for the tickets," said Ron Fifer. "I kept a fund. Mac gave me the money and I kept it in a shoebox." Mac was leery of alumni having close contact with his players. He knew that times were changing and wealthy alumni had gotten out of control with cash and gifts to athletes at other schools.

McCracken was definitely not a person who believed in overindulgence. Yet he also had a big heart and wanted the best for his players, so in Kansas City he decided to give the players a special treat. He asked Fifer how much money was in the shoebox and Fifer told him that there was almost $200. Mac said, "Split it up." So Fifer gave each player about $12 spending money. It was a rare splurge from Coach McCracken.

"[The players] didn't have any money," said Fifer. "They were all poor kids." The spending money allowed them to buy souvenirs for their family, see a movie, and enjoy their time in Kansas City. One of the players even used the money on a teammate. Bobby Leonard used part of his spending money to buy a new shirt and tie for Ron Taylor, who came to Kansas City to watch the Hoosiers play but was not on the team's active roster for the NCAA Tournament and had to watch the games in street clothes. Thanks to Leonard, Taylor didn't have to do it in the same clothes he wore at the regionals in Chicago.

On Monday, March 16, the IU squad worked out at the Municipal Auditorium at 2:00 PM to begin preparing for LSU. The Hoosier players, who had been dead tired on Saturday night, now had an extra bounce in their step, and several of them remarked that they felt better than they had in weeks. The Notre Dame win had re-energized the team and rekindled the players' confidence. They couldn't wait to get a shot at LSU. The NCAA semifinals were a little more than twenty-four hours away.

That night, Indiana freshman Charley Cogan—the kid who unknowingly ran into Branch McCracken in December and stood with Mac to watch the IU Fieldhouse floor get reassembled—was in his dorm room at the Men's Quad on campus. At 10:00 PM, Charley was in his pajamas, sitting on his bed poring over a textbook. Charley's roommate was sitting at the desk with a lamp shining over his study material. Like most freshmen, they had the door to their room sitting open. "You studied with your door open," said Cogan, "just because you didn't want to miss out on anything important that was going on."

Cogan's bed was the one closest to the door so he was the first to notice when three guys walked in dressed in street clothes as if they were ready to go somewhere. The leader of the pack was Dudley Miller, a friend of Cogan's, who said, "Come on Charley, get dressed. We've got a trip to make."

Charley said, "I'm not getting dressed. I'm ready to go to bed. I'm studying here!"

Dudley responded, "We've got an opportunity to see Indiana play for the national championship and you're sitting here? Come on, we're gonna go to Kansas City."

Cogan was still in shock that these guys were ready to leave right then and there and drive to Kansas City, and he repeatedly told Miller he wasn't going with them. "We went on for three or four minutes arguing," said Cogan. "I kept telling him he was crazy and that there was no way I was gonna go do something like that. . . . Eventually, [all three of them] said, 'This is too good of a chance to miss' and I said, 'Well, okay, maybe I should think about it.' The next thing I know I'm getting dressed and I'm wondering, 'What in the hell am I doing?' By midnight, we were on the road to Kansas City."

Dudley Miller said, "We took off in the middle of the night and I wasn't even sure [about the directions to] where we were going. It was just a bunch of guys kind of grabbing each other and saying, 'Let's go do it.' And all of a sudden it dawned on us, 'We're actually doing this.' We had no tickets. We had nothing but the desire to be out there and be part of it."

Cogan remarked, "We didn't have tickets, but we figured we'd be able to get tickets and they wouldn't be too expensive. . . . So we're en route, and after filling up the gas tank a couple times, we start talking about how much money we've got left, and it was like, 'Uh oh, we've got a problem.'"

Cogan had his checkbook, but the account didn't have a whole lot of money in it and checks weren't going to help them pay for food or gas. So they looked at the map and Dudley Miller saw that the road they were on—U.S. Route 40—went right by Columbia, Missouri, on their way to Kansas City. A girl Dudley knew from high school (his best friend's girlfriend) was at Stephens College in Columbia and Dudley said he could borrow some money from her. Cogan was horrified by that idea. "I remember thinking, 'I couldn't borrow money from someone else's girlfriend. I couldn't borrow money from my own girlfriend—if I had one—let alone someone else's girlfriend,' " he said. "But [Dudley] insisted that it was no big deal, that they were great friends and had been great friends all through high school, and it would be no problem. So, sure enough, we drove out of the way a little bit to go to Stephens College and he went to see her and she had to have money wired to her [from her parents] to give to him. So he got the money and thanked her and we took off."

After taking turns driving through the night and sleeping in the car, they pulled into Kansas City on Tuesday, March 17. The national semifinals were set to start that night, but none of the four guys actually knew where the games were being played or where to go in Kansas City to find out, so they parked the car downtown and started walking around looking for someone to ask. Fortunately, as they were walking on one side of the street, they spotted Charlie Kraak, Dick Farley, and Burke Scott walking on the other side of the street. Cogan, who had a class with Scott, yelled across the street, "Hey Burke!"

Scott looked over and said, "Hey, you're from Indiana!"

So the four guys ran across the street to talk to the IU players. Cogan and the guys told about how they'd just decided to come to Kansas City the night before and drove through the night to get there even though they didn't have tickets yet. The players thought it was terrific that they came so far and said that the IU ticket manager was in the Hotel Continental where the team was staying.

Since Cogan had a checkbook, the plan was for him to buy the tickets by writing a check, so Charley and his friends set out for the Hotel Continental. He didn't have trouble finding the ticket manager, but getting tickets wasn't quite as easy as he expected. The ticket manager explained that tickets were rare and they didn't have many left. However, Charlie explained that he and his three friends had driven all night to Kansas City for the games and he was prepared to write a check for four tickets. Gene Gedman, IU's star halfback from the football team, came to see the ticket manager about picking up his tickets while Charley was telling his story, and Gedman said, "Jesus, you guys [drove] all the way from Bloomington to see the game and you run into roadblocks like this." Then Gedman turned to the ticket manager and said, "Why can't you just go ahead and give them the tickets?"

The ticket manager, who appeared to be swayed by Cogan's story, said he could get four tickets but that the check would have to be countersigned by an IU staff or faculty member, to which Charley replied, "Well geez, how am I going to do something like that?"

"Do you know anyone in an official position at the university?" the ticket manager replied.

"No," Charley said. But after a slight pause, he said, "Well . . . Branch McCracken."

That drew a blank stare and several moments of silence. "You know Branch McCracken?" the ticket manager skeptically asked.

"Well, yeah, we speak," Cogan replied. "I chatted with him before the season. We're not old buddies, but he knows me." In fact, Charley had not only had his chance encounter with Coach McCracken in the IU Fieldhouse in December, but he also regularly passed Mac on the way to and from the IU Fieldhouse and often exchanged friendly greetings. To Cogan's small-town mentality at the time, that made them friends.

When Charley explained that he knew Coach McCracken, the ticket manager said, "You can't disturb him. He's resting for the game tonight."

Cogan simply responded, "Well, how am I going to get this signed if I don't?"

Gene Gedman chimed in again and tried to persuade the ticket manager to simply take Cogan's check, but the guy said, "I'd do it, but it would be my neck if I did."

So Charley decided that the only way for him to get the tickets was to get Branch McCracken to countersign his check.

The ticket manager still thought that wasn't a good idea. "You shouldn't do that," he said.

"I don't think he'll mind, really," said Charley. "He's always been very friendly."

"Well, I can't tell you what room he's in," said the ticket manager, "but if you get it countersigned we'll have the tickets."

So Charley went back down to the lobby and explained the situation to the other three guys, and they couldn't believe that Charley was thinking of asking McCracken to countersign his check. "Are you really thinking of doing this?" one of them asked. Charley told them about how insistent the ticket manager was about having the check countersigned and that he had four tickets ready for them, but the only way to get them was with cash or a check that was vouched for by an IU faculty or staff member. Then one of the guys turned to him and said, "You've got to do it. That's the only way we're going to get in to see the game."

With no other options available, Charley went to the front desk and asked if they would tell him what room Branch McCracken was in. He explained that he knew the coach and that if he wasn't able to see McCracken and ask him to sign his check then he wouldn't be able to see the game that night. The clerk at the front desk said he couldn't give out the room number but he could ring Coach Mc-Cracken's room and ask if he would see Charley.

Cogan nervously sat down in one of the lobby chairs and the clerk made the call. Mac picked up and the clerk said, "There's a gentleman that says he knows you" and then briefly explained the situation. He hung up the phone, walked over to Charley, and said, "Coach Mc-Cracken said to come on up." The clerk told him the room number and Charley went up to Mac's room and knocked on the door. Sure enough, McCracken had obviously been taking a nap because he opened the door in a white T-shirt and a baggy pair of white boxer shorts and his hair was all tussled. He recognized Charley, or at least was kind enough to act as if he remembered him, and he told the freshman to hand over the check. While he was signing it he asked, "So you drove all the way out here?"

Charley said, "Yeah, we just got in a few hours ago. We drove all night."

"Well, that's great," said Mac. "I'm glad to see that you could come. Here you go." McCracken handed him back the countersigned check, and Charley thanked Coach McCracken and wished him good luck, then promised that he and his friends were going to cheer so loud that the coach would hear them all night long.

Slightly stunned but very happy, Charley sped back down to where the ticket manager was and presented his countersigned check. The ticket manager looked at it and started shaking his head in disbelief. "That's his signature all right," he said. He took the check and handed Charley four tickets. Not only that, but they were pretty good seats— on the side of the court near one of the baskets and about halfway up the arena.

It had been less than twenty-four hours since Dudley Miller had talked Charley into making the trip to Kansas City. Since then, Charley and his friends had traveled more than 450 miles by car, nearly run out of money, stopped along the way to borrow money, arrived in Kansas City without knowing where to go or how to get tickets, got stonewalled when they finally tried to buy tickets, and then got an assist from none other than Branch McCracken himself in finally getting tickets to the Final Four. The four of them would have to sleep in the car for the next two nights, but they didn't care. They were having an experience they would remember for the rest of their lives.

The opening game of the 1953 Final Four featured Indiana against Louisiana State. It was a 7:45 PM tip-off, with the Washington-Kansas game to follow at 9:45. WDAF-TV in Kansas City was set to broadcast all the Final Four games, but the Chicago television stations decided not to pick up the games, so WTTV in Bloomington was unable to get the signal. That meant the fans back in Indiana had to catch the game on radio. The IU Radio and Television Service was doing a broadcast of the game that would be picked up by radio stations across the Hoosier state, including WTTS and WFIU in Bloomington, WIRE and WIBC in Indianapolis, WANE in Fort Wayne, WIOU in Kokomo, WBOW in Terre Haute, WBIW in Bedford, WSRK in Shelbyville, WKBV in Richmond, and WJPS in Evansville.

The LSU Tigers quietly invaded the Final Four as one of the hottest teams in the country. At 24-1, they had the best winning percentage in the nation among major colleges. While most of the headlines throughout the college basketball season revolved around teams like Illinois, Kansas State, Seton Hall, and Indiana, LSU dominated the Kentucky-less SEC, going 13-0 and sweeping through the conference's postseason tournament. The Tigers also broke the century mark three times during the season, including a 124-33 bombardment of Southwestern Tennessee.

In the NCAA Tournament, LSU made its way through the southeastern regional in Raleigh, North Carolina, with an 89-76 win over Lebanon Valley—the smallest school to ever play in the NCAA's round of sixteen. Then the Tigers opened up an eighteen-point third-quarter lead on Holy Cross and fought off a late rally by the Crusaders for an 81-73 win in the regional final.

The win over Holy Cross was largely saved by a great performance from LSU's star center Bob Pettit, who came through with several clutch plays down the stretch. Pettit, a 6' 9" junior, was a home-state superstar from Baton Rouge and was the centerpiece of the LSU attack. LSU also featured three Hoosiers on their roster, including starting forward Don Belcher from New Albany and reserves Don Loughmiller (also from New Albany) and Bob Freshley (from Rockport). Belcher was LSU's second-leading scorer behind Pettit, and Freshley was Pettit's backup.

LSU had a highly respected coach in Harry Rabenhorst, and the Tigers ran a balanced combination of fast break and half-court basketball. No one expected LSU to try to run with the Hoosiers, but just about everyone expected a major-league battle between the Big Ten champ and the SEC champ—similar to the Big Ten–SEC showdown in the 1951 Final Four when Kentucky won a 76-74 thriller over Illinois. The oddsmakers made Indiana a seven-point favorite over LSU, while Washington was just a three-point favorite over Kansas in the late game. However, the talk around the Hotel Continental, which hosted all four teams and the basketball coaches who were in town for the national meeting, was that the Indiana-LSU game would likely be the more competitive of the evening's doubleheader. Many of them expected the clock to strike midnight for Kansas in the second game. The undersized Jayhawks had defied low preseason expectations and ridden an underdog hot streak all the way to the Final Four, but most figured the jig was up for them against the Washington Huskies, whose mammoth frontcourt featured a 6' 7" forward, a 6' 7" center, and a 6' 8" forward.

For Indiana, LSU was scouted by IU freshman coach Joe Thomas, who later went on to fame as the general manager who built the legendary 1972 Miami Dolphins in the National Football League. Thomas went to Raleigh, North Carolina, for the southeastern regional, then arrived in Kansas City on Monday morning. He quickly had a conference with Branch McCracken and Ernie Andres and, prior to the Hoosiers' 2:00 PM practice in the Municipal Auditorium, the three of them devised IU's strategy for beating LSU.

For the first three minutes, the IU-LSU game was the extremely competitive showdown everyone expected. The opening sequence was beautiful for the Hoosiers. Bob Pettit won the tip from Don Schlundt and 5' 10" LSU guard Benny McArdle rushed the ball upcourt to probe the defense. He threw the ball to the wing, got it back out front and then drove the lane for a twelve-foot pullup jumper that was blocked by Burke Scott and recovered by Charlie Kraak, who took a few dribbles and flipped the ball ahead to Bob Leonard. When the LSU defense didn't aggressively pick up Leonard as he crossed half-court, the IU sharpshooter pulled up at the top of the key and released a twenty-footer that softly landed in the back of the net.

Next, Pettit missed on one end of the floor and Schlundt missed on the other end. Then the Tigers' 5' 10" guard Norman Magee swished a one-hander from fifteen feet to tie the game at 2-2. Burke Scott broke the tie with a free throw to make it 3-2 IU, but Pettit grabbed an offensive rebound and hit a turnaround jump shot to give LSU its first lead at 4-3. It didn't last long. Leonard came down and used a Burke Scott screen near the top of the key to uncork a step-back shot from twenty-two feet that rattled home just above the out-stretched arms of Pettit and made the score 5-4 Indiana.

LSU came down and tried to work the ball into Pettit, but the Hoosiers sagged in on him, which left Benny McArdle open for a two-hander from twenty feet and he sank it to give LSU a 6-5 advantage. On the next sequence, Schlundt got called for pushing off on Pettit and Pettit sank a free throw to put the Tigers up 7-5. But then Schlundt scored on an offensive rebound and was fouled on the play.

He missed the free throw but the ball was deflected out-of-bounds and awarded to IU. On the out-of-bounds play, Dick Farley scored on a pretty left-handed hook shot, and just like that, IU was back in front 9-7.

Then Burke Scott grabbed a defensive rebound, built up a full head of steam, ducked in and out of defenders, and went coast to coast for a layup right over Pettit. IU 11, LSU 7. The Tigers then decided to slow the game down and started walking the ball up the floor. After a free throw from Bob Leonard upped the Indiana lead to 12-7 with 5:52 left in the first quarter, LSU coach Harry Rabenhorst had seen enough, and he called for a time-out to try to put an end to the Hoosiers' 7-0 run. It worked. LSU missed a jump shot, but Pettit went over Schlundt and tipped the ball three times. The third one went in to cut the lead to 12-9, but then Schlundt caught the ball deep under the basket and easily scored over Pettit to push it back to a five-point lead at 14-9. On the next trip down, Schlundt tried to deny the ball to Pettit and got caught for reaching around, picking up his second foul with 5:13 left in the first. Nevertheless, McCracken gambled and left the big sophomore in the game.

Since Lou Scott had been lost at midseason, Schlundt had gotten used to playing with foul trouble. After Schlundt picked up his second foul against the Tigers, Leonard helped protect the big man by keeping the ball in his own hands out on the perimeter. Bobby nailed three straight long bombs, and on the third one he was hit on the elbow by Norm Magee and drew a foul. He stepped up and swished the free throw to make it a 21-12 Indiana lead. After LSU turned the ball over, Leonard raced up the floor and pulled up for another long jumper that he swished—his sixth-straight field goal without a miss—to put IU in control at 23-12. On the Hoosiers' next possession, Leonard finally missed his first shot, but he still was 7-for-8 from the field during the first quarter and sank two free throws to finish with sixteen points. Leonard had jump-started the IU attack, single-handedly outscoring the Tigers 9-2 during that key stretch and carrying the Hoosiers to a 31-20 lead at the end of the opening period. As a team, IU made fourteen of sixteen shots (.875) in the first quarter. LSU was lucky to be down by only eleven. If it weren't for twelve points from Pettit, most of them on tip-ins, the score could have been much more lopsided.

Leonard continued his hot shooting in the second quarter as IU quickly extended its lead to 35-23. LSU tried to tighten up its defense but ended up committing fouls and putting the Hoosiers on the free throw line. However, things also got a little dicey for IU as Leonard picked up three fouls in the period and Dick Farley and Don Schlundt each picked up his third. Both Leonard and Schlundt left the game with 4:59 left in the first half, and LSU soon cut the lead to 45-39 at the 2:25 mark, thanks to some hot shooting from Indiana native Don Belcher. At the half, IU clung to a 49-41 advantage.

With IU's top three scorers in foul trouble, LSU looked like it had a golden opportunity to wrestle back control of the game in the second half. But Leonard and Schlundt wouldn't let it happen. Leonard canned a twenty-two-footer to open the scoring in the third, and Schlundt had eleven points in the period. IU started the quarter with a 12-6 run and extended it to an 18-9 streak with 2:40 left in the third. At that point, Indiana led 67-50 and the game was all but over. Leonard had already retired to the bench with four fouls and wouldn't be needed for the rest of the night as a group of mostly second-team Hoosiers played ball control basketball for the fourth quarter and closed the game in solid fashion.

LSU had cut the lead to 69-56 at the end of the third quarter and closed it to 77-67 with four minutes remaining. But Indiana scored the final four points of the game to tuck away an 81-67 victory and earn the first spot in the national championship game the next night.

For the game, IU seared the nets by shooting 56 percent from the field. The Hoosiers put up a season-low forty-five shots, but hit twenty-five of them. Leonard had the hottest hand on the floor as he made nine of twelve shots (.750), all of them from beyond eighteen feet. Bobby also hit four of five free throws and finished with twenty-two points in twenty-five minutes of play. It was Leonard's sixteen-point net-scorching performance in the first quarter that pushed the Hoosiers into a lead they never relinquished, and his outside shooting exhibition left mouths agape and heads shaking throughout the Kansas City Municipal Auditorium. It remains one of the greatest first-quarter performances in the history of the Final Four.

Don Schlundt also made history. He finished with twenty-nine points on 8-for-13 (.615) from the floor and 13-for-17 (.765) from the line. The thirteen free throws he made gave him forty-one for the tournament, surpassing Clyde Lovellette's record of thirty-five set the previous season, and Schlundt still had one more game to bolster his new record.

IU's forwards also came up big against the Tigers. Charlie Kraak finished with nine points and nine rebounds, Dick White came off the bench and grabbed eight rebounds, and Dick Farley chipped in ten points (on 4-for-5 from the field) and seven rebounds. Farley also harassed LSU forward Don Belcher into a 4-for-15 shooting performance. Norm Magee had seventeen points for LSU on 6-for-15 from the field. The lone Tiger who had a big game was Bob Pettit, who finished with twenty-nine points and fifteen rebounds. Schlundt had a difficult time containing Pettit, who showed great versatility and athleticism, but Schlundt was much more efficient on offense. Pettit shot 10-for-24 (.417) from the floor and 9-for-18 (.500) from the line, so Don matched Pettit's twenty-nine points with eleven fewer field goal attempts and one fewer free throw attempt.

Following the IU win, the Hoosier players came back out into the arena to watch the next game. "After the semifinal game with LSU, we stayed and watched the Kansas game with the University of Washington," said Dick White. "We were honestly thinking we were going to play Washington, and we watched that game and about 10 minutes into the game we didn't think we were going to be playing Washington anymore."

Kansas had the dream season the year before in 1951–52. The Jayhawks went 26-2, won the Big Seven conference, and rolled through the NCAA Tournament. Then, three days after locking up the national championship, the team played in the U.S. Olympic Trials. The Jayhawks trounced NAIA champion Southwest Missouri State and came from behind to beat NIT champ LaSalle in New York

City. Kansas finished as the runner-up to the Peoria Caterpillars, a semipro AAU powerhouse at the time, and seven Jayhawks were selected to play on the 1952 U.S. Olympic basketball team, which swept its way to the gold medal that summer in Helsinki, Finland. That was precisely the script Kansas coach Phog Allen had written for his stellar recruiting class of 1948—and achieving it was Allen's greatest triumph as a coach.

Indiana native Clyde Lovellette was the centerpiece of that recruiting class and of the 1952 Jayhawk team. Lovellette led the nation in scoring (28.4 points per game) in 1952, led the Big Seven in scoring for the third-straight season, broke a slew of NCAA Tournament records, and finished his career as the all-time leading scorer in college basketball with 1,888 points. Lovellette was one of four senior starters on the 1952 Kansas team. The others were Bob Kenney, Bill Hougland, and Bill Lienhard. When the four of them left Lawrence, Kansas, they left a gaping hole in the basketball program.

There were eleven lettermen on the 1951–52 team and only four of them returned for the 1952–53 season—Dean Kelley, Charlie Hoag, B. H. Born, and Dean Smith. Kelley was the only returning starter and Hoag was the only other player who had seen significant minutes on the floor. Then, in the fall of 1952, the lightning-quick Hoag tore up his knee while playing halfback for the Kansas football team. His season was done—for both football and basketball. That left just three returning lettermen and only one experienced player coming back for the Jayhawks' 1952–53 season. It looked like a rebuilding year in Lawrence, and naturally expectations were extremely low.

"We were picked sixth in the [Big Seven]," said senior guard Dean Smith, who later went on to become a college basketball legend as the head coach of North Carolina.

To everyone's surprise—including the Jayhawks themselves—they had a terrific season. The Jayhawks' archrivals, the Kansas State Wildcats, were supposed to be the class of the Big Seven and one of the top teams in the nation. But during conference play, the Jayhawks swept the Wildcats and finished at the top of the Big Seven with a 10-2 conference record.

The Jayhawks were successful because several inexperienced players unexpectedly stepped up and provide major contributions. Junior forward Allen Kelley, the younger brother of Dean Kelley, became the team's second-leading scorer at 12.9 points per game. Harold Patterson, a 6' 1" junior forward, averaged 9.5 points per game and provided another pleasant surprise. West Point transfer Gil Reich, a 6' 0" senior guard, averaged 8.0 points per game and provided additional tenacity in the backcourt. But the biggest surprise of them all was also the biggest player of them all, 6' 9" junior center B. H. Born. During his first two seasons at Kansas, Born functioned primarily as a big body to guard Clyde Lovellette in practice—and that task never went very well for him. Lovellette dominated Born every day, just as he did most of the other centers in college basketball. But Lovellette also physically thrashed Born on a daily basis.

"[Clyde] was a tough man to be around in those days," said Born. "He liked to win and he was a bully. He outweighed me by about seventy or eighty pounds. I used to count the black spots on my body where he had gotten me with an elbow. He used those elbows like hammers." On two separate occasions, those elbows also broke Born's nose.

"It was terrible," said Dean Smith, "He'd beat on [Born]. In the shower, Clyde would even hit him with a [wet] towel. Clyde said he was trying to toughen him up."

Because they had seen Born get manhandled by Lovellette on a daily basis, the Jayhawks' two senior leaders, Dean Kelley and Dean Smith, went to Kansas assistant coach Dick Harp at the beginning of the 1952–53 season and appealed to him to give 6' 7" sophomore Eldon Nichols a shot at the starting center spot in front of Born. Kelley and Smith said that Nichols was more talented and was a better passer and shooter than Born. Dick Harp was annoyed by the suggestion and told the two seniors, "Would you mind letting us coach the team?"[2]

Born went on to lead the Big Seven in scoring and rebounding that season and was named the conference's MVP. "It was a huge shock to all of us," said Smith. "He really improved. He was awkward, but he really came on. . . . B. H. had a great year." Part of the shock of Born's success was that there wasn't anything flashy about his game.

He was a tall, skinny kid who didn't have a reliable go-to move in the post. He didn't really shoot the hook shot or the turnaround jumper. He simply scored from close to the basket on layups, short face-up jumpers, and tip-ins. He ended up averaging 18.9 points per game for the season and helped power Kansas to a lot of big wins.

The Jayhawks were also successful because they changed from being a team that relied on a dominant frontcourt that could overpower opponents to an undersized team that had four starters who were 6' 1" or shorter. As a result, they relied much more on their quickness and their defense.

"We changed the philosophy of how we played," said Born.

Smith remarked, "In '53, our defense really made the difference."

The defensive scheme the Jayhawks used was later called the "pressure defense." It was devised by Kansas assistant coach Dick Harp, who got the idea from the defense that Henry Iba's Oklahoma A&M Aggies played during the final minutes of games in which they trailed by six points or more. The Aggies played "one pass away" defense in which they closely guarded the players that were most likely to receive the ball from a passer. This type of ball denial was fairly new, especially the idea of denying passes on the perimeter. Previously, except for denying passes into the post, the defense didn't usually start until a player received the ball. There were quick guards who would try to step into the passing lanes and steal passes, but there were not defensive systems that focused on denying the passing lanes. Harp wanted to take Iba's defense a step further than just using it at the end of games. "Dick just said, 'Why not do it all the time?'" remembered Dean Smith.

Kansas implemented it halfway through its 1952 championship season and used it to finish the season on a thirteen-game winning streak that culminated with the NCAA title. As much as it had helped the 1951–52 team, the 1952–53 Jayhawks were even better at it because they had smaller, quicker players who could shadow opponents and keep them from running their offense. As a result, the 1953 Kansas squad could be a frustrating team to play against.

Harp's scheme worked, and it changed college basketball. The University of San Francisco would adopt it and use it to win national championships in 1955 and 1956. Two decades later, John Wooden would point to the arrival of the Kansas pressure defense as one of the turning points in college basketball. In 1991, Dean Smith remarked that all four teams in the Final Four—UNLV, Kansas, North Carolina, and Duke—used defensive schemes derived from the original Kansas pressure defense in 1952.

Dick Harp's role in developing and implementing the pressure defense highlighted the key position that Phog Allen allowed him to take in leading the Jayhawks. By the early 1950s, Allen had turned over most of the Xs and Os and everyday management of the team to Harp, while Allen himself focused on recruiting and motivating. Allen was also a doctor of osteopathic medicine, and he treated his players' injuries himself and often gave his starters "adjustments" before games. Allen didn't have his own practice, but he privately treated a number of professional athletes from various sports. Allen always felt that being a doctor and being able to treat his own players gave him an advantage over other coaches, and he loved to be called "Doc." He would often tell his players, "Just call me 'Doc'."

"Dr. Allen didn't do a lot of coaching," said B. H. Born. "Dick Harp was doing a good share of the coaching. [Allen] did the speeches and the recruiting. He went around and shook an awful lot of hands. . . . He was a doctor and he used to treat the players. He would give a manipulation before the games and some of the players went for that and some didn't. He would almost have to chase Charlie Hoag down to catch him to adjust him."

Dean Smith remarked, "Doc was more the motivator and into the fundamentals. Dick Harp, who had played for him, was a really bright individual in my opinion. . . . [Doc] was the motivator and Dick was the X and O guy."

By the 1953 Final Four, Phog Allen was also advancing in age. He was sixty-seven years old and suffered from occasional absentmindedness and memory problems, which was another reason Dick Harp was so important. In one incident in 1951, Doc Allen marched off the team bus to question the bill at a restaurant in Omaha, Nebraska, where the Jayhawks had just eaten. "After a while, Doc came back out of the restaurant," remembered Dean Smith, "but instead of getting on our bus, he took a wrong turn and got on a city bus. The players roared with laughter, but Harp leaped out of his seat and told us to be quiet. He sent a manager to rescue Doc from the city bus, and turned to the rest of us. 'If any of you utter one word, if I hear one laugh or even a murmur, you'll answer to me tomorrow,' he said. That was typical of Dick's loyalty."[3]

While Phog Allen didn't have the same mind for the details of the game that he did when he was younger, he had lost none of his charisma for storytelling and motivating. During the spring of 1952 when the Jayhawks were charging toward the national championship, Allen pulled out several emotional speeches. Allen was so effective that he even affected tough guy Clyde Lovellette. Remembering the speeches, Lovellette said, "We'd start crying, and want to break through walls."[4] However, Allen saved one of his most motivational—and most effective—speeches for the 1953 Final Four.

In the regionals, Kansas had defeated Oklahoma City 73-65 and then barely squeezed by Henry Iba's sixth-ranked Oklahoma A&M Aggies 61-55. When the Jayhawks arrived at the Final Four, Doc Allen publicly downplayed his team's chances. He said his underdog team was living on "borrowed time" and that they didn't belong "in this strong field" with Indiana, Washington, and LSU.[5] Privately, Allen's message to his team was much different.

Before the Washington game, Doc conjured up the perfect anecdote to motivate his players so they wouldn't be happy to just *be* at the NCAA finals. He told them the story of his 1940 team that made it all the way to the NCAA championship game and lost it right there in Kansas City in front of all their fans. He told of how his son, Bob Allen, a star guard on that team, had broken down and wept afterwards.

"He certainly motivated us for the Washington game," said Smith. "He was one of those Knute Rockne types, but usually we'd kind of just smile at some of his pep talks. But that time he told the story of 1940 when they lost in the finals and how his son cried and all that. I had a tear in my eye and I looked around and I think everybody else did too."

Allen finished with a flourish, saying that the players "had an opportunity like this once in a lifetime."[6]

The emboldened Jayhawks came flying out of the locker room and jumped all over the Washington Huskies in the opening minutes of their semifinal game. The Kansas defense forced multiple turnovers and made Washington look confused and unsteady.

"I don't think Washington even bothered to scout us because they thought we'd lost everybody from the year before and weren't that tough," said Born.

"The first ten minutes [against Washington] were unbelievable," said Smith. "They had a hard time getting a shot."

"We scored eight points before they even shot the ball," said Born.

After jumping out to an 8-0 lead, Kansas led 45-34 at the half. Washington's Bob Houbregs picked up four fouls in the first half and then fouled out in the third quarter. The Jayhawks were up 58-44 by the end of the third, and without Houbregs in the lineup for the Huskies, Kansas completely dominated the fourth and won by a final score of 79-53. Houbregs, who averaged 25.0 points per game, scored eighteen points. Kansas center B. H. Born, who averaged 18.0 points per game, scored twenty-six. Dean Kelley also stepped up and scored eighteen points for Kansas and Harold Patterson added seventeen. Besides Houbregs, the only other Husky in double figures was guard Joe Cipriano with eleven.

The Jayhawks' surprising blowout of Washington meant that Indiana and Kansas would square off the next night to settle the national championship. Although a showdown between No. 1 Indiana and No. 2 Washington would have made the perfect scenario for the 1953 NCAA title game, a rematch of the 1940 title game also offered an enticing subplot, especially since the game was once again being played in Kansas City.

Branch McCracken had his way of doing things. By 1953, he was set in his ways and had a well-defined pattern for how certain things were done with his basketball teams. One example was Mac's approach to road trips. He didn't like to travel to big cities. He was well aware of the troubles that even small-town schools ran into when traveling to New York City in the early 1950s. In the Big Apple, players from schools such as Bradley and Oklahoma were propositioned by gamblers or mafia agents to shave points.

When IU did go on the road, McCracken almost always rotated which players would room with each other for the road trip. He did that to prevent cliques and divisions on the team.

Mac also did not want his players hanging out in the lobbies of hotels. "He didn't like [players down in the lobby] at all," said Dick White. "I think Branch thought there might be a betting element. Or he didn't like the press talking to us. I think he was just trying to keep us out of trouble."

In general, Mac didn't like the players wandering off, unless it was for a short walk. For anything longer than that, there were generally three acceptable chaperones—the senior manager, an assistant coach, and Mary Jo McCracken. All three of them essentially reported to Mac.

The senior manager often took the players to a movie when the team was on the road—usually the night before the game. On the day of the NCAA championship game against Kansas, senior manager Ron Fifer lined up a different type of gig. Ever since the team had arrived in Kansas City, several of the players had been joking with Fifer about when he was going to take them to see former president Harry Truman, whose office was in the area. After the team finished eating lunch together on the day of the Kansas game, Fifer announced that he was going down to Truman's office and asked who wanted to join him. Seven players decided to go along: Jack Wright, Jim Schooley, Dick White, Jim DeaKyne, Dick Farley, Goethe Chambers, and Ron Taylor.

The group only had to go about ten blocks to the Federal Reserve Bank Building on the corner of 10th and Grand, where Truman had an office on the eleventh floor. When they arrived, Truman's secretary Rose Conway asked, "Who are you?"

"We're the Indiana basketball team and we'd like to see the president," Fifer said.

"Well, he's busy right now," Conway replied, "but be sure and wait because he wouldn't want to miss you. Sit down."

So the players waited several minutes and before long an energetic Harry Truman popped out of his office and invited the IU group to come on in. Truman, who was originally from Independence, just east of Kansas City, broke the ice by saying with a smile, "I don't want to sit on the fence about this. I want to tell you Indiana boys that I'm going to be yelling for Kansas tonight. I want you to know where I stand."

One of the IU players responded, "The reason we came down here was that we thought maybe Margaret would be here." Margaret was Truman's beautiful twenty-nine-year-old single daughter.

Truman let out a hearty laugh at that and said, "Ah, that's just like you guys!"

Then Truman's secretary ushered in two other IU students who were in town for the Final Four and who coincidentally showed up at the office and asked about seeing President Truman. One of them had a camera, and Truman said, "You'll want a picture." So he gathered the entire IU group around his desk and had his secretary snap a picture.

After they said their good-byes and left Truman's office, Fifer pulled aside the student with the camera and said, "I want an 8×10 of that picture this afternoon and I don't care what it costs."

When the group that went to see Truman got back to the hotel, it was time for McCracken's mandatory afternoon nap time, so the players dispersed to their rooms. But that didn't last long. Even before regular season games many of the players were too charged up to nap on game-day afternoons. In the hours before they were about to play for the NCAA championship, the anticipation was nearly unbearable, so Bob Leonard and Jack Wright set up a card game in Wright's room to pass the time. "We started a five and ten poker game," said Wright. "Pretty soon, one or two guys lit up cigarettes. Mac got wind that something was going on and sent Spike Dixon up to check it out. Spike came in the room and he just flat out told us, 'Mac knows something is going on up here and you guys better hit your rooms.' And boy we scattered. So he goes back down to McCracken's room and he was just going to go in and out and tell him everything was okay and get out of there. So he went in and said, 'Everything's fine. They were just up there playing a few cards. No problem. They're all in the bedrooms now.' And then Spike started to go out the door. And [McCracken] said, 'Well what kind of cards were they playing?' Spike said, 'Oh, I don't know what kind of cards they were playing.' And he started to go out the door again. Then [Mac] asked him, 'Who was in the game?' Spike realized this was starting to get serious and he was getting scared so he mentioned a couple substitutes and started to go out one more time. About that time he heard a big bang and [Mac] had come down on the desk and slapped it [real loud] and said, 'I want to know everyone who was in that game!' And [Spike] said, 'Well, to tell you the truth Mac, I don't know. There was so much smoke in there I couldn't see anything.' And then McCracken pointed at the door and yelled, 'Get out of here!' "

When the team gathered for its light pregame dinner, Spike told some of the guys about what had happened in McCracken's room. The guys involved were a little worried about what Mac might say or do when he came down for the dinner. However, when the Big Bear arrived, he was surprised to see a package on his plate.

The student who had taken the picture of the IU group with Harry Truman got the 8×10 that Ron Fifer had requested and brought it to Fifer that afternoon. "We wrapped it up and put tissue paper around it and put it on Branch's plate at dinner that night," said Fifer. "He was deadly serious about this time anyway [right before the big game] and he looked at that [wrapped present] and you could tell he didn't like it very much. But he opened it up and looked at it and, of course, there was Harry and all of us. And I never will forget, he stood up and looked around [holding up the picture] and said, 'Back home in Monrovia we'd have hung this in the outhouse to scare the rats away.' And that broke everybody up. That was one of the few light moments that we had before the final game."

Mac never brought up the card game or the cigarettes. It was time to focus squarely on the task at hand.

On the afternoon before the game, the Hoosiers received a ton of telegrams from well-wishers. One of them was from Sammy Esposito, the guy who just a year earlier McCracken had envisioned as the leader of the '53 Hoosiers. Espo's telegram was short and to the point: "Go get 'em gang."[7]

The opening sequence of the IU-Kansas tilt foreshadowed the type of intensity that this NCAA championship game would have from the opening tip until the final gun. B. H. Born and Don Schlundt both got a hand on the opening tip. The ball popped into the hands of Dick Farley, who rushed the ball up the floor and dumped it off to Burke Scott, who tried to force it into Schlundt on the inside. B. H. Born stepped around Schlundt and deflected the ball, and Gil Reich darted down and recovered the ball for Kansas. When the Jayhawks came down on their first offensive possession, they were much more patient, but the result was much the same. After ten passes, Kansas finally got the ball into Born, but as soon as he made a move to turn into the lane he had the ball stripped from him by Burke Scott, and the Hoosiers took back possession.

That was the kind of intensity, hustle, and heart both teams showed all night. Fans of the Hoosiers or the Jayhawks could not have been prouder of the effort and desire their teams showed throughout this game. Neutral observers were treated to a furious tug-of-war that featured fourteen ties and eleven lead changes. Kansas took the lead nine times, while Indiana owned the lead ten times, and neither team could ever build more than a six-point advantage. It simply could not have been any closer and it remained anyone's ball game until the final gun went off.

IU struck first when Don Schlundt turned away from a triple team and into the lane and then flipped in a little hook shot to give IU a 2-0 lead. A couple of possessions later, Born tied the game with two free throws to make it 2-2. Then Leonard missed a twenty-footer and Schlundt missed the tip-in. Born rebounded and quickly threw an outlet pass that was relayed ahead to Dean Kelley, who pulled up and banked the ball off the window to give Kansas its first lead at 4-2. Indiana quickly answered. Born deflected another entry pass into

Schlundt, but the ball ended up in the hands of Dick Farley, who whipped a pass over to Schlundt, who pivoted and laid the ball off the glass to tie it at 4-4. Then Farley missed a short shot in the lane and Dean Kelley rebounded and threw the ball ahead to his brother Allen Kelley, who streaked all the way through the Hoosier defense and scored to put the Jayhawks back on top at 6-4. Charlie Kraak then missed two free throws and Born came down and scored on a put-back to put Kansas ahead 8-4.

Kansas led for the next several minutes until Burke Scott swished an eighteen-footer from the baseline to put IU back on top 14-13. Dean Kelley tied it at 14-14 with a free throw, but Burke drew a foul with 2:52 left in the first quarter and hit a free throw to put IU up 15-14. Kansas ran off five straight points to snatch back a 19-15 lead, but Schlundt hit a layup and a free throw and Burke Scott scored on the fast break and was fouled by Allen Kelley. Scott converted the free throw to finish the three-point play and Indiana closed the first quarter with a 21-19 lead.

There were several surprises in the opening quarter. The biggest surprise may have been that Kansas showed no reluctance whatsoever to push the ball and try to run against the Hoosiers. The conventional wisdom was that the easiest way to play into IU's hands was to try to get in an up-and-down game with them. Any team that attempted to do that throughout the 1952–53 season had almost always regretted it, and had often gotten blown out. While Kansas pulled back its defense and did not try to extend full-court or half-court pressure the way it had against Washington, the Jayhawks also pushed the ball on offense and used long outlet passes to look for easy scores in transition.

Another surprise was that the smaller Jayhawks held their own on the backboards. In fact, B. H. Born dominated the boards in the first ten minutes and allowed Kansas to control the pace of the game. And although Indiana had sent IU golf coach Chili Cochran to scout Kansas in the NCAA regionals and all the Hoosiers had watched the Jayhawks' defense dismantle Washington in the national semifinals, IU still looked surprised and tentative when trying to deal with the Kansas pressure defense. Even sure-handed Bobby Leonard had several passes picked off by the Jayhawks. Kansas made it extremely difficult for IU to get the ball into Schlundt, and Dean Kelley never allowed Leonard to have an inch of daylight to get off a shot. Kansas also showed a lot of respect for Dick Farley and did its best to deny him the ball.

But while the Kansas strategy for holding down Schlundt, Leonard, and Farley had worked in the opening minutes, they also got a big surprise from IU guard Burke Scott, who scored six points in the first quarter and had three steals—including two strips from Born. The pesky Scott had also harassed the Jayhawks into a couple of other ballhandling errors.

In the opening minutes of the second quarter, the Jayhawks retook the lead at 25-23 on a short hook shot off the glass by Born. A few minutes later, Born drew Schlundt's third foul and converted the free throw to push the Kansas lead to 29-24. Dick White came in to replace Schlundt, and Dick Farley moved over to center and used his quickness to slice through the Jayhawk defense for two straight scores and cut the lead to 29-28. Then Burke Scott picked up his third foul when he charged Dean Smith. Smith nailed the free throw to put Kansas up by two, but Charlie Kraak scored on an acrobatic tip-in to tie the score at 30-30.

Kansas made a strong 9-3 run, led by Allen Kelley from the outside and Born from the inside, to take its biggest lead of the game at 39-33. McCracken saw the tide turning against his team and took a risk to counteract it by putting Schlundt back in the game. That was when Kraak started taking over the boards. Charlie scored on another tip-in to cut the Kansas lead to four, then he rebounded a Born miss on the inside and cleared it out. Back on the other end of the floor, Schlundt faced up and hit a fifteen-footer to trim the lead to 39-37, then Kraak pulled down the rebound of another Born miss and Dick White pulled up in transition to bury an eighteen-footer that capped a 6-0 Indiana run and tied the game at 39-39. In the final minutes of the half, Dean Kelley scored on a pull-up jumper in the lane, and Schlundt got hacked by Born and buried both free throws to make the score 41-41 at the half.

In the second quarter, Kansas again played very well and put the Hoosiers back on their heels for most of the period. However, just as

Burke Scott stepped up in the first quarter, Charlie Kraak stepped up for IU early in the second quarter. Kraak, a rebounding and defensive specialist who normally averaged just seven points per game, already had twelve points at the half, and his domination of the boards during the closing minutes of the second quarter enabled IU to come back and tie the game going into the locker room.

The battle between Born and Schlundt was the obvious headliner, and the two giants pretty much fought to a standstill in the first half, with Schlundt more effective in the scoring column but Born much more active on the glass and on defense. However, the more intense battle taking place was the one between Bobby Leonard and Dean Kelley. Leonard had almost single-handedly carried IU to its big win over LSU in the semifinals, especially in the first half. But Kelley was a senior and was a returning member of the All–Final Four team from 1952, and he was one of the few players in college basketball who could match Leonard's competitive drive. Kelley used his experience to get the best of his younger counterpart in the first half. The Kansas pressure made it hard for Leonard to get the Hoosiers' offense set up, and Kelley's flypaper defense gave him little room to set up for his own shot. Leonard went into the half with just two points.

But as he had done throughout the season when he had had a tough first half, Leonard quickly came back in the second half and played much more aggressively. He immediately came out and drained a twenty-two-footer at the start of the third quarter to give Indiana a 43-41 lead. Leonard's aggressiveness also served as a cue to his teammates, and all the Hoosiers started playing with more urgency and passion. The normally mild-mannered Schlundt even got called for a technical foul early in the third quarter. Schlundt drove the baseline and got hit by Born, who was called for a foul on the play. However, Jayhawk guard Gil Reich slid over for the double-team and Schlundt received the technical for planting an elbow on top of Reich's head.

At the 7:08 mark, Kansas reclaimed the lead at 48-47 on a Harold Patterson free throw. Dean Kelley hit a twenty-footer to put Kansas up by three, but Leonard answered by driving to the middle and pulling up for a fifteen-footer that trimmed the Jayhawk lead to 50-49.

On the next play, Dean Kelley tried to go right back at Leonard by driving all the way to the basket, but Leonard cut him off halfway there and a whistle blew. Leonard felt like Kelley had dropped his shoulder and banged into him, so when the referee raised his arm and pointed at Bobby, Leonard exploded and ended up drawing a technical foul. A few minutes later, Dean Kelley swiped at the ball as Leonard brought it across half-court. Kelley knocked it loose for a moment before Leonard recovered, and Kelley fouled him. Bobby made the free throw to pull Indiana to within three at 53-50. Next, Born faced up and missed a ten-foot jumper and Schlundt rebounded. On the other end, Schlundt caught the ball just inside the top of the key, took one long dribble, and sank a twelve-footer with two Jayhawks hanging all over him to cut it to 53-52.

Then things really got interesting. Dean Kelley pushed the ball up the court, probing the defense. He tried to drive down the middle but Leonard cut him off, so he scooped the ball to Gil Reich, who dribbled around to the wing and whipped an overhead pass into Born. Schlundt made an attempt to get around Born to deny the entry pass but was late, and that left Don out of position. Born immediately pivoted toward the baseline and found himself all alone for a layup, but he banked the ball too hard against the glass and it bounced off the front of the rim. Charlie Kraak was in perfect position for the rebound and he went up and grabbed it off the front of the rim with two hands. Born, who quickly realized his shot was going to miss, leapt for the rebound and crashed into Kraak. The referee's whistle blew and his arm pointed in the direction of the two players. Born instantly raised his arm and pointed at Kraak, but the ref walked toward them and clarified his call by pointing squarely at Born's chest. With 3:59 left to play in the third, the big Jayhawk hung his head and walked up the court. As he did, the official scorer blew his whistle and indicated that Born had just picked up his fifth foul and was out of the game.

The Kansas bench immediately protested. Phog Allen quickly rose out of his seat to approach the scorer's table, telling the official they had Born down for only four fouls. Allen appealed for him to check with the members of the press, and nearly all of them were in agreement that Born actually had four. So the official scorer changed his call and said Born could stay in the game.

As soon as he did that, a roaring sound rose up from the Indiana bench. Branch McCracken stormed up to the scorer's table and asked for an explanation. The official scorer explained that Born didn't have five fouls, as originally announced, but only had four and could stay in the game. Mac couldn't believe it. He protested that the official scorer's book could not be changed. It looked as if the official scorer might change his tune again and send Born to the bench, but he apparently thought better of it when it was pointed out that nearly everyone else had Born with only four fouls. McCracken pounded his fist on the scorer's table and shouted, "Your book shows five personals. Born should be out. You had five on him and you changed it to four. You know you did. We come out here and are supposed to be your guests and you're robbing us."[8] Then a disgusted McCracken reluctantly went back to the IU bench. After a five-minute delay to decide Born's fate, play resumed with the Kansas big man back on the court.

Kraak stepped to the line and hit his free throw to tie the game at 53-53, then Kansas ran a play similar to the one in which Born had picked up his fourth foul. Gil Reich again whipped the ball into Born in the low post, but this time Schlundt held his ground. Born pump faked and then went up for the shot, but he shuffled his feet in the process and was called for traveling. Leonard set up the Hoosier offense and went right after Born by pounding the ball into Schlundt, but Born forced Schlundt into a contested turnaround shot that missed badly. On the other end, Allen Kelley took a screen from Gil Reich and sank a seventeen-footer to put the Jayhawks back in front 55-53. After several empty possessions, Indiana patiently worked its half-court offense with four players on the perimeter and Schlundt in the middle. From the top of the key, Paul Poff delivered a perfectly timed pass to Schlundt, who caught it in the lane and then swept to his left and banked in a hook shot all in one motion to tie the game at 55-55. A Harold Patterson free throw made it 56-55 Kansas, then, with under two minutes left in the quarter, Leonard stole the ball at half-court and streaked down the floor for a layup that put IU ahead 57-

56. Kansas then ran the clock down and dumped the ball into Born, who made a strong move into the lane and scored with a little hook that he dropped over the front of the rim, and Kansas retook the lead at 58-57. Then IU inbounded the ball to Paul Poff, who tossed it to Leonard. Bobby looked up at the clock and then jogged the ball across the half-court line as if he wasn't in a hurry. Dean Kelley took the bait. Leonard got the room he needed, and he launched a high-arching forty-foot jump shot that swished through the net just before time ran out in the third quarter, giving Indiana a 59-58 lead heading into the final ten minutes.

The start of the fourth quarter was more of the same. The lead yo-yoed back and forth and neither team could gain an advantage over the other. The only difference was that the intensity increased and the pace became more methodical. Early in the fourth quarter, Dick Farley and Burke Scott returned to the game after long stints on the bench because of foul trouble.

With IU leading 62-61 with 5:36 left in the game, Kansas swung the ball into the corner and then dropped it into Born, who caught it and scored inside. But the basket was waived off because Born had used a forearm to clear out Schlundt and free himself. This time, Born was gone for good. When he went to the bench, he was the game's leading scorer and rebounder with twenty-six points and fifteen boards. As B. H. slowly walked to the Jayhawk bench to take a seat, he got a handshake and a smack on the rear end from Doc Allen.

Schlundt missed the first free throw but made the second, and IU led 63-61. Even without Born, the scrappy Jayhawks kept fighting. Replacing Born was 6' 3" sophomore forward Jerry Alberts, and Kansas got the ball into him. Out of instinct, Dick Farley mistakenly doubled down on Alberts and left Allen Kelley open in the corner. Alberts kicked it out to him and Kelley swished an eighteen-foot jumper to tie the game at 63-63.

Bobby Leonard didn't waste any time exploiting the Jayhawks inside. He drove straight down the court and dropped a pass to Schlundt just inside the free throw line. Schlundt went right to his hook shot and calmly buried it over Alberts. Indiana 65, Kansas 63.

With 3:57 left in the game, Kansas called a time-out. After the time-out, the Jayhawks worked the ball around until Allen Kelley made a great move to the basket, but his bank shot went in and out and Schlundt grabbed the rebound. Then Indiana ran a little clock. Leonard stood in the middle of the court holding the ball for five seconds while Dean Kelley jab-stepped toward him and poked his hands toward the ball, feigning a steal attempt. After a couple of passes, Burke Scott got the ball near the top of the circle and blew by Allen Kelley all the way to the basket, but he missed the layup.

With 2:41 left, Farley was called for a foul while going for a loose ball. It was Farley's fifth so he was done for the night, and Dick White returned in his place. Allen Kelley sank both free throws (he got two because there was less than 3:00 remaining) and the game was tied again at 65-65. But Leonard once again orchestrated a pass into Schlundt and Big Don caught the ball in the lane and went strong to the basket, scoring and drawing a foul on Alberts. Schlundt's free throw hit nothing but net and IU led 68-65 with 2:25 remaining. On the other end, Allen Kelley missed and Kraak tipped the ball to Dick White for the rebound.

The Hoosiers were now in command. Leonard once again held the ball out high with Dean Kelley swatting and posturing at him. Then Leonard passed it out and got it back. Harold Patterson came over to track Leonard, and Bobby tossed the ball to Patterson's man, Charlie Kraak, who took the opening and drove straight to the basket. Gil Reich stepped up to cut Kraak off just in front of the basket, and when he did Patterson bumped into Kraak's back and Kraak elbowed him to push him off. The referee whistled a foul on Kraak, and Charlie had a few heated words with him. Then Kraak threw the ball in the air and earned a technical, which meant Kansas would have three straight free throws and a chance to tie. It was also Kraak's fifth foul, so he had to go back to the bench and face McCracken.

Patterson hit one of two free throws and Allen Kelley missed the technical, so IU held on to a 68-66 lead, but Kansas still had possession of the ball with 1:21 left to play. Kansas worked the ball around, probing for a good shot. Dean Kelley finally grabbed the ball and made a quick move toward the baseline that cleared enough space to get by Leonard, and he lofted a little runner with Schlundt in his face. The ball kissed gently off the glass and banked in, and the game was tied one final time at 68-68.

Leonard brought the ball up the floor and tried to lob it into Schlundt, but Jerry Alberts curled around Big Don and tipped the ball away, nearly coming up with the steal before the ball went out-of-bounds. Leonard then inbounded it to Schlundt and Don tossed it right back to him. Bobby held the ball on the wing, then faked a pass and made a quick first step to get by Dean Kelley and go all the way to the rim. Kelley caught up with Bobby and hit him with a shoulder while Gil Reich met him at the basket and tried to prevent the layup. The foul was called on Kelley, and Leonard stepped to the line for two shots with 0:27 left and the championship hanging in the balance.

As Mac often instructed his players to do, Leonard didn't take a lot of time at the foul line. He just stepped up and shot it. The first free throw hit the front of the rim and never had a chance, but Leonard didn't think about it. He just quickly stepped up and took the second one. Bobby let it fly and started backpedaling. It swished through and IU led 69-68.

Kansas called time-out and drew up one final play. Dick Harp and Doc Allen outlined the Jayhawks' strategy, which was to run as much time off the clock as possible and then get the ball to Dean Kelley or Allen Kelley for one final shot. In the IU huddle, Mac told his boys that he believed Kansas would try to hold the ball until the very end and then run a double-screen for Allen Kelley, who was by far the best outside shooter on the Kansas team. The Hoosiers' job was to not give him a clear shot, but also not to foul him or leave another player wide open near the basket.

As the Indiana players walked back onto the court, they were all filled with desperation. That desperation was not only fueled by their own competitive fires but also by the memory of losing on several buzzer-beaters earlier that season. And they were still haunted by all the tough breaks that had denied championships to McCracken teams in past years. They took all that desperation and channeled it into thirty seconds of the best defensive effort they had ever given.

Kansas didn't hold the ball on the perimeter for long. Allen Kelley suddenly broke free under the basket with twenty-three seconds left and he called for the ball. Patterson delivered it to him, but Dick White held his ground with Kelley, and Burke Scott darted in and nearly stole the ball. Then Schlundt came over and trapped him as well. Kelley quickly tossed the ball back out to Gil Reich on the perimeter. Reich swung it to Alberts at the top of the key and he swung it to Dean Kelley on the opposite wing. Dean couldn't find any space, so he tossed it to Patterson at the top of the circle and he swung it to Allen Kelley who ran out to meet the ball. Kelley took a dribble but Dick White was right there to meet him again, and Schlundt stood by ready to double-team. Kelley desperately swung the ball into the corner to Alberts and yelled for the sophomore to shoot it. With Schlundt running at him, Alberts uncorked a solid-looking one-hander.

On the opposite side of the floor, Charlie Kraak stood in a spot where he could see both Alberts and the basket in a perfect line, and he saw the ball traveling straight toward the hoop. During the previous minutes, he had stood paralyzed along the sidelines after being charged with an offensive foul and a technical foul and letting Kansas back in the game just as it looked like IU would finally put the Jayhawks away. All Kraak could think about was that if the final Kansas shot went in, he would be the goat.

Out on the floor, Bobby Leonard couldn't even bear to watch the ball to see whether it would go in or not. "I saw that ball going into the corner," said Leonard, "and I saw him take that shot and I just put my head down. I thought, 'If it goes, that's four games we lose at the gun.'"

With that ball hanging in the air, there also hung two separate destinies. One of the two teams would go down in history as legendary, while the other would go down as a really good team that almost won the national championship. If the Hoosiers won, it would be the perfect coronation to a record-breaking season and an unprecedented romp through the Big Ten. If the Jayhawks won, they would have gone down as one of the greatest Cinderella stories in college basketball history and, coupled with their 1952 NCAA title, would have been only the second repeat champion in the history of the NCAA Tournament up to that point.

If Alberts's shot went in, then the 1953 Indiana Hoosiers would have ultimately been one more hard-luck IU basketball story, to join the many that had gone before them. They would have been the talented IU team that once again *almost* won the big one—and this time the close call would have come on the national stage.

However, Alberts's shot flattened out when it got to the rim. It hit the iron and bounced up off the backboard. Dick White, Harold Patterson, and Alberts all went for the rebound, but it bounced off their hands and went out-of-bounds. The final gun sounded and Indiana had officially captured the 1953 NCAA championship with a thrilling 69-68 win over Kansas.

A small contingent of IU fans rushed the floor—among them Charley Cogan and Dudley Miller—and they celebrated with the team. They joined IU players, managers, and other fans in lifting Branch McCracken and Bobby Leonard onto their shoulders and parading the two of them around the floor. Then awards were handed out, nets were cut down, and lots of photographs were taken.

As modern as the Kansas City Municipal Auditorium was for the time, it did not have its own dressing rooms or showers, so after the game the players had to get back into their warm-up pants and jackets and walk back across the street to their hotel to shower and get changed. However, before the team walked back to the hotel, McCracken and Leonard answered a few questions for the reporters. They asked Leonard about stepping to the free throw line for those final fateful tosses. He said, "I wanted to make the shots as much as anything I've ever wanted in my life. In fact, I had to make them."[9]

A reporter told Leonard that he had just spoken to McCracken, and Mac had said that he wasn't worried at all because Bobby had "ice water in his veins" (one of Mac's favorite expressions). "If that was ice water," said Leonard, "it sure as hell felt awfully warm when it was running down my leg."

Leonard finished with twelve points while Schlundt had thirty points and ten rebounds. Both of them made the All–Final Four team, joining B. H. Born, Dean Kelley, and Bob Houbregs, who led Washington to a third-place finish in the consolation game. Born was named the Most Outstanding Player because of his surprisingly strong performances against both Houbregs and Schlundt. Charlie Kraak added seventeen points and thirteen rebounds for the Hoosiers, while Allen Kelley fired in twenty points for Kansas.

Afterwards, Phog Allen remarked, "Indiana deserved to win. They had us outmanned, nine good players to our six. But our kids fought their hearts out, as always, right down to the last second."[10]

On the way back to the hotel, the IU players were serenaded by honking horns and loud cheers from the 350 IU fans who had attended the game and then lined the streets or cruised the downtown area afterwards. The celebration lasted well into the night, but it was only a prelude of what was to come back in Indiana.

After the players showered and changed, it was time to meet for one last postgame dinner. Once everyone had sat down at the table, Charlie Kraak tapped his glass for attention and, doing his best Mac impersonation, said, "Now boys, you played a pretty good game. I want you to enjoy it—but we made some mistakes. Now, we have some games coming up in a few months. Let's get ready for them."

Everyone erupted in laughter. "Suddenly, all the tension, the tiredness, and the long season was over," said Mary Jo McCracken. "We could laugh again."[11]

The next morning, the Hoosiers flew out of Kansas City and landed in Indianapolis at 1:25 PM. McCracken and the team got a surprise at the Weir-Cook Airport when members of Indiana's 1940 NCAA championship team met them on the runway to congratulate them. But the surprises didn't stop there. The team took a chartered bus from Indianapolis to Bloomington, and about halfway in between, in Martinsville, they started noticing cars parked along the side of the road. Pretty soon, both sides were completely lined with cars and Indiana fans were waving and cheering as their Hoosiers drove by. Once the bus reached the Bloomington city limits, McCracken and the players were transferred to convertibles that were flanked by fire engines and the IU marching band. The caravan then paraded the team through downtown Bloomington, where more than four thousand people—students and local fans—saluted the conquering heroes. Eventually, the caravan took them through Bloomington, across the

IU campus, and finally deposited them at the IU Fieldhouse, the place where their journey had quietly started five months earlier. That night the team had its final official function together, the team banquet in Alumni Hall at the Indiana Memorial Union.

Throughout the day, a smiling Branch McCracken patiently answered question after question about his team and its performance throughout the season and against Kansas in the NCAA championship game. In the end, Mac summed up his thoughts by saying, "The boys were marvelous. I've never seen such spirit and determination. But the [championship] game could have gone either way."[12] He was right, of course. But this time, it went his way.

EPILOGUE

It's been more than five decades since the 1953 Hurryin' Hoosiers were on the IU campus in Bloomington. Today, the IU Fieldhouse where they won all eleven of their home games during the 1952–53 season is the Wildermuth Intramural Center, part of Indiana's School of Health, Physical Education, and Recreation (HPER). On Saturday nights—the nights the 1953 IU team played many of their home games—there are now ten full-court basketball courts packed with highly competitive, no-holds-barred pickup games, some of the most competitive pickup games you'll find anywhere in America. On the large track that encircles those courts, you can see an internationally diverse group of joggers and walkers, most of whom have probably never heard of Branch McCracken or know him as little more than a name from the distant past.

However, when the track and the courts clear at 9:00 PM and lights begin to dim, you can look across that vast old fieldhouse and envision a raised basketball floor in the middle of it, with infinite rows of wooden bleachers stretching high up toward the rafters. If you look closely on that old court you can see the big red "I" in the middle and a spry young Bobby Leonard at one end practicing jump shot after jump shot, saying "We've *got* to win this. We've got to win. We've got to *win!*" And you can hear the echoes of the voice of Branch Mc-Cracken, roaming the sidelines in his navy blue suit and red tie with his hands cupped over his mouth, yelling, "Go! Go! Go!" and "Run! Run! Run!" as his boys rip the ball off the backboards and speed it down the court for an easy score in a pivotal Big Ten game.

This was a place where basketball dreams were made and realized by the 1953 Hurryin' Hoosiers. Their court is gone now and the details of all they did that season have slowly faded from the memory of most Hoosiers. Yet their accomplishments firmly established IU basketball as the Hoosier state's most beloved sports team. Their team unity and basketball precision live on as an example, and their championship dreams have been passed on and fulfilled again and again by new generations of Indiana Hoosiers basketball teams.

Appendix: Stats and Records

1952–53 Indiana Hoosiers Roster

Head Coach: Branch McCracken
Assistant Coach: Ernie Andres

No.	Player	Hometown	Class	Position	Height
14	Phil Byers	Evansville, Ind.	So	G	5' 11"
20	Goethe Chambers	Union City, Ind.	So	F	6' 3"
22	Jim DeaKyne	Fortville, Ind.	Jr	G/F	6' 3"
31	Dick Farley	Winslow, Ind.	Jr	F	6' 3"
33	Dick Hendricks	Huntington, Ind.	Jr	C	6' 5"
42	Don Henry	Evansville, Ind.	So	F	6' 2"
13	Charlie Kraak	Collinsville, Ill.	Jr	F	6' 5"
21	Bob Leonard (Capt.)	Terre Haute, Ind.	Jr	G	6' 3"
31	Paul Poff	New Albany, Ind.	So	G	6' 1"
34	Don Schlundt	South Bend, Ind.	So	C	6' 9"
19	Jim Schooley	Auburn, Ind.	Sr	F/C	6' 5"
25	Burke Scott	Tell City, Ind.	So	G	6' 0"
35	Lou Scott	Chicago, Ill.	Jr	C	6' 10"
23	Ron Taylor	Chicago, Ill.	Jr	F	6' 3"
41	Dick White	Terre Haute, Ind.	So	F/G	6' 1"
24	Jack Wright	New Castle, Ind.	Jr	G	5' 10"

1952–53 Season Results

Date	Court	Opponent	Result	Score
12/1/1952	H	Valparaiso	W	95–56
12/6/1952	A	Notre Dame	L	70–71
12/13/1952	A	Kansas State	L	80–82
12/20/1952	H	Michigan	W	88–60
12/22/1952	A	Iowa	W	91–72
1/3/1953	A	Michigan	W	91–88
1/5/1953	A	Michigan State	W	69–62
1/10/1953	H	(#19) Minnesota	W	66–63

1952–53 Season Results (*continued*)

Date	Court	Opponent	Result	Score
1/12/1953	A	Ohio State	W	88–68
1/17/1953	H	(#4) Illinois	W	74–70
1/19/1953	A	Purdue	W	88–75
2/2/1953	H	Butler	W	105–70
2/7/1953	A	Northwestern	W	88–84
2/9/1953	H	Wisconsin	W	66–48
2/14/1953	H	Michigan State	W	65–50
2/16/1953	A	Wisconsin	W	72–70
2/21/1953	H	Ohio State	W	81–67
2/23/1953	H	Purdue	W	113–78
2/28/1953	A	(#10) Illinois	W	91–79
3/2/1953	H	Northwestern	W	90–88
3/7/1953	A	Minnesota	L	63–65
3/9/1953	H	Iowa	W	68–61
NCAA Tournament				
3/13/1953	N[1]	DePaul	W	82–80
3/14/1953	N[1]	(#17) Notre Dame	W	79–66
3/17/1953	N[2]	(#7) Louisiana State	W	80–67
3/18/1953	N[2]	(#5) Kansas	W	69–68

1. Chicago, Ill.
2. Kansas City, Mo.

1952–53 Big Ten Standings

	W	L	PCT
Indiana	17	1	.944
Illinois	14	4	.778
Minnesota	11	7	.611
Michigan St.	11	7	.611
Wisconsin	10	8	.556
Iowa	9	9	.500
Ohio State	7	11	.389
Northwestern	5	13	.278
Michigan	3	15	.167
Purdue	3	15	.167

INDIANA'S RANKING IN THE 1952–53 ASSOCIATED PRESS POLLS

12/16	12/23	12/30	1/6	1/13	1/20	1/27	2/3	2/10	2/17	2/24	3/3	3/10	3/24
19	15	12	7	6	2	2	2	2	2	2	1	1	1

1952–53 INDIANA HOOSIERS SEASON STATISTICS

Team Statistics	G	FG/A	PCT	FT/A	PCT	R	TP	AVG
Indiana	26	737–2019	.365	638–910	.701	45.7	2112	81.2
Opponents	26	611–2041	.299	586–937	.625	36.0	1808	69.5

Player Statistics	G	FG/A	PCT	FT/A	PCT	R	TP	AVG
Schlundt	26	206–477	.432	249–310	.803	10.0	661	25.4
Leonard	26	164–503	.326	96–144	.667	4.2	424	16.3
Farley	26	94–212	.443	75–108	.694	6.7	263	10.1
B. Scott	26	76–206	.369	55–85	.647	3.5	207	8.0
L. Scott	10	28–83	.337	18–28	.643	5.7	74	7.4
Kraak	26	63–177	.356	60–102	.588	10.7	186	7.2
White	22	40–128	.313	43–58	.741	3.5	123	5.6
Poff	13	14–45	.311	12–19	.632	1.2	40	3.1
Byers	23	25–72	.347	13–24	.542	0.9	63	2.7
Wright	3	2–11	.182	4–4	1.00	0.7	8	2.7
DeaKyne	20	20–87	.230	5–12	.417	1.5	45	2.3
Chambers	2	1–1	1.00	0–0	.000	0.0	2	1.0
Henry	2	0–1	.000	2–4	.500	0.0	2	1.0
Taylor	2	1–2	.500	0–0	.000	1.0	2	1.0
Schooley	16	3–14	.214	6–12	.500	1.9	12	0.8

Appendix

1953 NCAA Tournament Bracket

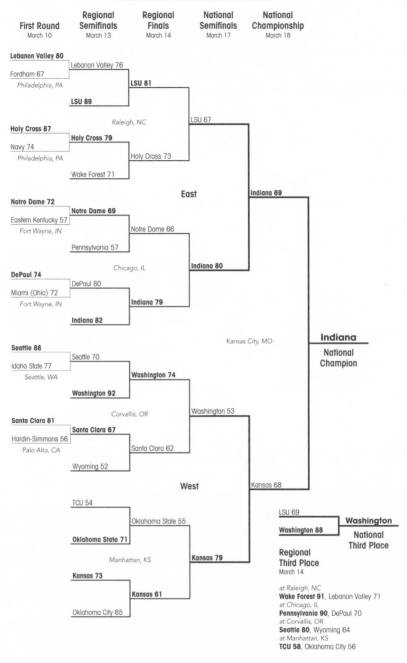

First Round March 10	Regional Semifinals March 13	Regional Finals March 14	National Semifinals March 17	National Championship March 18

Lebanon Valley 80
Lebanon Valley 76
Fordham 67
Philadelphia, PA
LSU 81
LSU 89
Raleigh, NC
LSU 67

Holy Cross 87
Holy Cross 79
Navy 74
Philadelphia, PA
Holy Cross 73
Wake Forest 71

East

Indiana 69

Notre Dame 72
Notre Dame 69
Eastern Kentucky 57
Fort Wayne, IN
Notre Dame 66
Pennsylvania 57
Chicago, IL
Indiana 80

DePaul 74
DePaul 80
Miami (Ohio) 72
Fort Wayne, IN
Indiana 79
Indiana 82

Kansas City, MO

Indiana
National Champion

Seattle 88
Seattle 70
Idaho State 77
Seattle, WA
Washington 74
Washington 92
Corvallis, OR
Washington 53

Santa Clara 81
Santa Clara 67
Hardin-Simmons 56
Palo Alto, CA
Santa Clara 62
Wyoming 52

West
Kansas 68

TCU 54
Oklahoma State 55
Oklahoma State 71
Manhattan, KS
Kansas 79

Kansas 73
Kansas 61
Oklahoma City 65

LSU 69
Washington 88

Washington
National Third Place

Regional Third Place
March 14

at Raleigh, NC
Wake Forest 91, Lebanon Valley 71
at Chicago, IL
Pennsylvania 90, DePaul 70
at Corvallis, OR
Seattle 80, Wyoming 64
at Manhattan, KS
TCU 58, Oklahoma City 56

328

Notes

1. Expansion and Crisis

1. Charley Rosen, *Scandals of '51* (New York: Seven Stories Press, 1999), 26. The epigraph that opens this chapter is from the same source, pp. 133–134.

2. Blair Kerkhoff, *Phog Allen: The Father of Basketball Coaching* (Indianapolis: Masters Press, 1996), 142.

3. Ibid., 143.

4. Ibid.

5. Ibid., 144.

6. Ibid.

7. Ibid.

8. Ibid., 145.

9. Rosen, *Scandals of '51*, 43.

10. Ibid.

11. Ibid., 44.

12. Ibid., 28–29, 37.

13. Ibid., 48.

14. Ken Rappoport, *The Classic: The History of the NCAA Basketball Championship* (Kansas City, Mo.: Lowell Press, 1979), 68.

15. Rosen, *Scandals of '51*, 17.

16. Ibid., 65.

17. Ibid., 129.

18. Ibid., 134.

19. Ibid., 139–140.

20. Ibid., 6.

2. Bobby

1. *Terre Haute Spectator*, September 29, 1979, 16.

2. Ibid.

3. Ibid., 17.

4. Rappoport, *The Classic*, 88.

5. Phillip M. House, *Hoosiers: The Fabulous Basketball Life of Indiana, 2nd Edition* (Indianapolis: Guild Press of Indiana, 1995), 112.

6. Ibid.

7. Ibid., 114.

8. Rappoport, *The Classic,* 88.

9. Ray Marquette, *Indiana University Basketball* (New York: Alpine Books, 1975), 133.

3. The Ox

Epigraph opening this chapter: "Basketball great Don Schlundt dies at 52; services will be Monday," *The Indianapolis Star* (October 12, 1985), 2.

1. Rappoport, *The Classic,* 87.

2. Ibid.

3. Ibid.

4. Pete DiPrimio and Rick Notter, *Hoosier Handbook: Stories, Stats, and Stuff About IU Basketball* (Wichita, Kans.: Midwest Sports Publications, 1995), 109.

5. Kerkhoff, *Phog Allen,* 167; and Dean Smith, *A Coach's Life: My 40 Years in College Basketball* (New York: Random House, 2002), 23.

6. DiPrimio and Notter, *Hoosier Handbook,* 109.

7. "Basketball great Don Schlundt dies at 52," 2.

8. Branch McCracken, *Indiana Basketball* (Englewood Cliffs, N.J.: Prentice-Hall, 1955), 1.

4. Big Mac and the Firewagon

1. Jay T. Smith, producer, "Coach for Life" (Bloomington, Ind.: WTIU, 1989).

2. Ibid.

3. Ernie Nims, "Branch McCracken—Profile of a Great Sportsman," WFIU Radio, 1965.

4. Smith, "Coach for Life."

5. Todd Gould, *Pioneers of the Hardwood: Indiana and the Birth of Professional Basketball* (Bloomington: Indiana University Press, 1998), 44.

6. "Branch Wins the Big One: The Pupil Beats the Teacher in a History-Making Win," *The Indianapolis Star Magazine,* April 2, 1978, 46.

7. Smith, "Coach for Life."

8. Marquette, *Indiana University Basketball,* 103.

9. Smith, "Coach for Life."

10. "Mary Jo McCracken: IU's No. 1 Fan Has Family Ties Here," *Wabash Plain Dealer,* February 14, 1975.

11. Bill Woods, "A History of Hoosier Hysteria: One Woman's Story" (n.p., n.d., article from the McCracken family collection).

12. Ibid.

13. Marquette, *Indiana University Basketball,* 97.

14. Woods, "A History of Hoosier Hysteria."

15. Ibid.

16. Nims, "Branch McCracken—Profile of a Great Sportsman."

17. Ibid.

18. Woods, "A History of Hoosier Hysteria."

19. Marquette, *Indiana University Basketball,* 89.

20. Nims, "Branch McCracken—Profile of a Great Sportsman."

21. Marquette, *Indiana University Basketball,* 89, 95.

5. The Second-Place Curse

1. DiPrimio and Notter, *Hoosier Handbook,* 97–98.
2. Rappoport, *The Classic,* 18.
3. Ibid., 19.
4. Marquette, *Indiana University Basketball,* 121.
5. Rappoport, *The Classic,* 15.
6. Ibid., 19.
7. DiPrimio and Notter, *Hoosier Handbook,* 99.
8. Ibid.
9. Smith, "Coach for Life."
10. Ibid.
11. Jason Hiner, "McCracken Represented Indiana in World War II," *Inside Indiana,* November 13, 2004, 20.
12. Jason Hiner, *Indiana University Basketball Encyclopedia* (Champaign, Ill.: Sports Publishing LLC, 2005), 250.

6. The Race and the Free Throw Contest

1. McCracken, *Indiana Basketball,* 85. The epigraph that opens this chapter is from the same source, p. 16.
2. Ed Frank, "Branch Admits IU Will Win A 'Few' Games," *Indiana Daily Student,* December 5, 1952.
3. Ibid.
4. "Varsity Cagers Turn Harriers," *Indiana Daily Student,* October 12, 1952.
5. McCracken, *Indiana Basketball,* 58.
6. "Major Recruiters Pay On For Players, Allen Says," *Indiana Daily Student,* October 21, 1952.
7. "Guard Prospects Cheer McCracken," *Indiana Daily Student,* October 29, 1952.
8. Rappoport, *The Classic,* 16.
9. McCracken, *Indiana Basketball,* 19.
10. Rappoport, *The Classic,* 16.
11. "Branch McCracken," Broadcast Sports Radio (Indianapolis), 1958.
12. Ibid.
13. McCracken, *Indiana Basketball,* 76.
14. Frank, "Branch Admits IU Will Win A 'Few' Games."
15. Ibid.
16. Ibid.
17. Jack Sellers, "Branch Takes Cagers to Big Floor, Works on Offense and Defense," *Indiana Daily Student,* November 20, 1952.
18. Charles S. Cogan, "Branch and Me," *Indiana Alumni Magazine,* March/April 2003, 42.
19. Ibid.

7. Here We Go Again

Epigraph opening this chapter: Herb Michelson, "Bitter Herbs," *Indiana Daily Student,* October 24, 1952.

1. McCracken, *Indiana Basketball,* 29.

2. "IU Five to Visit Two Toughies in Week," *Indiana Daily Student,* December 4, 1952.

3. Ed Frank, "Spirited Irish Drop Hoosiers, 71-70," *Indiana Daily Student,* December 9, 1952.

4. "Indiana Gets Rid of the Bad One," *Bloomington Daily Herald-Telephone,* December 9, 1952.

5. Ed Frank, "Mac Praises IU Comeback After Irish Victory," *Indiana Daily Student,* December 9, 1952.

6. "Victory-Minded Cagers Lay for Kansas State," *Indiana Daily Student,* December 12, 1952.

7. "Lou Scott Valuable to Hurryin' Hoosiers," *Indiana Daily Student,* December 18, 1952.

8. Bob Gildea, "Hoosiers, Gaining in Defeat, Ready for Big Ten," *Bloomington Daily Herald-Telephone,* December 15, 1952.

9. Jack Sellers, "Branch Praises Team Despite Defeat by Cats," *Indiana Daily Student,* December 17, 1952.

8. Kiss It Goodbye

1. Jon Stine, "The '53 champs: The Hoosiers Were Hers, Too," *Hurryin' Hoosiers,* 42.

2. McCracken, *Indiana Basketball,* 22.

3. Ibid., 23.

4. Ibid., 22.

5. Rappoport, *The Classic,* 87.

6. Jack Sellers, "Gopher Tilt Called Toss-up," *Indiana Daily Student,* January 7, 1953.

7. Ibid.

9. Speed versus Power

1. Pete Waldmeir, "A Note to Tom Amaker: UM's a Football School, First and Always," *The Detroit News,* March 31, 2001.

2. "Sincerely Bvon," *Indiana Daily Student,* January 10, 1953.

3. " 'Half-A-Step Saved IU,' McCracken," *Indiana Daily Student,* January 12, 1953.

4. Ibid.

10. The Game Neither Team Could Afford to Lose

1. "Coach McCracken Ill with Flu," *Indiana Daily Student,* January 14, 1953.

2. Jack Sellers, "Leonard May Miss Illinois Contest," *Indiana Daily Student,* January 15, 1953.

3. Robert Gildea, "Leonard Breathes Easier; So Does IU," *Bloomington Daily Herald-Telephone,* January 15, 1953.

4. Ibid.

5. Jack Sellers, "Leonard 'Weak But Ready' After Cold," *Indiana Daily Student,* January 16, 1953.

6. Bob Gildea, "Combes, McCracken Call This One 'Big One,'" *Bloomington Daily Herald-Telephone*, January 16, 1953.

7. Ibid.

8. Mary Horner, "'Star Dust'er Recalls Past At Indiana," *Indiana Daily Student*, January 17, 1953.

9. Ibid.

10. Ibid.

11. "IU Squeezes by Illini To Pad Big Ten Lead," *Indiana Daily Student*, January 20, 1953.

12. "Illinois Coach Performs Post-Mortem," *Indiana Daily Student*, January 22, 1953.

11. Century Mark

1. *Arbutus* (Indiana University yearbook) 1953, 2.

2. "Hoosiers Invade Purdue Tonight," *Indianapolis Star*, January 19, 1953, 17.

3. "Indiana 'Hurricane' Hits Here Tonight," *Lafayette Journal and Courier*, January 19, 1953.

4. Ibid.

5. Ibid.

6. "Sincerely Bvon," *Indiana Daily Student*, January 21, 1953.

7. Robert Gildea, "Big Don, Bobby Revising Records," *Bloomington Daily Herald-Telephone*, January 22, 1953.

8. Jack Sellers, "Hoosiers Relax After Winning Eight Straight," *Indiana Daily Student*, January 22, 1953.

9. Jack Sellers, "McCracken Clears Bench as Two Records Fall," *Indiana Daily Student*, February 4, 1953.

10. Herb Michelson, "Bitter Herbs," *Indiana Daily Student*, February 11, 1953.

12. A Knife in Wisconsin

Epigraph opening this chapter: Judy Williams, "House Cleaning On Agenda for Mrs. McCracken," *The Indianapolis Times*, March 21, 1965.

1. Mike Leonard, "Mary Jo McCracken Was a Big Part of Branch's Success," *Bloomington Herald-Times*, October 31, 1996.

2. Marquette, *Indiana University Basketball*, 109, 114.

3. Stine, "The '53 Champs: The Hoosiers Were Hers, Too."

4. Marquette, *Indiana University Basketball*, 81.

5. Henry McCormick, "Hoosiers Edge Gallant Badger Cagers, 72-70," *Wisconsin State Journal*, February 17, 1953.

6. Bruce Temple, "Indiana Thumps Ohio State 81-67 As Illinois Loses," *Louisville Courier-Journal*, February 22, 1953.

7. Charles Beal, "Indiana Netters Rout Ohio State, 81-67," *The Indianapolis Star*, February 22, 1953.

8. "Burned Up! IU Cagers Too Hot For One TV Set," *Bloomington Daily Herald-Telephone*, February 24, 1953.

9. "Seton Hall Retains Top Position; Says IU Schedule 'Weaker,'" *Indiana Daily Student*, February 25, 1953.

10. "Seton Hall Pilot Says Big 10 Not So Tough," *Bloomington Daily Herald-Telephone*, February 25, 1953.

11. "Seton Hall Retains Top Position; Says IU Schedule 'Weaker.'"

13. THE CLINCHER

Epigraph opening this chapter: Jack Prowell, "Prowling Around with Jack Prowell," *Champaign-Urbana News Gazette*, March 1, 1953.

1. Stu Huffman, "Illini Battle Rates TV As Hoosiers Reach for Title," *Indiana Daily Student*, February 27, 1953.

2. Herb Michelson, "Bitter Herbs," *Indiana Daily Student*, February 28, 1953.

3. George Bolinger, "IU's Champions Host NU Tonight," *Indiana Daily Student*, March 2, 1953.

4. Herb Michelson, "Bitter Herbs," *Indiana Daily Student*, March 4, 1953.

5. "IU Tops, Even Coach Says It," *Indianapolis News*, March 2, 1953.

6. Herb Michelson, "Bitter Herbs," *Indiana Daily Student*, March 4, 1953.

7. Ibid.

8. T. O. White, "Hoosiers Reign As Big Ten Kings, 91-79," *Champaign-Urbana News-Gazette*, March 1, 1953.

9. Ibid.

10. Ibid.

11. Ibid.

12. Ibid.

13. Ibid.

14. Ibid.

15. Herb Michelson, "Bitter Herbs," *Indiana Daily Student*, March 4, 1953.

16. Ibid.

17. Ibid.

18. Ibid.

19. Ibid.

20. Ibid.

21. Ibid.

22. "IU, Big 10 Champ, Practices 'As Usual,'" *Louisville Courier-Journal*, March 2, 1953.

23. White, "Hoosiers Reign As Big Ten Kings, 91–79."

24. Bruce Temple, "Thousands Brave Blizzard To Honor Big Ten Cage Champs," *Bloomington Daily Herald-Telephone*, March 2, 1953.

25. Ibid.

26. Ibid.

27. Ibid.

28. Ibid.

29. Ginny Krause, "A Coach's Wife Leads a Zany Life," *Crimson Bull* (IU basketball scrapbook), 1953–54.

30. Ibid.

31. Stine, "The '53 Champs: The Hoosiers Were Hers, Too."

14. A Record Night in Chicago

1. Rappoport, *The Classic,* 89.
2. Jack Sellers, "Regional Play in Chicago Tonight," *Indiana Daily Student,* March 13, 1953.
3. George Bolinger, "Macmen Hang On In Hectic Closing Minutes For 82-80 Win In NCAA Regional," *Bloomington Daily Herald-Telephone,* March 14, 1953.
4. Ibid.
5. DiPrimio and Notter, *Hoosier Handbook,* 113.
6. "Trounce Notre Dame; 'Big Don' Sets Record," *Indiana Daily Student,* March 17, 1953.
7. Herb Michelson, "Bitter Herbs," *Indiana Daily Student,* March 17, 1952.
8. Ibid.
9. Ibid.
10. Ibid.

15. Kansas City Coronation

1. Will Grimsley (Associated Press), "IU, Washington, Kansas, LSU In NCAA Finals," *Louisville Courier-Journal,* March 16, 1953.
2. Smith, *A Coach's Life,* 28.
3. Ibid.
4. Kerkhoff, *Phog Allen,* 171.
5. George Bolinger, "In the World of Sports," *Bloomington Daily Herald-Telephone,* March 17, 1953.
6. Kerkhoff, *Phog Allen,* 178.
7. Herb Michelson, "Bitter Herbs," *Indiana Daily Student,* March 20, 1952.
8. "KU Cinderella Dreams End With One Shot That Missed," *Kansas City Times,* March 19, 1953; "Indiana Beats Kansas 69-68 for NCAA Crown," *Louisville Courier-Journal,* March 19, 1953.
9. "Big Welcome Given IU Champions," *The Indianapolis Times,* March 19, 1953.
10. "Hoosiers Stop Kansas, 69-68, In Final Seconds," *The Indianapolis Times,* March 19, 1953.
11. Stine, "The '53 Champs: The Hoosiers Were Hers, Too."
12. "Big Welcome Given IU Champions."

Index

Index

JASON HINER

is an Indiana University graduate, journalist, and
historian. In his day job he manages a team of technology
editors for CNET Networks. He has written many
articles on the history of IU basketball for *Inside Indiana*
and is the author of *The Indiana University Basketball
Encyclopedia*. He is a member of the Society of
Professional Journalists and the Indiana Historical Society.